ROGER FULLINGTON SERIES IN ARCHITECTURE

*Production of this book was made possible in part by
support from Roger Fullington and a challenge grant from
the National Endowment for the Humanities.*

CINEMA HOUSTON

FROM NICKELODEON TO MEGAPLEX

★ ★ ★

DAVID WELLING

Foreword by Jack Valenti

University of Texas Press

AUSTIN

★

For my parents,
who indulged my many flights of
fancy.
If life is a movie, they raised the
curtain,
lit up the screen.
They were there,
and experienced it all firsthand.
With love.

★

COPYRIGHT © 2007 BY DAVID WELLING

Printed in the United States of America
First edition, 2007

Requests for permission to reproduce material
from this work should be sent to:
    Permissions
    University of Texas Press
    P.O. Box 7819
    Austin, TX 78713-7819
    www.utexas.edu/utpress/about/bpermission
    .html

(∞) The paper used in this book meets the
minimum requirements of ANSI/NISO
Z39.48-1992 (R1997) (Permanence of Paper).

LIBRARY OF CONGRESS
CATALOGING-IN-PUBLICATION DATA

Welling, David, 1958–
    Cinema Houston : from nickelodeon to
megaplex / David Welling.—1st ed.
    p.   cm. — (Roger Fullington series in
architecture)
    Includes bibliographical references and
index.
    ISBN: 978-0-292-71700-8 (cloth : alk. paper)
    1. Motion picture theaters—Texas—Hous-
ton. 2. Houston (Tex.)—Buildings, structures,
etc. I. Title.
    NA6846.U62H689 2007
    725'.823097641411—dc22   2007001066

CONTENTS

FOREWORD

In 1936, I was fifteen years old, freshly graduated from Sam Houston High School, when my uncle, Fred Cannata, general manager of the Horwitz theatres, hired me to work at the Iris Theatre as an usher–concession-stand operator and assistant to the projectionist, replacing the reels in metal containers at the end of each evening.

The Iris Theatre was not a movie palace. It was a second-run theatre, specializing mostly in westerns and Saturday serials. But for me it was a kind of paradise. I got to see every western movie produced at the time as I watched Ken Maynard, Hoot Gibson, Bob Steele, and a host of other gun-slinging good guys chase the rustlers. But it was a seven-day-a-week job, and my salary was eleven dollars a week. At the time it didn't seem that onerous. I worked steadily at the Iris for a year until I

★ got a job as an office boy at the Humble Oil Company and immediately enrolled in night classes at the University of Houston.

As I roamed the aisles of the Iris, manned the concession stand popping the corn, and did a bit of janitor work, I could never in my wildest conjuring of the future have forecast that some twenty-five years later I would be one of the leaders of the Hollywood movie industry.

I met on several occasions a unique figure in the theatre business, Will Horwitz. He owned, at the time, the Uptown, the Texan, the Ritz and the Iris, all managed by my Uncle Fred. Mostly I saw Mr. Horwitz at his annual Christmas party at the downtown Sam Houston Coliseum, giving away toys and food to disadvantaged kids in Houston. As I look back, I view with mounting admiration the philanthropy of Will Horwitz, unmatched in Houston, and on a scale rarely to be found today. He was also an implacable foe of the major studios and their distribution arms, fighting them tenaciously, accusing them of antitrust violations. The Supreme Court in the early fifties would agree with Horwitz and his colleagues. Their decision marked the slow undoing of the studio contract system, the collapse of the corporate embrace that nurtured stars, directors, and writers.

These were the glory days of the movie palaces in Houston. In downtown Houston could be found the Majestic, the Metropolitan, Loew's, and the Kirby—large and inviting, their ornate architecture and vast auditoriums singularly equipped for movie viewing. It was an Olympian theatrical environment. It never got any better, though at the time we had no idea of the radical, sweeping changes to come, not only in theatrical design but also in the shape and form of the major Hollywood studios, whose fortunes and changes I presided over for almost thirty-nine years.

But it is all fastened in my memory. I can still see those westerns at the Iris, still fascinated by the sounds of horses galloping and gunfights on the plains. It was a halcyon era for theatres in Houston. For me, the nostalgia still brims over with a boy's awe and wonder.

JACK VALENTI
Former Chairman and CEO,
Motion Picture Association of America

ACKNOWLEDGMENTS

Some books come together in a blink of an eye. This was not such a project. Initial research began in 1991, involving digging around in numerous files and archives, talking with people, and many, many eye blinks. Because many of the theatres referred to have long since been demolished, and a good number of those who worked at them are no longer around, the prime source of information has been newspaper accounts from years past, along with a large number of secondary sources.

Above all, thanks goes to the two newspapers that reported day-to-day life in Houston during the last century: the *Houston Post*, the library and photo files of which were explored during the early part of the project, and the *Houston Chronicle*. Most of the dates, details, and accounts were culled from these two vital sources.

★ Thanks also go to the other local newspapers, which helped to fill in the gaps, including the *Houston Press*, the *Leader*, the *Houston Business Journal*, the *Metropolitan Civic News*, the *Pasadena Citizen*, and the *Public News*.

The Metropolitan Research Center at the Houston Public Library was invaluable in helping assembly the background information and photographs for the book. Joel Draut deserves knighthood, or at least an Indiana Jones archaeology award, for his astute ability in uncovering long-forgotten photographic antiquities. His knowledge and darkroom wizardry is beyond measure. Other individuals and institutions that were of great benefit include Steven Fenberg with Houston Endowment Inc.; Alfred Cervantes with the Houston Film Commission; the archives of the Museum of Fine Arts,

Houston; the Woodson Research Center at the Fondren Library, Rice University; the University of Houston Special Collections and Archives; and two archives at the University of Texas: the Harry Ransom Humanities Research Center and the Center for American History.

To Jim Burr, my great editor at the University of Texas Press, major thanks for guiding me through all of the inherent crests and valleys. My heartfelt appreciation also goes to manuscript editors Mary LaMotte and Lynne Chapman, and copy editor Kip Keller for crafting this into a far better book. To Teresa Wingfield, a special thanks for her superb design ability. I know all too well the effort involved in this craft; her creative vision has made this book complete.

My heartfelt thanks to former Houstonian Jack Valenti, who without hesitation consented to write the foreword, but did not live to see the final book. From the Horwitz theatres to his leadership of the MPAA, motion pictures were a central part of his life. He passed away on April 26, 2007, and I would like to think that with his words, he came home one last time.

Invaluable to this project was Gary Warwick, who generously shared a wealth of photos, many hours of his time, and stories of the Ritz, Will Horwitz, and Eddie Miller (to name just a few). Thanks also to Al Zarzana, who played a big part in Houston's theatrical past. By sharing with me numerous photos and stories, giving me leads on new areas of research, and clarifying portions of the text, he contributed enormously to the book. My profound appreciation as well to Ray M. Boriski, who partnered with Al Zarzana on numerous theatres, helped out with

finding many elusive photos, and played me some great tunes. Special thanks also goes to Roy Bonario for his aid and historical knowledge and for generously allowing many of the photographs and clippings from his collection to be used in this book—and to his wondrous Memory Shop, which, during the seventies and eighties, caused me and countless others to wholeheartedly embrace the endless aspects of collecting. Photos and stories also came from other invaluable sources: Alvin Guggenheim, whose father played a major role in theatre operations in Houston; Charles Paine of both the Jefferson Amusement Company and Tercar Theatre Company; Carroll A. Lewis, who shared stories and photos of the Post Oak Drive-in and Movieland Golf, and of finding diamonds in a truckload of dirt; Jim Ohmart, for details and pictures from the world of Cinema West; Jim Koehn, whose theatre paintings I have admired for many years; Ray Hugger, for sharing his family photos; and Becky and Parker Riggs—his passion for drive-ins surpasses my own. Thanks also to Story Sloane III of Story Sloane's Gallery, who graciously offered some amazing images from his collection.

Thanks to the KPRC Channel 2 group for unearthing the Post Oak Drive-in photos: Ron Stone, Lyn Salerno, Lois Samford, Von Johnson, and Evelyn Hunt.

Other individuals who have helped out, by way of information, interviews, photographs, or random acts of kindness, include Jan Bettis, Earl Blair, Bryan Boudreaux, Chad Browning with the Regal Entertainment Group, John Coles, Keith Curtis, Al Davis, Mike Dean, Louis De Rose, Cary Dier, James E. Fisher, Tom Hannegan, Ed Henderson, Gus and Sha-

ron Kopriva, Clare Lagroue, Dan Lub-
bock, Robert Mireles, Bob Mortensen,
Greg Neumann, Steve Schmid, Tom
Seiler, Anthony Smith, Rick Staudt,
Bryan Talley, Dick Willson and the Hous-
ton Area Theatre Organ Society, Shawn
Welling, and Pamela Winfrey.

Love and thanks also to my father, Al
Welling, my mother, Bettye Welling, and
brothers Ken and Vince Welling. Lauryn
and Dylan, the world is at your fingertips
if you set your mind to it. Each day with
you is a joy. And finally, all my love and
thanks beyond measure to my wife,
Denise, who patiently put up with my
decade-plus obsession.

This has been a journey of discovery
for me. I hope it will be equally entertain-
ing for you. Let the film roll.

DAVID WELLING
July 2006

RICK
STAUDT

*The 1926 Ritz Theatre in
its later incarnation as the
Majestic Metro. It is the
only Houston movie theatre
from the silent era to have
survived, and now serves as
a special-events hall. Photograph by Rick Staudt.*

INTRODUCTION

We sell tickets to theatres, not movies.

MARCUS LOEW

★ THIS IS a book of shadows.

Recollected through words and pictures, it embraces a time gone by, places that no longer exist, and the people who made it happen. Mostly it is about rose-colored glasses—which is, after all, what the cinema has always been about. Movies offer a touch of the fantastic to a sometimes too harsh reality.

This sense of wonder is magnified when experienced through the eyes of a child, for whom the surrounding world seems exaggerated and extra large—perhaps because the smaller we are, the bigger everything around us appears. Is it any surprise that people's memories of their first movie experience are awash with more than the usual rose tinting?

Understandably, the screen—for that matter, the whole auditorium—seemed huge at that age. As the smell of candy and popcorn permeated the air, we sat in chairs way too big for us, some with spring-loaded seats that we could barely weigh down. The fear of darkness swelled uncontrollably as the house lights dimmed, plunging the auditorium into black—only to be dispelled as that first image appeared before us on the screen.

I remember—if only in bits and pieces, which is to be expected from a five-year-old. Early childhood recollections are elusive and slippery, not quite tangible in the way of later experiences. They come in flashes of half-formed moments.

Yet I remember the theatre clearly . . . and as much as I would like to claim that those early memories were of a spectacular picture palace, with its grand antique-filled foyer leading to a massive auditorium adorned in gold trim and deep, plush velvet curtains—my recollections instead are of a worn-out small-town movie house not far from Houston.

The old Alvin Theatre had long since seen its glory days. The seats were worn and torn, the floors sticky from the layers of candy mixed with soda syrup, the air reeked of stale popcorn—and age. It had accumulated a lot of that. The passing years had slowly diminished whatever magic had been entrusted to those walls. This was a modest, unpretentious, barebones kind of affair. The darkness that enveloped the auditorium helped mask the neglect that the theatre had endured over its three decades of existence.

In short, the theatre was a rattrap. That was what my brother called it, and even joked of the tug-of-war he had waged with an oversized rat after dropping his Mars bar to the ground. The tug-of-war was dubious; the oversized rats were not. The place was a dump.

Of course, none of that mattered to us kids. The Saturday matinee was the never-never land for us. Movies offered escapism, and it made little difference whether the cinematic fare was a western—naturally popular in a small Texas town—cartoons, or cheap science fiction.

The attraction on that particular day was *Godzilla vs. the Thing*, featuring a man in a rubber monster suit and some really bad dubbing. I had tagged along with my older brother, who more than likely had been given parental orders to take me with him.

After a visit to the cramped concession stand, positioned in the matchbox lobby behind the ticket window, we took our seats in the kid-filled auditorium. The lights dimmed. The projector lit up the screen. My life has never been the same since.

Eventually, my parents forbade us from going to the Alvin movie house—some-

Auditorium of Johnny Long's Alvin Theatre, 1987. Photograph by David Welling.

thing to do with its nasty condition. This reason made little sense to us kids. What did we care if the floors were sticky and the walls were destined to fail the white-glove test? Regardless, it was deemed off-limits. The old theatre would close soon after that, leaving Alvin without an indoor theatre until a new one was built in 1968. When the old theatre eventually opened its doors again, it was as a place for religious revivals, and people came for prayers and sermons, not cowboys and Indians. Eventually, it would close for good, falling into disrepair before facing demolition in 1996.

LONG'S ALVIN THEATRE, as it was originally called, was quite a big deal when it opened in 1936. A story ("New Alvin Theatre to Open Friday, Feb. 28th") in the *Alvin Sun* touted its modern design and construction, which featured a vaudeville stage accented with rich, crimson velvet curtains and large dressing rooms on either side. The townsfolk flocked to the February 28 gala event, paid their twenty-five-cent admission, listened to a mayoral dedication, and then watched the Harold Lloyd comedy *The Milky Way*. The Alvin High School girls pep squad presented the patrons with spring flower arrangements as they entered.

As a second newspaper story ("Completion of New Theatre Is Source of Pride to Citizens of Alvin and Community," *Alvin Sun*, February 28, 1936) noted, this was the fifteenth theatre in Johnny G. Long's theatre circuit, which included houses in Texas towns such as Bay City, Port Lavaca, El Campo, and Beaumont. His was an independent chain that booked second-run films, usually after their initial showings in the Houston

movie palaces. Long had previously bought the Alvin Grand Theatre, which had been showing flickers since 1919.

For Alvinites, Long's theatre was a center of activity, back in much simpler times. People would "go downtown" on Friday and Saturday nights for a movie or just to sit in their cars and watch the crowds go by. That was Saturday-night entertainment.

Aside from a steady stream of motion pictures, live appearances by such luminaries as Tex Ritter and his Musical Tornadoes, Ramblin' Tommy Scott, and Luke McLuke were also common occurrences. A Bonnie and Clyde stage show, complete with a bullet-ridden Model A Ford parked in front of the theatre, would sell out the house. Midnight spook shows with live productions were also held, as were occasional church services.

The popularity of television, among other forms of entertainment, took its toll, not only on the old Alvin Theatre but also on Long's entire theatre chain. By the sixties, the Alvin Theatre was a pale ghost of its former glory. Finances were thin, repair and upkeep difficult, and for the wages paid, janitors did a bare minimum. Finally, the roof that had long been weakened by water damage gave way. It came crashing down into the auditorium during an evening feature. Amazingly, only one minor injury occurred. As for recompense, the patron was quite satisfied with the theatre management covering her doctor bill, and never was heard the discouraging word "lawsuit." Again, those were simpler days.

The roof was rebuilt, but the theatre's end was in sight. Long's closed down, and except for its brief stint as a place of worship, sat dormant, neglected, and forgotten. The roof would eventually collapse again, exposing the balcony to the elements. A few years shy of demolition, the balcony itself would fall, effectively barricading the lobby entrance. Rusted theatre chairs and torn remnants of the movie screen were all that was left inside.

The old Alvin Theatre was razed in 1996 as part of a downtown-revitalization program.

TALES OF THE BIG CITY were not that different from those of its small-town cousins. In an early-seventies edition of the *Houston Post* there ran a short paragraph paying homage to one of Houston's great movie houses. Accompanying the text was a series of photographs of the abandoned theatre, taken by a staff photographer. Below these images ran the following copy:

> *In January 1923, reporters hailed the new Majestic Theatre at 908 Rusk as the "playhouse the duplicate of which cannot be found in America." On opening night, Houstonians from Rev. Peter Gray Sears to Mayor Oscar Holcombe flocked to the Majestic to see Henry B. Walthall starring in* The Unknown. *This week— after almost 50 years of vaudeville, musical productions, dramatic performances and movies—little is left from the Majestic except for the rubble of demolition crews. Modern economic conditions and contemporary entertainment trends had taken their toll. Now the broken and discarded remains of Greek statues, Roman pillars, Italian Renaissance fixtures and electric exit signs are mute testimony to the years gone by.*

Architectural obituaries such as this

are rare. Unless they are noteworthy landmarks, most buildings fall with little or no fanfare. This is especially true of Houston's movie houses, which die without the crowds, reporters, or klieg lights that heralded their ribbon-cutting births. Instead, there may only be a passively curious onlooker as the demolition crews do their work.

Left behind are memories, along with newspaper clippings and photographs, for a legacy. Reduced to rubble, these structures are swept away to make room for newer structures, freeway construction, and that ever-popular use for property, the parking lot. Some are converted to retail space, their innards ripped out and discarded in the name of commerce. Euphemistically, it is called progress. For historians, it goes by another, less favorable word, but by any name, the buildings are forever lost.

What remains today of the downtown Houston theatres can be counted on one hand. The 1926 Ritz/Majestic Metro Theatre is the only downtown movie house to have been restored, and now functions as a venue for special events. The artistic integrity of the restoration rivals that of the suburban Alabama Theatre, which was restored and reopened as part of the Bookstop chain of bookstores. In both cases, though no longer commercial cinemas, they succeed for other uses because the architecture remains faithful to its original intent. In fact, they are more appreciated now for their "theatre-ness" than they were during their final years of running flicks.

The building that housed the Isis, Houston's first deluxe theatre, sat unused for years before undergoing a restoration in 1998 (although the theatre itself was

The 1912 Isis Theatre after reopening as the Mercantile Brewery in 2000, with the upper-wall ornamentation still intact. Photograph by David Welling.

long gone). Only a few architectural remnants remained from its movie house days. The Zoe/Capitol building, at 719 Main, still stands, but the theatre is gone. The Scenic, at 113 Travis, was neither glamorous nor expansive, merely a nickelodeon-style business operating in the early teens. It is now part of Treebeard's Restaurant in Old Market Square. The eatery takes up the former 113, 115, and 117 lots, and the space for the former movie house is still visible on the floor.

Historical respect is an elusive thing, especially when dealing with the intangibles that make something historic. If the qualifying factor is age, then at what point does a building make the transition from just old to historic?

In Houston, a structure is eligible for historic status after fifty years; the ill-fated Shamrock Hotel (1946–1986) was razed after only forty. Other buildings don't last even that long, falling quickly to the wrecking ball.

Dallas, San Antonio, and Austin have all held on to their Majestics, refurbishing them into performing arts centers. Efforts to raise public interest, find sponsors, and secure much-needed funds can effectively turn a losing proposition into a profitable one. Houston missed the boat in this area. Yet with the current revitalization of the downtown area, and the conversion of previously vacant buildings into private lofts, the prospect of such a restored performance center could have been quite feasible. The downtown theatres originally died off because of the push toward suburbia. Now the downtown district is rediscovering itself, but sadly, none of the original showplaces still stand. More's the pity.

Likewise, the original suburban theatres, which lured patrons from the downtown area, have also faced extinction. These were never palaces on the grand scale of their predecessors. Instead, they offered what is now considered the stereo-

A weathered wall advertisement for the Zoe Theatre (home of Paramount Pictures), c. 1995. Courtesy of Greg Neuman.

typical theatre design, rich in art deco and exteriors of bold neon.

Of this period, from roughly the thirties through the fifties, only the River Oaks has survived intact and active—and at the time of this writing, its future is uncertain. Some others still stand, either gutted and serving other functions or closed and abandoned. The rest have been demolished.

Taking the place of these theatres are the multicinemas and megaplexes, which have grown to as many as thirty screens. After a long period of throwing up matchbox theatres, movie-house owners are slowly rediscovering spectacle. Stadium seating, the reappearance of large-scale auditoriums (and large-scale lobbies), and food bars are all part of the redefining of the modern cinema.

Still, even the most expansive of these new cinemas can't hold a candle to the palaces of the twenties. Nowadays, they would simply cost too much to build. No more Greek statues, mezzanines filled with fine antique furniture, or Egyptian temple interiors. All this was of a different time, when movies, along with the places that showed them, were magic—palaces of light that did not stand the test of time.

But a wealth of photographs does survive. It is these photographs, along with a wide variety of other documentation, that form the heart and soul of this book. For those too young to have known the Metropolitan, Loew's State, or the Majestic, this is as much of their grandeur as we will ever get to experience. Going to the movies was meant to be a spectacle, both on the screen and in the theatre itself. It was meant to be larger than life. It was meant to be remembered.

Here, then, is a celebration of what once was and will never be again, of an age when going to the movies was a magical experience. If you look hard enough, you may very well find that the photographs here still contain that magic.

Sit back, enjoy, and don't forget the popcorn.

CINEMA HOUSTON

★ ★ ★

The Sweeney & Coombs Opera House. Courtesy of the Houston Metropolitan Research Center, Houston Public Library, MSS 114-805.

ONE

STAGED ORIGINS

★ ★ ★

★ ★ ★

The art of acting consists in keeping people from coughing.

SIR RALPH RICHARDSON

I didn't like the play, but then I saw it under adverse conditions—the curtain was up. GROUCHO MARX

★ "I RECALL GOING TO A MOVIE back in 1898," reminisced former Houston mayor A. E. Amerman in a 1948 *Houston Press* column by Paul Hochuli.[1] "And a Mr. E. E. Taylor—who ran the movie—told me that when he operated it, the movie was the first in Houston."

Recollections such as this, found in yellowed newspaper clippings, represent all that is left of Houston's introduction to motion pictures. According to Amerman, the movie house was on the east side of Main Street between Rusk and Capitol, right next to a rose garden.

Amerman died in 1958. The theatre is long gone. So are the roses.

In the same article, Joseph Hornberger told of his first movie, also around the turn of the century. "The first one I attended was on Congress Avenue, on the (then) present location of Zindler's, and was

1

about in the middle of the block. In order to make the room dark, they had black-painted canvas stretched around the room. There were a few chairs, and a sheet was used as a screen. Admission was 10 cents.

"In those days, when a picture was finished, the house was cleared. If you wanted to see it again, you had to pay again. I saw it four or five times."

The Houston of 1900 was a fast-growing city with a population of 44,600, an increase of over 17,000 from the decade before. Cotton and lumber were the major sources of commerce, as was rail transportation, Houston being a junction for fourteen railroads. Water connections through Buffalo Bayou and the Gulf of Mexico served as the other factor in the city's growth. As with most cities, the hub of activity was the downtown area, and this is where the first motion pictures appeared.[2]

"The film I saw," continued Hornberger, "was about a fisherman sitting on a plank extended over a small stream. Along came a fellow in a covered wagon, who stopped, picked up a big rock, and threw it at the opposite end of the plank. Up in the air went the fisherman, coming down in the water. This caused a great deal of laughter, and that's all there was to the show."

What Hornberger remembered was typical of both motion pictures and the houses in which they were shown. Movies were new to Houston—and the world—and would not gain legitimacy for years to come. While opera and dramatic performances had their own venues in town, it would take time for the motion picture to find its own home. Movies would be sandwiched between live performances as filler or left to the small storefront rooms as described by Hornberger.

Once introduced to Houstonians, the movies would play an integral part in redefining downtown architecture. The Houston movie theatre would evolve from the performance hall to the nickelodeon and reach its grandest heights in the opulent palaces of the twenties. Still ahead would be the deco-based neighborhood theatres, the drive-ins, the multicinemas, the large multiplexes of the eighties and nineties, and the stadium-seat auditoriums of the new millennium.

However, the roots of Houston's movie houses date back to the 1830s, well before the first motion picture, with the establishment of live theatre. Before the flickers, the stage reigned supreme.

HOUSTON'S FIRST PERFORMANCES
John Carlos and Henri Corri

The foundations of Houston's movie theatres began in the 1830s. The playhouses from this period, although crude at first, served a multitude of functions: as entertainment venues, as lecture halls and forums for subjects ranging from literature to politics, and as centers of social activity for much of the population. Plus, an opera house brought respectability and culture to a city. For Houston, support for the dramatic arts was strong at the outset, and much of the patronage came from the political wing of the population, the city being the capital of a new republic. Support would continue with some difficulty after 1839, when the capital was moved to Austin.[3]

In 1837, an early attempt to start a theatrical venue in the city ended in tragedy. G. L. Lyons, an actor from the East, had posted a notice in the March 28 issue of the *Telegraph and Texas Register*, announcing plans to establish a "dramatic temple" in Houston. After assembling a troupe, he and his players set sail in the *Pennsylvania*. A gale capsized and sank the schooner, leaving only two survivors.

The city's first true dramatic performances occurred the following year, when merchant John Carlos furnished a building for use as a theatre. At the same time, the Saint Charles Theatre troupe of New Orleans, under the management of Henri Corri, was sailing to Houston from Louisiana. Corri had placed a notice in the *Telegraph* on May 30, stating that as soon as he had made arrangements for a theatre, the city would be given "amusements worthy of their patronage." Initial attempts to lease a building called Hubbard's Exchange led to a problem: to get the playhouse, Corri would have to make Carlos a partner. Carlos lacked Corri's knowledge of theatrical matters, and therefore grudgingly agreed to be coproducer. Houston experienced its true first night on June 11, 1838, with the presentation of J. Sheridan Knowles's popular comedy, *The Hunchback* (1832). Absent from opening night was the orchestra, still en route from Mobile, Alabama.

The Carlos-Corri partnership was shortlived. On August 15, Corri bought a fifty-foot-wide lot in the middle of the block of Congress, between Milam and Travis, opposite Market Square. Meanwhile, financial setbacks forced John Carlos to sell his theatre building. It was bought by Samuel G. Powell in a sheriff's sale on July 15, 1844, and renamed the City Exchange.

Corri's Houston Theatre

The year 1839 started off well for Henri Corri. His new theatre—the first true theatre building in the republic—opened on February 25 with Richard Brinsley Sheridan's *School for Scandal* (1777). During the 1839–1840 season, his theatre took on the permanent name of the Houston Theatre.

The Houston Theatre's operational history was uneven. In October 1839, the theatre closed after a presentation of *The Golden Farmer* and *The Romp* because of the "indisposition" of some of the company—or, said the *Houston Star*, because of the "indisposition of the people to attend and see good pieces murdered." Attendance slowly dropped over the next several years, in part because of the relocation of the capital. On April 30, 1841, Corri filed for bankruptcy, and by year's end he and his wife, Eliza, had booked passage back to New Orleans.

The Houston Theatre building and property was bought by Robert P. Boyce, the contractor who originally built the playhouse. After completing repairs to the building, A. S. Newton, a member of Corri's original acting troupe, reopened Corri's theatre in 1845 with a new company of players.

Perkins Hall (Pillot's Opera House)

The February 16, 1860, issue of the *Telegraph* announced a new building under construction on Franklin near Main, being built for Captain E. S. Perkins and James H. Perkins. Perkins Hall, as it became known, would go on to feature most of the great contemporary American performers during its nearly thirty years in existence and to establish itself as the first great playhouse in Houston. In 1879 its name was changed to Pillot's Opera House when Eugene Pillot undertook a complete renovation of the building.

Although Perkins Hall was finished just before the Civil War erupted, it apparently did not open until 1866, when James Perkins—popularly known as "Brother Perkins"—presented *Camille* on April 12.

In December 1867, the spectacular play *Under the Gaslight* by Augustin Daly was brought to Houston from New York, where it had opened in August. The five-act melodrama dazzled the audience with such stunning effects as New York lit by gaslight, a ferryboat powered by real steam, a climactic rescue from the wheels of an oncoming locomotive (the first use of what would soon become a clichéd suspense device), and a plot turnabout in which the heroine rescued the male.

About a year later Perkins Hall was lit with gas for the first time. In 1870 it was remodeled and its seating capacity increased to 1,000. However, by the end of December the theatre had succumbed to the "disease of empty benches," as described by playhouse actor Edmund D. Langley.

Despite this slump, during the early 1870s the theatre hosted such performers as Edwin Forrest, Maurice Barrymore (father of John, Ethel, and Lionel), Buffalo Bill Cody's company, and Joseph Jefferson.

City Hall Opera House (Scanlan's Folly)

In the 1870s, Mayor Thomas H. Scanlan decided to tear down the old Houston City Hall and replace it with a fancy combination city hall and market house. Several additional square miles of territory were annexed to acquire the tax base to support the bonds for the project. Originally estimated to cost $250,000, the project became a $470,000 fiasco because of overruns and miscalculations, garnering nicknames such as Scanlan's Folly, Scanlan's Palace, and Scanlan's Scandal. The ground floor contained the city market. An upstairs auditorium, officially titled the Academy of Music, was commonly known as the opera house. According to Dr. S. O. Young, vaudeville was first established in Houston by Ed Bremond.[4] The building was completed in the summer of 1874, and then burned in July 1876. Since the structure had been insured for only $100,000, the insurance company made some repairs, but the building burned again a few years later.

After Scanlan's death, his daughters spent a part of their legacy on the construction of a memorial office building—the Scanlan Building. Stella and Lillian Scanlan were also responsible for constructing the Ritz Theatre in 1926.

With the city hall opera house gone, only Perkins Hall was left to service Houston's stage-entertainment needs. However, the hall had become outdated, causing many performers to refuse to appear there. In January 1879, Eugene Pillot announced he would completely renovate Perkins.

Gray's Hall

Another new theatre was announced for the 1879–1880 season: Gray's Hall, located on the west side of Fannin across from the courthouse, was to be converted into a usable playhouse. With Gray's and Pillot's, the public was given twice the amount of theatrical entertainment as well as the prospects of a theatrical rivalry for the first time since the Carlos-Corri wars.

At the end of 1882 a new contraption was added at Pillot's—a telephone, allowing playgoers to reserve seats by phone. In 1884, Pillot's was wired for electric light, as was Gray's the following year.

In 1887, after years of waiting, Houstonians finally were able to see the great actor Edwin Booth. For his performance of *Hamlet* on February 23, tickets quickly sold out far in advance; in an early example of ticket scalping, seats originally priced at $2 and $3 went for as much as $24 before the show. His Houston engagement also included *Othello* and *Julius Caesar*.[5]

The final performance at Pillot's Opera House was on April 14, 1886. On May 3 the building burned to the ground. The fire appeared to originate from the Bell Variety Theatre, later called the New Variety, around eight in the evening. Within half an hour, both houses were consumed by the blaze.

The Sweeney & Coombs Opera House

Gray's Opera House, now the only playhouse on the block, was never well suited to theatrical needs. It did, however, encourage the building of a new house. On January 15, 1890, new owners J. J. Sweeney and E. L. Coombs announced plans to tear down the existing house and build a new opera house to be ready for the 1890–1891 season. Sweeney declared that by the next season's opening, Houston would have the "neatest and prettiest opera house in the south."[6]

The Sweeney & Coombs Opera House opened on November 3, 1890, with the Grau Opera Company performing Gilbert and Sullivan's *The Gondoliers*, but patrons nearly froze when the heating system failed to work. As reported in the next day's *Houston Post*, "There was a large audience present, but it was not a good natured one, the house being too cold to render those present thoroughly sensible to the divine charm of music."

The divine Sarah Bernhardt appeared on February 4, 1892, and many were surprised when instead of the lean figure shown in photos of her, there appeared a short plump individual. Many disappointed patrons left before the play was half over, and some even suggested that madam was walking through her part.

NEW OWNERS TOOK over Sweeney & Coombs in 1904: Hyman Prince, who had previously built the Olympia Opera House in Houston in 1903 (see Chapters 2 and 10 for details), and Harvey T. D. Wilson. The opera house underwent renovation and reopened on Thursday, September 29, 1904, under the new name of the Houston Theatre. Construction was not complete, and chairs for the lower area would not arrive for another week, but the show went on regardless. *Two Men and a*

Girl, with Tim Murphy, was the premiere play. At his curtain call on opening night, Murphy said, "God knows you needed a new opera house," which garnered enthusiastic applause from the crowd.

The building would stand only three years before falling victim to fire. A massive blaze swept through several blocks of downtown Houston late in the evening on Sunday, December 1, 1907—beginning in the Dunn Building, where an explosion raised the roof several feet. Evidence suggested arson as the cause. Ironically, great lengths had been taken against fire in the renovation of the theatre, including installing an alarm system and encasing the auditorium in brick firewalls.

Performances were moved to the Winnie Davis Auditorium, which required extensive remodeling to accommodate the demands of the detoured performances.

The Winnie Davis Auditorium and the City Auditorium

The Winnie Davis Auditorium had been opened in 1895. The hall, located at the corner of Main and McGowen and named after the daughter of the former Confederate president, Jefferson Davis, sported electrical connections, but the plumbing was primitive at best. It served its function for the next fifteen years. The Metropolitan Opera appeared there in 1901 for a performance of Richard Wagner's *Lohengrin*. Two hundred and fifty extra incandescent lights supplied additional illumination. After a repeat performance four years later, the Met did not return to Houston for forty-two years.

In 1910, the new City Auditorium replaced Winnie Davis. A well-proportioned hall that featured a grand proscenium arch, the City Auditorium was used for conventions, society balls, and occasional performances by theatrical stock

The Winnie Davis Auditorium. Courtesy of the Houston Metropolitan Research Center, Houston Public Library, MSS 1248-2027.

companies. It was also headquarters for the annual No-Tsu-Oh festivities. No-Tsu-Oh ("Houston" spelled backwards), also known as the Houston Carnival, was the big social event of the year and included horse and auto races, poultry and pet stock shows, rodeo events, and daily band concerts, all leading up to a spectacular parade and ball.

A highlight of the City Auditorium's history was the 1920 appearance of Enrico Caruso. Caruso disliked performing live, and therefore asked for exorbitant fees for his solo appearances. He demanded, and received, $12,000, which was placed in a bank thirty days before his appearance. The ticket office was swamped by hundreds of people for the sold-out show. Unwilling to turn them away, concert organizer Edna W. Saunders asked the ushers to open all

Interior of the 1910 City Auditorium. Postcard, author's collection.

the doors and windows of the hall. The evening air was filled with the voice of the most revered tenor of the day, heard by hundreds of people on the sidewalks outside the auditorium.[7]

The City Auditorium was razed in 1963 and replaced by Jones Hall.

AFTER THE Houston Theatre fire, Prince and Wilson laid out plans for a new theatre, to be built on the site of the destroyed playhouse. The Prince Theatre, as it was christened, became Houston's true transition venue from live entertainment to motion pictures—and in the coming years the two would oftentimes be intertwined, sharing bills and auditoriums.

The picture palaces were still years away; after all, motion pictures, still in their infancy, required time to grow.

The Cozy Theatre, 1919.
Courtesy of Houston
Endowment Inc.

THE
NICKELODEONS

*I consider the greatest mission of the
motion picture is first to make people
happy . . . to bring more joy and cheer
and wholesome good will into this world
of ours. And God knows we need it.*
THOMAS A. EDISON,
MOTION-PICTURE INVENTOR

*Young man, you should be grateful,
since, although my invention is not for
sale, it would undoubtedly ruin you. It
can be exploited for a certain time as a
scientific curiosity, but, apart from that,
it has no commercial future whatsoever.*
AUGUSTE LUMIÈRE,
MOTION-PICTURE INVENTOR

★ THE ALLURE OF THE CINEMA has
always been more than merely the sight of
moving pictures on a white screen; it is
the shared experience, wherein the viewer
communes with the movie as well as with
the other members of the audience.

For the exhibitor, group participation is
simply good business sense: more money
can be made selling a single product to a
group than to an individual. The original
peep-show movie loops of Edison's
Kinetoscope suffered from that basic limi-
tation; only one person could watch at a
time. Realizing this, numerous inventors
and entrepreneurs quickly forged ahead to
create a form of motion picture that could
be shown to a large group of people, and
Edison and the Lumière brothers led the
pack.

Edison's answer was the Vitascope,

which served as a blueprint for most of the other movie projectors that followed. After the 1896 premiere of both the Vitascope and the Lumière Cinématographe, projected moving pictures quickly spread across the nation. These early movies became part of the entertainment programs in opera houses, music halls, and early vaudeville theatres, whereas storefront theatres opened up to showcase film as the primary attraction. Traveling exhibitors would set up tent shows or find empty store space for their exhibits. Others would set up in parks or use the side of a downtown building. Little was needed to go into business: a vacant storefront, chairs, a projector, a white sheet stretched across the wall, and a sign painted on the exterior window.

This new form of entertainment blossomed in Houston much as it did in other major cities. In a 1940 *Houston Post* interview, P. W. Cain spoke of a movie house he opened with his brother, T. E. Cain. The year, according to Cain, was 1902: "We rented a store building in the 300 block of Main for—believe it or not—$20 a month, but the people just didn't seem to care about motion pictures, and our overhead was eating into our capital fast."

They decided to hold free open-air shows and sold advertising to local merchants. They moved operations to a leased lot at Elysian and Carter, two blocks from the Southern Pacific Roundhouse. After several successful weeks, largely because of merchant cooperation, they moved again to a site on Congress.

"It was a tough section over there near the roundhouse in those days," said Cain. "The neighborhood boys thought it was great fun to toss rocks through the screen and perpetrate other bits of their brand of humor, which proved to be embarrassing at times. One night one of the playful lads brought in from the woods one of the striped-back kitties and turned it loose in the crowd. There was no more show that night."[1]

For Houstonians at the beginning of the new century, most of the theatrical entertainment could be found in three places: Sweeney & Coombs, the Standard Theatre, and the Grand Theatre. Sweeney & Coombs booked legitimate productions, while stock companies played the Grand. The Standard handled vaudeville, usually two shows a day.[2] The Grand would later reopen as the first of the three Majestic theatres that Karl Hoblitzelle established in Houston (see Chapter 4 for a full account of Hoblitzelle's Houston Majestics).

To honor the opening of Hoblitzelle's third Majestic, in 1923, the *Houston Post* ran a special section recounting Houston's early theatrical days. According to the account, one of the earliest motion-picture showings took place in the empty top floor of the building on Congress that later housed Zindler's store. Inside the projector, a three-foot-diameter flywheel carried a continuous film loop. Power for the projector was brought in from the street-railway wires and reduced to a usable voltage by passing it through two barrels of water. A canvas screen was stretched across one wall, and the audience stood behind a roped-off area.[3] This may have been the same theatre that patron Joseph Hornberger recalled in his 1948 *Houston Press* interview with Paul Hochuli (see Chapter 1).[4]

In the same Hochuli column, Natalie Carlisle recalled seeing *The Pied Piper of Hamelin* in 1902: "I had seen it in Dallas, and when I found out it would be in

Houston, I made a trip here. I don't recall exactly where the theatre was, but it seems to me it was either the Isis, or a forerunner at the same location on Prairie between Main and Fannin."

Carlisle's remembrances point to the main difficulty—fallible human memories—in accurately presenting a chronology of these early theatres. The Isis Theatre was indeed located on Prairie between Main and Fannin, but it did not open until 1912. Carlisle may have been thinking of the Theato at 912 Prairie; however, it was not around until 1910. There also may have been a storefront theatre prior to the Isis around 1902, but documentation for that time is vague. (In addition, *The Pied Piper of Hamelin* was not released until 1903.)

THE FIRST MOTION PICTURES were void of story—merely a moving snapshot—but narrative soon became an essential part of film and its marketability. Edwin S. Porter, a cameraman and director for the Edison Company, created *The Great Train Robbery* (1903), an eleven-minute tour de force that told a definite story, ending with the startling shot of a cowboy aiming a gun directly at the viewer and pulling the trigger.

The public quickly developed an appetite for these short films. While the upper class firmly avoided such lowbrow entertainment, immigrant populations, whose lower incomes matched the affordability of this new medium, flocked to it. Nickelodeons, so called because admission was usually five cents, appeared throughout the downtown districts of all the major and midsized cities of America. In addition, films began to find their place in the larger live theatres of the day.

THE OLYMPIA OPERA HOUSE *(also known as the Standard, the Lincoln, and the Majestic)*, 711 PRAIRIE

The Olympia Opera House first opened its doors in 1903. During its history, the Olympia was known under various names—the Standard, the Texan, and the Majestic—but it was best known as the Lincoln. This may have been the movie house that Natalie Carlisle remembered in the 1948 *Houston Press* interview.

It was constructed in 1903 for Hyman Prince—owner of Sweeney & Coombs (the Houston Theatre)—who intended the showplace to feature vaudeville exclusively. Principal architect for the Olympia was Henry Cook, whose other works included the old Central Fire Station as well as the Rice and Pillot residences in Westmoreland Place. The Moorish-style two-story building was originally designed as an aerodome (or airdome, an open-air theatre) with wooden ceiling slats that could be cranked back during the hot summer months. It was later converted to a fixed ceiling. Seating was approximately five hundred, and the interior illumination was most likely by gaslight.[5]

By 1905 it had changed hands. The new operators, Alvido and Lasserre, renamed the theatre the Standard. Now functioning as a burlesque venue, it developed a rather scandalous reputation. Already considered an eyesore, it was raided numerous times, only to reopen shortly after each raid. It was eventually shut down by the city.

From 1907 it functioned as a brewery warehouse. In 1916 it became an early black professional building, housing lawyers, dentists, and insurance agents. As the Lincoln, the theatre ran a variety of "all colored" films for years to come (see Chapter 10 for a full account of its later history).

WHILE THE LINCOLN did not start off as a motion-picture house, others did. The nickelodeons were initially considered a novelty. They would, however, expand the social, moral, technical, and business boundaries of the time. The patrons of 1896 were shocked by the wanton sexuality of *The Kiss*, a brief film that featured a mustachioed man planting a smooch on the object of his affection. Such scandalous things were not meant to be seen in public, at least not by respectable people.

The five-cent picture theatres found homes across the downtown landscape but gained little recognition otherwise. The *Houston City Directories* initially lumped vaudeville theatres, opera theatres, and nickelodeons together under one heading. Only in 1907 was there a separation into "theatres" and "moving pictures." As opposed to a grander opera house, a nickelodeon was a simple affair, usually a converted retail space with banners and posters hung outside and a ticket booth next to the door. The interior was generally a long rectangular room measuring some twenty by eighty feet. Seating was either wooden benches or auditorium chairs, and a central aisle ran down the center of the room. Ceiling fans offered the basics of climate control. Occasionally, patrons would have to step up one or two steps to the sloped wooden floor, installed to improve sightlines to the screen. The screen might be fabric or a painted wall. The projector, originally set

up openly in the auditorium, was later moved to an enclosed booth opposite the screen. Because of the flammable nature of the early nitrate film stock, projection booths often included an escape window for the projectionist.[6]

A SHORT DETOUR TO GALVESTON

At this time, Galveston gained its first true moving-picture venue, the Globe Theatre on Market Street. Owner-manager Claude Brick had operated a struggling music store at that location, but was enamored of the movies. All the instruments were moved to the front of the store, and down the center was positioned a wall with three openings—a box-office window, an entrance, and an exit. "By this simple process, Claude Brick became Galveston's first motion picture exhibitor," said legendary director—and Galveston native—King Vidor, who worked at the theatre, taking tickets for $3.50 a week.[7]

In his 1953 autobiography, Vidor gave a full account of the Globe's operations, revealing the day-to-day functions of an early show place. He worked from ten thirty in the morning to ten thirty at night, tearing tickets and running the projector when the operator went to lunch. Access to the projector was limited. He would climb up a ladder and through the sixteen-by-sixteen-inch opening in the cramped galvanized-iron projector booth. The box had an opening for the projector lens, another for the operator to view the screen and focus the image, and another on the opposite side that looked down on the music store. This last opening was there in case of an emergency in either the theatre or the projection box. The box itself was so small that only someone who weighed less than 130 pounds could maneuver inside.

Since the projector had no take-up reel, the projected film would spill out into a large cloth hamper below. During reel changes, an intermission slide was shown, stating: "Just a moment, please, the operator is changing the reel." Such slides were quite common, and would be used in between features well into the twenties. A second reel would be loaded into the projector, to be fed into another cloth hamper. He would then hand-crank the original film back onto its reel, using a separate rewind.

Said Vidor, "This crude process presented a tremendous fire hazard, since sparks from the sputtering arc often fell from the flimsy lamp-house into the hamper of loose film. The resulting explosive flash rarely gave the early operators time to scramble down through the sole means of escape."[8]

The Globe ran split-reel comedies and dramas, the "split" referring to two or more stories on the same reel. Many of the comedies were French imports, starring the great Max Linder, France's Chaplin. At a later date, the two-reel Italian epic *Ben-Hur* was shown. Admission was raised for the event, from five cents to ten.

Vidor's first exposure to motion pictures was Georges Méliès's *Trip to the Moon* (1902) at the Grand Opera House. After his stint with the Globe, he worked as a newsreel photographer before moving to Hollywood. Vidor's films include *The Big Parade* (1925), *Ruby Gentry* (1952), *War and Peace* (1956), *Northwest Passage* (1940), and *The Fountainhead* (1949).

Electric Park: an outdoor venue that featured a combination of vaudeville and moving pictures. Houston Post, June 1907.

LIGHT AND HEAT

The term "electric" soon found its way into theatre verbiage as a way to distinguish motion-picture houses from those that featured strictly live performances—although a number of show places included both. The term was also tied in with the overabundance of lights used to showcase the exterior of these early cinemas. The Electric Park, on San Jacinto between Caroline and Prairie, was an outdoor vaudeville space. Billed as the coolest place in town, it featured 3,000 seats, 50 private boxes, and prices ranging from twenty to fifty cents. Tickets were available in advance at Spencer's Drug Store.[9] Motion pictures were often used as the concluding act of the bill. By December, the venue had changed its name to the People's Theatre. A separate Electric Park Theatre, at 314 Dallas Avenue, was in operation around 1912, operated by the Vaudette Amusement Company.

Main Entrance Electric Park, San Jacinto Street

There was also the Electric Theatre on Main, which featured such acts as the dancing, performing Filipino Midgets. Yet another People's Theatre, at 211 Milam, was listed in the 1910–1911 *Houston Directory* and was owned by Thomas F. Loftus. While some theatres merely changed locations, the tendency to reuse old theatre names would occur time and time again in the city.

The Texas summer heat, then as now, could be torturous. Adequate ventilation proved to be an obstacle for any indoor entertainment venue, and would remain so until the advent of air conditioning. This, along with the ease of putting up a theatre, led to the creation of the air-domes. These open-air theatres consisted of an outdoor space set up with benches, a projector, and a screen. In the evenings, when the temperature cooled off, the overall experience at an airdome could be quite pleasant.

One such venue was the Lyric Theatre, located at the corner of Capitol and San Jacinto. It too featured motion pictures on a vaudeville bill, and referred to this attraction in its advertising as the Lyricscope. The Lyric was leased by Claude Z. Brand and Henry Hoffman in December 1907, and then outfitted with heating, flooring, and a roof. Brand and Hoffman were already operating vaudeville houses in Galveston and San Antonio at the time.[10] It also was the object of court hearings between the owners and manager John Dickey, who had allegedly not fulfilled his part of the verbal contract.[11]

Most noted in 1908 was the opening of the New Houston Theatre, better known as the Prince. Lesser houses, such as the Alhambra Theatre and the Cozy, were also unveiled during that time. The Alhambra, located at the corner of Rusk and Fannin, was apparently under the same management as that of the Lyric, and was later managed by Robert Sutton.

The Cozy, at 1018 Texas, was built by M. F. "Mefo" Foster, then editor of the

Auditorium of the Prince Theatre. Courtesy of the Harry Ransom Humanities Research Center, University of Texas at Austin.

Houston Chronicle. The dailies publicized the gala premiere with the headline "It's out at last! The near theatre with the real show!" The October 11, 1908, opening night featured the singing and dancing comedienne Louise Hess, Richard Hamlin ("the medley man in brown"), and comedian Garry Owen. The tiny showplace, located in the Light Guard Armory, originally seated 250 people, and would be enlarged on two separate occasions during its brief life.

The theatre was run by Maurice Wolf, who, along with his brother, also operated another theatre, the Happy Hour, in the same building at 1022 Texas. The Happy Hour was a tab house, the name referring to the tabloid program, which spotlighted eight to ten attractive girls and a comedian.

THE PRINCE THEATRE
320 *Fannin*

The Prince Theatre, successor to the burned-down Houston Theatre (the former Sweeney & Coombs Opera House), opened on Thursday, September 24, 1908, with *The Land of Nod*, a play inspired by Lewis Carroll's *Alice in Wonderland*. Also featured on the bill was *The Salome Dance* by Marie Fauchonette.[12]

The interior was luxurious for its time. As described in *Houston Post* clippings, "The approach to the main entrance of the new theatre is through a long foyer, the walls of which are white porcelain tiling with a richly artistic frieze of landscape paintings done in oils." For opening night, ferns and tall palms lined the foyer, and red roses decorated other parts of the theatre. Patrons were greeted by a 2,000-seat auditorium of dark green and cool gray, accented by brass bars and bronze brushwork. The stage utilized two curtains: the asbestos drop curtain featured a central medallion and two tall flame-bearing urns on either side of the stage, while the stage curtain featured a Greek court scene, accented by heavy green velvet drapery. Ceiling and sidewall frescos, plus a great circular light in the ceiling's center, completed the effect.

Over the following years, the Prince would play host to vaudeville acts, melodramas, and movies. Houstonians saw live performances by Sarah Bernhardt, Al Jolson, Fanny Brice, Otis Skinner, John Drew, Lillian Russell, Anna Pavlova, Al G. Fields, James K. Hackett, Mary Mannering, Viola Allen, James T. Powers, Murray & Mack, DeWolf Hopper, Chauncey Olcott, Weber & Fields, and Anna Held.

In October 1915, the Prince featured a road show of D. W. Griffith's *Birth of a Nation*, complete with a thirty-piece symphony orchestra. It returned for a repeat engagement the following February; the ticket prices advertised in a local newspaper ranged from twenty-five cents for gallery seats to two dollars for the lower floor.

The Prince featured its own orchestra during the teens and twenties, under the baton of Professor Steinfaldt. On March 3, 1919, a new $10,000 organ was unveiled during a presentation of live acts and film, along with a two-hour recital given by Professor Piller.[13]

Business slowly dwindled as newer, more elaborate theatres opened. A 1920 newspaper ad showed it, along with the Liberty, Queen, and Zoe, under the management of the Paramount Theatre Corporation. Eventually, the doors were closed, opening only for an occasional road show. It was then taken over by Loew's Interests, using the theatre as a showplace for Loew's vaudeville. This continued through 1922, when the Lewis Worth Stock Company secured it. The building eventually became the property of the Massachusetts Mutual Life Insurance Company.

In the thirties, the building was leased to the Classified Parking System and converted into a four-story parking garage, at an estimated cost of $50,000. The building, before the conversion, had become a ghostly, abandoned shell. Chairs were still in place, as was the stage curtain, adorned with advertisements for Cheek & Neal's Maxwell House Coffee, Lewis's Fish and Oyster Cafe, and Krupp & Tuffley's buttoned, bulldog-nosed shoes for men. The dressing rooms were covered with autographs of the personalities that had graced the Prince's stage.

All this disappeared when the Prince became a twenty-four-hour hotel for cars. This, too, would eventually be razed.

SMALLER VENUES OF THE TIME

The 1908–1909 period gave rise to a number of smaller theatres: the Happy Hour, at 1022 Texas, managed by Harry Bonn; the Superba, at 403 Main; the Victor, at 412 Milam; and the Scenic, at 313 Travis, owned by Charles F. Bode. Its structure still stands as part of Treebeard's Restaurant in Old Market Square. Another Scenic was listed in the 1910–1911 *Houston Directory* at 507 Main, under the proprietorship of Bode and Isenhour.

The Bijou, at 413 San Jacinto, was an open-air theatre with a top constructed of a gas-pipe framework and a black tarpaulin that could be thrown back on sunny days. The auditorium was heated by gas stoves during the colder periods.[14]

The Vendome, featuring "polite vaudeville," was owned by W. F. Box and located at 406 Fannin. Its grand opening took place on April 18, 1909, with six high-class acts. As advertised in a newspaper of the day, admission was ten cents, and reserved seats cost an extra dime. It reopened in 1910 under new management. Movies featured there, such as those by Pathé and Biograph, were advertised as Vendomescope. It offered special bargain matinees on Wednesday and Saturday afternoons at two thirty.[15]

Another "polite vaudeville" house was the Passmore, at 414 Fannin. By December 1909, it changed names after being bought out by A. Schwartz, who had worked with the London Hippodrome and the New York Columbus Theatre. It was renamed the Imperial Grande, and later still it would change to the Orpheum, under the management of John B. Kelly.[16]

The year 1910 marked the opening of two important structures: Karl Hoblitzelle's second Majestic Theatre, which opened in February, and the new City Auditorium, which opened on December 8. The new Majestic was, for its time, the grandest of the local theatres. Upon its opening, a *Houston Chronicle* reporter stated that it would be "compared favorably with the gilded palaces of ancient kings" (see Chapter 4 for a full account of Hoblitzelle's Houston Majestics).[17]

Another smaller-scale theatre was the

Giuseppe de Liguoro's Dante's Inferno (1909) was Italy's first full-length feature film, and it became an international hit when released in America in 1911. Courtesy of the Houston Metropolitan Research Center, Houston Public Library, MSS 145-159.

Dixie, at 603 Main. It would entertain patrons throughout the twenties, eventually changing its name to the Feature #2. The Dixie was managed at various times by Fred Peters, Anthony Kornmann, and V. H. Hulsey, and at one time employed Fred Cannata as a combination doorman and usher for three dollars a week. In his spare time, he played the clarinet in the orchestra pit. Cannata would go on to become Will Horwitz's right-hand man in later years. The Dixie was one of four theatres that would be controlled by Moye Wicks, the others being the Star, at 507 Main; the Vaudette ("The little house

with the big program"), next to Sweeney's at 417 Main; and the Gem, at 505 Main, across from the Rice Hotel. Wicks would eventually give up the theatres for the confectionery business, which he operated while handling the movie houses.[18]

John De Brueys, in Paul Hochuli's 1948 *Showcase* column, said that the Star was right next to the Great Atlantic & Pacific Tea Company store, adding: "We kids always called the Star the 'Rats,' which was Star spelled backwards."[19]

The Gem opened on March 6, 1912. Listed also at that address in the 1912 *Houston Directory* was the Bil-Sol Theatre, under the proprietorship of Solan and Billings.

Associated with Wicks was Anthony Xydias, who managed both the Gem and the Star, and later still, the Rex. Xydias would eventually quit as an exhibitor during the twenties and become a director of cheaply made western thrillers in Hollywood.[20] Many of these features, with titles such as *Buffalo Bill on the U.P. Trail* and *General Custer at Little Big Horn* (both 1926), would find a second audience in the thirties with the 16mm home-movie market.

Also dating from this time was the Theato, at 912 Prairie, in the Scholibo Building, which was originally constructed in the 1880s. During its brief history, it was managed by W. F. Hennessey. A fire destroyed the theatre in the spring of 1910. The building survived and no one was hurt in the blaze, but the fire created concerns on the city council, resulting in a safety ordinance that required all theatres without rear exits to have the seats face the entry door. This caused many existing theatres to shift the seats around, so patrons entering the house faced the audience. The council's attention was well founded, since the highly flammable nitrate motion-picture stock made theatre fires a harsh reality.[21]

The Scholibo Building would become better known as the Shoe Market Building, from the retail store it housed for many years. The building was modernized in the forties, but by the early 1990s it had fallen into abandonment and disrepair. Its last occupant was an adult-movie theatre. It gained a new lease on life in the later nineties, after a complete restoration won it a 1999 Good Brick Award from the

Greater Houston Preservation Alliance. By then the building housed the Shoe Market Gallery on the ground floor, which specialized in gifts, home furnishings, and ethnic arts and crafts. The upper floor served as community meeting rooms and office space for Treebeard's Restaurant.[22]

THE NEWER, BIGGER COZY
1112 Texas Avenue

By 1910, the original Cozy proved to be too small, so M. F. Foster agreed to build a larger showplace. It would become one of the early standards for theatres in Houston, ranking with the Majestic, Isis, Queen, and Travis as a solid entertainment venue. It began as a musical-comedy house, later advancing to burlesque, and finally becoming a movie house.[23]

The theatre was built at a cost of about $30,000; Gus Street was the general contractor. It shared the same building as the old Light Guard Armory. The two-story structure seated around eight hundred people. The auditorium featured a balcony, four boxes flanking each side of the broad stage, and dressing rooms in the

Advertisement in the Houston Chronicle *for the grand opening of the Cozy, October 16, 1910.*

rear. One of these contained a fireplace, the room most likely reserved for the star entertainer. It was acclaimed also as having the best ventilation in Houston; the air conditioning consisted of forty large openings that allowed a moderate breeze to pass. In later ads, it billed itself as the "almost open-air theatre" and the "house of exits."[24]

The theatre was operated by Maurice Wolf, who had run the older Cozy at 1018 Texas. The new Cozy opened on October 17, 1910, with six "big acts" and an orchestra led by Charles Lewis, of the Herb and Lewis musical team. Performers included Lola Milton and company, the Melrose Comedy Four, Will Beam, the Sharrocks, Torcat and his great trained roosters, and a Cozygraph feature. Regular admission was ten cents, while the reserved seats on the main floor and the balcony-circle seats were twenty cents. Reservations could be made in advance by calling Preston 178. Friday evening was amateur night. Meanwhile, the original Cozy continued operations for an additional week.

Wolf eventually moved to Boston, becoming the New England district manager for the Loew's theatre chain.

In 1913, the Cozy was rented to the Barraco brothers, Paul and Victor, for eight hundred dollars a month. The Barracos also operated the Best Theatre and the Crescent. Paul died in 1932; Victor found a career as an attorney and in the Marine Corps. He would also be instrumental in the construction of the Bellaire Theatre in 1949.

"I was in the show biz then," Victor said in a 1973 *Texas Monthly* interview.[25] "Owned five theatres and the Key vaudeville house on West Dallas where Bessie Smith used to play." Barraco also owned the property at Grant and Welch that eventually became Anderson Fair. He died in December 1990 at the age of ninety-seven.

Houstonian Denney Strad, in a 1941 interview, recalled performing there with the Pete Pate Musical Comedy Company during its heyday: "The Cozy was one of the best small theatres in Texas in those days and presented some of the country's best entertainers in one-night stands. We were here on vacation with Mrs. Strad's folks when we started playing the Cozy. We did an operatic singing and violin vaudeville act. Pete was packing 'em in and hanging out the 'Standing Room Only' sign almost every night in those days." The Strad and Legato act would pull down one hundred dollars a week—not bad money for the time. The Strads also played the Travis and Prince theatres, as well as on Broadway and abroad.[26]

The Barracos operated the Cozy for several years.[27] Gabe Laskin then took it over for four or five years, including the World War I years. Soldiers from Camp Logan and Ellington Field would come into town to see the shows.

By the late twenties, the Cozy had been taken over by Bill Lytle, a former San Antonio mailman who owned a chain of movie houses. During this time, the theatre presented movies exclusively. After Lytle, management of the Cozy became unstable, and the theatre would be open one week and closed the next. Charles Camp, who had previously operated the Prince Theatre, eventually became the manager.

On March 28, 1926, the Cozy reopened

as the Royal Theatre. The evening program featured comedian Sam Mylie and his "peppy review," along with the Culberson Orchestra.

The last gasp of the Cozy took place around 1932 or 1933. It was open for about three weeks. The Commerce Company eventually bought the property. During its remaining years, the front entrance and lobby were converted into a fruit stand. In September 1941, the Olshan Demolishing Company began work on the Cozy. The common lot of many of Houston's early theatres was eventual demolition. The Cozy was razed to make way for a parking lot.

JORGENSEN AND AIRDOMES

A 1940s *Houston Post* article by Mildred Stockard described a nickelodeon at 410 Main, where the Princess was located.[28]

According to Stockard, the house was opened by George K. Jorgensen on January 1, 1907. Jorgensen had trained himself in carnivals, street fairs, and circuses, touring the country with his own projector and films. When film distributors made it easier to obtain new merchandise, he rented a vacant storefront in Houston, filled it with 200 folding chairs, hung up a sheet as a screen, installed his Little Edison projector, and set up a ticket office in front. His capital investment came to eighty-five dollars.

The first day's business brought in 800 patrons and forty dollars, followed the next day by 1,200 attendees. He handled all operations, from selling the tickets to hand-cranking the projection equipment. At the end of each reel he would turn on the house lights for a five-minute intermission while he rewound the film. Jorgensen sold his enterprise one month later at a profit, moved to Galveston, and

The Isis Theatre on Prairie. The building still stands. E. V. Richards Collection, courtesy of the Harry Ransom Humanities Research Center, University of Texas at Austin.

invested $180 to open up the Crystal Theatre. When it was sold in 1939, it was worth $250,000.

Two airdomes opened in Houston in 1911. The Plaza, at 1101 Main, was under the management of Mrs. Cora E. Jones, and later that of Charles T. Brian, Jr., who had managed the Galveston Grand Opera House the previous year. The 2,000-seat showplace, which opened on June 18, was decorated with thousands of electric lights, ferns, and flowers. The entrance featured a shell walk bordered by benches, swings, and flowers. The Plaza's motto: "Stars above you—Stars in front of you."[29] Another open-air venue was the San Jacinto Airdome, at the corner of Prairie and San Jacinto. It opened on May 12.

Over a dozen houses debuted in 1912. Chief among them was the Isis.

THE ISIS THEATRE
1012 Prairie

The Isis Theatre was Houston's first truly deluxe motion-picture theatre. Built in 1912, it brought audiences from the nickelodeons into a larger, plusher world. When it opened on April 16, the world was still reeling from the news of the *Titanic*, which had sunk only four days earlier.

The theatre, on Prairie between Main and Fannin, was owned by Hermann Fichtenberg of New Orleans, who had operated similar houses in other cities. The structure itself was constructed by C. D. Hill and Company. Management of Fichtenberg's chain was handled by W. H. Gueringer, with Moe H. Goodman as the local manager. Goodman would eventually be succeeded by veteran the-

atre man Hal Norfleet. Fichtenberg planned the showplace to feature a combination of motion pictures and live musical entertainment. Absent from his itinerary were vaudeville acts and stage plays.[30]

The theatre's namesake—Isis, the Egyptian goddess of fertility and enchantment—and her symbol, a flaming torch, were incorporated into the exterior structure. Referred to as "the theatre beautiful," the Isis featured modern fireproof architecture, a spectacular $5,000 pipe organ, and live orchestral accompaniment for the films. The organ, fifteen feet wide, twelve feet deep, and twenty feet high, was positioned behind the mirror curtain on the stage. The console was located in the orchestra pit and connected by a set of trackers.

A ventilation system brought in a constant stream of fresh air from the outside. Known as the air-washing system, it was composed of a large fan that sucked air from the roof through a fine spray of water that "washed" the air before shooting it into the auditorium. During summer months, blocks of ice would be placed in the washing chamber, creating an early form of air conditioning. In addition, vents carried air into the projectionist's booth, much to the comfort of the operator, who normally had to endure the heat produced by the film projector. Three ventilators on the roof eliminated the dead air that collected in the upper reaches of the auditorium.

Seating capacity was 900, with 750 seats on the lower floor and 150 in the balcony. The opera-style chairs were upholstered in leather and finished with brass. The interior was decorated in green and gold, with paintings of the namesake

Egyptian goddess on the walls. Illuminating the auditorium were fourteen hanging lamps as well as three large circular domes fitted with electric lights.

In the opening-day newspaper ads, a footnote stated: "Balcony exclusively for colored." The Isis balcony was accessible from a separate entrance. Segregation was commonplace, and would remain so for decades to come.

The Isis grand opening kicked off at six o'clock. Admission was ten cents for adults and five cents for children. Once inside, the patrons were escorted to their seats by a trained team of ushers. A full program had been planned out for the evening, beginning with an overture performed by the Isis Orchestra and conducted by W. R. Patrick. Arthur J. H. Barbour was the featured organist. Next on the program was the drama *A Dangerous Model*, followed by singer John Baxter. Two split-reel comedies, *Checkmate* and *The Ranchman's Marathon* (both 1912, directed by Allan Dwan), were presented before singer Guy Harris, billed as "that eccentric fellow." The final entry in the program was another drama, *The Torn Letter* (1912, directed by Tom Ricketts).[31]

The Isis program changed every one or

Front and rear views of the interior of the Isis. The facial busts on the sidewalls survived into the current century. E. V. Richards Collection, courtesy of the Harry Ransom Humanities Research Center, University of Texas at Austin.

two days. A rare filmed appearance of the great stage actress Sarah Bernhardt in *Jeanne Doré* (1915, directed by René Hervil and Louis Mercanton) was shown for a four-day run beginning February 2, 1916. Another early film, *The Trey o' Hearts* by Joseph Vance, described as "the great serial problem play," was presented in installments, much like the later movie serials. On the bill could also be found a list of live entertainment, such as Frank Callon, the eccentric singing comedian; singer Bessie Walsh; and Neal Abel, the man with the mobile face.

Additions and improvements were con-stant. Within two years, a new marquee and electrical display, studded with bulbs and suspended arc lights, were integrated into the theatre exterior. Part of this was due to one-upmanship with its chief rival, the Queen, which E. H. Hulsey opened in 1913.

The Isis reached its peak in 1917, when it was taken over by the Saenger Amuse-ment Company, with Al Lever as its man-ager. Saenger was a Louisiana-based theat-rical chain, founded in 1912 by brothers Abe and Julian Saenger. The chain was purchased by Paramount in 1929.

Al Lever went on to become branch

manager for Interstate Theatres. Saenger would eventually let go of the Isis, and it fell under the control of Will Horwitz, who placed Fred Cannata in charge of its operations. Along with the Liberty Theatre, the Isis would run under the Horwitz Homefolks theatre banner for a short time, but its days as a showplace were coming to an end.

The twenties brought in an era of truly opulent movie houses. Once considered the finest theatre in Houston, the Isis became plain by comparison with the regal upstarts. The last to manage the movie house was Ed F. Barnes, who later went on to become city editor for the *Houston Post*.

By 1928, the Isis had closed down, having never made the conversion to sound. The last newspaper advertisement ran on Sunday, October 7, for the Janet Gaynor feature *7th Heaven* (1927, directed by Frank Borzage). The building was remodeled for retail; the last tenant before a long period of vacancy was McCrory's 5&10 Variety Store.

THE AFTERLIFE OF THE ISIS

In 1998, the structure was given a chance for renewal. The downtown area had recently experienced a surge of redevelopment, including a new baseball stadium and the conversion of the Albert Thomas Convention Center into Bayou Place (including two theatres—the Angelica Film Center & Cafe and the Aerial Theatre). A number of older buildings were being converted into residential lofts, the most notable being the Rice Hotel. Across the street from the Rice side entrance was the Isis building.

Plans for the three-story building featured office space on the upper floors and a ground-floor pub, established by Scott and Lauri Littlewood, owners of the Bank Draft brewery in the Rice Village shop-

Facial busts in the interior of the former Isis, 2000. Photograph by David Welling.

ping center. Although the original Isis Theatre was no longer intact, numerous architectural flourishes still remained, and plans were set to uncover and restore the original structure. Ironically, the *Titanic*'s ghost still seemed to hover about the structure. There was a burst of renewed interest in the ill-fated ship after James Cameron's blockbuster film was released the previous year, sweeping the Academy Awards and becoming the largest-grossing film to date.

The former theatre space was effectively divided in half. First to open was the Mercury Room, an atmospheric bar designed in shades of browns and oranges.

Icon Ventures LLP, headed by David Edwards, served as developer for the transformation. The terrazzo floors were refinished, and structural elements long hidden by the ceiling were exposed. Installed on the lower floor was the semi-private VIP Room, with lighting sculptures by Isaac Maxwell and custom-made furniture and accents by the design teams Spaw Maxwell, Whitney and Whitney, and Griffin Architects. However, the premiere architectural element was the original art deco master stairway. The staircase and decorative railings were restored, and an inlaid wood cap was added to raise the height in order to comply with current building codes. The work on the stairs alone cost $40,000. The Mercury Room's premier opening was held on October 12, 1999, as a benefit for the Theatre District Association's ArtStart outreach program.[32]

Meanwhile, work continued slowly on converting the other side into the Mercantile Brewpub, which offered some surprises as the space was cleared. A long-vacant upstairs room, which once served as the theatre's projection space, still had the wall opening left for the projector. But the real treasure was discovered after the drop-down ceiling was removed. On an upper sidewall was a highly detailed sculpture running the length of the room, with ornate flourishes and five faces spaced throughout. Although in need of restoration, this decorative element would become a highlight of the finished brewery, earning it the "Best Atmosphere" listing in the *Houston Press*'s 2000 "Best of Houston" issue.

Spirits at the Mercantile were sometimes more than just libations. General manager Jeff Ehrich commented in the September 2000 issue of *002* that the building was supposedly haunted, and noted that three of the bartenders and a waitress had all reported seeing a man standing on the staircase landing at closing time, after the bar had been emptied. "He wears a derby hat, slacks, a white shirt and tie," stated Ehrich. "They tell me you see him out of the corner of your eye."[33]

Unfortunately, the opening of the Mercantile brought about the downfall of both it and the Bank Draft. "The Mercantile never really fulfilled its potential, despite the revitalization of downtown Houston," reported one trade journal. It was eventually shut down.[34]

More successful was the neighboring Mercury Room, which was listed in the May 2000 *Playboy* as one of the best bars in America.[35]

HOUSTON'S LIST of theatres kept growing in 1912. The Crystal, at 407 Main, was operational in 1912, managed by William

Geibig. On April 22 and 23 of that year, it presented what was advertised as the only existing footage of the *Titanic*, taken on deck and from the landing stage ten minutes before sailing time. In truth, part of this footage was actually taken from the *Titanic*'s sister ship, the *Olympic*.[36] Also in May, the theatre installed a $5,000 Choralcelo electric piano.[37] In June 1914, the operation of the theatre was taken over by Pearce Theatre management, which put in a new picture screen, overhauled the projectors, and installed new lenses. It was later purchased and rebuilt by A. E. Kiesing and placed under the management of Hal C. Norfleet, who made his career in the amusement business. It reopened on January 21, 1915, as the Key, showing Francis X. Bushman in *The Bat-*

tle of Love.[38] As advertised, it was "always cool at the Key."[39]

The Royal, at 211 Main, next to the First National Bank, had been a vaudeville house owned by Maurice Newmann.[40] In January 1912, its name was changed to the Pastime, and it was managed by John D. Dunmyre. Later still, its operations were handled by A. Schulman, who would continue working in show business when this theatre eventually closed.[41]

Others that opened included the Mecca, on Texas between Main and Travis, and the Grand, owned by Connally and McTighe, at 3618 Washington. It would be later known as the Midway, and featured live entertainment. Meanwhile, the Barraco Brothers opened the Crescent

The Pastime Theatre. Courtesy of the Houston Metropolitan Research Center, Houston Public Library, MSS 145-139.

at 602 Main. Other theatres that they would control were the Best, at 212 Main, and the Cozy. The 1912 *Houston Directory* also listed the "Is It Is," at 2209 Congress. No further details are known.

The early theatres remained in a constant state of evolution. Storefront shells made way for bigger and better venues.

The 1912 Isis was a solid indicator of the future of motion-picture houses. With 1913 would come more new theatres, including one that would challenge the Isis on its own turf. The duel of the cinemas was about to begin, setting a trend that continues to this day.

The 800 block of Main
Street facing north, c. 1926.
On the left is the Liberty
Theatre, on the right is the
Capitol (previously the
Zoe), and farther back is the
Queen. George Fuermann
Texas and Houston Collec-
tion, courtesy of Special
Collections, University of
Houston Libraries.

THREE

★ ★ ★

BIGGER AND
BETTER

★ ★ ★

The coming of the motion picture was as important as that of the printing press.

WILLIAM RANDOLPH HEARST

★ THE YEARS 1913 AND 1914 were ones of great change in the movie industry as short films began to grow longer. *The Adventures of Kathlyn* (1913, directed by Francis J. Grandon) introduced the format of a serial film, and after the success of the nine-reel foreign epic *Quo Vadis?* (1912, directed by Enrico Guazzoni), American audiences seemed more accepting of longer lengths. Director D. W. Griffith cemented this new standard with his four-reel *Judith of Bethulia* (1914), before embarking on his grand vision, the twelve-reel *Birth of a Nation* (1915). And in 1914, the Keystone Film Company introduced a new comedian to the world: Charlie Chaplin.

Theatres across America reflected these movie-industry changes as nickelodeons evolved into larger, plusher movie houses. Films, still part of a vaudeville

program in many theatres, took on more prominence as the decade passed. In addition, theatres paid more attention to customers' comfort and satisfaction, striving to provide comfortable seating, quality music, soundproofed projection equipment, and attentive service staffing.

The smaller storefront houses were slowly replaced by more impressive venues designed either exclusively for film or for film–live performance combinations. The natural—and logical—inspiration for the new breed of theatres was the opera house, in a pared-down, more streamlined style. As the decade progressed, architectural opulence found its way into the design palette of the movie houses.

THE QUEEN
613 *Main*

The most noted of the 1913 openings was that of E. L. Hulsey's Queen. Hulsey had already established a string of theatres, including the Queens in Dallas and Galveston. The $200,000 Houston showplace, on Main between Texas and Capitol, opened one year after the Isis Theatre did, and while the Isis may have been Houston's first deluxe theatre for film and live performances, the Queen was the city's first theatre built exclusively to show motion pictures. Indeed, it set out to rival the Isis, and this competition would continue between the two for some time.

The architectural firm of C. D. Hill handled the work under the supervision of E. F. Glick. Construction began after Hulsey took out a ninety-nine-year lease from the property owners, the Levy brothers; total investments on the Queen sat at half a million dollars. F. W. Peters would manage the theatre.[1]

The Queen, according to opening-day ads, was "fit for a king or queen and not too fine for the comfort of their majesties, the good, plain American people."

The stone, terra-cotta, and brick exterior featured a front vestibule of marble and fresco work, mahogany panels and doors, and even a mahogany entry-stairs handrail. The interior consisted of a 25-by-50-foot lobby leading to the 50-by-100-foot auditorium, with green leather opera-house seats. Although fireproofed to the standards of 1913, the building contained fourteen separate exits for both safety and convenience.

The central feature was the $20,000 Pilcher and Sons pipe organ, located in the orchestra pit along with a baby grand piano. The taller pipes formed part of the decorative embellishments on the sides of the proscenium arch. The Isis countered this by adding its own ten-piece orchestra, the competition favorably raising the standards of music in Houston's movie houses.

As at the Isis, climate control was an important factor at the Queen. A $15,000 air-washing system was installed in the the-

Lobby and staircase of the Queen. Note the neighboring jewelry store, seen through the window on the right. Courtesy of the Houston Metropolitan Research Center, Houston Public Library, MSS 100-273.

atre basement to cool and condition the air, this being the best option in the days before true air conditioning existed. A large electric fan would draw the air into the "washing tanks," then back into the theatre by way of 400 mushroom-shaped air registers located in the floor beneath the seats. The unit could also heat the building during the winter months.

Opening day was to begin with an organ recital at three o'clock; however, this was postponed to a later date. The opening performance, the Vitagraph three-reel picture *Wreck*, began at six thirty. Admission was twenty cents for box seats, fifteen cents for the reserved-for-smoking mezzanine, ten cents for the lower floor, and five cents for the balcony.

Hulsey's Queen would remain the high mark in Houston's theatre scene for a number of years, eventually becoming one of Houston's Paramount theatres, along with the Liberty, Zoe, and Prince.[2] Yet by the end of the silent era, other much grander palaces would surpass its opulence. One of the last Queen ads ran in May 1932 for D. W. Griffith's *The Struggle*, a fitting choice for what had once been a premier showplace in Houston.[3] O. B. Thomas, the last of a long line of Queen managers, found his way to the Empire Theatre in San Antonio. The Queen ceased to exist in the midthirties, the site sold to Woolworth Interests.[4]

Auditorium of the Queen. Courtesy of the Harry Ransom Humanities Research Center, University of Texas at Austin.

THE QUEEN'S DEBUT overshadowed those of most of the other houses that opened during the year. The Garden, on Fannin between Capitol and Rusk, opened on May 7. Also opened around that time were the Texas, at 215 Main next to South Texas Commercial National Bank; the Jewel Theatre, at 505 Travis; and the Heights Airdome, at 402 West 19th Avenue in the Heights. The Top o'Houston, located on the roof of the Carter Building (later known as the Second National Bank Building), featured live entertainment, motion pictures, and a food menu that included cold drinks, ice cream, tea, juice, salads, deviled eggs, and cigars.[5] Also listed in the 1913 *Houston Directory* was the Deroloc ("colored" spelled backwards) Theatre at 609 San Felipe, most likely a movie house for black patrons. In the 1919 *Directory*, it was listed as the American Theatre.

The Rex Theatre, at 511 Main, in the Binz Building, was later known as the Rivoli. The Binz Building, Houston's first skyscraper, was built in 1894 by Jacob Binz, and towered a full six stories.[6]

Two other theatres were of note that year, the Pearce and the Travis. The Travis Theatre, at 614 Travis, held its opening on April 13, 1913, with a program largely composed of vaudeville and a moving picture. The first week's entertainment consisted of the Mayfair Trio, the Copelands, a musical presentation entitled *Musical Pikes*, and a "Traviscope" movie.[7] Under the management of William Geibig, it eventually became a known as a tab show—a tabloid, or a condensed, low-budget version of a major live show, often consisting of skits, singing, dancing, and a movie.[8]

In 1919, the Travis was sold to a young man for $150, a sum he had to borrow. He

Devil-suited ushers accented the Queen's promotion for A. E. Merritt's Seven Footprints to Satan, 1929. Courtesy of the Sloane Collection, Houston, Texas.

*The Liberty Theatre, 1924.
Courtesy of the Houston
Metropolitan Research Cen-
ter, Houston Public Library,
MSS 200-332.*

only had $13 in his pocket at the time.
The man was Will Horwitz, and he
would play a major part in the downtown
theatre scene and in the lives of thousands of Houstonians during the Depression (see Chapter 7 for a full account of
Will Horwitz and his theatres).

THE PEARCE/LIBERTY THEATRE
718 *Main*

Two months after the opening of the Travis, the Pearce Theatre held its premiere.
The theatre was advertised as one of the
most beautiful playhouses in the South,
and featured a new radium gold screen
and musical accompaniment by a live
orchestra. A large battery of electric fans
provided ventilation and cooling. The
opening-day presentation, on June 10,
featured *The Accusing Hand* (directed by
Romaine Fielding) and *The Forgotten
Latchkey* (directed by Ralph Ince).[9]

In 1916 the theatre changed management, and was rechristened the Liberty,
where it was "a dime—all the time." A
grand reopening was held on Sunday,
February 6, featuring the Pearl White picture *Hazel Kirke*. The reopening-day
newspaper advertisements promised a theatre that was as "clean as a pin," as well as
willing to honor old coupons. Some theatres at this time sold books of admission
tickets. If the cinema was sold, it was left
to the discretion of the new owners
whether to honor the old tokens. The Liberty management decided to honor the
old Pearce coupons as a buy one–use one
deal. The ads also stated that the child's
admission was "half a dime. A slick for
you. A jitney for your kid."

Also in the ad was a notice of nonhos-
tility: "To our esteemed contemporaries:
The Liberty opens in the friendliest of
spirit. It has no fight to make on anyone.
It believes in co-operation—in harmony.
It bears malice toward none and good will

toward all. It will do everything in its power to promote the moving picture business as a whole—realizing that in helping others, it is only helping itself." This may have been either an indication of bad blood between the former owners and the neighboring movie houses or merely a publicity ploy.[10]

On April 12 and 13, 1922, the Liberty featured the then-controversial film *Are You Fit to Marry?* (released in 1917 as *The Black Stork*, directed by Leopold and Theodore Wharton), which dealt with eugenics. Ladies-only showings were held during the day, and presentations for men were at night. A lecture by Martha E. Lavacek, a nurse and social worker, was included at the matinee shows. Dr. H. J. Brooks addressed the men in the evenings.[11]

According to a 1938 *Houston Chronicle* article, the Liberty, in 1925, featured what may have been Houston's first talking picture, a few years before the Al Jolson phenomenon. It used the old phonograph system, which was unpredictable at best—synchronization was rarely precise, resulting in a character's voice continuing after the mouth stopped moving, and the volume was never quite loud enough.[12]

Will Horwitz later operated the Liberty for several years, beginning in 1926, but by the end of the twenties the theatre had ceased operations. The Liberty was eventually razed during a block-wide

Auditorium of the Liberty. Courtesy of the Harry Ransom Humanities Research Center, University of Texas at Austin.

demolition to make way for the Gulf Building.

THE CROWN (717 *Main*) AND THE ZOE (719 *Main*)

The year 1914 heralded the openings of the Crown and Zoe theatres. The Crown was located at 717 Main, in the Mason Building, and bore the name of its manager, Pete Crown, who eventually went into the dairy business.[13] Ads for the theatre invited the public to "come and spend a pleasant few moments." The Crown would later relocate to 305 Main, lasting into the twenties and surviving an unsuccessful attempt to revive the house as a tab theatre. In the thirties it reopened as the Joy.

The Zoe Theatre was located at 719 Main, directly across the street from the Pearce. The grand opening feature on October 14 was *America* (directed by Lawrence B. McGill), complete with souvenirs and an orchestra.

Theatres would help out the community whenever possible. When a fire, caused by a petty thief, destroyed the Bayland Orphans' Home, the Pearce and the Zoe held benefit screenings to raise money for the institution. The Pearce ran the two-reel Thanhouser film *Under False Colors*, a Keystone comedy entitled *A Colored Girl's Love*, and the Biograph comedy *His Jonah*. Lois Weber's *False Colors* was run at the Zoe.[14]

By 1916 the theatre was known as Hulsey's Zoe Theatre, showing such features as *Salome* (1918, directed by J. Gordon Edwards), starring Theda Bara. In March 1922, its name was changed to the Capitol, and would continue operations

through the midtwenties. The structure still stands, with a few architectural remnants of its theatrical past intact.

THE ONGOING EVOLUTION OF THEATRE DESIGN

The Zoe, like the Queen and Isis, used interior design and decorative flourishes to set itself apart from the older storefront nickelodeons. Its auditorium included an arched ornamental ceiling, accented moldings surrounding the screen, and organ pipes set to either side. As Linda Anderson Courtney pointed out in an article on Houston's early theatres, the evolution in both live-performance and motion-picture theatres took place concurrently, making it difficult to distinguish in which type of venue certain design aspects originated. She observed that live theatres encouraged deeper balconies, sightline formulas, and decoration. Motion-picture theatres were largely responsible for such things as space planning, building codes, and fire codes; the last was especially important because of the flammable nitrate film stock.[15]

John Klaber, writing for the November 1915 issue of *Architectural Record*, noted, "Design has been bad in these early picture theatres because [1] the vulgar tastes of the theatre owners and [2] their disinclination to pay the commission of competent architects."[16] He further pointed out the importance of screen and seat position, ironically falling prey to limited conceptions of the "language" of film. "The screen," he wrote, "should not be too high from the floor, in order that the figures may

*Auditorium of the Zoe The-
atre, 719 Main. Courtesy of
the Harry Ransom Humani-
ties Research Center, University of Texas at Austin.*

appear to walk on the ground and not in
the air." Early movies were shot like a
stage play, in one continuous long shot
and no close-ups. The audience quickly
came to understand how a medium shot
or a close-up strengthened the impact of
a scene, regardless of their not being able
to see the actor's feet. The walking-on-air
issue would likewise be overcome.[17]

Another change that would evolve over
the next decade was the redesigning of box
seats into balconies. In stage productions
before the 1870s, the action took place on
a wide forestage in front of the proscenium
arch, providing easy visibility for those in
the side boxes that lined the left and right
walls. Later, the "box set," in which the
action occurred behind the proscenium,
in a setting more akin to a room, was in

widespread use. This shift created sightline
problems for those sitting in the boxes
closest to the stage. As a result, boxes were
moved to the rear of the auditorium.

Seating structure changed again with
the advent of motion pictures, since the
optimum viewing area was situated per-
pendicular to the screen, right down the
center of the auditorium. The horseshoe
shape of the balcony evolved into a
deeper rectangular shape that extended
over the lobby or the rear of the auditorium. In some cases, the balconies held
more seats than the main floor.[18]

BY 1915 the star system had been established, allowing Mary Pickford to earn a
$104,000-a-year salary. The number of
film theatres in the United States

reached 17,000. Houston, according to the 1915 *Directory*, could account for 21, including legitimate stage venues. This was the year of *The Birth of a Nation*—Houstonians would experience the road-show engagement of it in October at the Prince Theatre, complete with a ten-piece orchestra.

While the true move to the suburbs would not occur for several more decades, an occasional picture house could be found outside of the downtown area. The 1915 *Houston Directory* listed the Arcadia, at 1902 North Main.

Between 1916 and 1917, the following movie houses opened: the Beacon, at 2514 McKinney; the Best, at 212 Main; the Douglas, later known as the Rao Rocco, at 2519 Live Oak, and the Northside, at 1016 Hogan. The Lyric, at 211 Main; the Victory, at 1011 Congress; and the Odin, in the 2700 block of Odin Avenue, all first saw life in 1918.

The Boulevard Theatre, at 6633 Harrisburg, opened on June 5, 1919. The opening attraction was D. W. Griffith's *Greatest Thing in Life*. Opening day ads ran a jingle that read:

So come on, Mary; don't fuss up the kids;
Just wash off their faces and put on their
*   lids;*
We'll attend the new show, it opens
*   tonight,*
On Harrisburg Boulevard, right in plain
*   sight.*

Wear your new gingham dress; it's neat
*   and clean,*
And, I saw Uncle Bill, he has cut out the
*   Queen;*
Their crowd is going and so's Uncle

John.
So hurry up Girlie, and don't be so long.

No crowded trolley nor carfare to pay,
We can save up our coin and go every
*   day,*
The best high-class pictures are booked
*   to run,*
Full of life, love and nature with oceans
*   of fun.*

The manager, he's a right thoughtful
*   young man,*
And, equipping the show, has done the
*   best he can*
To make a cozy, homelike retreat,
So come along, Mary; Let's get a front
*   seat.*[19]

The Boulevard would stay in operation for the next forty-three years. It was consumed by fire on Friday, December 21, 1962. Seventy-five firemen fought the blaze, which apparently started in the projection room. Frank D. Wilke, who had owned the theatre for the last thirty years, said that it was so badly damaged he would

The Liberty Theatre at Camp Logan. Courtesy of the Houston Metropolitan Research Center, Houston Public Library, MSS 114-600.

not try to reopen it. The final feature was a triple bill of *War of the Satellites, Day of the Outlaw,* and *The Tartars.*[20]

The Teatro Amado Nervo was a Spanish-language house at 1520 Liberty Avenue (according to a listing in the 1920 *Houston Directory*). Another theatre of note during this time was the movie house set up at Camp Logan in what is now Memorial Park. The camp was operational from July 25, 1917, to March 20, 1919, serving as a training ground for soldiers during the war. Details on the theatre are sketchy. According to writer Sarah Emmott, soldiers were able to see some of the latest motion pictures, sent over by the Prince Theatre.[21] A set of tracings and blueprints indicate that Alfred Finn was commissioned to design the Camp Logan structure for the Majestic circuit.[22] Will Horwitz, who would later have a profound effect on the downtown movie theatre scene, was said to have run the Camp Logan theatre.[23]

The year 1922 marked a change in the style of American movies as Hollywood established a censorship and regulation code. A trio of sex, murder, and drug scandals—Fatty Arbuckle's series of trials stemming from the death and alleged rape of Virginia Rappe, the drug-related death of Wallace Reid, and the William Desmond Taylor murder—forced the film industry to take drastic measures to avoid possible government-imposed censorship. Postmaster General Will Hayes was appointed czar of all that was moral and decent.

On March 4 of that year, Houstonians witnessed the opening of the Strand, at 508 Travis, in the Chronicle Building

block. The year also marked the opening of the Rialto.

THE RIALTO
608 *Main*

The Rialto Theatre lived and died within the silent era, operating for around five years. The theatre was built between Texas and Capitol, across the street from the Queen. Fred B. Chambers was the general contractor. The Houston Art Stone Company and the Salt Lake Marble and Supply Company did the ornamental work, W. A. Wiese handled the plasterwork, and C. A. Seymour finished the painting. The theatre was initially managed by Louis N. Weiner and Sam Abrams.[24]

The auditorium was decorated in shades of ivory, with fresco-ornamented walls, and the seats were constructed with wicker backs and soft cushions. An automatic cooling system, now becoming a standard amenity for any theatre, was installed.

The Rialto screen was located directly behind the ticket office in the theatre front. Thus, patrons faced the street instead of the rear of the building. This was done to comply with the 1910 city council safety ordinance, passed after the Theato blaze, requiring that all theatres without rear exits to have the seats face the entry door.

The theatre's original opening date, Wednesday, April 12, 1922, was pushed back twenty-four hours so that work on the interior could be completed. Opening day filled the house to capacity, and at times a surging line of patrons stretched half a block. Shortly after the doors

*The Rialto Theatre, 1924.
Courtesy of the Houston
Metropolitan Research Cen-
ter, Houston Public Library,
MSS 200-331.*

opened at four, the "Standing Room
Only" sign was hung outside. Tickets
were thirty cents for adults and ten cents
for children.

The theatre lobby and auditorium
were banked with baskets of roses, carna-
tions, and other flowers, sent as opening-
day gifts from friends, associates, and
other theatres.

The opening presentations were the
Harold Lloyd comedy *A Sailor-Made
Man* and Florence Vidor in *Woman,
Wake Up*, along with a newsreel. The

Rialto Symphony Orchestra supplied the
musical accompaniment. Ladies were
handed an opening-day program as they
entered, along with a floral souvenir,
while children were given special Harold
Lloyd sailor hats.

One of the Rialto highlights was a one-
week run of *The Phantom of the Opera* in
November 1925. Prices for the Lon
Chaney thriller ranged from fifteen cents
at the bargain matinee to a full seventy-
five cents in the evening.

The Rialto never made it into the

sound era. From the evidence of newspaper advertisements, it appears to have closed in February 1927. The last daily advertisement—dated February 16—was for *The Cheerful Fraud* (1926) with Reginald Denny. The Lon Chaney film *Flesh and Blood* (1922) had finished its run the week before.[25]

NOT ALL OF HOUSTON'S theatre projects reached completion. One such example was the Esperson Theatre and seventeen-story office-building complex on Main Street. Architect John Eberson, along with the Adams and Adams architectural firm of San Antonio, designed the structure.

The Beaux Arts–style auditorium, designed before Eberson's atmospheric period (the style for which, beginning with the 1923 Houston Majestic, he is best known), would have seated 2,570. A planned full basement would have been spacious enough to accommodate the hot-air furnaces, cooling equipment, orchestra pit, chorus dressing rooms, instrument room, carpenter shop, poster room, nursery, and animal room, which was used to house animals used in traveling vaudeville shows. Lavish embellishments of ornamental plaster, with heraldic designs and cherubs, would have adorned the interior.[26]

For reasons unknown, the Esperson Theatre was never built.

Theatre openings of 1923 included the Ideal, at 504 Milam; the Olympian, at 217 Main; and the Pastime, at 2514 McKinney. Yet the highlight of 1923 was the opening of Karl Hoblitzelle's third Majestic Theatre—certainly the most acclaimed of all of Houston's movie houses and the nation's first atmospheric theatre. More than any other single Houston theatre before or since, the 1923 Majestic would sum up the mystique of the motion-picture palace.

Advertisement in the Houston Post for The Phantom of the Opera *with Lon Chaney, showing at the Rialto, November 1925.*

Advertisement in the Houston Post *for the Majestic Theatre, January 28, 1923.*

★ ★ ★

THE
MAJESTICS

★ ★ ★

Back to the very first beginning,
Out to the undiscovered ends,
There's nothing worth the wear of winning,
But laughter and the love of friends.

He has achieved success who has gained
the respect of intelligent men, and the love
of children, who has filled his niche, and
has left the world better than he found it.

THE TWO ENGRAVED QUOTATIONS
ON THE EXTERIOR OF THE
1923 MAJESTIC THEATRE; THE FIRST IS
ADAPTED FROM HILAIRE BELLOC
("DEDICATORY ODE," 1910),
THE SECOND FROM
THE POEM "SUCCESS" BY
BESSIE ANDERSON STANLEY.

★ BY THE TIME of Karl Hoblitzelle's death—March 8, 1967—he had gained a reputation founded on decades of good-will to his community. At his passing, a telegram of condolence was sent by President Johnson, which read, "Karl Hoblitzelle was a generous and true friend. And with his death dies something in the hearts of each of us who knew him well."[1]

These thoughts were echoed by many others who had been touched by his influence. During his lifetime, Hoblitzelle was a businessman and civic leader; a director of various bank, gas, light, and insurance companies; and a chairman of medical institutions and universities. He had had a hand in oil production, farm and ranch operations, and was an honorary member of the Sons of the Republic of Texas.

And there were his theatres. His Interstate Amusement Company spread out from Texas to become an empire across the southern United States. Most of Houston's best-remembered movie theatres were Interstates—including three bearing the name "Majestic."

Karl St. John Hoblitzelle was born in St. Louis, Missouri, on October 22, 1879, one of ten boys and three girls born to parents Clarence Linden Hoblitzelle and Ida A. Knapp. Clarence was a war veteran who had been originally brought to St. Louis as a confederate prisoner. After the war, he remained in the city, finding work in the saddlery and harness business. Ida came from a prominent St. Louis family; her father, Colonel George Knapp, published the *Missouri Republican* (later the *St. Louis Republican*) newspaper.[2]

Ida had been raised with a classical education, and she passed on an appreciation of art, literature, and music to her children, especially Karl. Though he had only a high school education, he was well served by this enjoyment of the arts as the years progressed. His mother's influence was equally felt in other areas, such as the Christian principles of caring and sharing with one another. Her one inflexible rule, according to Hoblitzelle's sister, Mrs. John Tritle, was that there was no excuse for unpleasantness; and none could remain in the room unless they were pleasant.

Sunday dinners became forums for discussing issues ranging from politics and economics to art and literature, and there were seldom fewer than twenty people gathered at the table (Ida herself came from a family of twelve). George Knapp's background in newspaper publishing, Clarence's interest in politics,

Portrait of Karl Hoblitzelle, inscribed to the boys of Local 279. For many years, this photo hung in the union hall of the Projectionists' Union, Local 279, in Houston. Courtesy of Gary Warwick.

contributions from uncles educated at Harvard and Brown, and a healthy dose of the arts made for conversations that would extend for hours after the table was cleared. "Most of we children would drift away from the table to our own Sunday afternoon pursuits," recalled Tritle, "but Karl always stayed. It seemed that he never could soak up enough knowledge of the things that were being discussed."[3]

After Karl graduated from high school, he worked briefly in real estate and at a soap factory before taking up poultry raising and farming (using a plot of land leased from his father). He was soon selling potatoes and cucumbers to the St. Louis markets at top-dollar prices. This came to an end when the elder Hoblitzelle refused to renew the lease.

At the age of twenty he took on the position of office boy for Isaac Taylor, director of works for the 1904 Louisiana Purchase Exposition, passing up a $125-a-month salary in the auditing department.

While the salary was only $5 a week, he was fascinated with the activity around him. Taylor was a towering six-foot four-inch giant, whose presence Hoblitzelle immediately felt when he first appeared with a letter of introduction. "Is this the young man who wants to take $5 a week instead of $125 a month?" roared Taylor. "Send him in."

Hoblitzelle explained how he wanted to be where the fair was actually being built. In the years that followed, he was promoted first to secretary, then to acting director of works in charge of demolition at the close of the fair.

Hoblitzelle was approached by a group of concessionaires to invest in a feasibility study to bring vaudeville to the Southwest, an area still void of popular variety shows. With his brother George, he invested $2,500 to create the Interstate Amusement Company. In the fall of 1905, he leased five Texas theatres, intending to bring quality vaudeville to the state: the Majestic theatres in Dallas, Fort Worth, and Waco, and the Empires in San Antonio and Houston.

At that time, theatres were of the same standing as saloons—places that good, decent citizens avoided. Ministers called them the "gateways to hell." One often-told story was that of a Fort Worth mayor on his way home for lunch. After he left city hall, he detoured across the street, walked up a block, down, then back to his original route. His reasoning was to avoid the newly built Majestic Theatre, which stood in his path, and as a good citizen and politician, would not sully his reputation by being seen near such a place.

Hoblitzelle faced an uphill battle to sway public opinion. "It was a heart breaking job," he recounted, "to convince the good people of Texas in those early days that we were presenting only clean, wholesome entertainment. A good many of the men connected with the theatre of that day occupied questionable positions in the community. They had graduated out of saloon or gambling business and the public looked askance at them."[4]

Hoblitzelle set out to change both the reality and the perceptions. Determined to establish Interstate as a family-oriented establishment, he set up methods of screening the talent and material. The orchestra leader was assigned the job of censor. Managers at other theatres were then sent lists of the deletions. Since many of the acts came from the East and North, where the deleted passages were acceptable to audiences, "the actors couldn't understand the objections, "and we had a rough time for a long time," according to Hoblitzelle.[5]

An act would occasionally be hired and brought down, only to be told after arriving that its material was totally unacceptable. Hoblitzelle's rule was to pay them off and send them back East, a policy that proved to be expensive but necessary. "Often it meant that we'd have to stand off some creditors a few days to do it," said Hoblitzelle, "but the policy brought families to our theatres who wouldn't have come had we been less vigilant."[6]

There was a moral opposition to Sunday showings, which were decreed by churches to be a "desecration of the Sabbath." This was a hardship for audiences and theatres alike, since in the years before the five-day work week became standard, Sunday was the only day that

GRAND OPENING—MAJESTIC THEATRE

MATINEE DAILY	8:15 P. M.	TOMORROW	8:15 P. M.	EVERY NIGHT
EXCEPT ON SUN-DAY and MONDAY 2:15 P.M		FIRST SEASON OF MODERN VAUDEVILLE IN HOUSTON		EXCEPT ON SUNDAY AT 8:15 P.M.

TEN ALL STAR ACTS——NO INTERMISSION——SPECIAL DEDICATION EXERCISES

| DEDICATION PRICES 50c $1.00 $1.50 | MYSTERIOUS CRUCIBLE—A real snowstorm and other seeming impossibilities, by PROF. VAN HORN, the scientific manipulator of liquid air. GUS BRUNO—The "Eddy Foy" of vaudeville, in his laughing skit "Happy Hooligan and Gloomy Gus." GARDNER & STODDARD—In musical jingles and Interpretations of some noted stage folk. | THOS. J. KEOGH & CO.—One of the highest salaried acts in vaudeville. Mr. Keogh will present his successful playette. "The Way He Won Her. ORGERITA ARNOLD—A "hit" from Australia, new clever songs and impersonations. PROSPER TROUPE—Five in number. Secured from the Ringling Bros. Circus for this opening. | RICE'S ANIMAL CIRCUS—A miniature tent show on the stage. Trained dogs, ponies, Peru monkeys, etc. Two car-loads of apparatus. MLLE. PATRICE LA FAVRE—The favorite sweet voiced soprano, in her own diversion of illustrated songs. JOSEPHINE JACOBY—Remarkable violinist, graduate of Leipsic Conservatory, pronounced the world's musical wonder of the year. | REGULAR PRICES 15c, 25c, 35c and 50c |

CONCLUDING WITH EDISON'S LATEST INVENTION, THE "KINETOGRAPH," PRODUCING PICTURES WHICH "MORE THAN MOVE"

many families could see a quality show. When Hoblitzelle opened his new Dallas Majestic, he arranged for a minister of a different denomination to speak from the stage on each night of the opening week. The family-entertainment policy soon smoothed the Sunday waters.

Like those in Dallas, Houston's theatrical beginnings could be found in both the saloons and the legitimate stage. Hoblitzelle entered the city by way of the old Grand Theatre, which had been in existence since the turn of the century.

THE GRAND/EMPIRE/MAJESTIC
1306 Congress

The Grand Theatre, on Congress between Caroline and Austin, was built by George Kuhn and leased to Jake Schwartz, who would eventually work for the Will Horwitz theatre chain. In 1904 it was leased to Harry Colson Clarke, a popular comedian of the time. The showplace reopened as the Empire Theatre under his management on January 11 of that year. The first presentation was the popular farce *What Happened to Jones*. For the next two seasons, Clarke's stock company presented shows that had

already been performed successfully in New York and on the road.[7]

Hoblitzelle acquired the Empire as part of his initial theatre purchase. Extensive renovations took place during the summer of 1905, including a new, extended building front, an enlarged stairway, additional auditorium space, and three hundred more seats.[8] The theatre was then rechristened the Majestic.

The grand reopening, on November 6, 1905, featured a full presentation of high-class vaudeville acts, which included musicians Gardner and Stoddard, violinist Josephine Jacoby, soprano Mlle. Patrice La Faure, Orgerita Arnold, and comedian Gus Bruno. The opening presentation began with ceremonial speeches by manager Claude C. Cunningham and other celebrities. Cunningham would later achieve recognition as a candidate for United States president. The Thomas J. Keogh Company performed the playette *The Way He Won Her*, and Professor Van Horn, the "scientific manipulator of liquid air," conjured a magical snowstorm and other illusions. The Prosper Troupe, from the Ringling Brothers Circus, along with Rice's Animal Circus, also performed. The

Advertisement in the Houston Chronicle for the grand opening of the Majestic Theatre, November 6, 1905.

show concluded with an early film, described in advertisements as "Edison's latest invention, the Kinetograph," which produced pictures that "more than move."[9]

Yet despite the array of talent, the Houstonians of 1905 weren't sold on vaudeville. It would be many months before the Majestic became popular. Eddie Bremer, who was connected with Interstate in San Antonio at the time, and would become assistant manager of the Majestic a few seasons later, noted, "High class vaudeville acts were brought here, but the people of Houston had been prejudiced against vaudeville, and it took a long time to overcome this prejudice."[10]

Al Jolson graced the Majestic stage during its reign, as did the Colby singing act. Frank Colby would attain celebrity status in Houston in radio and advertising.[11] Another blackface performer was Ollie Debrow, whose wife, Jessie Reed, would gain recognition as a *Ziegfeld's Follies* girl. Ollie's brother, Bill, also did blackface, and both used the song "Hesitation Blues" as part of their act. The number, which had innumerable verses, all ended with the bridge line, "Can I get you now, or must I hesitate?"[12]

By 1909, Hoblitzelle was ready to expand the Houston branch of his Interstate empire, and plans were set in motion for a new Majestic. Once completed, it would be, for its time, the grandest of the local theatres. For its design, Hoblitzelle looked to the man who would play a pivotal role in a number of his future movie-palace constructions, including the 1923 Majestic—Austrian-born architect John Eberson.

THE 1910 MAJESTIC
807–811 Texas Avenue

Upon the opening of Hoblitzelle's second Houston Majestic, a *Houston Chronicle* reporter stated that the building could be "compared favorably with the gilded palaces of ancient kings." Houstonians simply called it the "Theatre Beautiful."

Eberson executed its initial design during the winter of 1907–1908. He had already garnered the nickname of "Opera House John" for his top-quality theatres. Ironically, electrical engineering, not architecture, was his original calling.

John Adolph Emil Eberson was born in 1875 in Cernauti, in eastern Austria-Hungary (now part of the Ukraine), to a successful timber merchant. After an education in Dresden and Vienna, he moved to St. Louis in 1901, taking on a job for an electrical supply and contracting company. His first project was to design and install the electrical system for a theatre in Vicksburg, Mississippi. This assignment was the catalyst for his interest in theatrical architecture and promotion. In 1910 he moved to Chicago—itself, a major center for theatre architecture—with his wife and three children. From this base of operations he continued to create theatres across the country for chains such as Butterfield, Loew's, and Interstate.[13]

The theatre was built by Jesse H. Jones on the site of the old Shearn Methodist Church, in the 800 block of Texas. Construction began in April 1909, and an October opening was planned. Building delays and other details eventually pushed the date back to February. The theatre reportedly cost $300,000.[14] Historian B. H. Carroll noted at that time that its price tag

"will doubtless prohibit its ever becoming a great revenue producer."[15]

According to *Houston Post* reports at the time, Eberson's design, which would not have been "strictly fireproof," was revamped into a less flammable structure of reinforced concrete.[16] The lobby was patterned after the House of the Tragic Poet at Pompeii, which had been unearthed several years earlier; the floor was paved with light-colored tiles; and the walls were finished in light marble. In the rear was the entrance to the foyer and auditorium, to the left was a telephone booth and the doors to the smoking room and balcony. The initial blueprints called for a single balcony, but a second one was added. To the right of the main entrance was the door to the ladies' parlor and dressing room, designed in Louis XIV style. In the rear was the ladies' retiring room, complete with electric fans and a writing desk. There was also a ladies' reception room, in the same style as the foyer.

From the lobby, gray steps led downstairs to the men's smoking room, which was designed in an old Dutch style: English red tile on the walls, rich velvet carpeting, a beamed and paneled ceiling,

The 1910 Majestic, 800 block of Texas Avenue. Courtesy of the Houston Metropolitan Research Center, Houston Public Library, MSS 19-947.

and a deep green mantel and fireplace. Opposite the fireplace were two locked doors. Hoblitzelle, in press releases at the time, said that the mirrored doors would forever be locked, since "they lead into the world beyond, and the prying eyes of the public will never learn the secret." More than likely they led to a storage area, or to the ushers' rooms, which were located in back of the smoking parlor.

A lush second-floor mezzanine, with leather-cushioned settees and a drinking fountain, offered access to Hoblitzelle's office as well as the nursery, which was complete with numerous toys and a nurse.

Four double doors, inset with plate glass, led from the lobby into the auditorium foyer. Finished in a German baronial style, similar to that of New York's Maxine Elliott Theatre, the foyer was lined with six large plate-glass mirrors, massive chandeliers, gilt brackets, and two stone drinking fountains.

The "modernized renaissance" auditorium displayed stucco decorative borders, floral designs, and soft colors on paneled walls. Ever opulent, the theatre featured 1,500 seats, 28 exits, 2,000 interior lights, and toilets on each floor. The boxes, equipped with chandeliers and individually controlled fans, were dressed in deep red cloth, offsetting the lighter tones of the auditorium. In total, 104 box seats were available. Nine boxes were attached to the front row of the balcony. To the rear of the upper balcony was the operator's booth. Beneath the stage was the green room, located at the northeast corner of the basement. South of this were bathrooms, dressing rooms, and lounges for the performers.

Charles A. McFarland was the original manager, having come from the old Majestic on Congress.[17] W. L. Sachtleben later filled the position through 1923, and then retired.[18]

The opening, on February 21, 1910, was one of the big social events of the season, and tickets sold out days earlier.

Lobby of the 1910 Majestic.
Postcard, author's collection.

Crowds gathered long before the doors opened, and many without tickets were there just to watch the festivities. The new theatre was heralded a block away by a mammoth electric sign that stretched across Main Street at the corner of Texas Avenue. Another similar display overhung Texas Avenue in front of the showplace. Then, at 7:30 p.m., the Majestic officially opened its doors.[19] As noted in the *Houston Post* shortly after the opening: "While the patrons had already named the new house 'Theatre Beautiful,' an equally appropriate name would be that of the 'palace of lights,' as there are so many lights that, upon first entrance, one is almost blinded."[20]

Patrons were dazzled by the opulence of the theatre. The foyer was filled with close to two dozen floral arrangements sent by well-wishing associates. Congratulatory telegrams were also on display behind framed glass. Beautifully embossed programs, printed on fine paper with white satin bows, had been prepared in advance for the event. These were to be handed out to the theatergoers upon their arrival; however, the programs came up missing the day of the opening. The event took place with only a handful available for the public. The elusive programs were uncovered the next day.[21]

This did not help Hoblitzelle's disposition, since he had worked long and hard that day. As the first patrons arrived, he dashed to the hotel to change clothes, and amid the rush, he forgot to shave. It was the classic scenario of theatrical life, when all goes wrong beforehand.

The Majestic employees were all uniformed, from the ushers and callboys to the stagehands. The stage manager, property man, electrician, and others behind the scenes wore white duck uniforms and blue caps. Doorkeepers and ushers were dressed in green. Hoblitzelle and his executive staff wore the customary tuxedos.

Hoblitzelle added unique touches to the evening, including two orchestras, the primary one in the auditorium and a second on the mezzanine. Boxes of candy were set out in the ladies' reception room. For the gentlemen, there were cigars— 1,500 of them—to be distributed throughout the rest of the week. Hot chocolate was to be served to the ladies during the upcoming week's matinees. Hoblitzelle also kept a hundred umbrellas on hand for use on rainy nights—available for a nominal deposit.[22]

At 8:15, the Majestic Orchestra, under the baton of B. J. Steinfeldt, began the evening with an eleven-part program: the march from the opera *The Prophet* by Meyerbeer, a selection from Victor Herbert's opera *Algeria*, followed by "The Dance of the Hours" from Ponchielli's opera *La Gioconda*, the "Wiener Blut" waltz by Strauss, the overture to *Raymond* by Ambroise Thomas, "The Opera Mirror" (selections from seven popular operas), and a final selection from Bizet's *Carmen*.

Congressman Daniel E. Garrett then took the stage as master of ceremonies, followed by Mayor H. Baldwin Rice. Finally, Hoblitzelle spoke, expressing appreciation to Jesse Jones as well as to the Houston theatergoers and their efforts to maintain a first-class vaudeville theatre.

With that, the curtain rose, and the first act to grace the Majestic stage, the

La Mothe Troupe, a family of acrobats and clowns, began. The rest of the bill consisted of singer Cecil Gordon, the LaZar and LaZar Company, comedian George Yeoman, the Three Richardsons, pianist-comedian Charley Olcott, Coin's City of Dogs, presenting *It Happened in Dogsville*, the Bootblack Quartet, and finally a Majestograph motion picture.[23]

"The new Majestic Theatre embodies in all its departments the brainy, breezy, modern answer to a long felt want among the best and most progressive citizens of Houston," noted Hoblitzelle, in a lengthy salutatory in the program book. "And this is, after all, what we have come among you for, to banish from your midst every bit of sadness and gloom possible, and

to give you back instead full measure of happy laughter, bright moments of enjoyment, a generally wholesome good time, and as Rosalind promised Orlando, a liver washed clean. If we succeed in this we will be satisfied, and you, sons and daughters of Texas, will feel that we have made some good return for your early welcome and encouragement."

He concluded by stating, "Thespis calls, the overture is rounding, and the curtain rises on our initial bow before you. Listen kindly, think warmly, speak as sweetly, our reputation is in your hands, and as Tiny Tim says, 'God bless us every one.'"[24]

Meanwhile the old Majestic was reopened for an additional season. It was eventually closed, and most top talent went over to the newer Majestic. From all available accounts, the old Majestic burned to the ground several years later and was never rebuilt.[25]

Hoblitzelle's new Majestic soon became a popular gathering place, where people came to be seen. Monday night was social night, and many patrons reserved season tickets for that evening, year after year. Performers who stood on its stage included Olga Petrova, Mae West, Al Jolson, Eddie Foy, and Alfred the Great (the world's greatest living chimpanzee). Will Rogers appeared there as a rope twirler before he hit the big time with the *Ziegfeld Follies*, and in October 1914, audiences were entertained by the antics of the four Marx Brothers.[26]

Feature films proved to be big draws, with titles such as D. W. Griffith's *Way Down East* (1920), *The Four Horsemen of the Apocalypse* (1921; directed by Rex Ingram) with Rudolph Valentino, and *The Shepherd of the Hills* (1919), directed by its author, Harold Bell Wright. As was the norm at the time, minorities were kept separate. As noted in the newspaper, an entire floor was reserved for "the colored people."[27]

The Majestic was also the birthplace of the Houston Symphony. Although finely trained musicians were abundant in Houston, the city was still dependent on imported symphony orchestras. In 1913, cellist Julien Paul Blitz approached the women's committee with the idea of his recruiting musicians if they found the supporters. Prominent Houstonian Ima Hogg, long a supporter of classical music, did just that.[28] A concert was held to gauge public response. The event proved

contagious, and soon every quality restaurant, vaudeville house, movie theatre, and socialite was assembling such events.

Theatres usually closed in July and August because of the grueling Texas heat. On June 21, 1913, at five in the afternoon, thirty-five musicians assembled at the Majestic Theatre. Conducted by Blitz, the first concert by the Houston Symphony was given, wedged between the matinee and evening vaudeville shows. The first official season began on December 19 of that year, to a capacity audience.[29]

This newer, glitzier Majestic quickly established itself as a major Houston showplace. As he did in other cities, Hoblitzelle gave the people what they wanted—sometimes before they even knew it—and the resulting Majestic Theatre would endure for well over a decade. By then, Hoblitzelle had begun planning a showplace that would be larger and more dazzling than the last. It would be this, the 1923 Houston Majestic, that would redefine the concept of a movie palace.

THE 1923 MAJESTIC
904–908 Rusk Avenue

Hoblitzelle's third and final Majestic is rightly considered the greatest movie theatre ever built in Houston. Credit for this largely rests with the vision of architect John Eberson.

Having begun with small opera houses, and moving up to larger vaudeville houses—including the Majestics in Austin (1915) and Dallas (1921)—Eberson had reached a creative impasse. He had

The grand 1923 Majestic on Rusk Avenue, 1936. Courtesy of the Houston Metropolitan Research Center, Houston Public Library, MSS 1248-2344.

become bored with the stuffy sameness of movie-theatre design, which in its short history had become merely a glitzier version of traditional opera-house standards. He looked for a new, informal, open-air style that would overwhelm audiences with color and light instead of ornamentation. By defying all the standards, the resulting design seemed not to be for a theatre interior at all, but for an outdoor garden in some exotic, faraway locale with a starlit sky overhead—set within the conventional indoor auditorium. This was the world's first atmospheric movie theatre.

The combination of an open Italian garden, ultra-Baroque columns, Roman temple parts, Spanish Mission bell towers, and side boxes effectively gave the auditorium the appearance of an exterior wall in some foreign village. The left and right walls were not identical, another broken rule. Rising above it all was the ultimate added touch: a Mediterranean blue ceiling inset with twinkling lights and clouds that floated lazily over the heads of the audience. The atmospheric ceiling consisted of blue plaster, perfectly smooth, instead of the normal ornamentation and filigrees. Said Eberson of the concept, "We credit the deep blue azure of the Mediterranean sky with a therapeutic value, soothing the nerves and calming perturbing thoughts."[30]

This innovation would soon attract assignments from movie-house moguls across the nation. Despite the more complicated technical considerations of an atmospheric theatre, the absence of ceiling ornamentation meant that a typical 3,000-seat atmospheric auditorium could be built for 25 percent less than the

traditional structures built by Thomas Lamb, Rapp & Rapp, and others. Instead of the costly filigrees and details was a gently curved, flat surface dotted with hundreds of quarter-inch holes set with dewdrop crystals. Several lighting units were installed in the space behind the ceiling, causing the individual holes to blink like stars.[31] Moving clouds were projected on the ceiling by way of the Brenkert Brenograph Jr., a magic lantern that passed negatives in front of a 1,500-watt light bulb.[32] Individual platforms set behind the wall architecture housed cove lighting for additional effects. A Majestic performance would begin with a sunset; light in the western corner of the auditorium that would slowly fade from view as

a nighttime blanket of clouds and twinkling stars set the tone. At the end of the presentation, the stars and clouds would fade as a dawn light arose from the eastern side of the interior.[33]

The auditorium details were both radical and unique: green vines, blooming flowers, Greek statues, and stuffed birds hung in mock flight. On both sides of the balcony were pergolas supported by caryatids, sculptured female figures that took the place of columns.[34]

Greek statues accented both walls. These reproductions were of Polyhymnia, the muse of sacred poetry; Euterpe, muse of music; the Venus of Arles and the Venus of Capua; the Winged Victory; the Apollo Citharoedus; a bust of Minerva

Interior of the 1923 Majestic. Unique to John Eberson's auditorium was having the two sidewalls designed around completely different themes. His trademark atmospheric blue ceiling looked down on it all. Courtesy of the Houston Metropolitan Research Center, Houston Public Library, MSS 1248-2357, 2364a.

on the proscenium arch; and a statue of Diana robing herself. Most of these figures were placed in the area above the second-level boxes.

Most prominent were the garden walls on either side of the proscenium. The left sidewall was an Italian palace facade, which concealed the pipe-organ loft. In front, the ornate proscenium arch was based on the Roman triumphal arch. Other features included advanced acoustics, an elaborate heating and ventilation setup, a hydraulic elevator, and a massive stage. Referred to as the Family Circle, the balcony area allowed a different perspective on the overwhelming architecture.[35]

The architectural influences were varied: the entrance resembled a Roman temple, the lobby floor was of multicolored faience, and above, the ceiling was one inspired by the famous Villa Cambiaso in Genoa. The door heads were designed after the ones in St. Peter's Cathedral.[36]

This visual cacophony was a reflection of Eberson's own vibrant personality. His daughter Elsa Eberson Kyle later commented, "He had a great flair for the dramatic, in his dress and in his surroundings. Never did things in an ordinary way. If he liked something, he didn't buy one . . . he bought five or six. His clothes were all custom made and designed by him . . . black velvet vests with many jet buttons and white pique edging along the lapels,

a brown cape with a velvet collar, black Homburg hat and flowing black artist tie. He had a strong, forceful character and when he entered a room, his presence was felt . . . a true showman."[37]

In later years, Eberson would take the stage at the grand opening of each of his completed palaces and present the new owner with a package of birdseed—to keep the stuffed birds happy.[38]

Such was Eberson's enthusiasm to create an interior wonderland that he neglected to include a box office in the initial plans. This oversight was remedied in time for the opening. Despite this, the atmospheric Majestic was to serve as a blueprint for all the Eberson theatres that followed.[39]

A three-story annex on the Travis Street side offered accommodations for musicians and performers. Likened to a hotel, it contained fourteen separate dressing rooms and two larger quarters for the cho-

rus girls. All rooms contained a heating and cooling system, large mirrors, dressing tables, soft carpeting, rugs, restrooms, and showers. The annex offered easy access to the stage.[40]

Eberson's son Drew worked closely with his father on many of his later theatres. Said the younger Eberson in a 1989 interview, "How did we build Atmospheric theatres? With imagination, organization, and hard work."[41]

The Houston Majestic was Eberson's springboard for innovation in theatrical design, and each successive structure became grander than the last. His Texas sweep culminated in the stunning San Antonio Majestic Theatre (1928, restored). The stock market crash of 1929 brought an end to all this—not just Eberson's major atmospherics, but to all grand picture-palace construction across the United States. The San Antonio Majestic had its grand opening just four months before the

The chief of service and his assistant on the roof, alongside the Majestic marquee. Courtesy of the Sloane Collection, Houston, Texas.

A program book handed out on opening night contained the Hoblitzelle declaration of policy. It read: "No act has been accomplished or word spoken that would bring a startled blush to a maiden cheek, or direct the unsullied mind of youth into ought but paths of purity. This beautiful Majestic Theatre has been emphatically a 'Ladies and Children's Amusement Temple,' a veritable Gibraltar of clean entertainment, surrounded by all the accessories dear to Dixie's daughters."[44]

The doors opened at 6:30 p.m. for the initial reception, with the dedica-

start of the Great Depression. After the nation recovered, Eberson's designs took on a less extravagant quality as Art Deco became the accepted style. By his death, in 1954, he had over five hundred theatres to his credit.[42]

ON MONDAY, January 29, 1923, the new $1 million Majestic Theatre, at 908 Rusk, opened to capacity crowd of 2,500 people. *The Houston Post* had featured a special section on the Majestic the day before. Said one reporter, "It is a playhouse, the duplicate of which cannot be found in America."[43]

John J. Galvin was the house manager for the new showplace, and Eddie Bremer acted as assistant manager and treasurer. W. L. Sachtleben was in charge of programming for both the new Majestic on Rusk and the older Majestic on Texas Avenue, which would continue operations under a different name.

Advance advertisement in the Houston Post *for the "million dollar" Majestic, January 28, 1923.*

tion ceremonies to follow at 7:45. Dr. Stockton Axson, head of Rice Institute's English department, served as master of ceremonies, giving an impressive verbal history of drama from Shakespeare to the present (ignoring ancient Greek drama, one reporter noted).[45] Other notables in attendance were Mr. and Mrs. Jesse H. Jones as well as *Houston Chronicle* president-editor (and builder of the two Cozy Theatres) M. E. Foster and Mayor Oscar Holcombe.[46] This was the first of many theatre galas that Holcombe would take part in during his eleven terms as mayor. His other theatre openings included the Loew's State, Uptown, Stude, River Oaks, Tower, Eastwood, Alabama, and Almeda.

Highlighting the evening's performances was the appearance of Henry B. Walthall, now best remembered for his role of Colonel Ben Cameron in *The Birth of a Nation*. Billed as the "Southland's Greatest Dramatic Actor," Walthall starred in a sketch entitled *The Unknown*. Also featured were pianist Huston Ray, the musical team of George Whiting and Sadie Burt, the Keno-Keyes-Melrose trio, and Boy, the musical pony. The DeMarcos, a dancing troupe from Buenos Aires, performed as well. The lineup finished with the Larry Semon feature *The Counter Jumper*.[47]

Lloyd Finlay conducted the house orchestra. His reputation from having worked at the older Majestic was high enough that offers to go to Broadway were numerous. His skill was one of the reasons that the Houston vaudeville venues were so highly praised on the coasts.

Despite the presence of all this talent under one roof, the real star of the evening was the theatre itself.

THE SECOND LIFE OF THE 1910 MAJESTIC

Meanwhile, the 1910 Majestic was rechristened the Palace, and became a stock theatre, home of the Palace Players. It held its reopening on January 29, 1923—the same day as the new Majestic's opening—with the comedy-drama *Up in Mabel's Room*.[48]

Other stock companies that would play the Palace included the Gene Lewis Stock Company, Olga Worth, the Baldwin Stock Company, and the Arthur Casey Players. At the time, Clark Gable was an inexperienced juvenile lead for the Gene Lewis Stock Company. According to biographer Lyn Tornabene, for Gable to simply walk across the stage or open a door was a challenge, and it took numerous rehearsals to smooth out his performance.[49]

The theatre was also rented out on occasion to the Rice Dramatic Club for its 1929–1930 season.

The theatre's latter days were uneven: it was used as an independent church, and later as a radio theatre for station KTRH. In the fall of 1937 it was remodeled and opened as the Zoe, featuring primarily westerns.[50] Then in 1938 it was leased to Will Horwitz for the showing of first-run foreign films. When the theatre reopened under his Homefolks banner on October 31, 1938—Halloween—it featured five vaudeville acts, *Phantom Gold*, and the Richard Dix feature *Blind Alibi*. Audiences were warned to arrive prepared to be frightened by a midnight spook show and the feature *The Shadow Strikes*, all for 25 cents.[51]

In 1945 it was reopened by Horwitz-

The former Majestic Theatre, renamed the Palace, showing the Buster Crabbe feature Nabonga, *1944. Courtesy of the Houston Metropolitan Research Center, Houston Public Library, MSS 200-188.*

Texan Theatres as the Nuevo Palacio, running Spanish-language films. It was managed by E. Valero. The theatre shut its doors on April 3, 1946. Shortly before its closing, Hoblitzelle and Bremer revisited the theatre and mulled over old times. They had already seen some of their other theatres fall to the way of progress. This would not be the last.[52]

The 1910 Majestic, once the toast of Houston, vanished, giving way to progress and the expansion of the Chronicle Building.[53]

A GALAXY OF STARS AT THE 1923 MAJESTIC

The 1923 Majestic quickly settled into a regiment of top-notch entertainment.

Special nights were scheduled for various organizations: Tuesdays were for the Shriners, the Elks on Wednesday, Thursdays were for the Advertising Club and the Lions, Friday for the Rotary and Kiwanis clubs, and Saturday for organized labor.[54]

The talent showcased under the Majestic banner read like a virtual who's who of the period. Patrons were treated to a live performance by virtuoso pianist Ignace Jan Paderewski within the first month of the grand opening. Talents such as Jack Benny, W. C. Fields, and cross-eyed comic Ben Turpin graced the Majestic stage. So did Cab Calloway, who received little hospitality outside the theatre. Fred Wyse, the operator of the Majestic Grill next door, found out about Calloway and sent food to his dressing room. Some of Wyse's customers were so

incensed that they vowed never to patron-
ize his place again. Wyse, however, was
unconcerned about any loss of business—
he also owned a team of racehorses. It was
Calloway who opened up the door for
future black performers.[55]

Another notable show was the Theatre
Guild's live production of *Mary of Scot-
land* by Maxwell Anderson, on April 8
and 9, 1935. Heading the cast was Helen
Hayes.

There was an art to bookings. Interstate
manager R. J. "Bob" O'Donnell would
always book a Randolph Scott western
when a stock show was in town; it always
packed them in. He missed the mark during the 1928 Democratic National Convention. Figuring that delegates would
pass by the theatre to get to the convention center, he booked composer and
singer Little Jack Little and Billy Purl.
"He was right. They passed right by," said
Eddie Miller, a spotlight operator at the
time.[56]

The Richard Dix film *Man of Conquest*, detailing the life of Sam Houston,
had its world premiere at the Majestic on
April 6, 1939. Cast, crew, notables, and
celebrities were in attendance; O'Donnell
was the master of ceremonies; and the
Houston Symphony Orchestra, under
the direction of Ernst Hoffmann, supplied music. In attendance were stars
Richard Dix, Gail Patrick, and Joan Fon-
taine along with director George Nich-
ols, Jr., who died later that year in a car
accident.[57]

The Majestic played host to events
both big and small, such as the 1939
Majestic Car Hop Contest. Newspaper
ads of the day read: "Meet Houston's Most
Glamorous GLAMBURGER Girls."[58]

Other features over the years included
The Sea Wolf, *Kitty Foyle*, *The Mark of
Zorro* with Tyrone Power, *Citizen Kane*,
Captain Blood, *Breakfast at Tiffany's*, *The
Road to Zanzibar*, and *The Greatest Show
on Earth*.

The Majestic experienced a number of
structural changes over the decades. The
Majestic was fitted for air conditioning
in 1924—one of the first Houston buildings to undergo the conversion. The Rice
Hotel cafeteria and the Second National
Bank lobby had been converted in 1922–
1923 (although there is still debate on the
order and exact dates).[59] New Movietone
sound equipment was installed in December 1927, making way for the advent of
the talkies. The Movietone process was a
forerunner of the modern sound-on-film
standard. Interstate spent $100,000 on the

*Interstate's Al Lever stands
next to the lighting controls
of the Majestic Theatre,
which brought about sun-
sets, twinkling stars, and
other lighting effects, 1965.
Labels such as "footlights
on stage" and "blue cove,"
are still in place. Courtesy
of the Houston Metropoli-
tan Research Center, Houston Public Library, RGD6N
1965-2818.*

On March 14, 1964, just as Beatlemania was gaining strength, the Majestic featured a special closed-circuit presentation of the Beatles' concert in Washington, D.C. Courtesy of the Houston Metropolitan Research Center, Houston Public Library, RGD6N 6162 3-14-64.

equipment for the Majestic and two other Texas theatres.[60] Boxes were removed to make room for additional chairs. Hoblitzelle was reportedly saddened by their passing, but felt they had become unnecessary. Some of the larger statues were lowered behind the garden wall, and others were removed entirely. Many of the aged figures required occasional repair, usually rendered by Hyman Werner, an Interstate maintenance man who had been with the company for nearly twenty-five years.[61]

A $120,000 overhaul was completed in 1950. New carpets, drapes, and seats were installed throughout the building, and spacing between the rows was expanded. Seats were repositioned in a staggered pattern to allow for unobstructed sightlines. The vertical Majestic marquee and banner were also removed, replaced by a larger, more contemporary marquee that never quite fit the original architectural design.[62]

On June 16, 1960, a benefit performance of *The Story of Ruth* was held, including a Sakowitz fashion show and a live appearance by Jayne Mansfield (who was not, however, in the movie). Proceeds went to the Houston Center for Blind Children.[63] Then, on December 19, 1968, the theatre hosted the world premiere of *Hellfighters*, which told the life story of Houston oil-well-fire fighter Red Adair. Portions of Rusk and Travis were closed for the event, even though Mayor Louie Welch and councilman Frank Mancuso voted against the request at a city council meeting, feeling that heavy Christmas-shopping traffic would be an issue.[64]

The old Lincoln Theatre, rechristened the Majestic, c. 1976, found new life under the guiding hand of Alvin Guggenheim. Courtesy of Alvin Guggenheim.

Even though Jimmy Stewart appeared during the later sixties, the days of live promotions were ebbing. One of the last big events at the Majestic featured comedian Bob Hope, promoting his 1969 film *How to Commit Marriage*. In a contest staged by Interstate Theatres and the *Houston Chronicle*, prospective couples were encouraged to send in letters (of fifty words or less) stating why they wanted to be married alongside Bob Hope. The winning couple would be married onstage, with Hope as the best man. The newlyweds would also win a trip to Las Vegas, $25 worth of groceries a week for three months from the Lucky 7 supermarket, and a host of other wedding presents.

Bobby Bailey and Grace Davilla were the winning couple for the May 30, 1969, ceremony, which meant changing their original June 28 marriage date. It also meant Bailey demoting his former best man to the role of groomsman. Said Bailey at the time, "I think having him (Hope) as my best man is going to be the greatest." When asked where they had originally planned to go for their honeymoon, he answered, "McAllen."[65]

HOBLITZELLE operated the Interstate chain in Texas up through the late sixties. By the mid-1970s it was known as ABC Interstate. The original Hoblitzelle policy not to "bring a startled blush a maiden cheek" seemed ironic by the early seventies, when films such as the Swedish X-rated film, *Naked as the Wind from the Sea* (1968), were shown. In April 1971, the Majestic Theatre property was sold to Robert C. Howell for an estimated $1.45 million. The end was near.

Ironically, the theatre was doing "perfectly acceptable" business and was still in an attractive condition, according to a *Houston Chronicle* article of the time: "The Majestic will go out healthy. The place just had the misfortune to be free-standing on an exceedingly attractive piece of real estate in downtown Houston."[66]

The final presentation at the Majestic was on Sunday, September 26, 1971. Featured that night was *Clay Pigeon* (directed by and starring Tom Stern). While ABC Interstate made no attempt to note the theatre's passing, the daily papers did. A *Houston Chronicle* photographer documented the theatre for a September 1971 article, finding many vintage remnants still intact. Said reporter Jeff Millar in the same article,

"The Majestic was born as a vaudeville theatre; and although you have to look behind the movie screen to see it, it's going to die, unreconstructed, a vaudeville theatre."[67]

Still intact was the massive dimmer control board, with switches labeled "twinkle lights" and "cloud effects," used for the atmospheric ceiling. A rope-covered pin rail supported old scenery in the flies, eighty feet above the stage. Old vaudeville signs, announcing the acts, were stuck in corners. A clipboard held a 1952 cue sheet from a one-night vaudeville revival, with six acts listed. Upstairs were two floors of dressing rooms, a total of twenty. A four-by-four-foot shaft from the stage door to the upper floor contained an electric wench. This shaft was used by actors to haul their trunks up to their dressing rooms.[68]

The theatre was razed in February 1972. The property remained unused until May 1979, when construction began for the First Interstate Center Building.[69]

With this came the end of the Hoblitzelle Majestic era, and the beginning of another—that of the Guggenheim Majestics.

In 1972, Alvin Guggenheim took control of the old 1903 Lincoln Theatre and rechristened it the Majestic. Others under his operation were the O.S.T. Theatre and the 1926 Ritz, renamed the Majestic O.S.T. and the Majestic Metro, respectively. All three theatres ran a steady cinematic fare of kung fu and blaxploitation features.

Eventually, these too would close, ending the long Majestic history; only the Majestic Metro found new life, as a special-events hall.

Grand auditorium of the Loew's State. The curtained arch on the sidewall contained the sounding boards of the organ chamber and the louvres that regulated the volume of the music. Courtesy of the Houston Metropolitan Research Center, Houston Public Library, MSS 19-402.

FIVE

THE
MAIN THREE

THE METROPOLITAN, THE KIRBY, AND LOEW'S STATE

Don't "give the public what they want"—give 'em something better.

SAMUEL LIONEL "ROXY" ROTHAFEL,
CREATOR OF RADIO CITY MUSIC HALL
AND THE ROXY THEATRE

★ THE 1923 HOUSTON MAJESTIC is considered a pivotal landmark in cinema architecture for being the first atmospheric theatre. Eberson's concept redefined what the picture palace could be. Yet within a few years, the Majestic had company that rivaled it for opulence and popularity.

Over a ten-month period, from December 1926 to October 1927, Houston experienced a theatre-building boom that spawned a trio of neighboring structures, two of which would be the most impressive theatres the city would ever have to offer (the actual construction dates covered a two-year arc). These were the Main three—the Metropolitan, the Kirby, and Loew's State—all located on a two-block section of Main, two standing side by side and the other, one block down on the opposite side of the street. The architect

connected with these three giants would also be closely linked with many of Houston's most impressive buildings—Alfred C. Finn.

Business buildings, private residences, apartments, hotels, and other public structures were all part of the Finn résumé, built during a career that covered half a century. While other architects focused on design and appearance, Finn developed an uncanny business savvy for communicating with clients about rentable footage, construction costs, and investment returns. Texas businessmen grateful for this ability awarded Finn their contracts over other, higher-profile architectural firms.

As a result, from 1913 to 1964 the Finn office would be responsible for such structures as the Sam Houston Music Hall and Coliseum (1937), the Sakowitz Brothers

store (1949–1950), the Houston Scottish Rite Cathedral (1922), the Jefferson Davis Hospital (1937), the Shriners Crippled Children's Hospital (1950), the National Bank of Commerce and Gulf Building (1929), the Cullen Administration Building at the University of Houston, and the San Jacinto Monument (1937).

Alfred Charles Finn was born in Bellville, Texas, on July 2, 1883, to parents Edwin E. and Bertha Rogge Finn. At the age of seventeen, Alfred took on a job building boxcars for the Southern Pacific Railroad in Houston. After taking a correspondence course in architecture, he landed a job in 1904 as apprentice draftsman with the Dallas architectural firm of Sanguinet and Staats. He was transferred to Fort Worth in 1907, and then back to Houston in 1912 when he was promoted

Main Street, c. 1934. Left: Loew's State and the Metropolitan; right: the Kirby. Courtesy of the Houston Metropolitan Research Center, Houston Public Library, MSS 200-177.

to assistant to Alfred E. Barnes, manager of the Houston branch. During this time he also worked as a local architect on the Rice Hotel and, in the process, met Jesse H. Jones, who would have a profound effect on the rest of his life.[1]

Jones was a lumberman, developer, publisher, financier, statesman, and humanitarian who had been instrumental in Houston's development since the early years of the century. Finn would soon develop a strong working relationship with Jones, their agreements relying on handshakes and verbal contracts. After Jones became a steady client, one architect in the Finn office described the firm as being "owned" by Jones. "Finn's office did all of Jesse Jones work," said another Finn employee. "I can recall very simply, because it was of so much importance to me later, working one Saturday morning, Mr. Jones showed up at the office, whatever I was doing, he had me step off the stool and he got on and he made suggestions and corrections on whatever I was working on. Mr. Jones paraded in and out of Mr. Finn's office, with Mr. Finn following in his footsteps."[2]

Since Finn's livelihood was so strongly linked with Jones, his career waned with Jones's passing, in 1956. Thereafter Finn had to contend with a host of essential problems he had never had to deal with before, such as the necessity for written contracts. He had also, by this time, suffered a stroke, which left him partially paralyzed and unable to work. With his death on June 26, 1964, the Alfred Finn architectural firm died as well.[3]

In his fifty-one years of business, Finn produced a wealth of unique buildings, including, besides the picture palaces in Houston, the Fort Worth Hollywood (1930) and Worth (1927) theatres, the latter styled in an Egyptian theme. The art of the pharaohs served him well, for it was this look that he used with equal flair for the first of the Main three—the Metropolitan.

THE METROPOLITAN THEATRE
1016 Main

For Houstonians in 1926, the $2 million Metropolitan Theatre resembled nothing so much as a spectacular Egyptian pal-

The Egyptian-themed Metropolitan, c. 1927. The easel display next to the stairs is for The Show *with John Gilbert, at the time America's top romantic leading man. Courtesy of the Houston Metropolitan Research Center, Houston Public Library, MSS 19-424.*

ace that had been raised from the banks of the Nile and firmly positioned in the heart of the downtown district. It would remain there, sandwiched between the Lamar Hotel and Loew's State Theatre, for exactly forty-six years and six days.

The theatre was operated by the Publix Theatre Corporation, a company founded in the fall of 1925 as a joint venture of the Famous Players–Lasky Corporation and Balaban & Katz of Chicago. According to blueprint records, fellow theatre architect John Eberson had a hand in the design.[4]

Finn personally supervised the construction, assisted by designing architect Jordan MacKenzie and the artist responsible for the interior decoration, William Orth. Their Egyptian-based vision incorporated architectural motifs reproduced directly from reference photos of existing structures in Egypt.[5]

An intricately decorated ticket booth stood outside the theatre entrance. Through the entry doors, inset with art glass, patrons found a foyer adorned with large oil canvases illustrating historical events from the fifteenth dynasty. Scattered throughout the entire theatre were depictions of kings, queens, court followers, dancing girls, and chariot races with prancing steeds. Also incorporated were symbolic icons: the key of life, the lotus leaf, the sacred parrot and eagle, prayer gods, and sphinxes.

Once inside the foyer, patrons were greeted by an enormous sphinx at the base of the broad staircase leading to the mezzanine promenade. Thousands of brightly colored ceramic tiles formed the floor and the wall murals. Ingeniously designed floodlights were incorporated into the wall motifs, in effect becoming

part of the design. Plush chairs, urns, and vases finished off the decor.[6]

As in his later design for Loew's State Theatre, Finn avoided the use of high ceilings in the mezzanine, thereby exaggerating the visual impact of the expansive, 2,500-seat auditorium.[7] Egyptian symbols covered the walls, and a flamboyant design framed the proscenium. A massive doily design with petals that radiated out toward the walls was located in the auditorium ceiling, and soft light streamed out through the incorporated art glass. Around the borders were hidden air ducts, leading from the refrigerated air-conditioning system. Four immense lamps, closely resembling those in a sacrificial temple, were suspended from the ceiling.[8]

The Metropolitan was one of the first theatres in the South to feature a disappearing orchestra pit, which could be raised from a point fifteen feet below the theatre floor up to audience level. A separate elevator controlled the organ console, which housed a Mighty Wurlitzer human-voice organ.[9]

The Metropolitan opened on Saturday, December 25, 1926—Christmas Day—preceded by a special advertising section in the *Houston Chronicle* the day before. Patrons formed a long double line that stretched a block from the box office well before the two o'clock opening.

By three, the crowd was seated, and a trumpet blast heralding the first program was followed by the deep bass tones of the Mighty Wurlitzer, played by house organist George H. Latsch. The proscenium curtains were drawn, followed by a screen announcement, a prologue, and "The Star-Spangled Banner." Next came the first feature at the Metropolitan,

Interior of the Metropolitan. Courtesy of Houston Endowment Inc.

Stranded in Paris, with Bebe Daniels, as well as a Publix stage show, *The Inaugural Banquet*, performed by a cast of twenty. These Publix productions were created specifically for movie-theatre audiences and taken on the road after their New York debuts. Topping off the program was a performance by the twenty-piece Metropolitan Grand Orchestra, which was raised into public view from the hydraulic pit and then led by Alexander Keese. The entire performance would be repeated at five, seven, and nine.[10]

Live performances and grand movies filled the Metropolitan during the following decades. Films included *Rebecca of Sunnybrook Farm* (1932), *The Wedding March* (1928; directed by Erich von Stroheim), *Mr. Deeds Goes to Town* (1936; directed by Frank Capra), *She Married Her Boss* (1935; with Claudette Colbert),

Psycho (1960; directed by Alfred Hitchcock), *White Christmas* (1954; directed by Michael Curtiz), *Gidget Goes Hawaiian* (1961), and appropriately enough, *The Egyptian* (1954; directed by Curtiz). The Metropolitan also hosted the national touring productions of the Sigmund Romberg operettas *Blossom Time* (1921) and *The Student Prince* (1924), the *Ziegfeld Follies*, and the operetta *Rose Marie* (1924).

El Paso had its special premiere in April 1949, with all the principal stars in attendance, headed by John Payne and George "Gabby" Hayes. The world premiere had taken place in El Paso the previous week.[11] The American premiere of *Genghis Khan* was held on June 18, 1965, and Stephen Boyd flew in for a promotional media blitz. He did not make a stage appearance.[12] *Thrillarama Adventure* had its world premiere on August 9,

1956—Thrillarama being an elaborate, although short-lived, wide-screen process similar to Cinerama.[13]

The Metropolitan had a rich history of live appearances. Vic Insirillo was a popular house bandleader and trumpet player during the later twenties, having spent formative years at other Houston theatres before Publix hired him to head the Metropolitan ensemble.[14] Comedienne Zazu Pitts presented her own stage review in October 1938.[15] Mae West appeared for one week in a live Hollywood review in April 1939.[16] That August, Hollywood producer Jesse L. Lasky appeared live with his *Gateway to Hollywood* show, featuring Anita Lou-

ise, Wendy Barrie, and Edmund Lowe. Two lucky Houstonians were selected to receive a Hollywood contract. On the screen was the Lasky feature *Career*, starring Alice Eden and John Archer, themselves prior *Gateway to Hollywood* contract winners.[17] *The Lone Ranger*, with Clayton Moore, was presented in January 1956 with a special live appearance by the Lone Ranger.

The Metropolitan's history also was to include burglary, armed robbery, and murder. In December 1949, a man robbed the box office, unaware that the cashier had her finger on a buzzer that was signaling the ushers, some seventy-five feet away. As the robber was about to

Grand auditorium of the Metropolitan. Courtesy of the Houston Metropolitan Research Center, Houston Public Library, MSS 19-425.

leave, the cashier screamed, "That's the man!" An usher tackled the man, holding him down until a patrolman arrived. The twenty-nine-year-old robber was later identified as having also held up the Navaway and Sunset theatres.[18]

A year later, assistant manager Jay Raney was forced to open the safe in the third-floor manager's office shortly after he and the theatre cashier had counted the receipts. The armed, masked man escaped with $603. When arrests were later made, the heist turned out to be the work of four individuals, including a seventeen-year-old former employee.[19]

In December 1960, two burglars ransacked the theatre offices, after tying up and blindfolding the porter. Unable to open the safe, they looted the *Chronicle* Goodfellows jar, a donation bucket aimed to raise money for Christmas toys for needy children.[20] Then, in February 1962, a man was found shot to death in the theatre restroom while the Houston Livestock Show parade was going on outside.[21] A decade later, burglars broke into the theatre safe, only to find a secondary one inside, and gave up the effort.[22]

In 1926 the Metropolitan was the first theatre on the block, but it would not remain an only child for long. Within eight months, a second, less pretentious movie house would join it in the neighboring block. The theatre-building boom of 1927 was in full swing.

THE KIRBY THEATRE
911 *Main*

Simple but refined was the style of the Houston Kirby, its name honoring pio-

neer Houston lumberman John Henry Kirby. The construction became the fourth movie house operated by the Publix chain in Houston, the others being the Capitol, the Queen, and the aforementioned Metropolitan. The Kirby was smaller than the Metropolitan—it sat 2,000—and was distinguished by a simple classical decor of marble, rose, and gold.[23] Floyd K. Smith managed the theatre.[24]

The formal opening took place on August 12, 1927, and long before the eleven-piece Kirby Theatre Concert Orchestra struck the first chord of the

The Kirby Theatre, c. 1930. Courtesy of Houston Endowment Inc.

overture, the Standing Room Only sign had been hung up.[25]

The Kirby was designed in the Adams Colonial style, with carved white pillars, stately marble stairways and walls, and a spacious foyer and mezzanine promenade. A lobby of soft, pearly white with gold was decorated especially for the opening with a line of floral arrangements. The auditorium was detailed in subdued amber, with touches of sky blue, Pompeian red, and dull gold, and soft draperies adorning the stage.[26]

The evening's entertainment included *Beau Geste*, starring Ronald Coleman, Maurice Lawrence leading the orchestra, plus a selection from *Faust*, as performed by Julia Dawn, the singing organist.[27]

Following *Beau Geste* the next week was *Chang*. Others to follow included *The Big Parade* (1925), *Ben-Hur* (1925), *Wings* (1927), Chaplin's *The Circus* (1928), *Old Ironsides* (1926), and *Camille* (1926) starring Norma Talmadge.

The year 1927 was a pivotal one in the history of the cinema—a year when the movies learned to talk. The Kirby heralded this new age when it featured Warner Bros.' *The Jazz Singer*. With this one film, the talkies were here to stay. *The Lights of New York* ran at the Kirby a year later as the first all-talking picture.[28]

When the Depression hit, the Publix chain collapsed, and the Kirby and the Metropolitan were taken over by Karl Hoblitzelle's Interstate Theatres; Eddie Bremer took the reigns as manager.

When the George Arliss feature *Disraeli* opened in 1929, it created a financial obstacle for the nearby City National Bank (a merger of Gulf State Bank and Judge James A. Elkins's Guaranty Trust Company). It was also the bank of choice of Jakie Freedman, a professional gambler who may have been the bank's biggest depositor. On the morning of *Disraeli*'s opening, a line of enthusiastic moviegoers stretched around the block from the ticket booth, and some mistook the movie line as one for the bank. Rumors quickly spread that the City National Bank was on the verge of collapse—just as Freedman arrived to make his morning deposit.

Freedman marched into Elkins's office, and the judge said that if he had any concerns, he should feel free to withdraw his money. "If you go down, I go down. We'll start over together," Freedman replied, and made his deposit. Had he closed out his account, it may have started a domino effect, thus wiping out the bank's available cash as well as its credibility.[29]

Houston's first Saturday-morning kiddie shows were held at the Kirby, as well as Bank Nights—lottery events in which tickets were sold in advance for a weekly drawing. Actress Nan Grey, a Houston native, made her stage debut at the Kirby, telling of her experiences in Hollywood.

Front entrance to the Kirby, c. 1928. The feature film, The Lion and the Mouse, *was an early Vitaphone talkie. Courtesy of the Houston Metropolitan Research Center, Houston Public Library, MSS 200-130.*

Other famous alumnae of the kiddie shows were Gale Storm (*My Little Margie*) and Ann Miller (*On the Town*).[30]

The Kirby also became the clubhouse for Rice Institute football players. The Rice athletes had developed a weekend habit of catching the Saturday-morning matinee, complete with a western and serial, before their game. As the school year came to an end, they realized that they would be unable to see the entire current serial, *The Lone Ranger*.

Bremer arranged a private party late one night. The Rice athletes brought their dates to see a special screening of the remaining chapters. Afterward, the long, marble-floored lobby became a dance floor, and a barbecue buffet and a record player were set up to one side. What started out as a one-time gesture became a traditional farewell party for the football players each June and continued until Bremer moved to the Majestic Theatre during World War II.[31]

Featured films at the Kirby included *Casablanca* (1942), Hitchcock's *Stage Fright* (1950), *Grand Hotel* (1932), *Li'l Abner* (1940), and *The Song of Bernadette* (1943).

In January 1949, a robber held up two cashiers and stole $335 after standing patiently in line with the rest of the ticket buyers. He made a quick getaway into the Saturday-night shopping crowd. The robber was later apprehended and identified as a thirty-two-year-old ex-convict who claimed to have traveled with Bonnie and Clyde.[32]

The section of Main Street between the Kirby and the Metropolitan had become a mecca for Houston's avid moviegoing public, but one grand palace was left to be unveiled, with elegance never before seen in the city, or rivaled since. This ace card was the stunning Loew's State.

The Loew's State marquee, c. 1929, with an eye-catching prop display for the movie Flight. *Courtesy of Houston Endowment Inc.*

THE LOEW'S STATE THEATRE
1022 *Main*

On October 15, 1927—just two months after the Kirby's debut—the extravagant Loew's State Theatre opened its doors. For the Loew's Corporation executives, this was the newest addition to their worldwide chain of over three hundred theatres. For Houstonians, it was to be the largest and most elegant theatre to grace the city.

The State was the creation of Loew's founder, Marcus Loew, also head of the Metro-Goldwyn-Mayer Pictures Corporation. It would be Loew's first in Houston as well as one of the most elaborate theatres in the company's circuit, costing an estimated $1 million. The State would complete Loew's southern circuit: Atlanta, Memphis, New Orleans, and Houston.

When Marcus Loew died on September 5, 1926, Nicholas Schenck took control of operations.

Alfred C. Finn was again contracted to be the architect for the building, and he worked with designing architect Victor E. Johnson. Anne H. Dorman of Loew's supervised the interior. As with the Metropolitan and Kirby, the Hewitt Company of Houston performed the actual construction.[33]

The week before the State's opening, downtown had unveiled its latest grand hotel, located at the corner of Lamar and Main. The 500-room Lamar Hotel, also built by Jones and Finn, was within easy walking distance of Loew's, and the Metropolitan was sandwiched between them.

The grand opening of Loew's State took place on Saturday, October 15, 1927. The previous Friday, the *Houston Chron-*

icle had run a fourteen-page special section dedicated entirely to the State.[34] The opening presentation began promptly at twelve thirty and ran through eleven that evening. The feature presentation was the Lillian Gish film *Annie Laurie*. Jesse Jones made a principal address, and the dedication program included Mayor Oscar Holcombe. Several people dressed in colonial garb handed out Martha Washington chocolates while a Loew's cameraman was on hand to film the grand opening. The film was then quickly processed in order to be shown later that day and on through the week.[35]

A $10 gold souvenir piece was awarded to the first patron to buy a ticket, along with a signed commemorative letter. It was then customary at the opening of a new theatre to award the first patron a gift of gold. This was thought to bring prosperity to the theatre, and Loew's had followed this practice.[36]

After passing the ticket booth, the patrons entered the theatre through a series of marbled outer lobbies, each fronted by three sets of bronze doors. The flooring was of imperial marble from Vermont, a white marble with a faint golden vein, with inserts of verde antique (a green serpentine marble), and the walls were of Italian tavernelle marble resting on bases of verde antique. Rows of bronze doors separated the vestibule from the lobby, which was in turn separated from the foyer, and the foyer from the auditorium. The high vaulted ceilings of the outer lobby were suddenly reduced to a low flat ceiling in the foyer and mezzanine. As in the Metropolitan, this cloistered atmosphere meant that the entrance into the expansive auditorium made more of an impact.[37]

The journey to the auditorium was like a walk through a mansion full of French furniture, bronze statues, Meissen urns, and beautiful gilt mirrors. The furnishings had been purchased from the famed Vanderbilt townhouse in Manhattan when it was razed earlier that year. The collection, which had belonged to the Vanderbilt family for almost a century, contained original pieces from the time of Louis XIV, Louis XV, and Louis XVI. One of the most dazzling of the acquisitions was a four-by-six-foot Louis XVI mirror, which adorned the wall of the mezzanine. Other pieces included two Louis XIV tables and a massive nine-foot console that held a Dresden vase flanked by two original Meissen urns. The overall effect was more that of an exhibition at a fine-arts museum than that of a movie house.[38]

The best was saved for last—the auditorium. Carved panels alternating with silk damask decorated the walls. The central ceiling was a thirty-three-foot-diameter dome embellished with panels of dancing figures and a large central rosette. Concealed around the base of the dome were thousands of electric lights that cast a flood of indirect light throughout the auditorium. The principal colors of the auditorium were turquoise, gold, cafe au lait, and ivory.[39]

The orchestra pit contained a mammoth Robert Morton organ, an instrument that ranked with the Mighty Wurlitzer. The Morton was designed to be a full orchestra in and of itself, able to mimic sounds from a trumpet fanfare to a flute or a single violin. It also contained a number of percussion effects, such as sleigh bells, glockenspiels, harps, chimes, and xylophones, along with the more solemn tones of a pipe organ. Loew's officials claimed to have used more than five hun-

The Loew's State under construction, 1927. Note the painted wall advertisement for the Metropolitan in the top left. Courtesy of Houston Endowment Inc.

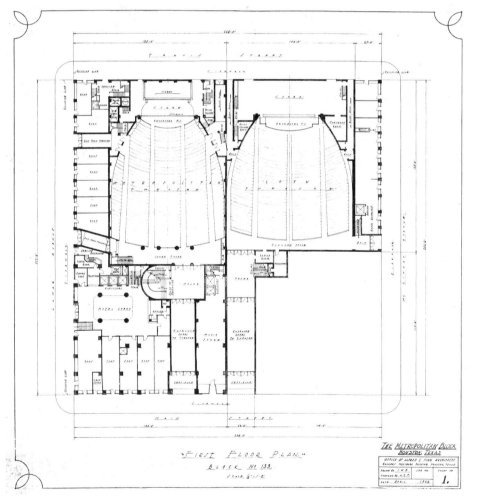

Blueprints from the office of Alfred Finn, dated April 1926, detailing the first floor of the Metropolitan, the Loew's State, and the Lamar Hotel lobby. Courtesy of the Houston Metropolitan Research Center, Houston Public Library.

dred miles of wire when hooking up this awesome instrument.[40]

"It was a lovely, beautiful theatre," said Homer McCallon, whose long career with Loew's began at the State. After a start in 1919 as reserve seat usher for the Bijou Theatre in Knoxville, Tennessee, he found himself in Birmingham, Alabama, as a theatre press agent. "I figured I'd better learn something about publicity," said McCallon in a 1972 *Houston Post* interview. "Back in those days, it was strictly flesh and flickers," he said. "We'd have a reel of comedy and a reel of news while the people got seated, then the stage show. Later, we split 'em—vaudeville and a feature picture both—and that went on a long time, until the talkies came in."[41]

The State ran movies for forty-five years. Celebrities who graced the stage included Edgar Bergen (with Charley McCarthy) and "Mr. Television" himself, Milton Berle. Judy Garland appeared in January 1938 to promote one of her MGM films.

"At Loew's, we had five acts of vaudeville and a big orchestra," continued McCallon. "With all the changes over the years, some of them were pretty drastic. Dropping vaudeville, for example. That was a pretty cruel thing to do to a lot of people, performers, stagehands, musicians. It was a pretty sudden adjustment for them to have to make and at a bad time, too, right in the middle of the Depression."[42]

Much of the talent came through in the form of touring companies. Among these performers were the Smith Sisters, Flossie and Fleda. The Houston-raised Smiths toured with the Loew's Theatre circuit for several years. "Sister teams were very popular then, and people thought we

were talented," explained Flossie Smith Jones to a *Houston Chronicle* reporter when she was sixty-six years old. "We did high kicking, tap dancing, singing—not much of anything. All we could do was look alike." Fleda eventually became an elementary school teacher, while Flossie joined the YMCA production office staff.[43]

In December 1927, just two months after the grand opening, Loew's State advertisements urged the public to "start the new year right. See Lon Chaney in *London after Midnight*" (now considered to be the most sought-after of all lost films). A more notable opening took place on February 7, 1940, when the State presented *Gone with the Wind* for a four-week run. The exterior of the theatre was remodeled to resemble a plantation, complete with white pillars and the *Gone with the Wind* banner across the top of the entryway. The newspaper ads that day were quite simple and uncluttered, advertising the 235 seats still available for the gala premiere that evening. The ticket price for the evening was $1.20 (including tax).[44] Of the 2,600 seats in the State, 2,521 were sold, according to a *Houston Post* article. This indicates a discrepancy common with theatre records—that of seat number. Loew's State originally listed its seat count as 2,500.[45]

In 1943, McCallon took over as manager of the State when the previous manager, Francis Deering, went into the navy. Deering would later return to a higher position in the Loew's Corporation before leaving to manage the Houston Symphony.[46]

On August 18, 1939, the State featured *The Wizard of Oz*. Other films presented at Loew's over the years included *A Tale of Two Cities*, *The Great Dictator* (1940),

The beautiful mezzanine promenade of the Loew's State contained a wealth of antiques from the Vanderbilt mansion. Note the Metro-Goldwyn trademark woven into the carpet design (without Mayer--the Metro and Goldwyn companies merged in 1924, but Louie B. Mayer's name did not immediately become an integral part of the banner). Courtesy of the Houston Metropolitan Research Center, Houston Public Library, MSS 19-394.

Balcony of the Loew's State. Clearly in view is the twenty-three-foot-diameter dome supporting the Czechoslovakian chandelier. Around the base of the dome are thousands of concealed electric lights. Courtesy of the Houston Metropolitan Research Center, Houston Public Library, MSS 19-399.

Waterloo Bridge (1940), *Dr. Jekyll and Mr. Hyde* (1941) with Spencer Tracy, *The African Queen* (1951), the 1946 version of *Cleopatra*, *The Courtship of Andy Hardy* (1942), *Singing in the Rain* (1952), *Spellbound* (1945), *North by Northwest* (1959), and *The Creature from the Black Lagoon* (1954; in 3-D).

There were numerous other special events over the years, such as a Shirley Temple look-alike contest. *Houston Chronicle* television critic Ann Hodges recalled being a contestant as a child. "I lost," she remarked. "I looked more like Jane Withers."[47]

McCallon oversaw all aspects of the business, handling managerial and press-agent duties as well as serving as theatre artist, his other ability. Promotional showcases in the foyer often included poster portraits that he painted of the stars.[48]

RELIEF FROM THE HEAT

The completion of the State, the Kirby, and the Metropolitan effectively established a distinct theatre district on Main Street between Lamar and Rusk. Many color postcards of the downtown area would feature this area prominently over the next four decades.

The recent development of air conditioning had tempered the misery of Houston's hot summer months, although only a few theatres offered it. To guarantee that theatre patrons could relax in total cooling comfort, Loew's spent over $100,000 on a specially created air-conditioning unit that could pump out air at a chilly sixty-five degrees.[49]

Air conditioning had a vital impact on the theatres that offered it. Before this time, many theatres shut down at the beginning of June and remained closed for the next three months. Movie producers figured this fact into their release schedule and held back their top pictures for the fall; theatre managers were forced to maintain empty, profitless theatres while waiting for the onset of cooler weather.

Early experiments with "washing" and recirculating the air to the auditorium helped ease the workload of the old standby, the ceiling fan. Both the Isis (1912) and the Queen (1913) boasted such equipment, but the 1923 Majestic (air-conditioning installed in 1924) and Will Horwitz's Texan (1925) are generally considered the first true air-conditioned movie houses in the city. By the time the big three were built, air conditioning had become much more advanced, allowing theatres to operate throughout the summer with no loss of attendance.

The refrigerating operators quickly learned the pitfalls of the new equipment while inadvertently freezing the ears of a few patrons. They discovered that the guide for proper temperature control was not the dry bulb of the thermometer—which measured the actual temperature—but the wet bulb, which displayed the humidity percentage.

"Thanks to experience," said W. V. Taylor, manager of Loew's State, for a 1932 newspaper article, "we have learned a few lessons about the proper handling of cooling plants. When they were first installed, the engineers did exactly what one would expect them to do—they turned on the cold. They did not realize at the time that being comfortable was one thing, and being cold was another. Like the man with the new automobile, they were anxious to see just how much energy they could squeeze out of their plants."[50]

A comfortable seventy-eight degrees became the standard. Loew's State was designed with zoned air conditioning, allowing the lobby to be a few degrees cooler than street temperature, the foyer slightly cooler than the lobby, and the auditorium to be coolest of all, so the patron became acclimated to the temperature in stages.

"In warm weather," stated Taylor, "just after a shower, the sun comes out and the humidity shoots up like a skyrocket. The engineer must then adjust the plant to remove the heavy moisture from the air, and substitute dry air."[51]

By the time the neighborhood theatres began appearing across town, proper air conditioning was as important to the operation of the house as the projector, screen, or seats—and it would continue to be advertised in local listings for many years to come.

MUSICAL ACCOMPANIMENT

Local musicianship was also linked with theatre operations. With vaudeville a vital part of the theatre program, there was a constant need for quality musicians, of which Houston had an abundance. According to a 1929 estimate by Robert Rice, president of the local musicians' union, the Houston membership at that time was somewhere around three hundred strong. While a number of them found work at various hotels and radio stations, many others found employment through Houston's numerous theatres. This was especially true before 1929 and the advent of the talkies, when musical

accompaniment for motion pictures was still a necessity.[52]

Survival as a musician was difficult, with most players depended on full-time jobs elsewhere just to get by. The best of Houston's talent usually found work directly in the theatres.

Legitimate orchestras found a home in the theatres as benefactors such as Edna Saunders worked to establish opera, classical music, and drama in the city. Groups such as the Nespoli Orchestra and Ellison Van Hoose's Little Symphony enjoyed premiere nights in 1931 at the Palace Theatre. Within a few years, entr'acte musical extravaganzas based on operas and symphonies were staged regularly at both the Majestic and the Metropolitan. Despite all this, and the recovery from the Depression, jobs for musicians were hard to come by.[53]

In an effort to offer musicians relief, Interstate Theatres city manager Eddie Collins established a new policy at the Metropolitan, which scheduled the nine-piece Metropolitan house orchestra to play for three weeks out of the month. The fourth-week orchestra was composed of a pickup group of local talent. Because of Interstate's expansion across the South, the company was able to offer musicians contracts for five-week work periods in Texas and longer options, up to twenty weeks, touring the southern states.

While the Metropolitan house orchestra was disbanded in late summer of 1935 because of a decline in vaudeville, local musicians were hired by touring entertainers such as Fanny Brice, Cab Calloway, Phil Harris, Perry Como, and the Mills Brothers. As movie theatres shifted to a film-only format, the Houston musician base would find employment elsewhere, but during the golden days of the movie theatres, live music was an integral part of the normal programs.[54]

BEGINNING IN THE THIRTIES, entertainment began to shift from downtown to the neighborhoods. Despite this, the downtown theatres remained prominent well into the sixties. The Metropolitan Theatre drew its largest recorded attendance during the December 1964 holiday weekend, when the James Bond film *Goldfinger* was released. During its six-times-a-day showings, the theatre hit the 12,000-patron mark. Theatres were doing phenomenal business at the time: Loew's showed *Father Goose* to sellout crowds while the Majestic showed *Sex and the Single Girl*. Conservative estimates at the time were that the three theatres cleared 50,000 people over the three-day weekend.[55]

However, by the end of the decade, the market collapsed for the downtown theatres as the first multicinemas began appearing around the city.

"Tempus fugit, as they say," commented *Houston Chronicle* writer Jeff Millar in a 1972 farewell article about the Main Street theatres. He had written a similar article about the Majestic Theatre only a year earlier. *Tempus fugit*—time flies.[56]

The first to go had been the Kirby a decade earlier. It was sold to the McKinney Avenue Realty Company in 1956. On April 15 of that year, a final double bill was shown at the Kirby: *Naked Dawn* and *Hold Back Tomorrow*.

One employee had lasted the life of the Kirby. Projectionist Jessie E. Hogue stood in the projection booth on opening night, when *Beau Geste* flashed across the screen—and shut down the projector on the final night of the Kirby. The theatre had survived for twenty-nine years. It was subsequently razed to make way for the expansion of the First City National Bank.[57]

As the sixties progressed into the seventies, the downtown palaces continued to die a sad slow death. By this time, the Metropolitan had acquired a large gaudy marquee ill suited to the style of the interior. The quality of films spiraled slowly down into the realm of exploitation. During its last year, the Met would additionally play host to live midnight rock shows on Friday nights. Said Millar, "Some of the energy seems to stick on the insane plaster sphinxes and linger."[58]

During this time, burglars broke into Loew's State and stripped the mezzanine of all that could be carried out, making their way down the marble stairs and out through the side exit. The remaining pieces would be sold later for large amounts after the theatre closed.[59]

The last several years for the State were marked by low attendance and low-grade films. In March 1972, the New York office of Loew's opted not to renew the lease on the building. The end finally came on October 15, 1972, exactly forty-five years to the day after the State first opened. The feature films that day were a double feature of *Black Belly of the Tarantula* and *The Weekend Murders*. The films ended, the lights were shut off, and the doors were closed for good. The elegant Loew's State, with its remaining antique furniture, its high vaulted ceilings and carved wall decor, went out not with a bang, but with a whimper.[60]

"I got all marshmallowy inside when the Majestic shut down," wrote Millar.

"I just don't think that the Majestic was quite ready to go. I can't get too worked up about Loew's and the Met. I guess it's because the owners have been playing nothing but crummy movies there in the last years. Both theatres are really pretty trashed now. They've outlived their era by 20 years and their practicality by about seven. They've been leaning on each other, very tired, and mumbling 'get it over with.'"[61]

"The thing about this show business," McCallon later said, "you don't live 48 hours on what you did yesterday, or last week or last year. Nostalgia is an interesting thing, but you can't sell it for a quarter."[62]

Millar described McCallon as a tall twinkle-eyed fellow who could "tell you stories about the movie business until the cows come home. He knows all about this tempus fugit stuff."[63]

McCallon spent forty-five years with Loew's, managing the State and supervising the building of the Sharpstown Drive-In in 1958, the Loew's Town and Country Theatre in 1972, and the acquisition and renovation of the Delman in 1969. After the Delman, he became city manager for Loew's. With the closing of the State, he was transferred to the Town and Country. He retired less than a year later, on February 2, 1973.[64]

The Metropolitan Theatre closed on December 31, 1972, sixteen days after the neighboring Loew's State shut its doors. The Mighty Wurlitzer organ was salvaged, ending up first in a private residence. During this time, it suffered in a fire, apparently caused by faulty Christmas-tree lights in the house, that melted half the stop tabs off the console. This was the second fire the organ had endured; the

first took place sometime between 1937 and 1941, above the main chamber on one side. The organ was left unplayable after the firemen went through the main chamber and stomped on the pipes. The Metropolitan Wurlitzer was eventually acquired by the Houston Area Theatre Organ Society, which installed it in the auditorium on the main campus of Houston Community College.[65]

The theatre lobbies of both the State and the Metropolitan were converted to retail space.[66] Shortly thereafter, in August 1973, wrecking crews came for their auditoriums, to make way for a parking lot for the same Lamar Hotel that had opened during the original theatre-building boom of 1927.

"I kept away from it," said McCallon. "It would have been a sad thing for me to see it go down. I loved that theatre. I would have been crying until now."[67]

Some portions of the Loew's interior were salvaged. Rare marble and ornamental plaster castings from the lobby and grand stairway were salvaged for Gary Warwick's restoration of the old Ritz/Majestic Metro.[68] During a sale of its fixtures, some of the State's velvet stage curtains were sold to a lady who made stuffed-frog pillows from the material.[69] The large brass door sets found their way into several different houses. One set adorned Lipstick's Cabaret, a men's club on the Southwest Freeway. This survived until 1994, when the club moved to a newer building next door. Gary Warwick acquired another set. More notable—and symbolic—were the six doors installed in the front of the Wheeler Avenue Baptist Church. The predominantly black congregation could walk freely through the very doors that were once off-limits to them.[70]

Despite his comment about nostalgia,

Debris from the auditorium of the Loew's State is in the foreground, revealing an advertisement for the Publix Metropolitan, Houston's $2 million palace of splendor, August 1973. Courtesy of the Houston Metropolitan Research Center, Houston Public Library, RGD6N 08-04-73.

McCallon kept a lobby decoration from the State, a bronze sculpture that adorned a small aquarium. "We kept goldfish in it when it was in the theatre," he said.[71]

Some twelve years after the Metropolitan and Loew's State were razed, the Lamar Hotel fell to a similar fate when 500 pounds of carefully placed dynamite charges reduced the building to rubble. A crowd of 4,000 spectators gathered on rooftops and intersections a block away, behind the secured area, to watch. Within seconds, an extended sonic-boom-like rumble shook downtown, followed by thick billows of dust.

"Golly, that was wonderful," said one spectator. "Let's do it again."[72]

THE CITY BLOCK formerly occupied by the Metropolitan, Loew's State, and the

Lamar Hotel became a parking lot, paralleling the "paved paradise" line from Joni Mitchell's song "Big Yellow Taxi." Downtown Houston was left without any of the original grand picture palaces; only the Ritz/Majestic Metro on Preston, diminutive by comparison, survived to see restoration. Had even one of the other grand palaces survived another decade, it might have been reevaluated for use as an entertainment facility, like the Majestics in San Antonio and Dallas or the Paramount in Austin. Instead, the rich classicism of Loew's State, the Metropolitan's Egyptian motifs, and the atmospheric ceiling of the 1923 Hoblitzelle Majestic are now but the stuff of memories and some black-and-white photographs.

Tempus edax rerum—time, which devours all things.

The Ritz Theatre, later to become the Majestic Metro. Although Sand Blind was released in 1925, this photo was most likely taken a few years later, after talkies had become the norm. Courtesy of the Houston Metropolitan Research Center, Houston Public Library, MSS 200-194.

THE
LATER 1920s

YOU AIN'T HEARD NOTHING YET!

Who the hell wants to hear actors talk?

HARRY WARNER

★ LEISURE AND RECREATION for Houstonians in 1925 were to be found on numerous fronts, from the comforts of the downtown theatres to the great outdoors. City parks proved to be an ongoing gathering spot for picnics and socializing. Others would make their road trips to Sylvan Beach and the gulf waters of Galveston for their communes with nature.

Another strong draw was Luna Park, which had opened in June of the previous year under a media blitz as the "Coney Island of Texas." The Luna's hype was equaled by its own ambitious concept; built at a price of $325,000, the twenty-acre park, in the 2200 block of Houston Street, aimed to compete with its New York cousin. Within were picnic areas, a large carousel, and a dance casino with a spring-supported floor that would bounce with the weight of the dancers.[1] Twice a day, folks could watch Dr. D. F. Carver and his diving horses, which were trained to dive from a forty-foot platform into a tank of water, or see an occasional bathing-beauty fashion contest.[2] Towering above the park was the Skyrocket roller coaster. The entire park was set aglow with 50,000 glittering electric lights. The park would survive for only half a decade, its ill-fated life drawn short by both the Great Depression and a roller-coaster accident, but for Houstonians in 1925, it was the hot ticket.[3]

The art of the silent film had reached its zenith. So had the movie houses that showed them. No theatre, before or since, quite matched up to the grandest of these houses, climaxing with Hoblitzelle's last Majestic in 1923, and the 1926–1927 trio of the Metropolitan, Kirby, and Loew's State. Through the remaining years of the decade, a number of smaller theatres would be built, including one that would survive into the next century.

The year 1925 offered up two new theatres, one being the Lamar at 2203 North Main. Also opening its doors that year was

the Texan, the second of Will Horwitz's Homefolks Theatres. Once the Depression swept across Houston, Horwitz's influence would extend far beyond his theatre walls (see Chapter 7 for a full account of Horwitz and his theatres).

The opening of the Metropolitan in 1926 would steal the thunder (and patron dollars) from older, lesser picture houses. One that held its own was the Ritz theatre, which opened the same year.

THE RITZ/MAJESTIC METRO
911 *Preston*

Of all of Houston's theatres built before 1930, only one has remained standing to see new life and restoration: the 1926 Ritz. While the theatre went under other names over the years—the Teatro Ritz and the Ciné Ritz—it is best known today by its final title, the Majestic Metro.

The theatre was situated on Preston between Main and Travis, next to the Kiam Building, home of the first Sakowitz department store. The medium-size theatre was designed by William Ward Watkin, whose credits include the Rice University campus (1910–1912), the original Miller Outdoor Theatre (1921), the Museum of Fine Arts (1922–1926), the Kinkaid School campus (1924), the Houston Public Library (1926), and Rice Stadium (1938).[4]

Watkin was born in 1886 and studied architecture at the University of Pennsylvania. After graduating in 1908 and spending a year traveling in Europe, he joined the Boston firm of Gram, Goodhue, and Ferguson. In 1910, he was assigned the Houston Rice Institute project, and then

Luna Park, the "Coney Island of Texas." Courtesy of the Houston Metropolitan Research Center, Houston Public Library, MSS 1248-2488.

The Ritz Theatre, restored as the Majestic Metro, 1990. Photograph by Steve Schmid.

remained in Houston to found the Rice University architectural department. He began an independent practice, designing houses for the South End and public structures as well as a number of unrealized jobs for the Scanlan estate. One Scanlan assignment that did reach completion was the Ritz.[5]

Construction on the theatre, on the former site of the Jemison Building, began in 1925. James Antill was the general contractor for the $50,000 structure.

The Ritz was owned by sisters Stella and Lillian Scanlan, daughters of Thomas Scanlan. When he died in 1906, he left a sizable fortune to his daughters. There is no indication that they were directly involved in the operation of the theatre.[6]

The Ritz held its grand opening on April 15, 1926, with the Buck Jones feature *The Fighting Buckaroo*. Also scheduled was a personal appearance from stunt double Le Moyne Veglee, the "daredevil doll of the movies," who told tales of her Hollywood experiences.[7]

Unlike the massive excesses of the nearby Majestic, the Ritz was an ornate but intimate theatre, with a seating capacity of 1,260. The red and gold auditorium was further enhanced by a large pipe organ, which served as accompaniment to the silent flickers. Very affordable admission prices of five cents and fifteen cents would remain in place through the thirties, eventually to be proudly displayed in bright lights on the exterior marquee.[8]

Space to the left and right of the lobby was built out as retail, a jewelry store on the left and an ice cream and sandwich shop on the right; the lobby proper was quite small. During renovation of the Ritz in the eighties, Gary Warwick found evidence that inset glass cases may have been visible on the left lobby walls, allowing Ritz patrons to see the jewelry in the neighboring store.[9] Likewise, an open window may have been constructed between the lobby and ice cream shop, creating an early concession stand.

Eventually, these two spaces were gutted and incorporated into the Ritz. The left space became a manager's office, while the wall for the right space was removed, thus adding to the lobby size. At this time, the right staircase, originally a mirror image of the left in the foyer, was repositioned to feed directly into the lobby.

During the thirties and early forties, B westerns were standard fare at the Ritz. Live acts could also be found on its stage during the midforties. Dick Daring, an old-time vaudevillian, staged a regularly changed live revue with dancing girls in colorful Hawaiian costumes, comedy skits, singing, and his special "stroblite" lighting effects. Among the performers he featured were Cleo Plunkett and Flo Del Garde, rotund comedian Chuck Sexton, vocalist Aleena Fowler, dancer Jean Fonda, and knockabout clown Chubby Swain.[10]

In 1930 it was taken over by local theatre man Will Horwitz as part of his Homefolks chain. Karl Hoblitzelle's Interstate Theatre chain also became involved when Horwitz formed an alliance, Horwitz-Interstate Theatres, with the organization. Horwitz was, at the time, married to his second wife, Agatha (also known as "Pretty Honey"), and had it not been for this marriage, the Ritz may not have survived into the twenty-first century.

After her divorce from Horwitz, Agatha married Eddie J. Miller, who was vice president and business manager of the projectionists' union, Local 279, IATSE (International Alliance of Theatrical Stage Employees). He was also the father of actress Nan Grey from a previous marriage.

Eddie Miller and his wife, Agatha "Pretty Honey" Miller. Agatha had previously been married to showman Will Horwitz. Courtesy of Ray Hugger.

When Horwitz died, ownership of his theatres was split; Agatha retained a one-fourth interest in the Iris, Texan, Uptown, and Ritz. Around 1946, Interstate offered her full possession of the Ritz in exchange for her partial interest in the other three—thus, the Ritz fell into the hands of the Miller family.[11]

Another minor partner in the Ritz was Frank "Red" Fletcher, a former vaudevillian with bright red hair who had managed the Horwitz-Texan Theatres. When air conditioning was installed in the Ritz auditorium, Fletcher helped out with the exorbitant cost of the equipment in return for an interest in the theatre.

The Millers lived on Hardy Street, next door to Agatha's cousin Hazel and Hazel's mother. When the mother died, the Millers invited Hazel, who was still single, to live with them. Then, in February 1958, Agatha (Horwitz) Miller died of multiple sclerosis. She had no children. Within a year, Eddie married Hazel. He, in turn, died around 1973.

During the early forties, the Ritz ran Spanish-language films, eventually changing its name to the Teatro Ritz and later as the Ciné Ritz.[12] The Millers also gained control of the North Main and Fulton theatres, and the Ciné Ritz moniker eventually ended up attached to the Fulton. Ray Hugger, a relative of Hazel Miller, worked the Ritz during college and took over its management after he graduated.[13]

In the seventies, the Ritz switched its name (to the Majestic, in 1972) and its type of screenings (to exploitation) under the guiding hand of Alvin Guggenheim, who had previously reopened the old Lincoln Theatre. Guggenheim named all of his theatres Majestic, in tribute to the Interstate Theatre he had ushered at in the forties. The Ritz marquee was covered up with its new name, the Majestic Metro (see Chapter 10 for a full account of Alvin Guggenheim).

Under the Guggenheim banner, kung fu and blaxploitation films were the order of the day. *Shaft* (1971), *Superfly* (1972), *Cooley High* (1975), and Bruce Lee films were all standard fare. During the 1976 holiday season, while other theatres were running the major-studio blockbusters, the Majestic Metro Christmas films were *The Monkey Hu$tle* (1976) and *Cornbread, Earl and Me* (1975).[14] Guggenheim eventually lost his lease and closed the theatre in September 1977 with audience-appreciation dollar shows. The final films were *Cooley High*, *Cornbread, Earl and Me*, and *Sheba, Baby* (1975).[15]

Later, the Majestic Metro ran porn films before closing its doors for good in 1984.

THE MAJESTIC METRO REVIVIFIED

In 1985, businessman Gary Warwick passed by the aging movie house and, curious, located owner Ray Hugger for a tour. Armed with a flashlight and a Coleman lantern, the two journeyed into the darkened auditorium. "We were like spelunkers," recalled Warwick during a *Houston Chronicle* interview. "It was like entering a cave. There were spider webs everywhere, no electricity, and water was standing six inches deep." Pulling away tattered shreds of fabric hanging from the walls, he found the decorative flourishes to be weathered but intact.[16]

Warwick had grown up with a love for the theatre, making 8mm home movies and shopping at nostalgia stores like Roy's Memory Shop. After college, he took a job in the real estate market with Gerald Hines Interests, thus gaining invaluable exposure to the downtown area. He then became vice president at Rader Companies and a subsidiary firm, Classified Parking, a position that gave him numerous opportunities to examine old buildings in the area.

Warwick took out a fifty-year lease with an option to buy and laid out a four-phase restoration plan. The first required structurally stabilizing the building, which had deteriorated over the years. A new roof was installed and the standing water bailed out. The second phase consisted of disassembly and demolition, which Warwick described as an archaeological dig. Previous "improvements," such as a dropped ceiling with acoustic tiles, fluorescent lighting in the lobby, and tacky fabric wall coverings, were removed. For-

Auditorium of the Majestic Metro, transformed for a gala dinner event. Note the plaster trim above the screen; it was deliberately left untouched for contrast with the restored auditorium. Courtesy of Clare Lagroue.

tunately, all of the essential elements of the theatre remained intact underneath the decades of makeshift remodeling. He also discovered the original Ritz marquee, its sunburst incandescent lighting intact, hidden underneath the Majestic Metro sign.[17]

Phase three involved creating a detailed set of architectural as-is drawings by friend and architect Tom Pollette of Charles Tapley and Associates. The flat Houston economy at the time put further work on hold.[18]

The final phase officially commenced in 1989. Architects Barry Moore and Kirk Eyring prepared the renovation plans,

and construction began in November of that year.

The ornate plaster moldings that lined the auditorium had deteriorated from age and neglect. Donald Curtis, a plaster and stucco expert, had sections removed so that he could cast new molds and duplicate the original work. A section of plaster molding directly above the screen would eventually be left unrestored to show the extent of the damage before the restoration.

The lobby had been altered the most. Since no photos of the interior existed, Warwick labored to keep the restoration as close to the period as possible. Antique lighting fixtures, wall sconces, stained glass, and other furnishings were added. The original candy counter was revamped into a bar area, and two minibars were located in the rear of the auditorium. The restrooms were beyond hope; the ladies room contained only three toilets and a minuscule sink. The whole area was reworked to include six fixtures, three sinks, and a large mirror.[19]

The house was rewired, the projectors repaired, and new air conditioning installed. The auditorium was restored in its original plush red and gold, and a new sound and light system was installed. Seats brought in from the demolished Tivoli Theatre in Aurora, Illinois, lined the rear and sides of the auditorium.[20] Other seats were bolted upright, serving strictly as decor, and the lower half of the sloped floor was left open. Around the periphery of the restored screen were placed spotlights capable of creating any number of lighting effects. Directly in front, Warwick added an elevated stage bordered with brass railings: a raised dance area.[21]

Rare marble and ornamental plaster casting had been removed from the lobby and grand stairway of the old Loew's State before its demolition in 1973. Warwick placed these items in storage with plans for their possible integration into the restoration of the large cantilevered balcony area. The original concept for this upper area called for a wine bar and a theatre-memorabilia museum.[22]

Knowing the futility of operating a single-screen downtown theatre in an age of home video and multiplexes, Warwick marketed the space as an events hall. The restored Ritz would cater to parties, recep-

tions, award ceremonies, style shows, and meetings, yet still retain all the capabilities of a movie theatre.

The cost of the restoration was $500,000; acquisition of land and the adjacent two-story Larendon Building (ca. 1890) brought the total cost up to $1 million. The Larendon Building would house executive offices, dressing rooms, and prop storage space, which was advantageous since the theatre, built primarily for movies and not vaudeville, had a shallow stage area and no backstage or wing space.[23]

A quandary arose about the dual names of the theatre. Said Warwick in a 1995 interview, "Was I going to call it the Ritz, and go back to the original name, or was I going to go with a new name. I decided to stay with the Majestic Metro. It was just a great-sounding name, and we really liked it because of what it denoted. When we would ask people, and do marketing surveys, the name projected images of something majestic to look at, and Metro gave them the thought that it was a downtown building."[24]

The Majestic Metro reopened on December 15, 1990, with the Merrill Lynch Christmas party, and the American Institute of Architects awards gala on January 31, 1991. This was followed by a party for the Page Parkes Center of Modeling, staged as part 1920s elegance and part 1980s MTV. A highlight of the evening was an old newsreel, located by Warwick, of 1930s models in swimsuits and fur coats. It was the first time in years that the old Ritz screen glowed with an image not containing hot, steamy sex or a karate chop to the chest.[25]

The balcony-restoration phase commenced during 1993 and 1994. Plans for the wine bar and museum were abandoned in favor of additional space for large-scale parties. All the chairs were removed except for five rows of seats in the balcony front; the floor was terraced; pony walls were installed; and ornamental trim work was added to blend into the original design. The structural antiques acquired from Loew's went unused in the restoration out of respect for the architectural purity of the original Ritz design.

For Warwick, the restoration became an ongoing project. "When you're doing something that's a labor of love, you're never really finished with it," he said. "There's always something else you can add or you can tweak or you can fix."[26]

To date, the former Ritz Theatre, one of a handful of buildings in the Old Market Square district to have survived, functions as a venue for special events. Intimate but opulent, the former silent-movie house managed to attain what the grand palaces could not: a new lease on life.

THE YEAR 1927 is best remembered for the openings of the Kirby and Loew's State theatres. Other, smaller theatres appeared during this time with far less fanfare: the Dunbar, at 2814 Nance; the Hidalgo, at 2213 Congress; the Houston, at 1011 Congress; the Family Theater, at 1413 Washington; and Lemuel E. Newton's Bluebonnet Garden Theatre, at 1015 Broadway. The Bluebonnet was a neighborhood theatre with a facade of sparkling white stucco and cool blue tile, and a quaint interior. In August 1936 it became a part of the Interstate Theatre circuit.[27]

THE COMING OF SOUND

With the widespread success of *The Jazz Singer* (1927), theatres across the nation were faced with an undeniable problem:

The Bluebonnet Theatre, c. 1937. Note the door to the right for the confectionery. Courtesy of the Houston Metropolitan Research Center, Houston Public Library, MSS 114-1964.

to talk or not to talk. Film production took a radical about-face, which in turn affected the theatres where those films were to be shown. Warner Bros. had been experimenting with the Vitaphone process—a phonograph record played alongside the film—although the original intention was not to show actors talking, but to standardize and replace the live musical accompaniment that most theatres supplied.

Warner Bros. hit pay dirt with *The Jazz Singer* and Al Jolson's declaration "Wait a minute, wait a minute. You ain't heard nothing yet!" To cash in on its success, the studio began to add talking sequences to silent films already in production. These "part-talkies" were released for a short time, followed by *The Lights of New York*, the first all-talking picture, along with Jolson's *The Singing Fool*.[28]

Meanwhile, Fox was developing its Movietone sound system, which applied sound directly to the film. Theatres were forced to choose between the two systems, and many opted for both so as not to limit either their options or profits. The major studios formed a yearlong committee to analyze and standardize the best technology. Sound-on-film would eventually win out.

While some sound films were released in both silent and sound versions to accommodate the theatres that had not switched over, the transition period moved rapidly. Theatres were forced to pay large amounts for this new technology: initial costs in 1927 ranged from $8,500 to $20,000. By 1929, the expense of installation would drop to $5,000–$7,000. As a result, all the major theatres converted to sound while many of the smaller houses closed their doors in silence.[29]

In Houston, the changeover to sound—and the Depression—brought construction of new theatres to a near standstill. A new Zoe theatre opened in 1928, at 502 Milam (although this may have simply been the Ideal Theatre reopened under a fresh name). This would be followed the next year by a small neighborhood theatre in the Heights that would survive in varying forms into the next century.

THE HEIGHTS THEATRE
341 *West 19th*

Now considered one of city's leading historical districts, Houston Heights was founded during the final decade of the nineteenth century. Located four miles from downtown, the Heights established itself as a separate town before its annexation into Houston. Three decades would pass before the community would have its own movie house.

The original Heights Theatre was, according to available accounts, nothing more than a small storefront space in the Simon Lewis Building, equipped with 350 folding chairs, a screen, and a projector.[30] The building, at the corner of 19th and Ashland Streets, was built around 1922 and would later house Ward's 19th Avenue Drugs, then function as a storage area for Harold's Men's Wear, located across the street. The building was completely renovated in 1989, and now operates as the Carter & Cooley Deli.

The second Heights Theatre was built in 1929, at the beginning of the Great Depression, by Charles Wygant, and was leased to his son Robert, then later to his grandson Richard. The movie house

The Heights Theatre, c. 1935. To the left is the Heights Confectionery and to the right is F. G. Kronberger Jeweler. Courtesy of the Houston Metropolitan Research Center, Houston Public Library, MSS 114-1969.

opened on May 14, 1929, with Zane Grey's silent western *Sunset Pass*.[31] The exterior facade resembled that of the Alamo, and the interior was a combination of Spanish colonial and what might be called "American Ritz." Dark red curtains and wooden seats covered with forest green and ruby-colored leather added to the decor. The front fifteen to eighteen rows of seats were wooden only, designed specifically for children. Total capacity was 750.[32]

Movies at the Heights Theatre—usually second runs and B westerns—ran for a two-day stretch: Sunday–Monday and Tuesday–Wednesday; Thursday was typically a one-day slate. The Friday–Saturday shows were usually westerns.

The ticket price was originally twenty cents, but after the stock-market crash, Robert Wygant collaborated on a price-slashing scheme with Julius Rosenstock, owner of the Heights One-Two, One-

Interior of the Heights Theatre. Collection of Gus Kopriva.

Newspaper ad for a week's shows at the Heights Theatre, Houston Heights Citizen, March 27, 1936.

Two Cab Company—an arrangement agreed upon at the steps of the theatre. Cab fare was reduced to fifteen cents for the first mile and five cents for each additional mile; movie prices were cut to fifteen cents for adults, five cents for children. Those prices remained intact until the government levied a movie tax that forced prices up to seventeen cents and nine cents respectively. By the fifties, kiddie admission would be a whole twelve cents.

There was no concession stand in the lobby. Instead, ice cream and candies were bought next door at Ebert Armstead's Heights Confectionery.

During the thirties, the theatre played the promotion game whenever possible; a bullet-ridden car might be parked in front of the theatre for a gangster movie, while a caged animal would be on display for a Tarzan flick. Live appearances included ones by Gene Autry and "Iron Eyes" Cody. Said Richard Wygant in a 1989 interview, "I can remember, as a boy, seeing the biggest lions and tigers in my life, out in front in cages."[33]

The theatre's motto, which ran on all the ads, was "Home Owned and Operated by Heights People."[34]

In 1935, the theatre was upgraded with air conditioning, an exterior facelift in an art moderne style, an interior redo of plush Americana, and a seating capacity increased to 900.[35]

Saturday westerns remained a favorite with the neighborhood kids who followed the adventures of Lash LaRue, Tim Holt, Bob Steele, the Durango Kid, and the "King of the Cowboys," Roy Rogers, whose color Republic films stood out in the days when most B films were black and white.

Occasionally, Heights residents would win tickets to the theatre; the *Houston Heights Citizen* newspaper ran the names of the winners, who could call the theatre for their free passes.[36]

In a 1992 *Houston Chronicle* article, writer J. T. Chapin reminisced about his boyhood at the Heights Theatre: "Even with low ticket prices, Mr. Wygant must have made a comfortable living. He owned a big black Cadillac (or was it a Packard?), wore black homburg hats, and smoked huge, foot-long cigars. When he drove up in front of the Heights, usually chauffeured by one of his sons, I regarded him with the same awe I would have accorded Cecil B. DeMille."[37]

When Robert Wygant died, in 1951, his son Richard took over the dwindling business. In January 1957, he shut the theatre down, and subsequently sold some of the auditorium seats.

The theatre was then bought and renovated in 1958 by John Scott and W. E. Coats, Jr. The missing seats were replaced, a snack bar was added, and excess space was rented to a jeweler who operated a store within the lobby area.[38] The theatre reopened on April 18, 1959, with *April Love*.

Within the first year, Scott ran afoul of the operator's union. The Heights union projectionist earned $125 for a thirty-five-hour week, and a second, $90-a-week relief man filled in the remaining hours. Because of financial problems—bank mortgage notes, expenses, and insufficient income—Scott asked the union for permission to operate the relief man's shift. The union's response was a predictable no, so he fired both union operators. The union picketed the theatre—Scott got an injunction against the union.

On October 10, 1959, a man broke three vials in the auditorium, each containing a combination of fatty acids and other chemicals, causing a vomit-like stench that effectively emptied the theatre. Five days later, the same foul stuff was poured into the exterior ticket booth, ruining the ticket machine and money-changer. A similar bombing took place the same day at the Don Gordon Theatre, another nonunion, family-operated movie house.[39]

Scott eventually leased out the theatre, which began showing R- and X-rated flicks. Area residents and civic groups were less than impressed with the subject matter, and the issue climaxed in May 1969.

The theatre booked the controversial Swedish film *I Am Curious (Yellow)*. With its brief flashes of nudity and loose approach to sex, *Yellow* was extremely hot, scandalous stuff for its time. It opened on May 21, much to the ire of the neigh-

borhood. On May 24, picketers from the Shady Oaks Full Gospel Church, 1501 West 23rd, claimed that the movie was obscene. The following day, a stink bomb was set off in the theatre and Ku Klux Klan literature was pasted outside. Another stink bomb exploded the next evening, followed by a bomb scare on May 27. The picketers returned on May 31. The cashier's life was threatened on June 1, and the manager's on the day after.[40]

In the morning hours of Friday, June 6, a fire gutted the interior and collapsed the roof. Firemen extinguished the blaze within an hour after a waitress from a nearby coffeehouse reported the fire at 5:15 a.m. Interior damage was valued at $90,000.[41]

The fire appeared to be deliberately set. Apparently, the arsonist hid between the seats at closing time, then walked up the attic boards on either side of the projection room, saturating it with kerosene.[42] An empty can of kerosene was found in the rear of the theatre. No one was ever arrested.

According to a person quoted in a newspaper interview, the theatre was "probably burned in the name of decency by some misguided moralist." Others surmised that the blaze had been set by unionized film operators in retaliation for the theatre's nonunion status.[43] Scott's hope to rebuild the theatre never occurred, since the property was underinsured.[44]

From 1969 to 1981 the theatre remained an abandoned shell, housing an occasional drifter from the cold. Scott ran a machine shop out of the front of the building. It was then sold in 1981 to John

Although the media suggested that showings of the feature film I Am Curious (Yellow) *were behind the Heights Theatre fire on June 6, 1969, it was just as likely that the theatre's union disputes were to blame. Courtesy of the Houston Metropolitan Research Center, Houston Public Library, RGD6-821.*

Holland, who planned to restore the old movie house.[45]

Holland's elaborate renovation ideas included a deli and a dining room in the lobby, a small screening room and a balcony on the second level, and on the third, a garden and a patio. Also on the second level would be a private club and bar (an interesting concept considering that the Heights had been a dry area since 1918). The estimated cost for the project was $500,000 over a three-year period. Holland secured a $150,000 bank loan, got another $150,000 in guarantees from personal investors, commissioned engineering reports, and had plans drawn up by architect Robert Morris.[46]

Holland's eventual improvements included an interior stage as well as exterior frames for glass blocks and circular

windows, but his grand plan was never completed, and the theatre remained roofless until 1988. It was, however, used on occasion, as when it hosted a benefit concert for Pacifica radio station KPFT in April 1982. The event included a showing of the 1956 movie *Rock Around the Clock*, with Bill Haley and His Comets, and a live musical lineup featuring Doctor Rockit, the Mydolls, Really Red, the Haskells, and others.[47]

In February 1988 the theatre was sold to Heights residents Gus and Sharon Kopriva, a local engineer and artist, respectively, who planned to reopen it as an art gallery and performance space. The theatre was Gus's fortieth-birthday present (instead of a stereotypical sports car). Having grown up watching movies at the old theatre, he did not want to see it demol-

Map of downtown Houston theatres. Map by David Welling.

A	**Azteca** – 1809 1/2 Congress Ave	L	**Lincoln** – 711 Prairie Ave.	RX	**Rex** – 511 Main and **Star** – 507 Main
B	**Best** – 212 Main	LS	**Loew's State** – 1022 Main	RZ	**Ritz** (Majestic Metro) – 911 Preston
BJ	**Bijou** – 413 San Jacinto	MET	**Metropolitan** – 1016 Main	RY	**Royal** (Pastime) – 211 Main
C1	**1908 Cozy** – 1018 Texas	M1	**1905 Majestic** – 1306 Congress (Empire/Grand)	SC	**Scenic** – 313 Travis
C2	**1910 Cozy** – 1112 Texas			ST	**Strand** – 508 Travis 3-4-22
CA	**City Auditorium** – Texas and Louisiana	M2	**1908 Majestic** (Palace) – 807 Texas	T	**Texan** – 814 Capitol
CC	**Crescent** – 602 Main & Texas	M3	**1923 Majestic** – 908 Rusk	TO	**Texas** – 215 Main
CK	**Crystal** (Key) – 407 Main	PE	**Pearce** (Liberty) – 718 Main	TH	**Theato** – 912 Prairie and Main
D	**Dixie** (Feature) – 603 Main	P	**Prince** – 320 Fannin	U	**Uptown** – 805 Capitol
G	**Gem** – 505 Main	PA	**Passmore** – 414 Fannin (Orpheum/Imperial Grande)	V	**Victory** – 1011 Congress Ave.
ID	**Ideal** – 504 Milam			VA	**Vaudette** – 417 Main
IR	**Iris** – 614 Travis	PC	**Princess** – 410 Main	VE	**Vendome** – 406 Fannin
IS	**Isis** – 1012 Prairie	PZ	**Plaza Airdome** – 1101 Main	VR	**Victor** – 412 Milam
J	**Joy** (Crown) – 303-05 Main	Q	**Queen** – 613 Main	Z	**Zoe** (Capitol) – 719 Main
K	**Kirby** – 911 Main	R	**Rialto** – 608 Main		

ished, as had happened to so many other Houston movie houses.[48]

In 1988, West 19th Street became one of the first two urban demonstration targets of the Texas Historical Commission's Main Street Program, in which the conservation and reuse of historic buildings was intended to lead to economic revitalization of the community. The Kopriva theatre renovation quickly became a focal point in this project. The Koprivas used the Morris-Holland facade design for the construction and brought in contractor Jay Dougherty, who had previously worked on the Bellaire Theatre restoration. They found that the second-floor projection area had survived the fire, as had the two restrooms. Air conditioning and heating were installed, the facade was repaired, the neon marquee was restored, and the long-awaited roof was finally added.[49]

The theatre was reopened on Friday, November 3, 1989, with a live production by Dreem Katz, *Pigs Dance II: Romp Thru Hell*. Playwright Kenny Joe Spivey and his theatrical troupe had already achieved local notoriety at Main Street Theatre with *Every Day at Dawn, the Pigs Dance in Ancient Ritual. I Know. I Dance With Them.*[50] Their Heights performances took place in an unadorned auditorium of exposed bare walls temporary theatre seats, folding chairs, and sofas. Dreem Katz would continue to use the venue for their shows even after Spivey's death in 1993.

Live productions by the Urban Theater and other groups, fashion shows, photography exhibits, a lecture by Dominican priest Matthew Fox, and a gala for the Greater Houston ACLU have all occurred at the revamped theatre.

In January 1993, the Koprivas, Morris, and Dougherty received the Gold Brick Award from the Greater Houston Preservation Alliance for their restoration of the theatre. Their work also allowed the building to be removed from the Texas Historical Commission's biannual Endangered Historical Texas Properties list.[51]

The second theatrical wind of the Heights theatre eventually passed, and the building became a retail antiques center.

ON OCTOBER 24, 1929, Black Thursday arrived — the crash of the New York Stock Exchange, which heralded the end of the roaring twenties and the start of the Great Depression.

With this, theatre construction virtually came to a halt. According to the *Houston Directory*, only a few would open in 1930: the Juarez, at 7320 Navigation; the Key, at 609 West Dallas, and the Aztec, also known as the Azteca Teatro and Maya Theatre, at 1809 1/2 Congress. Once theatre construction resumed, the houses would be smaller, simpler, and less pretentious. Art deco would be the rage. The age of the grand movie palace was over.

Will Horwitz, 1936: a single man can have a profound effect on the lives of countless others. Courtesy of the Harry Ransom Humanities Research Center, University of Texas at Austin.

★ ★ ★

WILL HORWITZ, PHILANTHROPIST

★ ★ ★

During this Depression, when the spirit of the people is lower than at any other time, it is a splendid thing that for just fifteen cents, an American can go to a movie, look at the smiling face of a baby and forget his troubles.

FRANKLIN DELANO ROOSEVELT
HONORING SHIRLEY TEMPLE, 1935

Mankind was my business. The common welfare was my business; charity, mercy, forbearance, and benevolence were, all, my business.

JACOB MARLEY IN CHARLES DICKENS'S
Christmas Carol

★ HOUSTON IN 1930 was a city comprising 68.6 square miles and an estimated population of 280,000. Within its boundaries could be found 21 banks, 29 parks, over 150 churches, and 60 hotels, with a total of 8,000 rooms. There were also thirty-six movie theatres, with a total of 13,000 seats.[1]

The Houston of 1930, like the rest of the nation, was also deep in the Great Depression. The coming years would see widespread unemployment, failed businesses, hunger, and hardships. To counter this, aid often came from individuals whose efforts could affect the destiny of those in need and make the turbulent times a little easier. One such person was Houstonian Will Horwitz—a flamboyant theatre man, radio station owner, floral enthusiast, and humanitarian. Some described him as Santa Claus. Because of

101

his movie houses, numerous community efforts, and innate compassion, the darkest days of the war years and the Depression contained a ray of hope.

Horwitz owned a handful of Houston movie theatres during the twenties and thirties. The fortune he amassed from the movie houses, he poured back into the city. He fed the poor, found them jobs, put clothes on their back, and entertained them, all at his expense.[2]

Will Horwitz was born in Benton, Arkansas, on June 25, 1886. After attending public school and receiving a master of arts degree from the University of Michigan, he entered the newspaper business. Horwitz arrived in Houston in 1917 and first worked for a newspaper before opening a

film exchange. His official debut as a showman began during World War I, when he ran a theatre at Camp Logan, possibly the Interstate-operated Liberty Theatre.[3]

In 1919, Horwitz bought the old Travis Theatre for $150, a sum he had to borrow, since he had only $13 in his pocket at the time. It was with the reopening of this old theatre that the era of the "homefolks" theatres began—modest, reasonably priced movie houses for ordinary people.[4]

THE TRAVIS/IRIS
614 Travis

In 1919 the Travis had been in operation for half a dozen years. It had originally

The Iris Theatre, c. 1929. Courtesy of the Houston Metropolitan Research Center, Houston Public Library, MSS 200-120.

The Iris Theatre, where "Every seat is a cool retreat," c. 1928. Children wait to get in for the Iris vacation party. Courtesy of the Houston Metropolitan Research Center, Houston Public Library, MSS 200-125.

opened on April 13, 1913, with a program largely composed of vaudeville plus a moving picture. Horwitz transformed the old Travis from a live-performance venue into a movie house, and to establish the theatre as a new entity, he opted for a new name. The old vaudeville house was renamed the Iris, after his daughter Ruth Iris Horwitz. He later delighted in telling how he didn't have the funds for a new marquee, so he changed the Travis T into an I and removed the A and V. The remaining letters were then rearranged to form the new name.[5]

The Iris, the first of the Horwitz "home-folks" theatres, reopened on June 7, 1919, with Norma Talmadge in *The Social Secretary*, along with a Mack Sennett comedy, a Hearst News Weekly, and accompaniment by the Lewis Iris Orchestra. In typical Horwitz fashion, opening-day admission was free.[6]

A year after his purchase of the Iris, he staged his first benefit: a vacation party for the twelve-and-under age group on their first day of summer vacation. A coupon from the daily newspaper entitled kids to free car rides, free peanuts, and a free movie. Thousands of children showed up. Not surprisingly, newspapers carrying the coupons often turned up missing from front lawns across town when these parties were thrown.[7]

Horwitz had found his niche in second-run family-oriented entertainment, and by 1925 he was ready to expand his homefolks empire.

THE TEXAN
814 Capital

The 1,393-seat Texan Theatre was Will Horwitz's answer to the grandeur of the

major picture palaces, although it strictly adhered to his concept of family-oriented pricing and entertainment. It unofficially opened on April 4, 1925, with a private screening for nearly 1,000 guests of the management. An orchestra, led by Max Fink, supplied music throughout the evening while a swarm of lovely usherettes, dressed in American Revolution period costumes, looked after the patrons. *Janice Meredith*, starring Marion Davies, was the feature attraction. All this, however, was merely a warm-up for the public grand opening at two the next day.[8]

Saturday was proclaimed Elks Day, and Houston Elks Lodge Number 151 was given the honor of opening the theatre. Actor J. Warren Kerrigan appeared in person for the formal dedication.

Befitting its name, the Texan incorpo-

rated various historical and regional motifs in a modified Spanish Renaissance style. The foyer was decorated with painted historical pictures of early Texas. Above the main entrance hung a mounted longhorn-steer head. The basement featured a nursery and playground for the kiddies. This included rocking horses and swings, as well as a merry-go-round in the middle of the room. The carrousel could hold a dozen kids at a time. Maids, dressed in white aprons, were on hand to look after the children. The Texan, along with the Majestic, was one of the first true air-conditioned theatres in the city.[9]

For those in the know, there was a penthouse with a blue-tinted picture window that looked out over Capitol Avenue. This area was accessible only through a "secret" door, which led to a small self-operated elevator. Said a *Houston Chronicle* writer years later, the secret passage and entrance gave "the place an air of mystery." Horwitz had originally planned to use it as a radio broadcasting station, but he never followed through, and it instead was converted into an office.[10]

It was hardly unusual for a downtown business to have living quarters nearby for the owners or manager of the establishment. The Iris had a similar apartment, and for a while Horwitz lived there with his second wife, Agatha.

The Texan, like the Iris, primarily featured second-run movies. Occasionally, a film such as the Al Jolson Vitaphone talkie *The Singing Fool* would garner first-run status.[11] Special guest appearances were also common, such as those by cowboy star Tex Ritter, the father of actor John Ritter, or Ernest Tubb and his entire Grand Ole Opry Show.

HORWITZ THREW his first Christmas party for the poor in 1926; more than 5,000 children showed up at the Texan. The Horwitz Christmas parties became a Houston tradition for two decades. The events, held for poor Houston youths, allowed him to give out bags filled with candy, toys, and fruit. For many children, this was the only Christmas gift they would receive.[12] Kids might get a ball, a glove, perhaps a sack of candy or fruit. Boys over twelve might get a BB gun. Girls usually got dolls, doll beds, or doll clothes.[13] The Texan eventually proved too small for the event—lines of children would sometimes run five to six blocks long—so the gatherings were moved to the City Auditorium. Theatre employees would spend hours wrapping and tagging presents for the annual event, which continued until two years after his death.

What began on a moderate scale eventually cost Horwitz thousands of dollars, but he replied, "I don't care what they cost. Houston built this theatre for me and I want to do something for Houston."[14]

He would celebrate his birthday, June 25, by giving the kids a free show, a bag of peanuts, and a refund on their carfare both ways. Kids would line up for blocks to get in.

HORWITZ WOULD eventually add more theatres to his roster. Both the Liberty and the Ritz would fall under his control, both structured according to his homefolks philosophy. Low prices, respectable second-run films, and community efforts were all part of his operation. At its peak, his theatres drew 75,000–83,000 patrons a week, rivaling the draws of the first-run Main Street theatres. Ever the innovator, he helped create a market for the art house with his support of foreign films.

His business principles led to constant disputes with film distributors, who threatened to cease renting him films if he didn't raise his prices. In response, Horwitz

When the Horwitz annual Christmas parties, like this one on December 23, 1935, grew too large to be held at the Texan, they were moved to the City Auditorium. Collection of Roy Bonario, courtesy of the Center for American History, University of Texas at Austin.

threatened to show independently made films if he were cut off from the major releases. To dramatize the price war, he staged a parade on Main Street, driving a truck loaded with live hogs bearing the signs "movie hog trust." The symbolic swine were also placed on exhibit in his theatre lobbies. The producers backed off.

HORWITZ AND THE GREAT DEPRESSION

During the Depression, those who had little to start with wound up with even less, and those ranks were joined by many more as the years progressed. Horwitz was especially active during these years. He financed a twenty-four-hour restaurant on Preston, the Grub Stake, across from the farmers market. Here, more than 100,000 free meals of soup, vegetables, meat, and coffee were served. A sign outside read "If you are hungry, come in and have a meal." Despite the fact that much of the food was donated by farmers who couldn't sell their produce, the eatery still cost him $500 a week.

Horwitz's "tin can days," held one day a week, allowed a person to go to the theatre for no other cost than a tin can of food. The canned goods were then stacked up and given to the needy at a store he opened at Capitol and Travis. This concept was later applied to clothing as well: the price of admission would be an article of good used clothing, also to be given to the poor. He filled an entire storeroom with clothing, and then handed it out to those in need. On other days he would accept an IOU from anyone eager to see a movie but without the money for admission.

Horwitz created jobs for the jobless, placing billboards around town that read "Let's Be Proud of Our City . . . Give the Unemployed a Job." An old bridge was purchased from the city for five cents, the price a mere formality. Men were then hired to tear the structure down.

He also operated a free employment bureau at Bagby and Walker in 1932 and 1933. During the eighteen months it was open, nearly 50,000 unemployed people registered for work. The agency would advertise for odd jobs and solicit work from door to door. He featured the trading of "one day's work for seven day's food supply for a family of five." The bureau was estimated to cost Horwitz around $1,000 a month to operate. According to Fred Cannata, Horwitz's general manager, "Those were the days when college men drove ice trucks and they weren't ashamed."[15]

Fred Cannata spent his life in and around the theatre business. He was born in Modica, Sicily, and immigrated to Texas with his parents when he was a boy. At the age of seven, he was singing songs in Italian (in accompaniment to slide shows) at the Electric Theatre in Beaumont.[16] Later he worked in a medicine show and as a roustabout and a clarinet player. He then took a job at the Dixie Theatre on Main, working as a ticket boy, bill poster, and, again, clarinet player. The clarinet followed him to the Isis after he tired of the three dollars a week he was making. He spent his time there as usher when he was not in the orchestra pit, until a twist of fate brought him notice. Word of mouth painted him as a hero when a fire broke out in the building adjoining the theatre. Although there was little danger, he calmly cleared the audience from the auditorium. He was offered seven dollars a week—plus a uniform—to usher for Horwitz at the Iris. He also found work at the Texas Theatre on Main. World War I intervened, and he was shipped overseas as part of the 111th Signal Battalion of the 36th Division. After the war, he returned to the Iris as a projectionist. By 1929, Horwitz had given him the position of general manager for the company.[17]

Cannata brought his nephew Jack Valenti into the Horwitz fold in 1938, and he worked at all four theatres, with duties ranging from ushering and janitorial work to preparing films for shipping. Valenti would later write speeches for Lyndon B. Johnson before becoming the president of the Motion Picture Association of America. "I had no idea in those days," said Valenti in a December 1989 *Houston Chronicle* interview, "that I would be so deeply involved in the movie business at its highest levels."[18]

"Horwitz was demanding," Valenti continued. "He used to come through the theatres and make sure that things were clean, and make sure that people were on duty, and that they were doing their right job. He didn't mind reprimanding you if you weren't, no matter who you were. He believed that the public had to be served well."[19]

"He was a civic-minded showman who was not dedicated to selling pictures, but to doing something worthwhile," said Cannata. "And in this business, that was sort of rare."[20]

THE 1940S

After the Depression, Horwitz was forced to raise admission price in his theatres. Adults were charged twenty-five cents for evening shows, though children's prices remained at five cents.

"There is nobody like him in the business today," said Valenti. "First, he was a small theatre-chain owner. Second, he was irreconcilably independent. He danced to his own drummer. Number three, he had this sense of civic justice about him. He had made a lot of money, and he wanted to give some of it back, so he would hold those big Christmas things."[21]

Saturday mornings meant group meetings at the Horwitz theatres. The Girl Builders met at the Iris for Bible verses, songs, talks, and a movie. The Boy Builders met at the Texan. The Buck Jones Ranger Club and the Knot Hole Gang also held weekly meetings at the Iris, and after the construction of the Uptown in 1935, a servicemen's club met there.[22] Coffee and cake were served free to the soldiers, and they were given writing paper and envelopes as well. Amateur nights were held at the Iris and Texan.[23]

During the 1928 Democratic convention in Houston, he sent Cannata to the Rio Grande Valley to round up forty-eight donkeys, one for each state in the union. Cannata arrived with fifty; two had been born en route.

One of the newborns was presented to the Democratic presidential candidate, Al Smith. After the convention, the remaining animals were given away. Some were gifts to Hermann Park and the Faith Home, where children could enjoy donkey rides. Faith Home had, in fact, received playground equipment from Horwitz the previous year.[24]

Horwitz provided care for a number of elderly people at St. Anthony's Home for the Aged on Almeda Road, many of whom were friends he had known for years. He purchased a portable projector and would send this to various institutions whose children would not otherwise have the opportunity to see a movie.

Horwitz supported organized labor. During the Southern Pacific Railroad strike, he advertised free admission to any strikers who exhibited a union card. His support was not without an edge. When the projectionists went on strike over a disagreement with Horwitz, the theatre musicians (who were not involved) decided to hold a sympathy strike and stage a parade. Feeling that they had no business in the matter, Horwitz bought a crate of rotten eggs on Commission Row. When the marchers reached the front of his theatre, he began lobbing the eggs at them. Innocent bystanders who got splashed were sent to a nearby laundry to get cleaned up at his expense. Showing appreciation (and a sense of humor), the musicians' union later presented him with a gold egg, and the machine operators gave him a gold-plated life membership to their union.[25]

He once conducted a "masher campaign," directed at men who molest women in shows. Pins were provided at the box office so that women could ward off any unwanted advances by poking them. A sign on the screen read "Mashers caught in this theatre will be whipped and then fined."[26]

Horwitz operated Houston's first radio station, WEAY, from the top floor of the Iris. The station was later consumed by KPRC. A second station was purchased in Reynosa, Mexico. The station, XED, would be the cause of very rough times for the Houston showman.

XED ran a radio lottery, which was legal in Mexico, but the United States government contended that the U.S. mail was being used to distribute the lottery tickets. Horwitz was summarily arrested upon crossing the border into Texas. A trial in Corpus Christi resulted in a prison sentence of eighteen months in the federal penitentiary in Leavenworth, Kansas. This was later reduced to one year and a day.

Public outcry was immediate. A petition campaign for presidential clemency garnered 100,000 signatures, but it did no good. In June 1932, Will Horwitz was sent to prison.

He handled business from his cell, wiring instructions to Cannata. When a hurricane devastated the Valley, he scheduled food drives, as well as clothing drives that brought in more than 10,000 garments. These were turned over to the Valley Co-operative Bureau. His wire read as follows: "Strip our commissary and give food supplies to the Red Cross for distribution among flood sufferers. Also give benefit stage and screen shows at all of our theatres Friday night. Charge no admission but take free will offerings from all patrons and turn all funds over to the Red Cross. Also suggest that you stop for a moment of grateful prayer that Houston was saved from the hurricane."

He was released after serving six months in prison. In 1940, he would receive a pardon and restoration of his citizenship and civil rights from President Roosevelt.

The City Auditorium was filled with 2,000 people for his homecoming party, which was sponsored by various labor and trade groups. The master of ceremonies, the Reverend William Stakes Jacobs, said "If all the mudslingers in the world were given the ocean for a bucket and comet for a brush, they could never blacken you in my eyes. There has never been a man who worked more heroically for Houston than you have."

Horwitz responded, "What I have done, I deserve no credit for. You, all of you folks sitting out there, have made these things possible by patronizing our theatres. I was only returning to you that which was rightfully yours."[27]

All this attention came to a man who, thirteen years earlier, had had to borrow the money to get his theatre business started. Once home from prison, Horwitz reinserted his fingers firmly into numerous civic and theatre-related activities, but he knew the time was near for the homefolks theatre family to grow. He had opened the Texan in 1925, and acquired several theatres already in business, but he was eager to build a better one. That one would be the Uptown, and it would be his last.

THE UPTOWN/RIVOLI
805 *Capitol*

The Uptown theatre began with Fred Astaire and Ginger Rogers dancing across the screen. It ended with live strippers and girlie films—not the fare that Will Horwitz would have approved of. Like many other theatres, the Uptown opened to much fanfare, then slowly slid down ladder of respectability, eventually becoming a burlesque hall before falling to the wrecking ball.

The Uptown project was to be a grand venture. Horwitz envisioned not a single theatre, but a minicity that included the Uptown Arcade—an enclosed set of shops and restaurants, all built into a tunnel system connected to the Uptown Theatre— a 500-car-capacity parking garage (and bicycle-checking area), and the newly

The crowning theatrical achievement of Will Horwitz: the Uptown, a combination multicinema, underground tunnel system, and shopping mall. Courtesy of the Houston Metropolitan Research Center, Houston Public Library, MSS 200-213.

*Will Horwitz, with tie
undone, stands with a line
of children in the Uptown
underground. Collection of
Gary Warwick, courtesy of
the Center for American
History, University of Texas
at Austin.*

renovated Iris Theatre. According to Cannata, it was the only downtown theatre built specifically for sound—the rest were adapted for sound after the talkies came in.[28] Other attractions were a flower shop, a post office, and a curio shop. In the heart of the basement, patrons could relax in the Old English–style decor of the Uptown Tavern. Other spots included the Uptown Lounge, also known as the Blue Room, and the Texas Fountain Room. The underground walkway connected the Texan lobby, the Fountain Room, and the Uptown Tavern, then joined a set of stairs to the Uptown. Horwitz was said to have been inspired by the Rockefeller Center tunnel when he extended his basement into this unique path of tunnels, the first such underground system in Houston. The temperature of the whole facility was maintained by a massive air conditioning system, from the auditorium on down to individually cooled telephone booths. On the upper floor was an additional miniature theatre, the International (also known

as Uptown Hall and the Uptown Little Theatre). This secondary auditorium was constructed for advance screenings and foreign films, in essence becoming an early art house.[29] The Hall held its opening day on December 3, 1935, with Upton Sinclair's *Thunder over Mexico* (1933; directed by Sergei Eisenstein).[30] The Hall also ran features such as the southern premiere of Charles Dickens's *Christmas Carol*, with Sir Seymour Hicks, during the holiday season of 1935.[31]

Construction began in January 1935, on the property bound on four sides by Capitol, Texas, Travis, and Milam. The architectural firm Jones and Tabor handled the design, with final decorations by Koetter and Arbing. This would be the last movie theatre built in downtown Houston for many years.

In February, Horwitz held a contest to name the new theatre, and was swamped with nearly 11,000 suggestions. After eliminating obvious names, such as "San Jacinto" and "Lone Star," as well as names

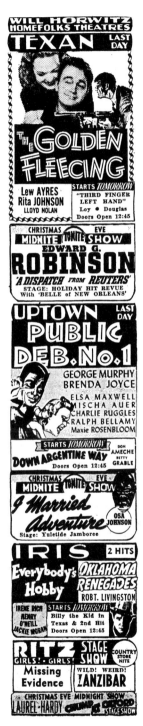

Newspaper ad for Horwitz's Homefolks Theatres, c. 1940. Collection of Roy Bonario.

too long for advertising purposes ("Temple of Happiness"), two finalists were decided on. The judges came up split 2–2 on the names, and Horwitz cast the deciding vote.[32] The winning name was submitted by thirteen-year-old Louise Price, who was awarded $50 and an elaborate floral bouquet for choosing the name "Tower."[33]

The choice was short-lived. When the theatre opened some eight months later, its name had changed to the Uptown—more than likely to avoid confusion with the Interstate Theatre of the same name on Westheimer, which opened three months after the Uptown.

Horwitz took advantage of any opportunity to publicize the Uptown. At one point during its construction, a massive I beam was delivered by truck to the theatre site. Allegedly, he paid the driver five dollars to have a motor breakdown at lunch hour in front of the Rice Hotel. The resulting traffic jam—and the newspaper publicity—was well worth his expense.[34]

On November 9, 1935, "Uptown Avenue" opened its doors to the public amid the standard publicity blitz. Harry Greer of KTRH broadcast the event, which featured such notables as Mayor Oscar Holcombe. After a presentation by Will Horwitz, the feature film began: *Top Hat* with Astaire and Rogers.[35]

The theatre auditorium incorporated a spacious, open design. Instead of an overhanging balcony, the interior featured an amphitheatre approach, the rear seats rising in ascending tiers from the main floor. The balcony section was especially ventilated for smoking, and a tier of seats was designed for the hard of hearing. A standard-size stage that included dressing and prop rooms faced the audience.[36]

Over the next twenty-four years, the Uptown kept the masses entertained with films such as *Steamboat Round the Bend* (1935) with Will Rogers, *High Sierra* (1941), and *The Invisible Ray* (1936). Other events included personal appearances by Gene Autry, Smiley Burnett, and Roy Rogers. Cowboy star Ken Maynard outdid them all by riding his horse, Tarzan, up on the stage.

HORWITZ THE FLORIST

As prominent as Horwitz was in show business, one of his hobbies brought him equal recognition—floral cultivation, which he started purely for recreation, and continued as a way to provide flowers for the sick. He built a greenhouse at his forty-six-acre estate in Dickinson so he could spend his spare time raising flowers. Huge gardens and floral borders surrounded his home. This way of taking his mind off the movie business eventually led to the creation of a horticultural paradise, costing an estimated $250,000. He later commented, "I found that I had invested so much money in the plant that I had to commercialize my hobby, so I opened flower stores."[37]

He opened a flower shop in the Uptown Building and ran a floral department at Sears, Roebuck & Company. Thousands would visit his Dickinson grounds on Sundays. In one instance, he extended an invitation to the public to see his 10,000 poinsettias. Asked which he liked best, the flower business or show business, he replied "I love both; flowers are the most profitable."

By the time he moved to Dickinson, Horwitz was married to Gladys Deason. This was apparently his third marriage: Ruth Iris was the offspring of his first, and his union with Agatha "Pretty Honey" Nolen was his second; the latter would later marry Eddie Miller, head of Local 279 of the projectionists' union (see Chapter 6 for an account of Agatha and Eddie).

In 1941, approximately 12,000 children attended his twenty-second annual Horwitz–Houston Post Christmas party. The December 24 event was always the highlight of the year for Horwitz. He was still active in aiding those in need, even though the Depression had passed, and the joy expressed by the hundreds of children at his party easily compensated for the cost and effort put forth. All the preparations were in place. All was ready to go.

It was an event he would never attend.

Three days before the party, he suffered a major heart attack. Unable to portray Santa Claus again, he instead dictated a letter to his guests from his hospital bed at St. Joseph's Infirmary. It read: "The show must go on, and I want to express to each and all of you my heartiest wishes for a merry, merry Christmas and a happy New Year." Cannata bore the news to the 12,000 children who attended.[38]

He rallied back from the first attack, and then suffered a second attack thirty-six hours later, at two in the morning. He died three hours later, at five on Christmas Day 1941—ten hours after his Christmas party had been held. He was fifty-five years old.[39] The Horwitz theatres—the Iris, Ritz, Texan, and Uptown—were closed on Thursday and through four thirty on Friday in tribute to Horwitz.

Will Horwitz was survived by his widow, Gladys Horwitz; his daughter, Ruth Iris; and her husband, Fred Gibbons. Fred, a well-known musician who played at a number of downtown theatres, originally supplied music for movies during the silent days. This musical talent was eventually handed down to his son Billy, who would form the group ZZ Top.

"(Fred had a) great, great musical background," said his later wife, Lorraine, in the KHOU Channel 8's *Houston: Remember When* series. "He could play for almost any scene, almost knowing what it was going to be before it happened. He was never at a loss to find a note on the organ."[40] Frederick Royal Gibbons died on July 19, 1981, at the age of seventy-three.[41]

THE END OF THE HORWITZ EMPIRE

With the passing of Will Horwitz, the

Horwitz at home with his beloved garden. Collection of Gary Warwick, courtesy of the Center for American History, University of Texas at Austin.

days of the Homefolks Theatres came to an end. In 1949, eight years after his death, the Ritz was sold. Then, in 1953, the Texan fell, having had shortest life of all his theatres. While it had continued to do good business to the end, the owners lost the lease on the property. The last regular performance, the Howard Duff feature *The Roar of the Crowd*, was on Labor Day.[42] This was followed by a special final-day presentation. The event attracted a fair amount of attention, and several hundred patrons of various ages, but not the school-age kids who normally populated the theatre. The first day of school kept them from attending the morning show. The doors opened at ten thirty, and Cannata, manager Valenti, and Mrs. Horwitz were on hand to greet their old patrons—and to say good-bye. Three features were scheduled for the day: *My Little Chickadee* (1940), *Destry Rides Again* (1939), and *Argentine Nights* (1940), with the Ritz Brothers.

Many of the fixtures and furnishings, including the old pipe organ, were to be sold the following day. In question were the painted murals in the lobby, which depicted the history of Texas. Said Cannata, "They are on Canvas, so we can save them. I think we will give them to some school or to a charitable institution. They should be where they will be appreciated."[43]

Initial plans were to clear the rear fifty by fifty feet of the site for a new eighteen-story Houston Club annex building. The front part of the site would be used for parking.[44] Gladys retained ownership of several of the theatres until about five years before her death, in 1972.[45]

Both the Iris and Uptown continued operations well into the sixties. The Iris

was closed for a short time in May 1959 while undergoing a $15,000 remodeling.[46] The following month, the Iris was both open and in the news when a thirty-four-year-old woman was raped in the ladies' lounge. An usher at the theatre stated at the time that she saw a young man follow the victim into the restroom. When the usher tried to order him out, the man barred the door, and then forced the woman to disrobe at knifepoint.[47]

The Uptown would eventually become something quite different from what Horwitz would have wanted for his theatre. In 1953, a panel discussion focusing on the Kinsey report on the sexual behavior of women was held at the Uptown after Mayor Roy Hofheinz pulled the event from the Music Hall. "Sex is here to stay, but not in the Music Hall," Hofheinz remarked, adding that the program did not meet the aesthetic requirements to be held on city premises. The panel consisted of actress Joan Blondell, actor Reginald Owen, author Lee Alden, and radio personality Lee Trent.[48]

By 1959, the Uptown became part of the Rowley United Theatre chain. With the opening of the 70mm epic *Solomon and Sheba* on December 25 that year, the Uptown switched its name to the Rivoli.[49] It, along with the Tower Theatre, became the first two Houston movie houses to install the special Todd-AO equipment.

The Rivoli featured stage productions, such as Mitzi Wayne in *Auntie Mame*, as well as a new process more dazzling than the previous Todd-AO installation—Cinerama. The theatre closed in August 1960 and underwent a $50,000 conversion, becoming the first Cinerama theatre in Texas. It reopened on August 25 with *This is Cinerama* (1952), followed by titles such as *South Seas Adventure* (1958) and the Lowell Thomas production *Seven Wonders of the World* (1956).[50] Sadly, these were the last glory days for the Rivoli. Attempts to make it a Cinerama house failed, and the Rivoli eventually turned to girlie films such as *Nude on the Moon* (1961) and *Virgin Sacrifice* (1959), as well as to live burlesque. Fred Cannata, who had managed the theatre since its opening in 1935, had little to say about the change. "I'm not too fond of it myself," he said, "but on the other hand, it was the only way to keep the theatre open."[51]

In June 1962, the Rivoli, together with the Paris Theatre, wound up in the Houston courts. At issue was a "nudie" film called *Not Tonight, Henry*, whose subject matter offended a portion of the Houston population. A 600-name petition submitted by the Reverend Lloyd Watson, then pastor of the Bellaire Christian Church, prompted an inquiry into whether such films could be considered obscene. Other films mentioned in the protest were *The Magic Spectacles* (1961) and *Mr. Peter's Pets* (1962). The storylines centered on, respectively, a pair of unique X-ray glasses and a pet-shop operator who changed into animals so he could sneak into bedrooms and watch women undress. Although highly scandalous for their time, these films would be sedate compared to the titles on today's adult-video shelves.[52]

The years progressed but little changed. Adult films continued to play. People watched. Others were outraged (sometimes after watching). The courts served as a battleground. Titles such as *Runaway Hormones* and *Passions* were the norm.

Entertainment was also served up in the form of live burlesque (stripteases)

and advertised as "the only burlesque live show in town." Admission had changed much since the Uptown days, having escalated to $1.50 plus the flash of a draft card. The Rivoli also had amateur nights for those aspiring to such a career. One story, told by a Rivoli cashier, was of a bank president's secretary who doffed her clothes on amateur night (under the name of "Diana Thursday"). This continued for several weeks until she was recognized and the theatre staff began receiving calls of inquiry from the bank. The secretary did not return.[53]

The Uptown Arcade continued to house tenants, who subleased space from the theatre. Benny Sebesta ran the Ace Photography Studio there for twenty years before moving it to 3304 Milam. Central Cleaners, run by William Kusakis, was

The Rivoli, with one of its featured attractions, 1965. Courtesy of the Houston Metropolitan Research Center, Houston Public Library, RGD6N 1965-2406.

another latter-day occupant.[54] There was also a rumor during the Rivoli days that a "tunnel of love" was operating beneath the auditorium.

The end was near for both the Iris and the Uptown. The Iris had fallen on bad times, and its lease was due to run out in June 1965; the Rivoli's was set to expire on October 31 of that year.

In 1964, Allright Auto Parks, Inc. announced the cash purchase of plots of land in the downtown area, including those occupied by the Iris and Uptown theatres as well as the adjoining arcade. The purchase price for the theatre lots, approximately 32,000 square feet of land, was estimated at somewhere around $750,000. Once razed, the property would be converted into a parking lot.[55]

On December 22, 1964, about thirty employees of the Rivoli and Iris gathered in the Rivoli auditorium for their last Christmas celebration together. As they sipped their coffee and snacked on donuts, they resigned themselves to the fact that both theatres would be torn down the following year—and they would be out of jobs. They talked of the Horwitz Christmas parties at the City Auditorium. The parties had long since been abandoned, and the auditorium no longer stood.[56]

For the final open night of the Iris, July 26, 1965, Fred Cannata scheduled a suitable finale. He located a print of *Top Hat*, the Fred Astaire–Ginger Rogers musical that opened the Uptown theatre in 1935. Admission was five cents for kids, fifteen cents for adults, just as in the early days. Also shown that evening was the Walt Disney feature *A Tiger Walks* (1964). With that, the Iris, the last of the "homefolks" theatres, closed for good.[57]

The Rivoli had shut its doors eight days earlier. The final night drew about 150 customers, mostly young males who sat quietly through the show. Entertainment that evening featured three scantily clad women and the singing master of ceremonies, Skip Cole. One of the performers, a tall, straight-haired girl with the stage name "Lisa," lived up to the true tradition of show business. As she took the stage, clearly visible on her left side was a strip of tape, a bandage to protect the three ribs she had broken in an accident three days earlier.[58] Cannata's attitude on the final night was controlled, yet bitter. "You want my true feelings?" he remarked. "I think it's a dirty shame. They talk all the time about building the town up, and what they are doing is tearing it down. The downtown is dead, dead, I tell you. This won't help the city."[59]

The Iris and Uptown theatres were demolished on August 15, 1965. With their demise came the end to the Horwitz theatre legacy. The city block is now the site of the Texas Commerce Tower.

IN REMEMBERING HIS BOSS, Cannata said "We won't know another man like Mr. Horwitz soon. He was a great character. As a showman, he will be ranked with the late P. T. Barnum. His reputation was nation-wide. The moving picture industry recognized him. He was a pioneer in many things for the betterment of the show business, and he was constantly called upon for duplicates of his campaigns that they might be applied elsewhere. He enjoyed the esteem of actors and actresses. They recognized him as a great showman."[60]

Fred Valerio Cannata passed away on February 16, 1990 at the age of ninety-three.[61]

Well before the Greenway, the Angelica, or the Rice Media Center came along, the Al*Ray Theatre, catered to the appetites of foreign-film connoisseurs. Courtesy of Al Zarzana.

★ ★ ★

THE NEIGHBORHOOD THEATRE, 1934–1949

★ ★ ★

Would you be mine? Could you be mine?
Won't you be my neighbor?

MR. ROGERS

★ WITH THE ONSET of the Depression, the building of movie theatres came to a halt. By the time theatre construction resumed in Houston, the Depression still had the country in its grip, and the rules of the entertainment game had changed dramatically.

Silent films had died out the previous decade. Those theatres that did not convert to the new sound technology simply closed down. The ornate grandeur of the pre-Depression picture palace evolved into a new streamlined architectural style, which would become stereotypically associated with the movie-theatre concept forevermore. Massive theatres were replaced by smaller, more intimate structures. Gone were the atmospheric cloud-and-stars ceilings, Egyptian temples, Roman statuary and flourishes, opulent marble interiors, live orchestral accompaniment, Wurlitzer organs, full vaudeville programs, ushers in uniform, and 2,500-seat auditoriums.

Geography played a part as well; as the city continued to expand, the distance from most people's homes to downtown increased. Houston's growth gave rise to theatre construction in its suburbs.

Although a few theatres during the previous decade had been constructed outside of the downtown district (such as the 1929 Heights Theatre), the thirties were the breakthrough years of the neighborhood theatre. The first one to open would be only a short jaunt down Main Street to Richmond—the Delman Theatre.

THE DELMAN
4412 Main

The Delman was a genuine sign of the times: movies would now go to the audience, rather than the other way around. It was also the first Houston theatre to be built specifically for sound pictures. The independent theatre was owned by I. B. Adelman of Dallas, and featured a design by architect W. Scott Dunne, who soon after developed the Interstate Tower Theatre.

The foyer and mezzanine were decorated in shades of orange, yellow, and blue. These tones were softened in the

The Delman theatre, c. 1935, with the George Arliss film The Guv'nor, *under its American title,* Mister Hobo. *Courtesy of the Houston Metropolitan Research Center, Houston Public Library, MSS 114-1966.*

1,000-seat auditorium with tan walls and seat backs accented by jade green, lavender, and rose.

The Delman opened on Wednesday, November 28, 1934, to a near-capacity crowd; Adelman, Dunne, and manager L. O. Daniel, Jr., were in attendance — along with the chief sound technician from RCA.

The foyer was decorated with flower baskets sent by friends and associates, and congratulatory telegrams were pinned to a bulletin board in the lobby. Ladies were handed flower souvenirs as they entered. Tinted glossy photos of Shirley Temple were given to the children over the next several days — appropriate for the opening Shirley Temple feature *Baby Take a Bow*.[1]

Most of the Delman's early features were second-run, a factor that eventually led from the auditorium to the courtroom. In 1948, Adelman filed suit against a group of movie-production companies and theatre operators over the right to compete for first-run feature films. The major features usually ended up at the top downtown three: Loew's State, the Majestic, and the Metropolitan. The district court ruled that the Delman was not in competition with the three in question, but was entitled to compete with the Kirby and River Oaks theatres. The Fifth Circuit Court of Appeals upheld the ruling.

The legal wrangling went on for years. In his 1962 request for a Supreme Court review, Adelman contended that the three downtown giants were in a conspiracy to monopolize first-run movies. The Kirby theatre had since closed down. Adelman suggested that with its closing, he was further cut off from any access to first-runs,

since those movies, formerly available to the Kirby, were now being absorbed by the big three.[2]

Named in the last petition were Paramount, Loew's, Radio-Keith-Orpheum, RKO Radio Pictures, Warner Bros., Twentieth Century–Fox, Columbia, United Artists, Universal, Interstate, and Texas Consolidated Theatres. The Supreme Court, in a decision on April 16, 1962, refused to hear his appeal.

In December 1960, the theatre spent over $50,000 to install Todd-AO widescreen equipment. Thus equipped, it held the Texas premiere of Stanley Kubrick's *Spartacus*.[3] In June 1960, the feature film *Chance Meeting* was targeted by the American Legion as un-American. Walter J. White, vice commander for Post 416, requested all true Americans to boycott the film, which was showing at the Delman, because its production involved personnel who had communist affiliations. "We have a list of 300 communist sympathizers," said White, "still working in Hollywood." He had not seen the film. On the double bill was the Hammer Studios horror film *The Man Who Could Cheat Death*. The Legion also voiced opposition to three other films at the time, *Spartacus*, *Exodus*, and *Inherit the Wind*, for similar reasons.[4]

Controversy arose again in April 1966 following a showing of the family-oriented film *The Trouble with Angels*. The French film *The Sleeping Car Murders* was shown as a sneak preview, but proved to be too sexy for the Houston audience. One male patron was so offended that he called the police. Assistant manager Allene McIntosh shut down the presentation, agreeing that it was not fit to be seen by the "adults only" crowd. The movie had not been previously screened. About fifty patrons demanded their money back—because they were not allowed to see the entire showing.[5]

For the most part, the Delman's fare during the sixties consisted of foreign films, such as those by Ingmar Bergman, and some repertory titles.

The Delman was bought and renovated by the Loew's Theatre chain in 1969; changes included a newly draped auditorium, rebuilt seats, updated restrooms, and, as stated in the newspapers, "mad, mod décor." The Delman reopened on Christmas Day as the Loew's Delman, showing the feature *The Secret of Santa Victoria*. Loew's would operate the movie house for the next nine years.[6]

By the 1970s, the Delman had hit hard times. Most of the downtown theatres were suffering, and the Delman, at one time considered a neighborhood theatre, was now perceived as a near-downtown house, and thus lost business to the new breed of suburban multiplexes. It closed its doors briefly in the midseventies, and then reopened in 1978 with the Clint Eastwood film *The Gauntlet*. Business was disappointing. Scheduled for February 15, 1978, was Martin Scorsese's documentary about the Band's farewell concert, *The Last Waltz*. At the last moment, the studio pulled the film, leaving Loew's empty-handed. It was the final straw. The Delman closed its doors on February 5, 1978, after a final showing of the Eastwood film.[7]

The Delman reopened briefly in 1986 as the Maceba Theatre. Planned as a black performing-arts center, the house opened on January 31 with the play *Diary of a Black Man (How Do You Love a Black Woman?)*. Maceba Affairs

president Danny Hodges envisioned the house as the Apollo Theatre of the South. The theatre was open only a brief time, and crossed into the twenty-first century unused and boarded up.[8]

In September 2002, the theatre was razed. The property, which included an adjacent strip center, had already experienced several fires over the previous year. Houston's Metropolitan Transit Authority had begun construction for the new Metro rail line, tearing down several buildings near the intersection—however, the Delman's demise was not part of that plan. Tivoli Realty of Dallas, owners of the Delman property, felt that the land would be worth more money vacant.

According to the *Houston Business Journal*, a last-ditch effort was made

The Park Theatre, c. 1938. Courtesy of the Houston Metropolitan Research Center, Houston Public Library, MSS 114-1970.

The Joy, 303 Main, c. late 1940s. The Joy often showed unusual films that no other theatre in town would exhibit. George Fuermann Texas and Houston Collection, courtesy of Special Collections, University of Houston Libraries.

to save the endangered theatre. John Michael Gonzales, chairman of the Midtown Management District, attempted to acquire the theatre for the local theatre company Infernal Bridegroom Productions. No agreement was reached.[9]

THE RANKS of the neighborhood theatres can be divided into two distinct groups: Interstate houses and all others. All the major releases and first-runs were channeled through those theatres with affiliations to the major studios; the independents had to settle for the leftovers. Most of the top films were sent directly to the big downtown theatres, but as Interstate expanded its theatre line, the first-runs found distribution into the various Houston neighborhoods. Beginning with the 1935 opening of the North Main Theatre, Interstate swept across the city, building more than ten theatres over the next twelve years. Less than two months after opening the North Main, Interstate opened the Tower, and the Eastwood Theatre a month later.

Between 1934 and 1950, Houston saw over two dozen independent theatres open. In 1935, the same year as the debut of Interstate's North Main, Will Horwitz built the final theatre in his mini-empire of movie houses, the Uptown.

The march of the independents was on. In 1937 the Park Theatre and the Joy began operations, and nearby Pasadena got its Pasadena Theatre. The Rice University district gained its first theatre at this time, the University.

The Park Theatre, at 2813 Dowling, opened around 1937 and would survive for a little over thirty years, closing down in 1969.

After sitting dormant since the start of the thirties, the old Crown Theatre, at 303 Main, reopened as the Joy Theatre, possibly as a live venue, as indicated by the 1937 *Houston Directory*. By 1940 the Joy had become a predominantly film-oriented venue, and for a time was known as the Joy-Tex.

Earl Blair, who later managed the Bijou Theatre, grew up at the movie house. Said Blair, "In the days before pre-school care, I would accompany my grandmother to work downtown, and she would deposit me in the hands of the Joy's manager (a woman), who would watch after me as I, literally, spent the entire day watching the same bill over and over again. Imagine my surprise . . . to learn in later years that the Joy was not the best of spots. To me, it was a palace."[10]

The last listing for the Joy Theatre was in the 1955 *Houston Directory*.

THE UNIVERSITY/NAN GREY
3636 *University Boulevard*

The 1936 opening of the University Theatre in West University Place came as a great relief to those residents who had been making the trek to either the Tower or the Delman for their movies. The modest independent theatre was built by D. F. Luckie in a small shopping center that included a neighboring grocery store.[11] The theatre operated for several years before undergoing a name change. By 1939 it had been renamed the Nan Grey Theatre in tribute to the local actress.[12]

Nan Grey was born Eschal Miller in Houston on July 25, 1918, to parents

Dolores Miller, a former stage actress, and E. J. Miller, a theatre projectionist for the Majestic Theatre who had advanced to union representative. At the age of thirteen, Eschal accompanied her mother to Hollywood and quickly landed a contract with Warner Bros., remaining active in films through 1941.[13] She married singer Frankie Laine in 1950.

The theatre's name change would be temporary, returning in 1940 to the University. In June of that year the theatre became a part of the Interstate Theatre chain, and D. F. Luckie took over operations from Hugo Plath, who had been running the theatre for the previous few months.[14] This takeover by Interstate allowed the house to acquire

The University Theatre, c. 1941. Collection of Roy Bonario, courtesy of the Center for American History, University of Texas at Austin.

first-run films, always a problem for the independents.

Despite stiff competition from the Interstate Village Theatre, which opened in 1941, the University remained operational. It closed down during the war years from a shortage of theatrical materials, but reopened in 1946; ads promised the best in wholesome entertainment for the people of West University Place. The University Theatre continued operations through 1948, when it finally closed for good.[15] The interior was gutted and converted into retail space, serving at various times as a barber shop, a Masonic hall, a ladies' clothing store, a resale shop, and a plastics development company. As of this writing, the structure still stands.

THE UNION
4001 Humble Road

"We believe Houston is another Los Angeles," explained Ernest Megowan to an invitational crowd at the 700-seat Union Theatre the day before its official opening.

When Glendale was established, it had about the same relation to Los Angeles as Humble has to Houston. There was a considerable stretch of country in-between. Today you can drive from the downtown business section of Los Angeles to Glendale and never know you are out of the city. We think in just a few years, it will be the same way from Houston to Humble. We believe this entire section will be city, and that the location of our theatre will be the union point for this growth. Therefore, we have decided to call this theatre the Union.[16]

Megowan was a business partner in the creation of the Union Theatre, along with owner Elizabeth Moody, and her son, Stewart Moody, who would manage the house. Located four miles from downtown at 4001 Humble Road, the building included a central movie house and two

The Union Theatre around the time of its opening in 1938. Courtesy of the Houston Metropolitan Research Center, Houston Public Library, MSS 200-212.

side wings designed to house a variety of retail shops.

An invitational opening presentation took place on October 7, 1938, with a newsreel, a cartoon, and a Jane Withers comedy. This was all a warm-up for the following night's showing of the Errol Flynn feature *The Adventures of Robin Hood*, followed on Sunday, Monday, and Tuesday by *Crime School* with the Dead End Kids.[17]

Humble Road would soon undergo a name change to Jensen Drive, and the Union Theatre adopted a new street address of 5408 Jensen. The theatre remained in operation for only seventeen years. By 1955, it was no longer listed as a functional theatre.

THE YEAR 1939 is generally considered Hollywood's true golden year. Within a twelve-month period, audiences were given *Gone with the Wind*, *The Wizard of Oz*, *Wuthering Heights*, *Northwest Passage*, *Mr. Smith Goes to Washington*, *Of Mice and Men*, *Ninotchka*, *Stagecoach*, and *The Private Lives of Elizabeth and Essex*. For Houstonians, this wealth of quality filmmaking found its way across the city screens, first in the major houses, and then the second-run independents.

During the course of the year, there were also a series of world premieres, various live productions, and the opening of four new movie theatres. *The Folies Bergere* stage revue was seen at the Metropolitan, and the world premiere of *Man of Conquest* at the Majestic in April was followed by the southwest premiere of George Bernard Shaw's *Pygmalion* at Loew's State. The State was also selected as a testing spot for gauging public reac-

tion to a film before its national release. Premieres for these advance screenings included the 1939 releases *The Housekeeper's Daughter*, *Babes in Arms*, and *Raffles*.[18]

Four new theatres would open that year, all during November, making the

This ad for Johnny G. Long's regional chain ran on April 19, 1947, just a few days after the Texas City explosions. Collection of Roy Bonario.

pre-Christmas season a busy one for moviegoers. Interstate's Alabama Theatre was the first and largest out of the gate and the only one that was not an independently owned house. This was followed by the Stude Theatre in the Heights, the Navaway, and the River Oaks.

THE STUDE
730 *East 11th Street*
Near Studewood

Comparatively small even by neighborhood standards, the 625-seat Stude theatre added competition in an area that already included the Heights Theatre and the North Main. Robert Z. Glass build the independent house at a cost of $50,000 and operated it himself.[19] Glass had already been in the theatre business for fifteen years, running three theatres in Dallas and two in Beaumont before coming to Houston. The Glass Theatre Corporation would go on to build the State

Theatre in 1941 and to acquire the Plaza theatre in 1948. The Stude, advertised as "Houston's new theatre of tomorrow," was a modest house, designed as a stadium-style auditorium with a semibalcony designated for smoking.

The grand opening was held on Thursday, November 16, 1939, with searchlights, a blaring brass band, and a live broadcast by radio station KXYZ. Featured inside: the Bing Crosby feature, *East Side of Heaven*, color cartoons, and a newsreel.[20]

The Stude operated as a theatre for less than twenty years. By 1956 it had been converted into a church, operating as the Stude Revival Center.[21] It remains a house of worship as of this writing.

THE NAVAWAY
6714 *Navigation Boulevard*

The Navaway Theatre opened its doors one week after the Stude did. The 725-

The Stude Theatre, functioning as a church, c. 1980s. Photograph by Jim Koehn.

The Navaway Theatre, 1939.
Collection of Roy Bonario,
courtesy of the Houston
Metropolitan Research Cen-
ter, Houston Public Library,
MSS 114-1968.

seat house was built by R. V. Ratcliff in a thickly populated industrial section near Magnolia Park and the Turning Basin district at a cost of approximately $45,000.[22] The building, designed by architect E. E. O'Donnell, featured a front and foyer of brightly colored glass and soft neon lights.[23]

The theatre opened on November 22, 1939, with the feature film *Only Angels Have Wings*, a comedy short, and a newsreel.[24]

By the early forties, a number of the independents banded together to advertise en masse as Houston Independent TheatreS (HITS): Your Hit Program. Those participating included the Navaway, Lindale, Northside, the Queen on Jensen, the Stude, and the granddaddy of the bunch, the 1919 Boulevard. Much of the movie fare shared among these theatres was of B quality.

The Navaway operated through the sixties before closing down; its last listing was in the 1965 *Houston Directory*. It has since been torn down.

THE RIVER OAKS
2001 West Gray

The November 1939 sweep of theatre openings, which gave Houstonians four new movie houses in twenty-seven days, came to an end with the opening of the River Oaks Theatre. The independently owned theatre was built by the River Oaks Corporation at a cost of $100,000, using a design created by Dallas architects Pettigrew and Worley.[25] The firm would also design four Houston Interstate theatres between 1946 and 1948: the Fulton, the Garden Oaks, the Broadway, and the Santa Rosa.[26]

Noted Texas artist Buck Wynn, Jr., was contracted to create various interior murals and decorations. Wynn's other credits included the Dallas Village Theatre, the Goliad Memorial, and works at the Texas Centennial in Dallas (1936) and the New York World's Fair.

Inside, a color scheme of straw, green, and coral accented the walls of the lobby and auditorium. The lobby also featured decorative glass and a mural painted by Wynn. The aluminum handrail on the stairway leading to the balcony was underlit by a neon tube. Two Motiograph projectors and a Western Electric sound system were installed and would remain in use until a restoration occurred in 1986.

In the auditorium, which had a seating capacity of 923, the chairs were arranged with extra space between the rows.[27] On every other row, the end seats on the center aisle were double width, which proved to be popular with wider patrons. Young couples were also very fond of these, since they made the perfect dating seats.

On either side of the screen were large bas-relief sculptures by Wynn, with figures representing the land and the sea. At one

The River Oaks Theatre, c. 1934. Note the separate ticket booth under the marquee. Courtesy of the Houston Metropolitan Research Center, Houston Public Library, MSS 114-1967.

Main auditorium of the River Oaks Theatre, 1986. Courtesy of the Houston Metropolitan Research Center, Houston Public Library, RGD6N 5-14-86 #23.

point during the following decades, they were covered by a curtain and remained hidden up through the mideighties. They were rediscovered by the then-current manager and unveiled once more. Like many other features of this theatre, they remain an integral part of the theatre to this day.[28]

It was originally leased to Paul Scott (who had previously managed the Varsity Theatre in Dallas), and was opened to the public on November 28, 1939, with the feature *Bachelor Mother*.

It was acquired by the Interstate Theatre chain in February 1947, and became an early art house, featuring foreign and stateside films for one-week runs. During many of those years, a sign hung in one of the exterior windows: "You will never see anything usual at the River Oaks."[29]

Shortly thereafter, the theatre became associated with the rise and fall of the Houston Players theatrical troupe. In

1949, director-playwright-composer Eddie Dowling appeared in Houston on a wave of advance publicity, aided by Ralph Mead and longtime friend and theatre manager R. J. "Bob" O'Donnell. When the original performance plans at the Shamrock Hilton fell through, a contract was drawn up with Interstate for use of the River Oaks. This required construction of a stage area for the first performance, *The Time of Your Life*. Between productions, the River Oaks would continue as a movie house.

During rehearsals, Dowling suffered from bleeding ulcers and soon moved back to New York to pursue other theatrical interests. The orphaned show was eventually produced, to mostly lukewarm response. All major business connections dried up with Dowling's departure. To make matters worse, he left the theatre's assets, the proceeds from the sale of $13,000 worth of season tickets, tied up in a joint account with Interstate. The Houston Players lasted only a short while longer.[30]

Interstate held on to the River Oaks for close to three decades, finally relinquishing it in late 1975. It was taken over by Trans-Continental, a chain that operated the Shamrock Six and Festival Six multicinemas. It was then acquired in 1977 by Movie, Inc., a repertory theatre chain out of New Mexico. The company had already acquired eleven theatres, including ones in Lubbock and San Antonio. Movie, Inc. eventually merged with the Los Angeles–based Landmark Theatre Company.

Many of the River Oaks architectural accents had been either covered up or left unused. Under new ownership, the theatre underwent a major restoration: modern Formica was stripped away to the original plaster; the neon handrails were refurbished; neon sidelights that ran from floor to ceiling were repaired; new carpet was added; and a new paint job, complete with appropriate murals, was done. Paul Richardson, a partner in Movie, Inc., said, "I found all kinds of neon decoration inside. We're going to put back all the '40s and Art Deco touches we can."[31] The Midwest-raised Richardson had attended the University of Houston from 1969 to 1971, and had been looking for a Houston theatre to purchase for the previous two years.

The most radical change came in the choice of film fare. Instead of first- or second-run films, the new River Oaks went repertory: old movies, rereleased movies, classic movies, foreign movies, cult movies, and almost anything out of the mainstream. Said Jeff Millar in the *Houston*

Chronicle, "Those of you who like the Alley Theatre's Summer Film Festival are going to love the new River Oaks Theatre. It's going to be the Alley 365 days a year."[32] The film lineup changed almost every other day. The double bills were usually unique, complementary pairings by genres, themes, stars (Bogart, the Marx Brothers), directors (Fellini, Kurosawa), or holidays. Exclusives on art and foreign films were also a mainstay of the River Oaks schedule.

In the prevideo-precable days, the repertory format was a godsend for the serious filmgoer, who was given the opportunity to see an ongoing lineup of diverse (and often hard-to-see) films. In addition, audiences were given a twofer—two films for the price of one—presented in what was one of Houston's few surviving classic theatres.

The theatre reopened on March 26, 1977, with a double bill of *King of Hearts* (the 1966 version, with Alan Bates) and *Bedazzled* (1967).[33]

Well remembered during this time were the River Oaks poster-sized film schedules, covering the features and run dates for a full three-month period. The schedules became standard decor for most movie buffs' walls and refrigerators. Another draw was the well-stocked concession stand, featuring herbal teas and fruit juices for the discriminating consumer. For popcorn lovers, the butter topping was the real thing. The menu would later be expanded to include espressos, cappuccinos, bagel dogs, Häagen-Dazs ice cream, and butter cakes and brownies from Treebeard's restaurant.[34]

The classic and foreign choices were always popular and sometimes controversial. The Jean-Luc Godard film *Hail Mary* (1985) caused much protest from local church groups because of its updated interpretation of biblical figures. In January 1983, a standoff took place outside the theatre between Ku Klux Klan members and an anti-Klan organization. At the center of the conflict was the film *Fire on the Water*, about the influx of Vietnamese fisherman in the Galveston Bay area. The incident ended without violence.[35]

The most controversial occurrence took place on September 9, 1982, when Houston vice officers raided the theatre during a showing of Pier Paolo Pasolini's *Salo*. The 1975 film, based on the Marquis de Sade's *120 Days of Sodom*, had become notorious because of its depiction of sadomasochism and extreme torture. The manager was arrested and charged with promoting obscene material, a misdemeanor offense. The police allowed the film to run in its entirety for the audience before seizing the print. Ironically, this was the third time that *Salo* had been shown over the last three years, a point officers seemed unaware of.[36]

In a trial that took place in April 1983, the jury found *Salo* not obscene. The manager, who had since moved to manage a Landmark theatre in New Orleans, was declared innocent of any wrongdoing.[37]

By the mideighties, the popularity of cable and video had killed the repertory forum, and the theatre turned increasingly to first-run films. Finally, the theatre gave in to economic needs and converted the balcony into two additional minitheatres, each seating 125 people. To accommodate the new screens, the balcony was extended out sixteen feet. The downstairs auditorium was left intact, minus a block

of chairs removed from the rear to provide for a projection booth, a change that reduced the capacity to 546 seats. A full renovation included elevators and handicapped-access restrooms, an upstairs café, a new blue and gray paint job, and platter-system projectors, which replaced the old carbon-arc equipment that had been used since 1939. Dolby sound was added downstairs and ultrastereo sound was installed

River Oaks theatre film schedule, c. 1980. Author's collection.

for the balcony screens. The renovation cost $400,000.[38]

The new screens opened on May 15, 1986, with *Smooth Talk* (1985) and the River Oaks' signature film, *Bedazzled*. Despite increasing competition, including the twelve-screen Cineplex Odeon multiplex in the River Oaks Plaza, which opened only blocks way in 1990, the purity of the River Oaks drew a loyal base of patrons. It has shown up year after year in the *Houston Press*'s "Best of Houston" issues under various categories: "The Best Theatre to See an Art Movie," "The Best Midnight Film Series," and "The Best Theatre Concession Stand," to name a few.

It remained a popular place for premieres. The Texas premiere of the locally shot film *The Evening Star* was held in December 1996, with Shirley MacLaine and director Robert Harling in attendance.[39] A month earlier, actor Kenneth Branagh had appeared for an advance preview of his four-hour interpretation of *Hamlet*. The theatre was at the time in the process of upgrading the sound system to digital sound. Plans were set to have the system installed in time for Christmas, but the *Hamlet* preview forced a rush job that was not completed until four that afternoon, leaving a two-and-a-half-hour window for testing before the doors opened that evening. "We literally couldn't open the auditorium until about half an hour before we had to," said manager Gretchen Myers. The film was presented without a flaw.[40]

The summer of 1999 brought in the last great independent film of the century. Costing $30,000 to film, *The Blair Witch Project* grossed more than $1.5 million nationwide over a three-day weekend . . . on only twenty-seven screens, an average of $57,047 a screen for its initial limited release. The River Oaks sold out almost every show during the three-day period, with long lines waiting outside the theatre. Said Sarah Gish to the *Houston Chronicle* at the time, "We're setting all-time house records. It's just incredible."[41]

The River Oaks successfully managed to survive in the era of the megaplex, and as was mentioned in the 2004 *Houston Press* "Best of Houston" issue, "There are only three screens here, but they're usually showing something smart."[42]

THE THREAT OF DEMOLITION is a constant for older theatres. In 2006, this became apparent for both the River Oaks Theatre and the Alabama Bookstop, formerly the Alabama Theatre. On July 22, 2006, the front page of the *Houston Chronicle* reported unconfirmed plans to raze portions of the River Oaks Shopping Center (including the River Oaks Theatre) and to construct a multistory Barnes

To preserve the integrity of the main auditorium, the River Oaks balcony was twinned into separate houses. Courtesy of the Houston Metropolitan Research Center, Houston Public Library, MSS RGD6N 5-14-86 #8.

& Noble on the site of the Black-eyed Pea restaurant; the latter plan would make the Alabama Bookstop obsolete, since it was owned by Barnes & Noble and located a few miles from the River Oaks. The two theatres, which had both opened in 1939, only twenty-six days apart, represented the last two pristine examples of thirties theatre architecture in the city.[43]

Weingarten Realty Investors, which controlled both properties, quickly came under fire in the media for its supposed intentions. To try to save the structures, local groups mobilized several efforts, including an August 1 appeal to Houston City Council and a petition drive that by August 31 had garnered 23,000 signatures.[44] Society philanthropist Carolyn Farb spearheaded a preservation effort in front of the River Oaks Theatre on August 30, her crowd of supporters wearing black "Save Our Shrines" T-shirts.[45] Three months later, the *Houston Press* gave the matter special attention in its annual "Turkeys of the Year" issue, suggesting a bleak outcome for the cinemas.[46] As of this writing, the future of both theatres is uncertain.

WITH WORLD WAR II came changes in theatre culture nationwide, beginning with the shorts produced by Hollywood's Motion Picture Committee Cooperating for National Defense. From promos for war bonds to war-oriented storylines, support for those fighting overseas found its way into all walks of life—even entertainment. Displays in the larger theatres, such as Loew's State, advertised war bonds and savings stamps. Small change from movie ticket purchases could be converted into savings stamps, and a book filled with these stamps could be turned in for a $25 war bond.[47]

What the war did not change was the continued expansion of both the Interstate and independent theatres across the city. In what was becoming an annual new-theatre event, Interstate unveiled the Almeda in 1940, and two independents theatres opened as well: the Queen and the Lyons, the latter for a minority clientele.

The year 1941 saw the opening of four new houses: the Lindale, the State, the Sunset, and the Interstate Village Theatre.

THE LINDALE/AL*RAY
5006 *Fulton*

The Lindale underwent several name changes during its lifetime, as well as changes in the caliber of its programming. As with most independent theatres, it survived on second-run features during its early days. In 1960, Al Zarzana and Raymond Boriski took over the theatre with the intention of founding a good art cinema and renamed it the Al*Ray, a combination of their two first names.[48] It reopened on April 20 with the French melodrama *Razzia* (1955), along with the award-winning short subject *The Mischief Makers* (1957; directed by François Truffaut).[49] Free coffee was available to the patrons. As Houston's only art house, the Al*Ray presented "distinctive films for discriminating people," as it touted itself in ads. The theatre ran a steady stream of foreign and art films such as *Shoot the Piano Player* (1960; Truffaut), *Man and Wife*, *The Collector* (1965; William Wyler), and *Samurai*. Later the theatre changed its for-

Auditorium of the Al*Ray Theatre, 1960s. Courtesy of Al Zarzana.

Among the great Al*Ray stories is the day that a horse was brought onstage as a publicity ploy. Once in front of a packed house, the horse raised its tail and gave an unexpected performance. The Al*Ray's owner gained his fifteen minutes of fame for cleaning up after the animal in front of the audience. Courtesy of Al Zarzana.

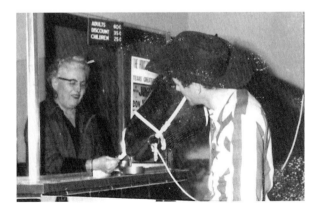

mat to Spanish titles before Al Zarzana let go of his part in the theatre.

In the later sixties and seventies, the theatre began showing X-rated films. Within its walls, patrons could experience such dubious fare as *Kama Sutra '71: The Book of Love*, *Catch 69*, *The Love Muscle*, *Slippery When Wet*, *Screwples*, and *The Desires of Wendy*. The Al*Ray showed such steamy products through the eighties before finally shutting its doors. The building has since been razed.

THE STATE
5913 *Washington*

R. Z. Glass expanded his Houston independent-theatre holdings past the Stude with the State Theatre, located in the West End on Washington. It opened on August 1, 1941, with the James Cagney feature *Strawberry Blonde*. The admission prices—five cents and fifteen cents—fit the needs of the surrounding working-class neighborhood.[50] The theatre was neither fancy nor distinctive in appearance—merely a small cinema for area residents.

The State was leased to Ed Henderson in the early fifties. His first inspection of the theatre was during a packed showing of a Donald O'Connor movie. Both the number in attendance and the theatre's condition were misleading. There was no snack bar. The amplifier went out shortly after he took control. Neighborhood kids

The former State Theatre as the Living Word Outreach Church, c. 1980s. Photograph by Jim Koehn.

would loiter in the theatre all day, usually after sneaking in through the rear doors.

Henderson tried varying promotional tactics to boost business, and drove around the neighborhood with a loudspeaker to advertise the movies. Local talent Johnny Ragsdale made a special appearance on one occasion. Yet problems continued to escalate; there were issues with the projectionists' union and with the IRS over the entertainment tax. Then a security service came by to offer burglary protection. Henderson declined the offer, and the following day, vandals forced their way into the office safe. A few teens threatened his business partner, promising to take his severed head home in a basket. The associate was not amused. When a hard rain filled the base of the auditorium with water, Henderson used the flood as justification to break the lease and got out of the theatre business.[51]

The State became a bar with dancing girls for a brief time, but by 1958 it had turned to religion. The Bethel Temple

Church served the community for several decades, finally closing in 1986.[52] It then became a series of musical venues; Adam Joseph opened it on December 8, 1990, as the Junkyard, the premiere featuring an evening of soul-funk-Motown-reggae.[53] On July 5, 1991, it reopened as the Vatican, with a grand opening party featuring the Toy Subs and the Chamberlains.[54] The roster of bands it showcased represented the finest in nineties cutting-edge rock and thrash — the Cramps, the Meat Puppets, Nine Inch Nails, the Butthole Surfers, Lush, Mr. Bungle, Curve, and My Life With the Thrill Kill Kult.

The interior bore little resemblance to the original design. A stage area was constructed in the front of the auditorium, and although the balcony area still remained, all the seats had been removed. Air conditioning was nonexistent. Gutted walls were painted black and featured Day-Glo logos of the bands that had played there. It shut down in 1993.

In January 1994, the space reopened as

the Abyss.[55] It also received a nod from the *Houston Press* in their 1995 "Best of Houston" issue as the best club for sweating: "You could swear the walls are sweating at this sauna. Unlike some other infamous hotboxes, it doesn't matter if the crowd is 50 or 500, or if the pit is active or empty, you're still bathed in your own liquids by night's end."[56] The Abyss also incurred numerous visits by the police department and fire marshal because of noise complaints, overcrowding of the 290-capacity venue, or other grievances. It finally shut down on August 31, 1998.

With the new century, the old State Theatre came full circle. According to a story by Deborah Mann Lake in the *Houston Chronicle* ("A 1930s Theatre Is Reborn," July 25, 2004), the building was renovated into offices for Media Systems, Inc., which specialized in designing home theatres. Featured in the heart of the building was its state-of-the-art model screening room—the return of movies to the old theatre.

THE SUNSET/ACADEMY/LYRIC
1711 *McGowan*

The opening of the Sunset was a point of fusion for two generations of theatre operators. Its owner, Albert Farb, had originally moved to Houston in 1923, opened a dry goods store, then sold it and acquired a drug and candy store at 715 1/2 West Dallas. As the Depression swept across Houston, Farb took ownership of the theatre next to his store, the St. Elmo, at 711 West Dallas. "I had saved up $2,500," said Farb in a 1966 *Houston Post* interview, "and had it in a savings and loan, but they would not let me withdraw it, so I got the money from a bank."[57] With that, Albert Farb officially entered show business. He explained his early success thus: "The price of admission charged was 25 cents—and no one had it. So we dropped the price to 5 cents, and sold more popcorn and root beer. We had a full house almost every night."[58]

After a good run with his sole theatre, he decided to build a second, the $70,000 Sunset Theatre. The 1,050-seat movie house opened on Friday, October 3, 1941, to a receptive crowd.[59] Featured that evening was *The Great American Broadcast*,

The Sunset Theatre. The identity of the girl in the foreground is unknown. Courtesy of Roy Bonario.

with Jack Oakie and Alice Faye, plus four shorts and a newsreel.[60] The Sunset property had been purchased from Joseph Hornberger, who said that the theatre would never succeed in that location. "A big chain had looked at the property," said Farb, "surveyed it, and decided it would never work. But the theatre was a sell-out."[61] He also operated the Rainbow Theatre on West Dallas.

Albert made the Sunset a true family business by handing the managerial chores over to his eighteen-year-old son, Harold. The younger Farb would continue the family flair for real estate after his father sold off the theatre business.

Both theatres were operated successfully throughout the war years. Afterward, Albert sold them and eventually concentrated his efforts in real estate. It proved to be the most profitable decision of his life. He took all the money he had and marched into the real estate department of the Houston Bank Trust Company. "They told me just to blindfold myself and stick a pin in the map," Albert said. "All the property was going to be a good investment."[62] The advice proved correct. After a long prosperous life, Albert Farb passed away in 1979 at the age of eighty.[63] His son, Harold, died on October 10, 2006, at the age of eighty-three.

After the Sunset was sold, it continued operations through 1952, including a grand reopening in March 1944 that included new seats.[64] It also underwent several name changes, first to the Academy in 1954, then to the Lyric in 1955. By 1956, the theatre had shut its doors, only to reopen first as a drugstore, and later as a bingo hall. By the nineties, the site had become part of the Memphis-based Shoe Warehouse chain.[65]

BY 1942, America was fully entrenched in the war. The ever-present Interstate Theatre chain opened the Wayside during this time. During that period, the Plaza, the Holman, the Rainbow, and the Deluxe opened their doors, the last three being ethnic houses.

The Plaza, at 3818 Broadway, operated throughout the forties. In August 1948, R. Z. Glass acquired the house, adding it to the State and the Stude on his theatre roster. The theatre underwent a redecoration: air conditioning, projection equipment, body-form seats, and a crying room for baby-restricted parents were added. The reopening program was *Always Together* (1947), with Houstonian Joyce Reynolds, *Robin Hood of Texas*, (1947) with Gene Autry, and a live stage show with the Bar X Cowboys. The Plaza would survive through the end of the forties. By 1951, its name changed to the Vogue Theatre. There was no further listing after one in the 1951 *Houston Directory*.

The theatre-construction scene slacked off through the 1944–1945 period, and then gained momentum the following year with three new houses. Interstate's Santa Rosa, opened in 1946, along with the independent Don Gordon and Globe theatres. The Globe, at 6901 Lyons Avenue, operated through 1952, according to the *Houston Directory*. As of this writing, the building still stands, operating as an automotive shop.

THE DON GORDON
4719 CANAL

The Don Gordon Theatre opened its doors on October 12, 1946, with the Barbara Stanwyck feature *My Reputation*.[66] "The Don Gordon name is interesting," said Roy Bonario, a local film aficionado who spent his childhood in most of the Houston theatres, "in that it is named after the owner's two sons, Don and Gordon." According to Bonario, the theatre lobby had a Coke machine.[67] The theatre

The Don Gordon Theatre, c. 1984. Courtesy of Al Zarzana.

remained in operation through the early seventies.

The features at Don Gordon were second-runs, oftentimes westerns or horror films such as *Northwest Trail* and *The Curse of the Mummy's Tomb*. By the early seventies, the theatre had been taken over by Alvin Guggenheim, who also operated the Majestic Metro and the Majestic O.S.T. Under his banner of exploitation, audiences could see flicks such as *Chinese Hercules* and *The Dragon Dies Hard* in all their kung fu glory. Eventually, Al Zarzana bought the lease from Guggenheim and ran Spanish movies for several years. It was then taken over by the Benitez chain. By the midseventies, it had closed down, and then, according to Bonario, it reopened as a church.

IN 1947, Interstate made up for its earlier slack period by opening three new theatres: the Broadway, the Garden Oaks, and the Fulton. While Pasadena saw the Garden Theatre open on Tarter Street that year, Houstonians embraced a single independent theatre—the O.S.T.

THE O.S.T./MAJESTIC O.S.T./PARIS
4010 Old Spanish Trail, near Scott

Originally named the Old Spanish Trail Theatre, it quickly became identified by its abbreviated name, the O.S.T. The $200,000 theatre was built for owners Mr. and Mrs. J. L. McKinney (who also co-owned the Navaway), Mr. and Mrs. H. S. Proctor, and Ron C. McKinney. The oval lobby was designed with a gold-flecked maroon terrazzo floor, walls rendered in

The O.S.T. Theatre, c. 1983.
Courtesy of Al Zarzana.

various shades of gold, and a wide curving stairway leading to the balcony. The 900-seat auditorium was finished in shades of maroon and light rose.[68]

The O.S.T. opened its doors on Saturday, February 15, 1947, with the feature film *Rendezvous with Annie*. By 1961, standard film fare had run its course, and the theatre reopened on September 1 as the "newly beautiful" Paris, billed in advertisements as "The ARTfilm Theatre." Also new was the regular admission policy: eighteen years of age and older only. Admission was a dollar. The theatre reopened with the Jean Seberg foreign film *Breathless*.[69] But the art-film fare at the Paris eventually turned to such titles as *Naked Island: The Land of 1,001 Nudes*, featuring scenes in "blushing color," and *The Ramrodders*.[70]

By the following decade, blushing nudes would give way to kung fu kicks and blaxploitation. Alvin Guggenheim took over the Paris, renaming it the Majestic O.S.T. and presenting a steady flow of *Shaft*, *Superfly*, and Bruce Lee. The gala opening on May 4, 1973, featured Isaac Hayes in the "foot-stomping, hip-shaking celebration," *Wattstax*. Guggenheim was already packing people in at his downtown venue, the Majestic Metro.[71]

In October of that year, radio station KYOK began presenting kiddie shows at the theatre on Saturday mornings, complete with cartoons, child-oriented features, and a stage show with prizes for the song-and-dance contest winners. "There aren't that many theatres in the black areas of town," said KYOK general manager Ed Howard at the time. "And the films that are shown, the blaxploitation numbers, deal with violence, pimps, and dope. That's not what the kids need to see." All of the money made from the shows, after operating costs, went into a charities fund.[72]

The theatre closed down after a few years. In 1985, plans were set for the theatre to be converted into the Juneteenth USA Cultural Arts Center. Democratic state representative Al Edwards took an active role in the project, but the plans for a lease-purchase agreement with owner John Brodsky fell through.[73] The theatre crossed into the next century unused.

AS THE FORTIES drew to a close, five new independent theatres opened. Lyons Avenue gained another theatre, the Venus, at 6515 Lyons. It, along with the Galena in Galena Park, was acquired in 1959 by Al Zarzana and Ray Boriski from Oscar Korn's O.K. Neighborhood Theatre circuit. First as a conventional theatre, and later as a Spanish house (Cine Venus), the Venus operated well into the eighties.

The theatre push extended outward on Jensen Drive with the opening of the Granada and North Houston theatres.

Originally listed at 8718 Humble Road, the North Houston would settle on the address 8720 Jensen as the name of the street changed. It survived into the seventies; however, the film lineup went from second-run features in the fifties to X-rated features such as *Deep Throat* and *Doctor Studley* in the late sixties before the theatre closing down entirely. The building crossed into the next century with its exterior completely stripped. A small front section of the building had last operated as a Spanish-language church.

THE AVALON/CAPRI/FIESTA
743 *South 75th*

X-rated features would also be the eventual substance of the Avalon, located in the East Side, but it began its days catering to other audiences. After a start as a traditional movie house, it became a live venue in 1955 under the hand of George Lee Marks. Marks was a New York theatrical distributor who owned a string of movie theatres around the country. He arrived in Houston with plans to open a live theatre, partially inspired by his brother's success as producer for *Matinee Theatre* for NBC.[74]

After extensive renovations, the improved Avalon reopened with *The Great Sebastian*, but with only mediocre success during a two-week run. It featured TV actor Paul Hartman, Ethel Shutta, and a backing cast that included Claire Van Erp, an actress and director who had previously lost interest in live productions. During the tryout period, her husband, Doug, had dragged the ailing actress from a hospital bed to audition. Not only

The Venus Theatre, c. 1961. Courtesy of Al Zarzana.

The Avalon Theatre in its later incarnation as the Capri, c. 1985. Photograph by Jim Koehn.

did she get the part, but the experience also reenergized her enthusiasm for the medium.[75]

The second production, *At War with the Army*, starred Morey Gossfield of the Phil Silvers television show, and was based on a Martin and Lewis movie. Gossfield's small role was expanded to take advantage of his name, but one evening he didn't appear at curtain time. The star, unaccustomed to driving, had lodged his rented car sideways in the theatre driveway, effectively creating a traffic jam for the patrons who couldn't park their cars.

Two more shows followed: *Will Success Spoil Rock Hunter?* starring Wally Cox, and *Cat on a Hot Tin Roof*, with Diana Barrymore and Clifton James, best known as Sheriff Pepper in the James Bond films *Live and Let Die* and *The Man with the Golden Gun*. *Cat* was successful enough to bring the Avalon into the black, partially because of the notoriety generated

by Barrymore's tell-all autobiography and the movie made from it. Despite this, the theatre closed.

Its failure was due largely to its distant location in a lower-income area. In addition, the theatre was undersized: it lacked an orchestra pit, backstage dress-

Lobby of the Capri. Courtesy of Ray M. Boriski.

The Bellaire Theatre, mid-1980s. Collection of Roy Bonario, photo by Al Davis.

ing rooms, and fly space. Lastly, the theatre just ran out of money. After a failed attempt to stage *Happy Birthday* with Joan Blondell, the theatre closed down, six months after opening and with only four productions to its credit.[76]

The Avalon then dived from legitimate productions into sex. Those seeking adult entertainment could see such saucy titles as *Hideout in the Sun: It Happened in a Nature Camp* and *Not Tonight, Henry* ("See the 15 'no-cover girls' that *Playboy* magazine gave three pages to," read the local ads).[77]

Al Zarzana and Ray Boriski took over the theatre as a showplace for Spanish-language films and renamed it the Fiesta. When Zarzana got out of the partnership, Boriski changed the theatre's name to the Capri. The theatre survived well into the eighties before eventually closing down. In a complete reversal of morality, the structure later reopened as the Living Hope Church.

THE BELLAIRE/BEL AIR
4020 Bellaire Boulevard

The Bellaire Theatre was an independent neighborhood movie house owned by Victor A. Barraco, Carl Tanner, and Frank R. Guinn. The 1,210-seat theatre was designed as the focal point of a commercial shopping center, and the exterior featured an impressive multicolored neon display, visible from blocks down Bellaire Boulevard. Nione Carlson rendered decorations and murals in the interior.[78]

The formal opening for the new center took place in the afternoon on Saturday, April 16, 1949, with the Fred Astaire–Judy Garland musical *Easter Parade* along with a cartoon and a newsreel. *The Adventures of Don Juan* followed on Sunday. For the kids, a Saturday-morning children's show preceded the opening festivities with cartoons, a serial, and *My Dog Rusty*.[79]

The Saturday-morning kids' programs were quite popular, and for a time they featured local personality Don Mahoney, a cowboy in the Roy Rogers mold.[80] He was best remembered for his TV program with Jeanna Claire and the Kiddie Troupers, which ran for several decades beginning in the fifties. Among those who performed or square-danced on his show were Johnny and Edgar Winter, and Annette O'Toole.

The Bellaire features were generally second-run. One of the rare first-runs was the magnificent Russian version of *War and Peace*, considered by many to be the definitive film version of the Tolstoy novel. When shown in May 1969, the epic 373-minute film was presented in two parts, each shown for a one-week period.[81]

Competition during the seventies drained much of the business away, causing the theatre to become at varying times a martial-arts house, an Indian theatre,

and briefly a showplace for magicians. The last incarnation took place in 1982, when Kirby Van Burch and Terry Ritter conducted a $30,000 restoration, adding a proscenium stage, dressing rooms, new wiring, equipment, air conditioning, and seats. They opened with a magical horror show, *Sorcery*, on October 23, with dance choreography by Glen Hunsucker.[82] Van Burch would eventually become a resident performer in Branson, Missouri.

In 1976, the Bellaire served as a dollar house, and was later taken over by the Tercar Theatre Company. Finally, it succumbed to running X-rated films before closing down in 1985.

In a 1984 *Houston Chronicle* article, Louis Parks flagged the Bellaire for having the most bizarre lobby. "What can you call this?" he asked. "Art decadent? How about Space Station 1950? If movie

Lobby of the Bellaire, 1970s. Courtesy of Charles Paine.

The renamed Bel Air Theatre, c. 1988. From the collection of John Coles, courtesy of Io Communications.

two 120-seat theatres. Two more auditoriums, seating 50 and 210, were constructed in adjoining retail space. The main auditorium held 420 seats, all of which were imported from France. The main projection booth was moved downstairs, and a glass rear wall was installed so patrons could view the equipment in operation on their way to the auditorium.[85]

The spectacular, multicolored neon exterior was restored to its former glory. Lost during this process were the second neon L and E from the fixture, which effectively renamed the cinema the Bel Air.

The bar area was partitioned from a section of the lobby with a glass-brick wall and a separate entrance. Several windows were installed between the bar and the smaller auditoriums, allowing the diners to view (but not hear) the movies. Menu items included pizza, deli sandwiches, and finger munchies, none of which were allowed in the auditorium.[86]

The Bel Air reopening took place on November 26, 1986, with three of the five screens completed. The features were *The Girl in the Picture*, Bertrand Blier's *Menage*, and a second run of *A Room with a View*. The remaining two screens opened on December 5, with *Twist and Shout* and *Dancing in the Dark*.

Competition from the other Houston art houses soon pressured the Bel Air to change its offerings from first-run specialty features to second-run mainstream bargain shows. Admission was $1.50, later raised to $2. The lease was eventually taken over by a group of investors under the banner of Bel Mar Limited; Coles remained the general manager.

In 1989, KLDE radio personality

theatres are dream palaces, this one is a fun nightmare." Of the exterior, he added, "Most of the neon is out at present, but that sort of adds to its charm."[83]

In 1986, Metro Cinema leased the property from InterCity Investments, planning to put in five auditoriums and a restaurant-bar. Company president John Coles of Houston and Dallas vice president Robert E. Berney, Jr., had already been successful with a similar conversion of the Inwood Theatre in Dallas.[84]

The Dallas-based ArchiTexas architectural firm carried out the renovation design. The main auditorium was left intact, and the balcony was converted into

Joseph Craig hosted classic movie nights on alternating weeks. The theatre was also host to the *Rocky Horror Picture Show* phenomenon. By this time, the bar had become known as Mars Restaurant and Bar, operated by the owner of the Blue Moon, and would later be called simply the Bel Air Bar.[87]

The theatre was a home for the Vietnam Veterans Film Festival, the Houston Association of Film and Television annual Academy Awards party, and a venue for the Worldfest Houston Film Festival.

By 1991, financial trouble was evident. InterCity served Coles an eviction notice in March when he was five days late on the rent. The issue was resolved, but in November they notified him that the lease, which would expire on the first of December, would not be renewed. It was rumored that Ye Seekers, a health-food store located at the far end of the center, had lodged complaints against the theatre—its grievance being that theatre patrons used too many parking spaces. This was apparently not a problem with any of the theatre's other neighbors, including a Black-eyed Pea restaurant.

Community support for the theatre was immediate, and spawned a "Save the Bellaire" letter and fax campaign. The petition, with over 2,000 names, apparently had some effect, since a temporary agreement was worked out. Coles himself finally decided to shut down the theatre.[88] The Bellaire closed for good on August 2, 1992.

The Bel Air Bar closed the same night with a musical bash featuring local hardcore bands Blender and Bleachbath. The

bands played on through the wee hours until the local police arrived to send the lively crowd home.[89]

The building reopened in June 1993 as a Discovery Zone kiddie park. Gone were the large neon B-E-L A-I-R letters above the marquee, replace by multicolored cartoonish letters that spelled D-I-S-C-O-V-E-R-Y Z-O-N-E. The interior was completely gutted, stripped, leveled, and converted into a playground. No trace of its former incarnation was left.

The Discovery Zone chain filed for bankruptcy in 1999, and the Bellaire location, among others, closed down.[90] The shutdown was abrupt, leaving many customers less than happy. One letter, taped on the front door after the store's closing, expressed a parent's dismay at how a company could operate is such a manner. She had arranged in advance for her little boy's birthday party to be celebrated there. When she arrived with her child on Saturday morning, she found the business closed. She had to wait for all the party guests, and then tell the children that the party was cancelled. This, she explained, was not the thing to do to a child on his birthday.[91]

The Austin-based Whole Foods Market converted the old theatre space into a 46,000-square-foot grocery store at the end of 2000. The organics-oriented market in effect replaced Ye Seekers, which had since closed down.[92]

THE CAPITAN
1045 *East Shaw*

The forties came to a close with the openings of the Capitan, in Pasadena, and the

Granada Theatre on Jensen, both owned by Phil Isley of Dallas, father of film actress Jennifer Jones.

For the citizens of Pasadena, moviegoing was divided into two camps. Seeing top-line movies meant a trip into Houston to one of the first-run houses. For those content with lesser fare—the second-run and B western titles—there were the local theatres. Pasadena in 1949 had a few to choose from: the 720-seat Rita, at the corner of Shaw and Shaver, had been in operation since the early thirties. Originally built by D. P. Rathbone, it was eventually taken over by Johnny Long, who changed its name to the Pasadena Theatre. Long's regional chain provided a constant supply of live and filmed entertainment to its varied theatres, including Long's Theatre, also located on Shaw.[93] In addition to the Pasadena Theatre, there were also the Garden Theatre and the South Houston Theatre.[94]

These movie houses would pale in comparison with the Capitan. The 1,600-seat venue was built in the Corrigan Center, on the former site of a one-acre pioneer homestead. Interior decorators Nat Smythe & Son were responsible for a stylish design and for executing the visually captivating interior. The auditorium walls were painted a deep blue-green, and mythological murals painted by Colville Smythe graced the sides. The right side depicted Europa riding a golden bull—Zeus in disguise—amid a sea of dolphins, Nereids, and Tritons blowing conch-shell horns. The opposite wall incorporated Neptune astride a golden sea horse, set in a similar background. The ceiling contained a recessed central area of deep sea green with a design of a seventy-five-foot

compass cord supported by an immense mermaid. The nautical concept was selected because of Pasadena's proximity to the Port of Houston.[95] At a later date, the frolicking bare-breasted nymphs would draw objections from a church congregation that felt patrons should not be looking at such a thing on a Sunday morning. The offending imagery was repainted.

The foyer and mezzanine continued the nautical themes and colors of the auditorium. Other amenities included a crying room for babies and rocking, push-back chair seats, which were becoming the new standard for theatres.

The November 19 grand opening offered the feature presentation *Impact* and a Tom and Jerry cartoon, plus guest appearances by western film stars Chill Wills and Monte Hale. The Wills film *Trailin' West* and Hale's *San Antonio Ambush* were also featured at the time. The following Thursday, the Capitan began a six-day run of David O. Selznick's *Portrait of Jennie*, starring daddy Isley's little girl, Jennifer Jones.[96]

The standard second-run fare at the Capitan would continue for several decades, but by the end of the sixties, the north end of Pasadena was no longer the central hub of town, and audiences were instead patronizing the early multiplexes. In 1970, the theatre switched to X-rated fare. Pasadena was already up in arms over the explicit movies being shown at the nearby Red Bluff Drive-In. According to a June 1970 newspaper article, the films presented at the Capitan were "far worse than those at the Red Bluff."[97] The Capitan would close in 1976, and then reopen as a church.

The Capitan's grand relighting ceremony, June 2000. Photograph by David Welling.

Faith Temple of Pasadena leased the theatre, with plans to hold services there on Sunday and Wednesday nights and to present movies and stage shows on Friday and Saturday nights. "Our aim is to spread the Gospel, and give people a decent place for recreation," said the Reverend Michael La Monica of the nondenominational church.[98]

The Capitan's usage as a church didn't last, nor did its use as a Spanish-language movie house in the eighties, and it was finally sealed up to wait for a new lease on life. In 1997, a group known as Our Neighborhood Association raised money for the theatre's restoration by selling a commemorative throw blanket, which featured an image of the Capitan in the center, surrounded by pictures of local churches, historic houses, and other buildings.[99]

The City of Pasadena eventually purchased the theatre and shopping center for just under $6 million and hired a market-research company to poll the community on how to best use the theatre. Almost everyone agreed that it should be a modern multipurpose venue with the ability to handle stage plays, live events, musical concerts, and the like.

On August 31, 1999, the Pasadena city council approved a $199,976 exterior restoration, certain that the facade would attract positive attention to the remainder of the project. The Sparkle Sign Company was contracted to remove, restore, and reinstall the marquee.[100]

A relighting ceremony for the Capitan's refurbished exterior was held on June 20 of the following year. Nearly three hundred people were on hand to see the newly luminous neon, which had remained dark for a quarter century. Mayor Johnny Isbell and other council members stood by as Edward Carleton, the original general manager of the Capitan, threw the light switch—just as he had done for the original opening in 1949.

"Isn't it beautiful," said his wife, Jo, to the *Pasadena Citizen*. "It looks just like it did when it opened."[101]

Don Carleton, director of the Center for American History at the University of Texas, told the *Houston Chronicle* in 1999, "The Capitan is one of the last of the great old theatres built in Texas. It was an incredible palace." He should well remember, since his father was the

general manager at its opening, half a century earlier.[102] In retrospect, it has fared far better than most other theatres, despite a future as yet unfinished. The old Pasadena Theatre is gone, the site now occupied by Norman's Furniture, and the Long Theatre building has been converted into the Pasadena Gun Center.

THE GRANADA
9231 Jensen Drive

"You won't believe your eyes . . . it's so beautiful," read the opening day ads for

The Granada Theatre on opening day, 1949. Courtesy of the Houston Metropolitan Research Center, Houston Public Library, MSS 200-113.

Phil Isley's Granada.[103] The distinctive exterior featured separate vertical and horizontal marquees inset with glowing neon, and a rider on horseback painted on the above exterior wall. An equally lush auditorium incorporated curving deco motifs, billowing curtains on either side of the screen, and scenic paintings on the sidewalls. The balcony and ceiling were included in the ornate decor.

The feature for the December 7, 1949, opening day was *You're My Everything*. The following weekend, Houston actor Monte Hale took the Granada stage for two live appearances while his latest film, *Prince of the Plains*, was featured. *Massacre River* was the second feature.

The Granada functioned for years as a standard independent. Double bills always served to pull in patrons, and the pairings were sometimes unintentionally amusing, as when the two big epics *Krakatoa, East of Java* (1969) and *King Kong Escapes* (1967) were shown together.

On February 1, 1970, it was taken over by Al Zarzana. The theatre attracted 3,000

Auditorium of the Granada. Courtesy of the Houston Metropolitan Research Center, Houston Public Library, MSS 200-118.

The relationship between theatre owners or managers and the projectionists' union was not always an amicable one. When the Al*Ray Theatre closed, Ray Boriski hauled the projectors out to the curb as scrap. Courtesy of Ray M. Boriski.

people on its opening day. At the time, Zarzana was operating the Santa Rosa theatre as a Spanish-language house, and would acquire the Garden Oaks in 1975. Under his control, the Granada would continue to focus on the Spanish-speaking market.[104]

The theatre would operate though the eighties before shutting the projector off for good in 1988. The building survived into the new century, its neon vertical marquee intact. It last served as a Spanish-language church.

OVER THE PREVIOUS twenty years, neighborhood theatres had firmly estab-

lished themselves as the new wave of moviegoing, effectively superseding the downtown movie palaces. Their biggest obstacle was the solidified power of the major theatrical chains, which managed to maintain a stranglehold on all first-run entertainment released by the studios. Most of the large first-run houses, such as the Loew's State, were, in actuality, exhibition arms of the studios. Yet one theatrical chain managed to sweep across the southern states, growing in size and scope with each passing year. This was Karl Hoblitzelle's Interstate theatre chain, and it would leave a lasting impression on Houston's theatrical landscape.

Karl Hoblitzelle. Courtesy of the Hoblitzelle Foundation.

NINE

★ ★ ★

HOBLITZELLE'S
INTERSTATE

★ ★ ★

Karl Hoblitzelle has been an empire builder—and his is a prouder achievement than the empires that have risen and fallen since he has been on the scene, for his is built not on conquest, but on service, not on the forces that divide men, but on the ideas that unite them.

CECIL B. DEMILLE, 1946

★ BY 1929, Karl Hoblitzelle's Interstate theatre chain had become one of the largest and most respected chains in the Southwest. Dallas, San Antonio, Austin, and Houston all had their own Hoblitzelle Majestics, Houston being home to three consecutive ones. Each of his theatres strove to offer the best in wholesome entertainment in an atmosphere of clean, safe comfort, and in the process, to bring respectability to motion-picture entertainment. "The Theatre," said Hoblitzelle, "belongs to the customer first, and to we who operate it second."[1]

As the twenties came to a close, Hoblitzelle felt it was time to retire and take a well-deserved vacation. He planned to take Esther, a former Broadway star who had been his wife since 1920, on an extended tour of Europe. He struck a deal with the RKO theatre chain, which was eager to expand into the southwestern market, by which he sold his interest while retaining several theatre buildings as real estate investments. The transaction was closed in May 1930.

Karl and Esther left for Europe in 1931, leaving his theatre empire in what he thought to be competent hands. But the Great Depression took its toll on RKO, and it and Interstate, along with Paramount Southern Enterprises, were forced into receivership in January 1933. Hoblitzelle arrived home to the possibility of RKO theatre closings, which would add hundreds of theatre workers to the masses of Depression-era unemployed.[2] Acting promptly, he reorganized the two companies as the Interstate Theatre Circuit. In addition, he acquired the Dent Theatre Circuit of Texas, which became Texas

Consolidated Theatres. Hoblitzelle would remain president of Interstate until his death in 1967.[3]

Houston's grand Majestic of 1923 remained the company's major showplace for the city, drawing crowds even as the Depression ran its course. With the end of the Depression came the first of the Interstate neighborhood theatres, and the company announced a building program for five more in Houston. The first of these would be a holiday event, delivered for a festive unwrapping in December.

THE NORTH MAIN
3730 *North Main*

The North Main was Interstate's first Houston theatre to be built outside of the downtown district. This would be

The North Main Theatre, c. 1942. To the left of the theatre is the popcorn stand where patrons could buy their popcorn from Shorty before entering the theatre. Courtesy of Parsley Studios.

Auditorium of the North Main. Courtesy of the Center for American History, University of Texas at Austin.

followed by the Tower, the Eastwood, and two other proposed, as yet unnamed houses, one to be located in the South End and the other positioned downtown at Main and Lamar. Initial estimated costs for the five together were predicted to be in the $750,000 range.

Dallas architect W. Scott Dunne handled the design; he would also be responsible for the other four planned structures, as he had been for I. B. Adelman's Delman Theatre the previous year.[4] The grand opening took place on Christmas Day 1935. Billed in ads as "Interstate Theatres' Christmas gift to the North Side and the Heights," the 1,000-seat North Main marked the new Interstate direction toward conveniently located, neighborhood theatres.[5]

The feature for the opening was *Page Miss Glory*, starring Dick Powell and Marion Davies. Managerial chores were assigned to John Arnold, a lifetime the-

atre man who for decades would serve as one of the pillars of the Interstate Houston branch before retiring in the early seventies.

For many patrons, attending the North Main included buying popcorn from "Shorty," a little person who operated a stand next to the theatre.

The theatre remained in operation for several decades. In the seventies, the North Main marquee was replaced with one that read "Ciné Ritz," and its movie format switched to Spanish-language films.[6] By the nineties, it was operating as a Hispanic church. The once-stylish deco interior had become a well-used, run-down shell. Floors that were once carpeted were now bare wood, and walls had been repainted a light baby blue. The projection booth had been gutted and was now used as a classroom. The exterior of the theatre, which was still somewhat intact in 1993, except for a painted-over marquee, was soon stripped down to the bare brick and cement understructure. It was later replastered into a stark white facade without any theatrical embellishments, sign, or marquee. At the end of the nineties, the building still functioned as the Centro Cristiano Alfa y Omega Church.

THE NORTH MAIN was no Majestic—far from it. Neither the neighborhood nor midthirties economics warranted such extravagances. However, it still held true to the standards that Hoblitzelle established from his earliest houses: cleanliness, comfort, beauty, and safety. "It has been a source of great satisfaction to me to see something come out of a barren stretch of land that is beautiful," Hoblitzelle had said. "To me, the greatest impulse in life is to create beauty. We strive to enhance our entertainment by a setting of beauty in which to enjoy it."[7]

While the Interstate theatres of the thirties may not have matched up to the palaces of the twenties, they still offered the setting he strove for. Over the next dozen years, Interstate would continue to expand across the Southwest, all the while improving on the art of theatre construction. If the North Main was a Christmas present to the city, then his next one would be a valentine.

THE TOWER
1201 *Westheimer*

The night sky on February 14, 1936—Valentine's Day—was sliced apart by a battery of Hollywood klieg lights and sun arcs. Those who followed the beams found themselves at the corner of West-

heimer and Waugh Drive and at the grand opening of Interstate's newest neighborhood theatre, the Tower.

Colorful banners decorated the adjacent streets for the occasion. The all-girl Black Battalion Drum and Bugle Corps, from Sam Houston High School, stirred the crowd with their marches, while radio station KTRH broadcast the event live. Looming overhead was the massive neon Tower marquee, visible from blocks away, with a revolving neon beacon that underwent fifteen color changes a minute.

Inside, the ceremonies continued with dedications from longtime mayor Oscar Holcombe and other dignitaries. Blackstone, the magician, wowed the mezzanine attendees with his hat-and-bunny wizardry—he also performed at a special kiddie matinee the next morning and gave away the 100 magic rabbits to the children. A thirty-piece orchestra under the direction of musician–conductor–house manager Lloyd Finlay entertained the crowd before the showing of the grand opening feature, *The Barbary Coast*.

Opening-night festivities such as this were standard for Interstate, and often included searchlights, fireworks, live radio broadcasts, souvenirs, and bands ranging from the Elkadettes and the Black Battalion to Cliff Breacher's Cowboy Band. Local celebrities, political figures, and studio chain officials often joined the Interstate heads and managers for these galas.[8]

The 1,200-seat Tower, like the North Main, was built from plans drawn up by architect W. Scott Dunne. Rich in art moderne motifs, the Tower's appearance maintained the "Interstate look."

The Tower shared the block with the Jack Roach Ford dealership, a relationship that was both "pervasive and elusive," according to writer Peter Papademetriou in a *Houston Home and Garden* article: "Theatres were often located as part of new strip commercial centers, a form of development generated by accommodation to the automobile. Both their flashy styling and the evolution of the pylon-marquee were obviously related to visibility from automobiles."[9]

Thus began the forty-two-year history of presenting feature films at the Tower. William Wyler's *Ben-Hur* was shown as an exclusive (all seats reserved, mail-order tickets available).[10] The 1970s gimmick "Sensurround" vibrated the auditorium walls for *Earthquake* (1974) and *Midway* (1976). Other films included *My Fair Lady* (1964), *Gigi* (1958), *Around the World in 80 Days* (1956), *Porgy and Bess* (1959), *And God Created Woman* (1956), *La Dolce Vita* (1960), *Exodus* (1960), and

The Rocky Horror Picture Show (1975), which began its midnight-movie reign at the Tower.

Wide-screen Todd-AO first appeared in Houston at the Tower with *Oklahoma!* (1955). Of special note was the newly installed curtain to accommodate the wider screen (which stretched from sidewall to sidewall). Since there was no room for a side draw curtain—and no room at the top for a waterfall curtain—Interstate devised an "upside-down" curtain, which was located at the bottom of the screen and opened and closed from the floor. Although Tower manager Ross Vallone was credited with the idea, other Houston managers also claimed to have had a hand in its design. The list of those who may have been involved includes Al Lever, John Smith of the River Oaks Theatre,

and Howard Skelton of the Alabama. Vallone, an Interstate institution, did managing stints at the Majestic, the Tower, the Eastwood, and the ABC Interstate twin on Westheimer, most likely the Woodlake.[11]

Like many theatres, the Tower suffered hard times in the seventies, culminating in its closing. The final feature, *Jaws II*, was shown on August 24, 1978.[12]

The Tower was sold to PACE Management and its new subsidiary, Tower Ventures. The master plan was to reopen the theatre as a venue for live productions, music, and plays. It underwent a major exterior restoration by Barry Moore Architects in 1988.

The theatre was revamped for live shows, which began on November 18, 1978, with a performance by minimalist composer Philip Glass.[13] *The Best Little*

Whorehouse in Texas, *Greater Tuna*, *Jesus Christ Superstar*, *Bottoms Up*, and *Hank Williams: The Show He Never Gave* were all notable productions. *Ipi-Tombi* did extremely well, although the last sold-out show was not performed because the South African cast members held invalid visas.[14]

The musical talent came in all forms, from the folk styles of John Prine, Judy Collins, and Nanci Griffith, to the Pretenders and performance artist Laurie Anderson. Other artists included Kim Carnes, the Mamas and the Papas, the Manhattan Transfer, Burt Bacharach and Carole Bayer Sager, Lee Ritenour, Jimmy Vaughan, Sarah McLachlan, Tori Amos, and Peter Allen. February 1990 also kicked off a celebration of disco nostalgia with "Decadance." Every Friday night the Tower would turn into a flashback dance arena.[15]

PACE eventually grew tired of the structure's shaky viability, opening it only for an occasional show. By March 1995 it had been put up for sale for $1.4 million.

The theatre was converted into retail space in 1995, and reopened in the later part of November as a Hollywood Video movie store. Although the T-O-W-E-R letters on the neon marquee were replaced with H-O-L-L-Y-W-O-O-D, the decorative neon was completely restored to its original dazzling glory. However, the impressiveness of the exterior restoration failed to carry through to the interior, which was gutted and remodeled to look like all the other stores in the chain.

To date, movies remain a part of the Tower, if only to be rented and watched elsewhere.

THE EASTWOOD
4537 *Leeland*

Little time was wasted between the Tower's debut and that of the Eastwood,

Opening night of the Eastwood Theatre, 1936. Collection of Roy Bonario, courtesy of the Center for American History, University of Texas at Austin.

which opened less than a month later—and slightly over two months after the North Main. The movie house was the third installment in Interstate's move to the suburbs.

The 1,100-seat Eastwood utilized a style similar to one that architect W. Scott Dunne had used in his previous theatres. The exterior sported a large triple-faced neon sign on the roof's center instead of on the front of the building, as was traditional. The featured film for the March 6, 1936, opening was *The Barbary Coast*, the same film that had opened the Tower three weeks earlier, along with a Mickey Mouse cartoon, *Band Concert*, and a *March of Time* newsreel.[16]

Despite its initial standing in the neighborhood, the theatre did not hold up under the test of time over the decades, its last listing being in the 1966 *Houston Directory*. The building no longer exists.

INTERSTATE CONTINUED to expand its line of new theatres as well as acquisitions and fifty-fifty partnerships with older independents. When the Depression brought about the collapse of the Publix theatre chain, Interstate picked up both the Metropolitan and the Kirby, placing Eddie Bremer at the helm of the latter. Other Houston theatres that came under Interstate's wings over the next few decades included the Bluebonnet in 1936, the University/Nan Grey in 1940, and the River Oaks in 1947. In the company's later incarnation as ABC Interstate, its banner would fly over a whole new set of theatres and drive-ins.

Hoblitzelle succeeded partly by surrounding himself with good men, one of whom was Al Lever, the chain's city man-ager for the Houston region. Before joining Interstate in 1925, the Brooklyn-born Lever worked—or played—as a circus clown for the Barnum and Bailey Circus. He first managed the Houston Isis, then owned by the Saenger Amusement Company of New Orleans. When Interstate bought the Isis, Lever joined the Dallas office, and then eventually came back to Houston. A *Houston Chronicle* reporter described him as "that rare breed: men admire him and women cherish him." Lever dressed in the "continental flavor of Adolph Menjou, but a peg more subdued. He spoke in the low-key caressing gambler's voice that pleased the ear. And the face was the face of a man who has lived life to its fullest measure . . . [he] is also one of the finest gin-rummy players in the city."[17]

At the time of his retirement, in April 1967, he had spent ten years training Art Katzen to be his successor. Katzen would, in turn, serve as city manager through 1976.

THE YALE
3906 *Washington*

Over a year passed between the East-wood's opening and that of a new Interstate theatre. Again, the company focused on the Heights district, adding another movie house to an area that already included the North Main and the Heights.[18]

On May 20, 1938, the 1,204-seat Yale, on Washington near the corner of Yale, opened its doors with the feature film *Navy Blue and Gold*, starring James Stewart, and a Donald Duck cartoon.

John Arnold moved over from the North Main to manage the new theatre. Arnold started at the Kirby at age eighteen while studying physics at Rice University. As usher, he developed the showbiz knack of tearing tickets with one hand, a handy ability when dealing with two lines of people simultaneously. He took a job as assistant manager in Austin as the talkies were taking hold before returning to the Kirby as assistant manager. During the Depression, he supervised bank nights, when lucky patrons had a shot at winning a twenty-five-dollar fortune.

Then came managerial chores at the North Main and the Yale while he was also serving as a lieutenant colonel in the Texas State Guard and chairman of the district YMCA, the Boy Scouts, and the Community Chest in the Heights. Civic duties also found their way into the theatre on occasion: during a hurricane, he transformed the movie house into a shelter, running films all night for the audience. As Yale manager, he often staged events to attract more business, such as a "battle of the cowboys" between Gene Autry and Roy Rogers films.

Arnold would eventually become the city office trouble-shooter, dealing with problems such as missing reels and plumbing mishaps. When a newsreel turned up in the middle of a feature at the Garden Oaks, "we bicycled the right reel out there," he explained to the *Houston Post*. "Everything went wrong but we always did something. We always got the picture on."[19] He finally took on a less hectic position as manager of the North Shore Theatre before retiring in 1973.

The best memories, he later claimed, were of riding cowboy star Ken Maynard's horse and chatting with Clark Gable, then just a struggling stage actor, in the Kirby lobby. "He was a big-eared ham," mused Arnold.[20]

The Yale remained a staple of the Interstate chain for the next fourteen years. Popular among the kiddies was the Saturday-morning Popeye Club, which showed three hours of cartoons, serials such as *The Green Hornet*, a feature film, and, on numerous occasions, a stage show—all for just a nickel. Before the show, ushers would pass out bubble gum to the kids. The Popeye Club became a standard weekend event at a number of Interstate theatres.

In 1952, a "consent decree," the result of a federal antitrust ruling, went into effect, forcing Interstate to sell off some of its theatres, including the Yale and the Broadway. (Note: This litigation is discussed fully later in this chapter.) Both were bought by William O'Donnell (the brother of R. J. O'Donnell). Alvin Guggenheim managed both theatres for the next two decades before striking out on his own with the Lincoln, the Don Gordon Theatre, and his trio of Majestics.[21]

The Yale survived for twenty more years. In January 1967, the Heights State Bank bought the Yale theatre property along with the neighboring John Allen

post office building. Just four years earlier, in November 1962, the new Heights Bank building had opened adjacent to the theatre, moving from the 3618 Washington location that would later house Rockefeller's nightclub. The added property would allow the bank to expand.[22]

The theatre was leased back to William O'Donnell, who operated it for a few more years before shuttering it on January 1, 1972, the same day that the Broadway closed. According to Guggenheim, 1971 was the most profitable year for the Yale since the property had been sold. The Yale was razed in January 1972.[23]

BY THE MID-FORTIES, Interstate's operations for theatre construction had become an intricate process—a far cry from the early days, when the general-office staff consisted of Hoblitzelle, a combination treasurer–general manager, a booking manager, an auditor, and a stenographer. The decision to build a new theatre had evolved into an elaborate process, beginning with the executive department, which chose a location by considering suitability, population, and distances to neighboring theatres. The legal department cleared any restrictions and handled all legal documents, and the real estate department closed the deal on the property. Decisions regarding building style, size, space usage, seating, parking, concessions, and additional retail space fell to the construction department. A separate purchasing agent was involved in the acquisition of everything from carpets and drinking fountains to ticket machines. Sound and air-conditioning engineers were involved in the process, as were the departments handling insurance, publicity and advertising, and booking,

Auditorium of the Alabama, 1950. Collection of Gary Warwick, courtesy of the Center for American History, University of Texas at Austin, e_bb_1495.

as well as, finally, the house manager and staff. Simplicity had become a thing of the past.[24]

From 1938 to 1942, Interstate opened a new theatre each year in Houston. The entry for 1939 remains the best surviving example of Interstate's theatre architecture of the period, and perhaps is fitting that it opened during Hollywood's *annus mirabilis.*

THE ALABAMA
2922 Shepherd

When it opened, in November 1939, the Alabama was Interstate's tenth theatre in the Houston area, the others being the Metropolitan, Majestic, Kirby, Delman, Eastwood, North Main, Tower, Bluebon-

net, and Yale. In addition, it was the first and largest of four openings that month, with the independent Stude, Navaway, and River Oaks theatres to follow.

The Alabama design was handled by John A. Worley, of Pettigrew and Worley. His unique touches included a freestanding street-side vertical tower sign that spelled out A-L-A-B-A-M-A, a distinct variation from the more common, attached variety. This striking landmark, designed and built by Texlite, Inc. of Dallas and the Texas Neon Sign Company, could be seen from blocks away on either side of Shepherd Drive.[25] Also freestanding was the box office, positioned below the Alabama marquee; this was removed during a later remodeling. Of special note was the inlaid design on the walkway immediately outside the lobby: a spiraling yellow motif that bore a suspicious resemblance to the yellow-brick road from *The Wizard of Oz*, which had opened at Loew's the previous August. Whether the similarities were deliberate or coincidental is a matter of speculation.

The 1,200-seat interior utilized a tan and burgundy color scheme, with a contrasting blue added. The lobby and foyer were finished in simulated wood paneling that was laid like wallpaper to fit the various curves and offsets of the room. Murals on the auditorium panels adjoining the proscenium arch served as accents, while a built-in light fixture extended from the center of the ceiling and ran down each sidewall of the auditorium. The auditorium floor was covered in broadloom carpeting with an acanthus-leaf pattern.[26] The dedication ceremonies took place on Thursday, November 2, 1939, with the usual Interstate festivities and the feature *Man About Town*, with Jack Benny.[27]

In later remodelings, the lobby was upgraded twice, the undersized concession stand was updated, and the box office

was rebuilt into the theatre front. Original plans for a shopping center surrounding the theatre eventually came to fruition. The space to the left of the theatre was first occupied by the A&P Grocery, later by Cactus Records. To the right was Walgreens, and on the far-left corner was C.O.D. Coney Island.

Howard Skelton managed the theatre during the later fifties and early sixties. During that time, horror-film double features would be shown on Halloween and Friday the thirteenth.[28]

In 1960, special Todd-AO equipment was installed for the October 26 opening of *The Alamo* starring John Wayne. Similar equipment had already been installed at the Tower and the Rivoli.[29] In 1974, the Clayton Foundation sold the shopping center to the Pete Kaldis Realty Company and Weingarten Realty, Inc. The Plitt chain leased the Alabama in the midseventies, along with a handful of other Interstate theatres.

Feature films during the Alabama's history ran the gamut from *The Glen*

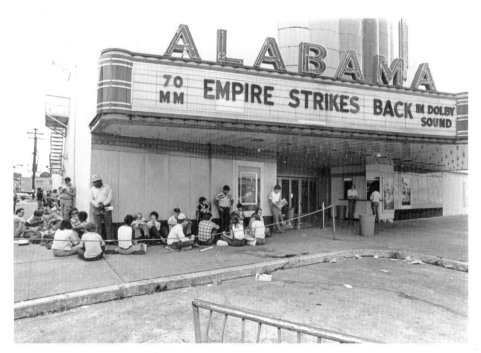

Star Wars fans await the first showing of The Empire Strikes Back, *May 21, 1980. Courtesy of the Houston Metropolitan Research Center, Houston Public Library, RGD6N 5-21-80.*

Commemorative Bookstop poster, created by Houston illustrator Mike Dean, 1984. Author's collection, illustration ©1984 Mike Dean.

Miller Story (1953) to blockbuster titles of the seventies and eighties, such as *The Sting* (1973), *The Omen* (1976), *The Towering Inferno* (1974), *American Graffiti* (1973), and *Reds* (1981). *The Sound of Music* (1965; all seats reserved) attracted audiences for over a year during its run.[30] Long lines of science fiction fans wrapped around the building for *Close Encounters of the Third Kind* (1977), *Alien* (1979), and *The Empire Strikes Back* (1980).

Competition from multicinemas, cable television, and videotape cut deep into the Alabama's attendance and profits. "One can only wonder how long the Rocky Horror Picture Show will sustain the Alabama," noted writer Peter Papademetriou in 1978.[31] The *Rocky Horror* phenomenon had been a midnight-movie staple on Friday and Saturday nights since moving over from the Tower in February 1978.

Plitt held on to the cinema until 1983, when Weingarten Realty bought the remainder of the fifty-year lease. Reportedly, one of the contributing reasons for the sale was Plitt's expenses for repairing damage caused by Hurricane Alicia, which plowed through Houston in August 1983.

According to *Houston Chronicle* reports at the time, the fifty-year agreement had six more years to run. Revenue from the ground lease, which had been negotiated at pre–World War II prices, most likely influenced Weingarten's decision. Art Katzen reported that the ground lease cost Plitt $175 a day, including half the parking lot.[32]

The movie era of the Alabama ended in early December 1983. Its final presentation was the low-budget horror flick *Mortuary*, a title that paralleled the theatre's final days.

The entire Alabama Center, now

owned by the Alabama Shopping Center Company, a partnership between Weingarten Realty and Kaldis Realty, underwent a facelift. Plans were drawn up for an elite mix of complementary businesses. The eventual lineup consisted of Butera's Deli, the Austin-based Whole Foods Market, the Whole Earth Provision Company, and longtime tenant Cactus Records.[33]

Bookstop, another company from Austin, leased the theatre. Gary Hoover, president of the chain, insisted on keeping the original decor of the building. He contacted Judith Urrutia, of the San Antonio-based Chumney/Urrutia design firm, whose work he had been impressed with. Although she was initially reluctant to take on the project, his enthusiasm won her over. She and fellow architect Billy Lawrence began the redesign.[34]

They found the theatre suffering from a lack of upkeep: the roof leaked, walls were water stained, and the paint was well worn. The chief priority was to maintain the integrity of the original design while optimizing its functionality for a retail space. Seats were removed, and a three-tier platform was constructed, leading down to the base of the auditorium. The neon light coves were left intact. The lobby was redesigned as a cashier area. Since the lobby had been altered twice since 1939, the team consulted original-era photographs from Bob Bailey Studios. The area was configured to work best as a checkout area.

Interior work included new lotus-pattern carpeting in shades of green, black, blue, and peach and a detailed interior paint scheme, which included the wall scallops and murals, in watermelon, green, beige, and brown tones. The paint job alone cost $40,000. Exterior remodeling was kept to a minimum. The original "Alabama" neon letters above the marquee were replaced with identical ones reading "Bookstop." The vertical "Alabama" street-side sign was left intact as indicating the name the entire strip center. The cost of the reconstruction exceeded $400,000.[35]

The new Bookstop opened on September 30, 1984. The store quickly became a popular spot because of its unique atmosphere, vast selection, discounts on all books, and midnight closing time. It also became something of a pickup spot for literary types.

Barnes and Noble bought the Bookstop chain in 1989. The Alabama Bookstop underwent another renovation in 1993, expanding out to the alleyway to the left of the theatre. The balcony was finally converted into retail space and an espresso bar, allowing customers and students to sip their coffee while browsing through a book or magazine. Tables and chairs were set along the balcony ridge overlooking the main floor and in other nooks and halls throughout the theatre. Once completed, the remodeling greatly enhanced the look of the old theatre space.[36] The old balcony seats were donated to Stages Repertory Theatre for its restoration of the historic Star Engraving Building.[37]

As of this writing, the Bookstop is still operational. As a remodeled former cinema, it is more appreciated now than it was during its final years as a movie house. The *Houston Press* acknowledged its appeal in the 1999 "Best of Houston" issue, describing it as one of the best bookstores for poetry: "Bookstop is the upscale boho dream shop in the upscale boho dream shopping strip. Plus, the good vibes left over from the many years of midnight *Rocky Horror Picture Show* screenings permeate the corporate bookstore atmosphere."[38]

Still, the July 22, 2006, issue of the *Houston Chronicle* cast doubt on the former theatre's continued existence, along with that of the nearby River Oaks Theatre (see Chapter 8 for a full account of their possible demolition).

THE ALMEDA
5614 *Almeda*

The success of the Alabama was followed up eleven months later with the unveiling of the smaller Almeda. A burst of fireworks marked the August 3, 1940 opening, along with the Hope and Crosby feature *Road to Singapore*.[39]

The property for the 1,000-seat theatre had been acquired through Isadore Adelman, who was responsible for the Delman on Main as well as the Interstate Tower. He sold part of the land to Interstate for the project and became a partner in the construction. Architectural chores were handled by the Houston firm of MacKie & Kamrath, which was a strong proponent of Frank Lloyd Wright's organic style of architecture.[40]

The Almeda ceased operations as a theatre around 1956. It quickly found new life as the Fred Astaire Dance Studio (1958–1964), and as the Prayer Temple Church in the later sixties. In its final years it served as an African American nightclub, then was razed in the eighties.[41]

AS THE NUMBER of theatres in the Interstate empire continued to grow, so did the number of its employees. Hoblitzelle set up employment standards that

were both generous and ahead of their time. "The entertainment industry," said Hoblitzelle, "more than any other business, is built upon good relations with the public. And your public relations can be no better than the relationship that exists between a company and its employees."[42]

He established a sliding vacation scale, allowing a week's vacation for each year worked, with up to three weeks paid and an extra week paid for those who had been with the company more than three years. Also set up was a holiday profit-sharing plan in which 10 percent of the profits were put into a bonus fund and paid at Christmas time. A loan fund was available for times of sickness or death, a general employee's welfare fund covered major emergencies, and Interstate paid a major part of the group insurance premium. Using the welfare fund, the company paid twenty-five dollars to each employee who became a parent. An additional provision,

Opening night at the Almeda Theatre, 1940. Collection of Roy Bonario, courtesy of the Center for American History, University of Texas at Austin.

set up during the war years, paid double if the parent was in the military. A leave-of-absence provision for college was also established for those wishing to resume their education.[43]

THE VILLAGE
2412 *University*

On Sunday, April 27, 1941, the *Houston Post* ran a picture of a steel framework under construction by the George P. O'Rourke Construction Company—the beginnings of the Interstate Village Theatre. Five decades later, on January 7, 1994, the same newspaper ran a photo of the same iron structure. This time the movie house was coming down. Between those two dates lie its fifty-two years of history.

Interstate again contracted the Houston firm of Mackie & Kamrath, which had worked on the Almeda the previous year. The 960-seat Village included a giant glass candy counter and a bright neon facade that could be seen from blocks away. It was this design that won a top industry design award in 1944. This was to be the last Interstate movie house to open in Houston before America's entry into World War II.[44]

The theatre opened on August 15, 1941, with the Hope and Crosby film *Road to Zanzibar* and remained a stable neighborhood theatre for many years.[45] Featured films ranged from *That Hamilton Woman* (1941) and *Barry Lyndon* (1975) to *Jaws* (1975) and the Joe Cocker concert feature, *Mad Dogs & Englishmen* (1971).

During Christmas 1973, screams echoed off the walls when the theatre hosted an exclusive road show of William

Friedkin's *The Exorcist*. According to a theatre spokesman, *The Exorcist* made more money at the Village that first week than any other movie in the history of movies in Houston.[46]

By 1978, the Village had become an X-rated movie house under the operation of the Universal Amusement Co., which also owned the Art Cinema at the other end of the Village center. On August 8, 1978, actress Leslie Bovee (real name Leslie Wahner) made a special live appearance to promote her film *Sex World*. She was arrested by the police while performing onstage and charged with indecent and immoral dancing. She declined to dance

The Village Theatre, 1945. Collection of Roy Bonario, courtesy of the Center for American History, University of Texas at Austin.

as scheduled on the following day.[47] A separate raid was staged on September 23, 1983, after the police received an anonymous letter stating that wild orgies were rampant in the balcony. Arrested for public lewdness were fourteen patrons and one employee.[48]

Local residents tried to shut down what they saw as a disgrace to their community. The city council listened to their grievances, and by 1984 an ordinance was passed that required any such adult-oriented business to pay a $350 permit fee. In addition, no sexually oriented business could be established within 750 feet of a school or church or within 1,000 feet of any other similar business.[49]

The community finally won out in 1987. The Oceanic Development Corp., which owned the theatre, bought out the remainder of the lease from Universal. All of Universal's other theatres, including the Art Cinema, had already closed down as the X houses fell victim to the ready availability of porn on home video. The last gasp of the Village took place on February 18, 1987. A raucous crowd of applauding kids, most likely Rice students, filled the house for the final two films: *Nibblers* and *A Taste of Money*. The theatre doors were then closed for good.[50]

After a period of sitting dormant, the property was acquired by Rice University. Plans were drawn up for a major reconstruction of the central Village shopping district, which would have required the demolition of the Village Theatre and neighboring buildings.[51] Several preservation groups expressed a desire to save the cinema. Their concerns were politely rebuked.

Jerry Bryant spearheaded an effort to save the theatre. While film director

for local TV station KTXH, Bryant had gained national attention for his film-restoration projects. In January 1993 he formed Cinemamento, a nonprofit organization whose goal was to save the Village. He assembled an impressive board of advisers, which included film critics Leonard Maltin and Robert Osborne, film-restoration specialist Robert Harris, MCA TV senior vice president Bill Vrbanic, and Fox Video director of research Bart Pierce.

Bryant's strategy was to seek $250,000 in corporate funding for the restoration process. The renovated theatre would host theatrical and musical performances, movies, civic affairs, and gatherings of Rice students.[52]

Rice and Weingarten were not receptive. To complicate matters, a city moratorium on the destruction of historic structures had been enacted by Mayor Lanier's administration a few years earlier. The theatre qualified for that protection because the Texas Historical Commission had declared it eligible for listing on the National Register of Historic Places.[53] Rice asked the state to remove the building from the list. That request was refused, so the university waited for the moratorium to run out.[54]

The moratorium expired on January 1, 1994. By January 15, the Village was gone. Also lost was the adjoining building, home to the World Toy Store, a demolition that caused as much consternation as that of the theatre. Originally opened by Adelaide Friedman and Rose Behar in 1953, the store had over the years become a local landmark as well as a magnet for toy collectors nationwide. At the time of the store's closing, Friedman was eighty-three; Behar had died the previous

December at eighty-one.[55] Phase two of the Village Arcade was finished in 1995.

THE WAYSIDE
3236 *Telephone Road*

With a screening of the Bob Hope feature *Louisiana Purchase*, Interstate opened the Wayside Theatre on April 24, 1942. The lobby featured a unique refreshment bar. During the short life of the concession fountain, patrons could get vanilla shakes and chocolate malts.[56]

The Wayside fared little better than some of its Interstate brethren, closing down in 1957 after some fifteen years of service. It was later converted into the Jimmy Menutis Lounge and Club for a short time before being razed.

When the Wayside opened, the world was a gloomy place, and the banners, lights, and festivities offered a brief reprieve from the news of the day. Movies offered the escapism that people wanted in order to forget the fighting overseas, yet the war remained in the forefront, even in the fantasyland of the theatre.

INTERSTATE DURING WARTIME

The American way of life changed radically during World War II. Truth and propaganda ran together in the news as well as in entertainment, and buying war bonds became the recommended use for income.

Well before America's entry into the war, Hoblitzelle had taken steps to aid those abroad. In 1940 he channeled one day's receipts from all Interstate theatres into aid for Jewish relief, raising $40,000

for the cause. The same year, he assembled twenty-five of Dallas's top leaders and laid out plans for a mass meeting to alert Americans to the Nazi threat. The gathering, some 25,000 strong, was held five days later to approve resolutions vital for the troubles abroad: repeal of legislation in order to offer all assistance—short of joining the war—to Great Britain and France; a reaffirmation of American principles; stopping the shipment of materials to those countries sympathetic to the "enemies of democracy"; providing material and moral support for those working against un-American activities; and requesting Congress to appropriate $50 million for refugee relief.[57]

The Wayside Theatre, 1944. Collection of Roy Bonario, courtesy of the Center for American History, University of Texas at Austin.

Then came Pearl Harbor. On December 7, 1941, an order was sent from the Interstate executive department to all Interstate theatre managers: "Drop everything and throw your whole effort into winning the war."[58]

Not since the days of the Depression were theatres used to such a degree. War bonds, sold in theatres across the nation, raised hundreds of millions of dollars. In many movie houses, a bond purchase served as admission to a movie. Hoblitzelle saw to it that movie premieres and live appearances by stars of both stage and screen were used to increase bond sales. As in the Depression, there were days when goods—a can of food, clothing, scrap iron, or tin cans—served as admission tickets; these items were used to aid either U.S. stockpiles of war materiel or those in need of food and clothing.[59]

In 1942 the U.S. treasury secretary asked the movie-theatre industry to take charge of the Fifth War Loan Drive. R. J. O'Donnell took the role of national chairman, spending over fourteen days touring film-distribution centers across the nation during the day and sleeping in airplanes at night.[60]

Interstate sent units to Texas army camps to entertain the thousands of soldiers in training as well as the wounded returning from overseas. The same year, Hoblitzelle was approached by mothers of servicemen abroad, frustrated over war delays, strikes at home, and personal and corporate greed. Repeating an earlier tactic, he assembled key Dallas figures and organized a citizens' rally of 5,000 people. "This is not a meeting," exclaimed Hoblitzelle to the crowd calling for action, "to direct any organized indignation at any

particular group, but to express the public sentiment so the President and Texas Representatives at Washington may know that the people of Texas will not tolerate further delay in matters involving the nation's safety. Too much time has been lost already and the whole nation is aware of it. The time for talking is over and the time for action is at hand."[61]

The group passed resolutions demanding the following: a law for cooperation by both management and labor in all essential industries to achieve total war production; a law that prohibited labor strikes and management lockouts and subjected anyone involved in such actions to be immediately drafted into either industry or the military; and a program to encourage worker contributions and prevent excess war profits.

With the end of the war, Americans came back from the front and life began to return to some sense of normalcy. In 1946, Interstate resumed its Houston construction blitz, beginning with the Santa Rosa. The expansion would be short-lived. Only four more Interstate houses would be built before the government stepped in and imposed strict guidelines on how major theatre chains could do business.[62]

THE SANTA ROSA
5607 *Telephone Road*

The Santa Rosa was Interstate's first postwar construction in Houston, and *Canyon Passage* was the December 20, 1946, debut feature. The following morning was set aside for the usual three-hour kiddie program.[63]

The Dallas architects Pettigrew and

Worley were contracted to handle the Santa Rosa project, and would go on to design the Broadway, the Fulton, and the Garden Oaks. The firm had previously worked on the River Oaks theatre, and John A. Worley had handled the Alabama design.[64]

In 1976, the theatre was sold to Al Zarzana, who also operated the Granada and Garden Oaks theatres as Spanish-language movie houses.[65] Zarzana eventually sold the theatre to the MGH Corporation, which changed the theatre's name to the Star and its specialization to X-rated features. With the advent of home video, the Star became a combination video-film adult theatre: the auditorium served up sex on the screen, and the lobby was converted into a video-rental area filled with aisles of saucy VHS tapes. The theatre continued to serve up adult entertainment throughout the nineties.

The Santa Rosa Theatre, 1946. Collection of Al Zarzana, courtesy of the Center for American History, University of Texas at Austin, e_bb_1777.

The unique circular lobby of the Santa Rosa. Collection of Al Zarzana, courtesy of the Center for American History, University of Texas at Austin, e_bb_1886.

ter, an innovation that would gain more prominence over the years. Entering the terrazzo-floored lobby, patrons were greeted by the music of Norma Ballard (the "virtuoso of the electric organ"). Ballard had previously performed in an extended run at the Metropolitan Theatre, and would subsequently appear at the Garden Oaks and Fulton openings.

The auditorium, with a seating capacity of 1,200, was decorated with floral wall murals by Dallas artist Eugene Gilboe.[66] Managing the theatre was L. C. Newton, previously the manager of the Wayside as well as of the original Broadway Theatre.

The Broadway remained a part of the Interstate circuit for only a short time. After the 1952 antitrust ruling, the theatre was sold to William O'Donnell, along with the Yale, and managed by Alvin Guggenheim. As with the Yale and others, the neighborhood surrounding the Broadway changed over the following years, thus affecting the theatre's bottom line. It was condemned in the early seventies for highway right of way, and closed on January 1, 1972, the same day the Yale closed.[67]

The Broadway Theatre at the time of its opening, 1947. Collection of Roy Bonario, courtesy of the Center for American History, University of Texas at Austin, e_bb_1532.

Auditorium of the Broadway in later years. Courtesy of Alvin Guggenheim.

THE BROADWAY
1325 *Broadway*

By the time that the Broadway opened, Interstate was operating fifteen other theatres in the Houston area. The doors opened on May 25, 1947, with the Disney feature *Song of the South*.

The exterior, decorated with green structural glass and enameled porcelain, featured a cashier's booth located to the left of the entrance instead of in the cen-

THE GARDEN OAKS
3750 *North Shepherd*

Less than two months after opening the Broadway, Interstate unveiled its second of three theatres for 1947: the 1,000-seat Garden Oaks. The grand opening took place on July 10, 1947, with the Spencer Tracy–Katharine Hepburn film *The Sea of Grass*.[68]

The Garden Oaks marquee, with bright flashing lines of orange, blue, and red neon, towered over the orange terrazzo entry and a tiled theatre front, its partial-turret ticket booth jutting from a corner.

Its lobby, considered large by later standards, featured an extra-high ceiling, a balcony staircase going up one sidewall, a massive candy counter, and large murals on the walls. The murals, having fallen victim to disrepair and water leaks, would, unfortunately, be painted over in later decades.[69] The sidewalls of the spacious auditorium also featured floral wall murals,which, unlike the lobby paintings, survived into the nineties.

In May 1975, ABC Interstate sold the Garden Oaks to Al Zarzana, who owned and operated the Granada and the Santa Rosa and at one time had ushered at the Garden Oaks.[70] His first double bill paired *The Texas Chainsaw Massacre* with Bruce Lee's *Return of the Dragon*.[71]

By 1987, economic hardships had forced Zarzana to take the inevitable step toward twinning the theatre. Unwilling to destroy the architectural integrity of the main auditorium, he converted office space alongside the theatre into a 300-seat auditorium, which opened on November 6 of that year. Patrons that week had a choice between *La Bamba* or *Robocop*, either one for a mere dollar.[72] He soon took to running Spanish-language films in the smaller auditorium. These screenings

The Garden Oaks Theatre, 1949. Collection of Roy Bonario, courtesy of the Center for American History, University of Texas at Austin, e_bb_1586.

Auditorium of the Garden Oaks, 1984. Courtesy of Al Zarzana.

quickly became his "bread and butter," doing better business than those in his main house. Eventually he began running English-language films with Spanish subtitles in the large auditorium, which helped business somewhat, but he had

As a dollar house, the Garden Oaks did brisk business, especially with blockbusters such as Jaws, 1975. Courtesy of Al Zarzana.

difficulties finding a steady supply of subtitled features.

The early nineties brought another hardship to the Garden Oaks: an eighteen-month road construction project that reduced Shepherd Drive, directly in front of the theatre, to rubble. Said Zarzana in a 1992 interview, "Basically, we have been struggling just to exist for the past 10 years. Then they had Shepherd completely torn up for almost two years and it just about did us in." The work was completed in the first part of 1992.[73]

The Garden Oaks garnered some much-needed attention from a pair of articles that ran in local papers. The July 1992 issue of *The Leader* covered Zarzana's attempts to keep the theatre operational. By this time, the movie house had acquired the distinction of being the only privately owned, independent theatre in the city.[74]

The Leader article was followed by a February 1993 *Houston Post* story focusing on Houston's various battles for building preservation.[75]

173

A final attempt by Zarzana to show second-run English-language films did little to help, and the building was then subleased to another group during its last year of operation. The Garden Oaks finally closed down in the first part of 1994, the marquee reading, "THAT'S ALL FOLKS." Zarzana leased the theatre to a Spanish-language church, and with the new century, he sold it to Evangelistic Temple, a nondenominational English-language church.

THE FULTON
3310 *Fulton*

The last of Interstate's 1947 theatre triad opened on September 26. The first feature was the Eddie Bracken–Priscilla Lane film *Fun on a Weekend*, along with a Donald Duck cartoon and Pete Smith's *Football Thrills No. 10*. The next morning, the children's fun club featured Roy Rogers in *Don't Fence Me In*, cartoons, the last chapters of the serials *The Black Widow* and *The Scarlet Horseman*, and a live appearance by ventriloquist Chester LeRoy.[76]

The Fulton operated for less than ten years. By 1958 it had become the Fulton Bowlers Lanes, lasting as a venue for keglers through the better part of the sixties; by 1969 it had changed again, this time to the Stardust Ballroom.[77] In the early eighties it once more became a movie theatre, this time under the name of the Cine Colonial, running Spanish-language films. It was eventually razed, and the property is now occupied by the Clemente Martinez Elementary School.

THE CONSENT DECREE

It had long been felt by the independents that the major film studios, which supplied their product only to theatres that they owned, had established an unfair monopoly. The small-time theatre owners, struggling on a diet of second-run fare, lacked leverage against the theatrical Goliaths.

In 1938 the Department of Justice filed suit against the majors, alleging illegal restraint of trade. After a decade of legal wrangling by the two sides in lower courts, the Supreme Court voted unanimously that Paramount and four other studios constituted an illegal trust. The 1948 ruling found that the "Big Five" studios—Paramount, Loew's/MGM, RKO, Twentieth Century–Fox, and Warner Bros.—along with the "Little Three"—Columbia, Universal, and United Artists—had established unfair control of production, distribution, and exhibition. Under this ruling, the studios agreed to divest themselves of their theatres, which would be sold to independent operators. Films were to be rented on a picture-by-picture, theatre-by-theatre basis.[78]

The effects of this ruling can still be felt today. Without the incentive to keep a yearlong flow of product in theatres, which were no longer their own, studios began to schedule their top films for peak seasons, namely, summer and the Christmas holidays. And while the consent decree ostensibly favored the independents, it created a whole new set of obstacles to be overcome. The studios and distributors found new ways to rake in high profits at the expense of the the-

The Fulton Theatre, 1947. Courtesy of the Houston Metropolitan Research Center, Houston Public Library, MSS 114-1971.

Circuit along with Texas Consolidated Theatres became part of the ABC organization, thus bringing a forty-year chapter of its existence to a close. With this amalgamation, the Interstate chain, which had grown steadily since its 1905 origins, suddenly hit a federal impasse. Its ownership of almost all the major movie venues in town, including the premium downtown palaces, its methods of obtaining films through the distribution line, and its ABC connection all served to place Hoblitzelle in a similar position as the major studios. The path was clear: Interstate would have to divest itself of some of its movie houses. "We had 21 theatres at one time," remembered Al Lever, "but the federal government action forced us to relinquish about half of them."[79]

Neighborhood movie houses were sold off and partnerships severed. With the exception of two drive-ins—the Shepherd and the South Main—Interstate added no new venues to its roster through the mid-sixties as other interested parties scooped up the relinquished theatres. The North Main, Eastwood, Yale, Almeda, Wayside, Bluebonnet, Broadway, University, and Fulton would all disappear from the Interstate listings, either through sell-offs or closures.

In its new incarnation, Interstate would continue to operate into the seventies. However, the true glory days of Hoblitzelle's multistate theatrical chain—from the time of the early movie houses to the pinnacle of Eberson's atmospheric Majestic and two decades worth of neighborhood expansion—had come to an end.

atres, such as the 90–10 split, in which 90 percent of gross ticket sales are returned to the distributor. Ticket prices went up, which caused more patrons to stay away, at a time when television was already beginning to affect business adversely.

In December 1949, the Interstate

Originally named the Olympia Opera House (1903), and then the Standard, it was best known as the Lincoln Theatre, seen here c. 1941. Courtesy of the Sloane Collection, Houston, Texas.

TEN

★ ★ ★

JIM CROW AND
THE ETHNIC THEATRE

★ ★ ★

Those who deny freedom to others, deserve it not for themselves.

ABRAHAM LINCOLN, 1859

There is no more evil thing in this present world than race prejudice . . . It justifies and holds together more baseness, cruelty, and abomination than any other sort of error in the world.

H. G. WELLS, 1907

★ THE HOUSTON OF 1928 boasted a multitude of downtown movie theatres, including the grand expanses of the Majestic, Metropolitan, Loew's State, and Kirby. Patrons could experience a motion picture in opulent, catered comfort while resting on soft, comfortable seats positioned for optimal viewing. The lobbies, designed like princely palaces, allowed customers to enjoy a touch of the regal while escaping the intense Texas heat for a few hours.

But if a patron happened to be black, such accommodations counted for nothing; luxuries were severely curtailed, or shut off altogether, because the pleasures granted to white patrons at the theatre, as in other places, did not apply to African Americans. Not until the mid to late sixties, when the civil rights movement successfully pushed through legal reforms, culminating in the enactment of the Civil Rights Act of 1964, would many Houstonians be able to enter a theatre and sit where they pleased, whenever they pleased. Until then, they would have to deal with segregated areas, separate screenings, and minority theatres.

In 1928, Houston had six black-oriented theatres and two theatres that catered to Mexican Americans. The ethnic theatre would be a constant for the following decades, continuing well past 1964, when anyone could attend whatever cinema he or she wished. Eventually, these theatres would come to include the so-called blaxploitation houses as well as the foreign-language houses for Hispanic, Indian, and Asian audiences.

In the first half of the twentieth century, doors were not open to blacks in most theatres, restaurants, or hotels. Although the Civil War had ended slavery, much of the United States became a legally segregated society, especially in the South. The 1880s saw a number of court decisions that narrowed the scope of the Fourteenth and Fifteenth Amendments to the Constitution, including the 1883 judgment by the U.S. Supreme Court in *Civil Rights Cases*, which allowed for private discrimination, including the exclusion of blacks by theatre owners. States quickly enacted laws that supported such actions.[1]

In 1876, the Texas Constitution had legally imposed school segregation, and other laws brought about statewide segregation on railroads in 1891. While Houston did not pass a comprehensive set of laws controlling black behavior, those enacted merely reinforced the existing

social order. A 1903 city ordinance segregated streetcars, followed in 1907 by one that covered public facilities—hotels, theatres, and restaurants. The end result was a total division of the races.[2]

The policies established by the theatre industry followed these standards in several ways. Some set up separate screenings, either on certain days or at certain times. The midnight movie originated partly during this time, when late-night showings would be held for black audiences. More commonly, owners would set aside a segregated area, usually in the theatre rear or balcony, the latter sometimes called the "buzzard roost" or the "peanut gallery." To add more distance, many of these theatres would have separate side or back entrances leading directly to the designated areas.[3] For example, the Isis, when it opened in Houston in 1912, incorporated the following blurb in its local paper publicity:

The entire lower floor exclusively reserved for white patrons. Balcony for colored, with separate entrance and exits. The most luxuriously comfortable opera chairs available. Nothing is too good for patrons of the Isis.[4]

While there was no indication of where the "comfortable opera chairs" were located, it is unlikely that they were to be found in the balcony. Instead of through luxurious lobbies and mezzanines, blacks would enter from a separate door, sometimes nothing more than a fire escape, to reach the balcony area. This was the standard for most mainstream theatres, and such second-class treatment was a way of life for most African Americans.

The consideration of race in theatres

was not just a southern prejudice. For those in business, it was a real concern, a matter of dollars more than individual rights. In *The Motion Picture Handbook for Managers and Operators*, a 1910 guide to operating theatres, movie-house owners were urged to accede completely to common prejudices:

> *The matter of race (nationality) must be looked after carefully, since some sections may be peopled almost exclusively by any one of half a dozen foreign-speaking nationalities. This, under some conditions, might prove disastrous. Take the lower-class Italians. If any considerable number of them patronized your house you would have to look to them entirely for your revenue, since a house patronized by any number of them will have to depend on them alone for support. Any considerable number*

> *of Negroes will queer a house with all other races; and there are other races to which you must cater exclusively or not at all, so that the matter deserves close investigation when seeking a city nickel theatre site.[5]*

On a rare occasion, segregation policies would be overridden. In his 1976 autobiography, Cab Calloway described touring throughout Texas and the vast crowds he drew. During his Houston dates at the Majestic Theatre, midnight shows were added to the four a day already scheduled, yet the box office was still turning people away. After the fourth day, the management had to open up the mezzanine to blacks to accommodate the crowd, the first time that the Majestic had done such a thing. It was, as Calloway described it, "the power of the buck . . . You put up $10,000 profit up in front of a man's face, even in a town as segregated as Houston was in those days, and the man will open doors quicker than you can blink."[6]

Given these restrictive policies, separate, ethnic theatres were a welcome alternative, even though they did not offer the comfort level or the first-run features of the major houses. The first of these was perhaps the finest, and although razed in 1977, it survived longer than any other.

THE LINCOLN/OLYMPIA OPERA HOUSE/STANDARD/TEXAN/ MAJESTIC
711 *Prairie*

The Lincoln was originally opened in 1903 as the Olympia Opera House, then later changed names to the Standard, and eventually became a brewery warehouse (see Chapter 2 for a detailed account of its initial history).

In 1916 several black entrepreneurs bought the building, converted it back into a theatre, and added two floors of offices above the lobby. This became an early black professional building, housing lawyers, dentists, and insurance agents. Several fraternities had offices there as well: the King Solomon Grand Lodge and the Queen Esther Grand Chapter of the Eastern Star. The theatre was operated by O. P. DeWalt, a real estate agent who also worked from the building.

As the Lincoln, it ran a variety of "all colored" silent films, usually from the Foster Photoplay Company and the Lincoln Motion Picture Company. A black-oriented movie would surface from the

major studios every once in a while, but these were rare. Occasionally a live performance would be thrown in for free, such as one by actor Stepin Fetchit, who performed there in the late twenties.[7] Friday- and Saturday-afternoon westerns were popular with the kids, who took in a steady dose of Tom Mix, Buck Allen, and John Wayne.[8]

"I guess he was the first black theatre operator in Houston," recalled DeWalt's son, Olen P. DeWalt, Jr., in the 1998 KHOU-TV documentary *Houston Remembers*. "The owners wanted it for colored people, back in those days. And he insisted in trying to operate it, but the owners said that it was a colored theatre, but they wanted it under white management. He persisted, and they threw him out one time, but he kept going back." The management eventually gave him a chance as manager. DeWalt ran the theatre, tearing tickets as well, while his wife worked the box office. "On several occasions, he had the children in free," continued DeWalt. "Showed how he appreciated the patrons and that was called appreciation day."[9]

In 1921, the local censor board banned several movies starring Galveston boxer Jack Johnson. The films—*The World Runs On* and *The Black Thunderbolt*—featured Johnson on-screen with white actors. In addition, the promotional handbills, called dodgers, were considered "incendiary and inflammatory." Johnson was the first black man to win the heavyweight boxing title—at a time when boxing was illegal in Texas—and would eventually be inducted into the Texas Sports Hall of Fame (1971) and the International Boxing Hall of Fame (1990).[10]

Front and rear views of the Lincoln auditorium. Courtesy of the Sloane Collection, Houston, Texas.

DeWalt was born near Livingston in 1886, and graduated with honors in 1910 from what would eventually become Prairie View A&M. After moving to Houston, he worked as a real estate agent and briefly as a principal of the Independence Heights School. (In 1915, Independence Heights, northeast of Houston, became the first incorporated African American city in Texas.) In 1913 he married Maud Pernetter and had one son. When the first Texas chapter of the National Association for the Advancement of Colored People (NAACP) was formed in Houston in 1912, DeWalt became a charter member, and later served as its president. As a civil rights leader, he stood up to the Ku Klux Klan and worked to establish a branch of the National Urban League in Houston. He was assassinated in the Lincoln theatre on April 24, 1931.[11]

After DeWalt's death, his widow managed the theatre for a brief time. Most of the offices in the building were vacant by the middle thirties, except for one occupied by a dentist who stayed there through the early seventies. When the talkies evolved, the Lincoln featured melodramas produced by Oscar Micheaux, who directed black films through the late forties.

Many of the black theatres began to disappear from black neighborhoods in the late fifties. By the middle sixties, the Lincoln had changed its name to the Texan, running grind action pictures. This format eventually gave way to softcore porn, and by 1970 the theatre was vacant.

The rise of suburban multicinemas lured white audiences away, leaving downtown theatres barren. However, a new film genre brought fresh life to the theatre giants: blaxploitation. Films like *Shaft* (1971), *Superfly* (1972), and *Blacula* (1972) as well as movies fueled by the kung fu craze all proved to be incredibly popular. So it was that the old Lincoln came under the control of exhibitor Alvin Guggenheim.[12]

The Guggenheim Empire

Alvin Guggenheim began his association with the movies before World War II, when he worked as an usher at the downtown Majestic on Rusk. By the age of sixteen, he had worked his way up to manager in the Interstate theatre circuit. After a brief stint in the U.S. Army in Europe during the war, he returned to work again for Interstate. Eventually he would leave to become city manager for Cinema Arts Theatres. "I worked at the Metropolitan," said Guggenheim in a 1994 interview, "then went to the Yale as manager. Bill O'Donnell bought the Yale from Interstate, and I worked there until I bought a theatre myself."[13]

Sensing a lucrative market, Guggenheim leased the old Lincoln in 1972 and invested $12,000 in remodeling. He then renamed it the Majestic, after the grand Interstate palace of his youth. Under his control, the new Majestic became one of the most successful downtown theatres in the seventies, running a steady stream of chop-socky, kung fu, action, horror, and blaxploitation features, hits like *Greased Lightning* (1977) and *Fists of Fury* (1971). The Majestic, he claimed at the time, was one of the most successful black-oriented theatres in the Southwest.

Houston Chronicle writer Barbara

Cleland made note of the reopening in June 1972, and how this Majestic recaptured "the flavor of old-time movie houses with red cloth-draped walls and replica chandeliers." Describing it as an intimate theatre of 600 seats, she added that it "definitely has more character than many modern movie houses–but less padding on the seats."[14]

Looking to expand his base, Guggenheim reopened several more theatres, again rechristening them under the Majestic banner. In 1973, the former O.S.T. Theatre on Old Spanish Trail opened its doors as the Majestic O.S.T. The following year, he reopened the old Ritz on Preston as the Majestic Metro. The Brazos Twin and the Long Point Cinema, formerly the Oak Village, also came under his control. He would eventually own and operate nineteen Texas theatres. Simultaneously, he started handling promotional appearance tours for the studios, a move that allowed Alvin Guggenheim and Associates to expand to Kansas City in 1971 and New Orleans in 1972.

Longtime associate Gerri Frasier began her work with Guggenheim at age sixteen, working the concession stand at the Yale. "Alvin just knew everyone," she said in a 1997 *Houston Chronicle* interview, "and the film companies would call him to set up itineraries for their stars." Up-and-coming performers such as Clint Eastwood and Jack Nicholson made promo stops in Houston through Guggenheim's arrangement. Over the years, his offices would come to be lined with autographed publicity stills of the stars who passed through his theatres. Guggenheim and Associates would eventually include his sons Alvin, Jr., Bill, and Bob.[15]

The Lincoln's Last Days

As the days of *Cleopatra Jones* and *Superfly* ebbed, so did the downtown theatres. Houston's final Majestic era came to an end, beginning with the closing of the Majestic on Prairie when Guggenheim's lease ran out. Its last features were *Cornbread, Earl and Me, Cooley High,* and *Sheba Baby,* all shown for a dollar on Sunday, September 11, 1977.[16] The Majestic O.S.T. and the Majestic Metro closed their doors around 1984,

The Rainbow Theatre, c. early 1940s. Courtesy of the Houston Metropolitan Research Center, Houston Public Library, MSS 210.

the latter having spent its final days as a porn house.

"Alvin was probably the last of that generation of movie publicists," said *Houston Chronicle* film critic Jeff Millar in 1997, "when hoopla was hoopla. That era of publicity that was still hanging on before the corporate bean counters of the motion picture world today."[17]

Alvin Guggenheim died in June 1997.

By the end of its years, the old Lincoln/Majestic was considered a dump. The upstairs office space had gone unoccupied for the last forty years. Many of the remaining details in the auditorium—a bas-relief of Lincoln on the wall, cast-plaster ceiling filigrees, and smiling gargoyles—were covered by layers of acoustical paint. The original 1916 lobby ceiling remained covered by a more recent dropped ceiling. The auditorium smelled, and rats could be spotted in the aisles. All this, hidden away in the dark, was demolished in late September 1977.[18]

MINORITY AUDIENCES had other theatres to choose from besides the Lincoln. The 1915 edition of the *Red Book of Houston* (a 150-page "compendium of social, professional, religious, educational interests" for Houston's black population) listed the New Sun Set Theatre, at 711 San Felipe, as one.[19] In 1918, patrons could attend the Odin Theatre, at 2705 Odin Avenue. The 1928 *Motion Picture Trade Directory* listed six Houston black-oriented theatres: the Lincoln, the Parkview, the Pastime, the St. Elmo, the

Washington, and the Zoe. An additional two theatres, the Azteca and Hidalgo, were oriented toward Mexican American audiences.[20]

Both the Pastime, at 2514 McKinney, and the St. Elmo, at 711 West Dallas, were under the management of Harry Schulman. The Pastime originated around 1917 under the name of the Beacon Theatre, and would survive through the 1940s. The St. Elmo lasted from around 1918 to the midthirties. Paul Barraco managed the Washington. The Zoe, at 502 1/2 Milam, was operated by A. Silverberg and Son.

Later came the Holman, the Rainbow, and the Deluxe. The Holman, at 3400 Holman, entertained the masses through 1949, while the Rainbow, at 909 West Dallas, remained open for a decade longer. The Deluxe, at 3301 Lyons, was owned by Mitchell M. Lewis, who also operated the Holman, Lyons, and Park theatres. It stayed in operation through the end of the sixties. While the structure survived into

the new century, it had been abandoned for years.

Segregated movie houses spurred the development of a black film industry. Unlike the stereotypically uncomplimentary portrayals that were seen in most Hollywood features, the African Americans shown in these films were part of well-developed character studies that covered all aspects of the black experience. What these films lacked in budget, they made up for in story line and intent. Many of these, such as the films of Oscar Micheaux, have become classics in their own right.

Even after civil rights legislation of the 1960s eliminated the necessity of their existence, a number of neighborhood ethnic theatres remained in operation because of the demand of patrons in the surrounding area. Yet as the decades passed, residential patterns continued to shift. The Fourth Ward, where the West Dallas area serviced over 95 percent of the businesses owned by blacks, was the economic center for the black community up through the midthirties. The focus then slowly shifted over to the Fifth Ward, especially around Lyons and Jensen Drive, where activity hit a peak in the early fifties. The pattern then shifted to the southern part of the city as well as to the Third Ward.

Many of the black-oriented theatres were located in the Fifth Ward, where Lyons Avenue hosted the Washington/Roxy, Deluxe, Lyons, and Globe. Lyons Avenue had originally been named Odin Avenue, after Bishop John Mary Odin, the first bishop of the Catholic Diocese of Galveston. In a touch of irony, the street was renamed Lyons Avenue around 1935

The remains of the Deluxe. Courtesy of James E. Fisher.

in honor of the saloon magnate John Lyons.[21]

When the Washington opened around 1920, the street was called by its original name. By 1926, the address had changed from 2711 to 2737 Odin Avenue. Around 1937, the Washington had changed its name to the Roxy, and would remain operational under that name through the midsixties. Little currently remains of the city block where the theatre once stood.

In *Sig Byrd's Houston*, writer Sigman Byrd tells of a young black preacher dressed in a blue denim shirt, dungarees covered with large patches of red gingham, gentle but empty eyes, and long hair sticking out in all directions. The man went by the name "Monkey-Bit," and was a familiar sight in the area. He acquired the nickname after a mishap at the Washington when a jungle feature was playing. Several monkey cages had been set outside for promotion, and the preacher almost got his thumb bit off after sticking his hand in the cage. Said Byrd, "Monkey-Bit never was the same again."[22]

The Lyons, at 4036 Lyons, opened around 1940 and operated through 1958. The building still stands, now functioning as the Latter Day Deliverance Church. The Deluxe, at 3303 Lyons, opened around 1943 or 1944, according to the *Houston Directory*, and operated through the end of the sixties. The Globe, at 6901 Lyons, opened three or four years after the Deluxe and remained open until around 1952, according to the *Houston Directory*. The building was eventually converted to retail space, operating as tire store.

A typical lineup, as indicated in a 1947 issue of the *Metropolitan Civic News*, listed the Rainbow Theatre on West Dallas as showing the Sunset Carson western *The Cherokee Flash*, along with *The Devil's Mask*. At the Roxy, patrons could see *Centennial Summer*, with Jeanne Crain, and *Shadows on the Range*, with Johnny Mack Brown. Meanwhile, the Dowling, at 2110 Dowling Street, featured Susan Hayward in *Smash-Up*.[23]

THE NAACP FOUGHT segregation through both state and federal courts throughout the fifties. Even in the face of court rulings against segregated facilities, many institutions continued to do business as they had in the past. An example of this is an interoffice letter dated June 10, 1954, from the home office of Interstate theatres to its city managers:

The Supreme Court has ruled against segregation of races in the public schools. As a result of this ruling, there is a possibility that some well-intentioned negroes [sic] will seek to

After its days as a movie house, the Lyons Theatre was converted into a church. Photograph by David Welling.

The Dowling Theatre, 1963. Courtesy of Ray M. Boriski. Auditorium of the Dowling Theatre. Courtesy of the Houston Metropolitan Research Center, Houston Public Library, MSS 210.

purchase tickets to some of our theatres in the days ahead.

It is Van Hollomon's opinion that the Supreme Court decision does not apply to theatres. Therefore, if your box office should be approached by negroes [sic] who wish to purchase tickets--you could simply say . . . "We do not cater to negro patronage at this time."

Any such incident should be handled as pleasantly as possible and the management should avoid any argument or discussion. After having made the above statement, he could thereafter simply take the position that these are his instructions from his Home Office, and that he is not in a position to explain or elaborate.[24]

Despite the efforts of the NAACP, it was not until the sixties that an upheaval took place in the structure of race relations. Student protests, court cases, direct involvement by President John F. Kennedy and Attorney General Robert Kennedy, his brother, all served to intensify the civil rights movement. Resistance was unyielding, especially in the South, and sometimes not without violence. During a 1961 convention for drive-in owners and operators in Texas, one speaker suggested that "killing them all" would be a simple remedy to the problem.[25]

In the end, the Jim Crow laws governing segregation were dismantled, thus allowing blacks an equal spot at lunch counters, restaurants, hotels, and theatres. Though other parts of the country experienced rioting and other forms of unrest, Houston made this transition in relative

calm as business leaders from both the black and white communities worked together.

The origins of this cooperation can be traced to August 1959 and the arrest of Eldrewey Stearns, a young law student at Texas Southern University. Stearns was driving home from a night job at the Doctor's Club when he was pulled over by two Houston policemen. When the officers saw a photograph of a white woman in his wallet, they arrested him for "lacking a valid driver's license." Once downtown at the police station, he was beaten by the policemen, who were joined by two other officers.

After Stearns lodged a complaint with city council, the story made front-page news, including a one-on-one interview on Channel 11 with Dan Rather, then a young Houston television reporter. More importantly, this incident served as a fuse, inciting a group of TSU students to actively protest the segregation of Houston's public lunch counters, theatres, and restaurants.[26]

Students took an in-your-face path of nonviolence to convey their message and, as a result, get arrested. They stood at the entrances of the Metropolitan, Majestic, and Loew's State theatres, attempting to buy tickets to the coveted "whites only" section. Lawyer Thurgood Marshall sent word through TSU president Samuel Nabrit that one way to get arrested was to block the theatre exit. "Well, the students wanted to get arrested, and they did just that," explained Nabrit in the documentary *The Strange Demise of Jim Crow.*[27]

While the students took their mission to the streets, a number of black business leaders acted behind the scenes in tandem with Houston's top movers and shakers, who greatly wanted to avoid the turbulence that had erupted in other cities during the first years of the sixties. Meetings took place behind closed doors and across phone lines, aimed at quietly solving the problem. Among those involved were *Houston Post* publisher Oveta Culp Hobby, Hobart Taylor, Quentin Mease, Curtis Graves, Dr. Earl Allen, Foley's executive Bob Dundas, Channel 2 president Jack Harris, Louie Welch, Roy Hofheinz, and John T. Jones (nephew of Jesse Jones). Jones was then owner of the Rice Hotel, chairman of the Houston Endowment, and owner of three downtown movie theatres.

The goal was to do it quietly; the solution was to impose a media blackout as Houston was methodically and slowly desegregated. The lunch counters were the first victory, as small groups of African Americans quietly entering, eating, and leaving--and as television, radio, and the newspapers all looked the other way.[28]

May 23, 1963, had been set as the date for an internationally televised ticker-tape parade in downtown Houston, honoring astronaut Gordon Cooper. The TSU students planned a protest around this event, announcing that their action would be halted only by the immediate desegregation of theatres and restaurants.

The theatres had already been approached on the matter, but had avoided any decision, instead passing the buck to their corporate offices in New York and Washington. Jones was in Washington that morning, scheduled to meet with the theatre executives. As former

student protestor Otis King described in *The Strange Demise of Jim Crow*, "The negotiations were going on, and I guess 11 o'clock was my fail-safe point, which was the last time the people were going to call in to ask us if it was a go. And at that point, we were to say go, and they would have passed the word to the people in the crowds, the signs would have come out from under the coats, and they would have rushed into the street."[29]

Less than an hour before the cutoff time, John Jones called Hobart Taylor and Samuel Nabrit with good news: the following Thursday, the theatres would be open to any and all patrons. Word was passed on to the students, and the parade proceeded undisturbed before a crowd of 300,000 Houstonians.

Theatres made the transition quietly, as had the lunch counters, and the media continued its blackout policy. The following year saw the passage of the Civil Rights Act, and with that, Jim Crow faded from view.

Since theatres were no longer restricted, African Americans were willing to travel longer distances, to nicer theatres outside their immediate areas. The ethnic neighborhood theatres continued to operate for a time, but most of them would eventually close down. Desegregation, the changing structure of theatrical releases, and the birth of the multicinema all played a part in their demise, and in the end, they closed for the same reasons as other neighborhood theatres did.

Some continued to operate, and other new ones came into being. The aforementioned Lincoln and Ritz theatres found new life for a short time under

the hand of Alvin Guggenheim, but by 1976, the blaxploitation craze had run its course. Fewer films were being made specifically for black audiences, and for those produced, revenues were dropping. It would be another decade before a new generation of filmmakers, including Spike Lee and John Singleton, revived the black film market with a new degree of depth and dynamics. In the process, they gave these new films something they had never before achieved–a level of equality in Hollywood.

SEGREGATION AND SIMILAR injustices were not targeted at African Americans alone; many in the Hispanic community endured the same forms of discrimination. They were, according to some blacks, "just a shade above us" in the way they were treated by the white community. While some restaurants posted signs that read "No Mexicans," others simply ignored any that entered. In a 1985 centennial edition of the *Houston Post*, a sixty-eight-year-old resident recalled her childhood: "They would not permit us in the bottom part of the the-

The well-attended Azteca Theatre. Note the ladder in the rear, the sole means of getting to the projectionist's booth. Courtesy of the Houston Metropolitan Research Center, Houston Public Library, MSS 11.

atre. They placed us up in the balcony with the colored people." Because of this form of treatment, she never went to see movies at the major downtown theatres.[30]

The Spanish-speaking community had its own series of theatres for both live entertainment and motion pictures. During the twenties, the Guadalupe Church operated a live theatre for local talent and visiting troupes, and another one was built in 1928 by the Sociedad Mutualista Benito Juarez (a Mexican American mutual aid society) in Magnolia Park. Another venue was El Salon Juarez and Teatro, at 7320 Navigation, the remnants of which still stand. The Hidalgo, which ran motion pictures, was located at 2213 Congress.[31] Yet the best known was El Teatro Azteca, the Aztec Theatre. The hall was opened in 1927 by the Sarabia family at 1809 1/2 Congress and featured live entertainment as well as motion pictures. Originally

from Guanajuato, Mexico, Socorro Sarabia arrived in Houston in 1914, and was joined by his mother, three brothers, and young sister in 1919 after their father was killed in the Mexican revolution. Once in Houston, the family played a considerable part in the development of the city's Mexican American community.

El Teatro Azteca served as one of the social hubs of the community, playing host to a number of Spanish-language celebrities on the touring circuit, as well as to vaudeville groups such as Los Hermanos Areu. In addition to vaudeville, audiences could watch silent Mexican movies throughout the twenties. After the Depression, the Congress Avenue business district began to decline, hastened by the movement of people to the suburbs. By 1957, the Azteca had closed, though it then reopened for a few more years as the Maya.

The Hispanic theatre survived well

As a Spanish-language house, the Granada packed them in when The Exorcist *was shown in the 1970s. Courtesy of Al Zarzana.*

The Bobo Lang Theatre, 1985. Photograph by Jim Koehn.

The former Liberty Hall, reopened as the Lido Theatre, 1985. Photograph by Jim Koehn.

into the later part of the century. The Ritz theatre on Preston became the Teatro Ritz, closed down, and then reopened as the Ciné Ritz, a name that was later transferred to the Fulton. The Venus, at 6515 Lyons, also turned to the Hispanic market, and continued to operate through the mideighties. The Epsom Downs Drive-In, at 9716 Jensen Drive, also converted to Spanish-language films, changing its name to the Peliculas Mexicano Auto-Cine. During this time, the Lindale would change names to the Al*Ray and feature Spanish films as well. It would later change to an X format.

The Garden Oaks Theatre, at 3750 North Shepherd, also functioned as a Spanish house. Under the control of Al Zarzana, it had struggled as a regular cinema, changing over to a dollar cinema before evolving into a venue for Spanish-language films. Eventually, it ceased showing films altogether, reopening as a Spanish-language church.

While most of the nonmainstream theatres were to be found in the African American and Mexican American communities, they were by no means the only houses in town. As other non-Caucasian groups grew over the decades, their representative theatres would take form.

Built in 1978, the Bobo Lang Theatre, at 2015 Walker, catered to the Chinese community. Its pagoda-style entrance led to a tiny lobby filled with video games and snack machines and connected to the midsize auditoriums.[32]

With recent population shifts, a newer Asian district evolved in the outlying part of Bellaire. The nearby Southwest Cinema, at 2610 Fondren, originally opened in 1972 as the Jerry Lewis Twin Cinema, then the Bijou. Later, as the Shalimar, it ran Hindi features.

The ethnic theatre has evolved with the times. Megaplex construction (and subsequent closures of the older multiplex theatres) has brought about a resurgence of such venues. Farooq Khan operated the Shalimar until its closing in 1984. In January 2004, he reopened the General Cinema West Oaks Central as the Bollywood Cinema, presenting a steady stream of South Asian films, including the restored version of the 1960 classic *Mughal-e-Azam*, considered by many to be the *Gone with the Wind* of Indian cinema. The West Bellfort cinema, formerly the Plitt Cinema 5, also played host to Bollywood fare.[33] Meanwhile, the Southmore, in Pasadena, reopened on May 18, 2005, as Cinema Latino de Pasadena, featuring dubbed and subtitled films for the Hispanic market.[34]

What is clear is that these theatres serve the same purpose now as they always have: to offer entertainment while embracing and preserving the bonds of a particular culture. The big difference now is that those who attend have a choice.

Advertisement in the Houston Post for Solomon and Sheba, December 25, 1959. By the end of the fifties — when the Uptown reopened as the Rivoli — practically every technique and gimmick had been used to lure patrons back into the nation's theatres and away from the dreaded television set.

ELEVEN

★ ★ ★

THE

FIFTIES

★ ★ ★

THE INCREDIBLE 3-D WIDE-SCREEN TECHNICOLOR STEREOPHONIC-SOUND BALLYHOO PARADE

Why should people go out and pay money to see bad films when they can stay home and see bad television for nothing?

SAMUEL GOLDWYN

★ THE FIFTIES were deadly years for the motion-picture business. In 1948, average weekly attendance at the movies was 90 million; this figure dropped by 20 million the next year, and another 10 million the next, resulting in a nearly 50 percent drop by 1953. Average weekly attendance reached its lowest mark in 1958, at 39.6 million. Theatres had movies to show, but people just weren't buying.[1]

A number of reasons contributed to this decline in attendance. Fewer films were being made, partly as a result of the aftershocks of the 1948 consent decree. Some claimed that the movies just weren't that good. Higher taxes, a rising cost of living, and the effects of the Korean War all contributed to the slump in the film industry. All this showed in the Houston attendance figures, with an estimated count of 166,000 patrons, com-

pared to the reported 195,000 in 1952.[2]

Competing diversions were also to blame for the theatres' woes. A growing interest in sports, bowling in particular, steered potential patrons away from the cinemas, as did the shift in the seasons. Winter was always a slow point, as attendance fell about 40 percent below the summer pull because of cold weather, fog, and rain as well as school. Parents tended to keep their children home on school nights and stay home themselves. Most wintertime activity tended to occur on weekends and school holidays. Some theatres, such as the O.S.T., remained closed during the week during this time, opening only for the weekend traffic.

While all these factors played a part in the attendance slump, one stood out

above them all: television. The new medium had been around as early as 1930, but by 1950 there were an estimated three million television sets in homes, and those families that didn't own one visited their neighbors who did.[3]

It was initially thought that television was a novelty, and that once it wore off, theatre attendance would again rise. This failed to occur, creating a widespread panic within the industry. It was clear that theatres had to offer more than they had in the past in order to compete.

First came color, which had existed in the movies since the beginning, initially in the form of hand-painted and tinted film. Early two-strip Technicolor found its way into feature films during the twenties, but it was the eye-popping richness of the

Wide-screen features needed big stories, thus came the epics of the period, such as King of Kings, *showing here at the Yale, c. 1961. Naturally, the bigger the movie, the bigger the promotion. Courtesy of Alvin Guggenheim.*

three-strip Technicolor of the thirties that brought the full spectrum of the rainbow to film. Television technology would eventually embrace color, and so Hollywood kept looking for other lures for the public.

Few indoor theatres were built in Houston during the fifties. The building boom had passed, the last major constructions being Interstate's Garden Oaks in 1947 and the independent Bellaire in 1949. Instead, the focus of theatre construction shifted to drive-ins as ten outdoor theatres were built during the decade, culminating in the elaborate Loew's Sharpstown Drive-In of 1958. The few listings for film and stage theatres during that time, according to the *Houston Directory*, included the Airway, at 5206 Airline, and the Centre, at 2920 Luell Street, both from 1951; the Clinton Theatre, at 9605 Clinton Drive, around 1955; and the Grand Theatre, at 12769 Market Street Road, around 1958.[4]

Wide-screen movies became the biggest hook used in the business, beginning in 1952 with those filmed in Cinerama. This elaborate three-screen system created an ultrawide image on a screen that curved 146 degrees. Showing Cinerama films meant huge expenditures for a theatre owner—outlays for extensive renovations to an auditorium, three synchronized projectors, a special louvered screen, and an elaborate sound system—yet the public fell in love with the spectacle.[5] The Rivoli, formerly the Uptown, became the first theatre in Texas to house the system, undergoing a conversion from Todd-AO equipment to Cinerama and reopening on August 25, 1960, with *This Is Cinerama*.[6] Subsequent films such as *The Wonderful World of the Brothers Grimm* and *How the West Was Won*, both released in 1962, made way for a streamlined "Super Cinerama," which managed to incorporate the whole image on one

The Airway Theatre, 5206 Airline, c. 1951. Courtesy of the Center for American History, University of Texas at Austin, e_bb_0945.

piece of film. The Rivoli never succeeded as a Cinerama theatre and spent its final days as a burlesque house. The Windsor Theatre, built specifically with Cinerama in mind, opened in 1962 with *The Brothers Grimm*.[7]

For the most part, Cinerama was far too costly and troublesome for all but a few specialized theatres. Twentieth Century–Fox offered an alternative process that proved to be more practical, requiring less initial preparation. In Cinemascope, the image is compressed on the film stock, and then expanded by use of an anamorphic lens when projected. Of all the wide-screen processes, Cinemascope became the most widely accepted, and is still in use to this day.

Despite its popularity, Cinemascope was not the only kid in town. In Paramount's VistaVision, filmed images are rotated ninety degrees and projected horizontally instead of vertically. VistaVision was introduced to Houston audiences at the Metropolitan in 1954 with *White Christmas*.

Todd-AO, named after showman Michael Todd, predated Cinerama by a few years. It was installed at the Uptown for *South Pacific* in 1958.[8] This presentation required special 70mm projection equipment to be installed; the Tower Theatre had previously made the conversion. By the following December, with the showing of the epic *Solomon and Sheba*, the Uptown had officially changed to the Rivoli.[9]

By 1961, Houston had three full-time theatres and one standby "road show" house equipped for Todd-AO motion pictures. The Tower had made the jump in 1956, for its showing of *Oklahoma!*[10] The Alabama underwent a $100,000 remodel-

ing in 1960 for the October 26 opening of *The Alamo* starring John Wayne. This was followed in December by the Delman Theatre, which spent over $50,000 in conversion costs to equip it with Todd-AO equipment. With the new system in place, the Delman held the Texas premiere of Stanley Kubrick's *Spartacus*, with Kirk Douglas.[11]

The wide-screen parade continued with a long list of other processes, or variations on the existing ones: Duo-Vision, Panascope, Spectrascope, Superama, Technirama, Ultra-Panavision, and so on.

Thrillarama was an elaborate and overblown wide-screen process similar to Cinerama. The Texas-based creators, Albert H. Reynolds and Dowlen Russell, premiered their travelogue feature *Thrillarama Adventure* on August 9, 1956, at the Metropolitan before moving on to other cities. The Thrillarama premiere festivities were just as big as the film itself, with a parade and an outdoor stage show featuring the Apache Belles of Tyler Junior College (a dance-drill team), Mexican stars Teresa Barcelata and dancer Viky Romero, a *charro* (cowboy) guitar group, the American Legion Band, a marine color guard, representatives from Quebec's Laurentian Winter Carnival, fifty Ford convertibles, and a decorated bus.[12] Reynolds and Russell's brainchild was short-lived, however, made obsolete by Cinemascope technology.[13]

To distinguish their product from television, the movie studios targeted sound as well, offering stereophonic sound, which reproduces the sound separation of live hearing. By the time of *The Brothers Grimm* in 1962, Cinerama was being presented in a seven-channel sound setup.

NEVER BEFORE ON THE SCREEN!

UNDERWATER SCENES . . . IN 3D AMAZING! EXCITING!

woman's beauty his prey!

RAGING UP FROM THE AMAZON'S FORBIDDEN DEPTHS!

CREATURE FROM THE BLACK LAGOON

NEW-TYPE VIEWERS FOR YOUR FULL ENJOYMENT!

Starring
RICHARD CARLSON · JULIA ADAMS
with RICHARD DENNING · ANTONIO MORENO

On **WIDE-VISION SCREEN** STARTS TODAY!

LOEW'S

Advertisement in the Houston Post *for a showing of* Creature from the Black Lagoon *at a Loew's theatre, 1954.*

Wide-screen movies gave theatres an edge they needed over television, and an increasing number of films were shot using the new, wider aspect ratios. Theatres, in turn, reconstructed their screens to accommodate the wider picture. While the best of the new Hollywood crop was shot in wide-screen, a misconception arose that the wide format alone would pull the crowds in—and as movie mogul Samuel Goldwyn once quipped, "A wide screen just makes a bad film twice as bad."

MANY OF THE OTHER processes were nothing more than ballyhoo, a trade term for publicity and gimmickry that blew everything out of proportion. Ballyhoo did not have to reflect either the film's merits or its contents; its primary goal was to get attention, lots of it, with as much fanfare as possible.

A true master of the ballyhoo kings, William Castle, used gimmicks to sell all of his low-budget shockers. One of the classic Castle effects was Emergo, a plastic skeleton that emerged from a casket during a film's climax and was hoisted by wire over the heads of the audience. Among the other notable (or notorious) tricks were: Illusion-O, Castle's variation on 3-D; Aromarama, which used a scent-dispensing system to perfume the theatre with seventy-two different odors; Smell-O-Vision, offered by Mike Todd, Jr.;[14] Percepto, the wiring of theatre seats to deliver

low-voltage shocks; and many more—Dinovision, HypnoMagic, Hypnovision, Mysti-Mation, Psychorama, Wondra-Scope, Supra Motion, Sin*ascope, Cinemagic, Perceptovision, and Fantamation, to name only a few.[15]

One of the true joys in movie gimmickry was 3-D, a process that gave the illusion of layered dimensionality. Beginning in 1953 with the film *Bwana Devil*, the list of films produced in 3-D ranged from the bottom of the barrel—*Robot Monster* (1953), *Gorilla at Large* (1954), and *The Mask* (1961)—to top-notch productions such as *Kiss Me Kate*.[16] This last film, released by MGM in 1953, was given a pair of Texas test screenings to determine the viability (and profitability) of 3-D. The 3-D version was shown in Dallas, while Houston hosted the standard version.[17] And *Creature from the Black Lagoon*, though not the clearest 3-D film to watch, had kids flocking to the Loew's State when it was shown in March 1954.

The added cost of 3-D films stemmed from the special glasses for the audience, a cost usually passed on to patrons. In a 1953 Interstate Theatres interoffice memo, Raymond Willie indicated the price breakdown for admission (Table 11.1).[18]

The gimmick has never quite gone away, despite the varying effectiveness of the process itself. Some 3-D features have excellent quality, such as *The Polar Express* (2004), which ran at Houston's

Table 11.1. Breakdown of Admission Costs to 3-D Movies at Interstate Theatres, 1953

	Net admission	Federal tax	3-D viewer	Total admission
Adults, anytime	58¢	12¢	15¢	85¢
Children, anytime	21¢	4¢	15¢	40¢

Marq*E theatre on the large IMAX screen. On the opposite end of the scale was *Spy Kids 3-D* (2003), which had processing marginally better than that of some of the dreck from the fifties. Other notable examples include the IMAX 3-D films shown at Moody Gardens in Galveston.

ANOTHER POPULAR EVENT was the spook show, a combination movie and live performance that featured magic acts, floating skulls, hypnotists, torture dungeons, people dressed up as monsters, and, as a high point, a minute of total darkness when the auditorium lights were turned off. Many times this type of show was held at midnight, another precursor to the modern midnight movie. These events had been staged since the thirties, but served their purpose well during the

fifties, when theatre attendance was down.

At times, the shows were so popular that they were held in two theatres simultaneously. This process, known as "bicycling," involved running the feature at one theatre and presenting the stage show in another. The two would then be swapped halfway through the program. Jack Baker's stage show "Asylum of Horrors" was once presented at both the Houston Majestic and Palace theatres using this method. At the midpoint, Baker walked his actor, in full Frankenstein's monster makeup, down the street to the Majestic, causing an unsuspecting woman to be scared witless when they turned the corner.[19]

The spook shows were nothing new; they had been quite popular in the thirties and forties. In a letter to Publix Theatres, Interstate executive vice president R. J.

The midnight spook shows first gained popularity in the 1930s. They were a perfect fit for the gimmick-filled '50s. This midnight show was at the Boulevard Theatre in the early 1960s. Photograph by Ray M. Boriski.

Children in costumes at a special Halloween show at the Venus Theatre, early 1960s. Courtesy of Al Zarzana.

O'Donnell once commented on the success of El Wyn's "Spook Party" shows, which were held at various Texas theatres. Initially opposed to this style of show, his attitude changed after seeing the response:

> *We eventually brought it into San Antonio on a Sunday night. We booked this attraction in conjunction with a very bad picture,* The Ghoul. *Despite that, we had to open two theatres in San Antonio, as we filled the Texas, with its 2,700 seats, and had to take care of the overflow at the Empire. The gross was $1,217.70. About three weeks later, we brought it into Dallas at the Majestic Theatre and played to capacity, grossing $1,203.00. We then put it into our best theatre in Houston, and grossed $1,100.00. I am sure that you will realize that these are practically New Year's Eve grosses, or better.*[20]

The fifties, despite all the innovation and gimmickry, remained a point of sagging revenues for movie theatres, but by 1961 the downturn had reversed itself. Houston's theatre attendance in 1959 rose to 168,000 from 166,000, and increased another 1,000 the following year. In just the first five months of 1961, business increased by 8 percent. Those in the business credited the increase to the output of better quality films. The Majestic recorded its longest run to date with *The World of Suzie Wong* (1960), which ran for eight weeks. The River Oaks broke its attendance record, previously held by *Julius Caesar* (1953), three times, each time with a Disney feature. *Swiss Family Robinson* (1960) ran for multiple weeks, and its record was shattered twice in 1961, first by *101 Dalmatians* and then by *The*

Absent-Minded Professor. Said River Oaks manager Johnny Smith in June 1961, "It [*Absent-Minded Professor*] could run for weeks more, except that we are definitely committed to opening another Disney picture, *The Parent Trap*, on June 29. And I will not be surprised if it beats *The Absent-Minded Professor.*"[21]

The most notable thing about the public's movie-viewing habits during the fifties was the surroundings in which a great deal of it occurred. Moviegoers sought out newer, increasingly larger venues for their entertainment when they went out—if they went out, away from the television set. Despite the air conditioning and plush interiors offered by indoor theatres, patrons flocked to a new type of cinema, one in which they never had to step out of their cars. With all its appeal as well as its drawbacks and sometimes questionable reputation, the drive-in was the fifties' main moviegoing venue.

—World's Most Beautiful Outdoor Theatre!

Sharpstown OPEN-AIR THEATRE

BELLAIRE BOULEVARD at HILLCROFT AVE.

10 GOOD REASONS WHY YOU AND YOUR FAMILY WILL ENJOY LOEW'S NEW SHARPSTOWN!

1. MINIATURE RAILROAD
The children will love the FREE rides on our streamlined MINIATURE RAILROAD—"The Sharpstown Flyer." On their trip around the 1600-ft. track, they'll pass through the Magic Tunnel. Nearby is the KIDDIE ZOO—with its collection of domestic animals, and Fairy Tale Land!

2. BRILLIANT PROJECTION
The highest-powered mirror-type projection lamps yet developed will insure an even, brilliant picture reproduction on the huge 52 ft. x 122 ft. specially surfaced screen. The giant screen will accommodate Cinema-Scope, Vista Vision and all other picture sizes.

3. HI-FI SOUND
Loew's new Sharpstown will service hi-fi sound to each car speaker. Thanks to the newest electronic developments, you'll hear true reproduction of dialogue, music and sound effects.

4. CIRCUS PLAYGROUND
Our colorful Circus Playground offers all sorts of free play devices including a full-sized MERRY-GO-ROUND, slides, swings, rides and sand-boxes. There are comfortable benches for Mom and Pop. Boffo the Clown, will entertain the tots!

5. TASTY REFRESHMENTS
Our air-conditioned, spic-and-span four-lane cafeteria will provide fine food and refreshments speedily. Featured are barbecued hamburgers, hot dogs, chili con carne, tamales, shrimp rolls, French fries, hot buttered popcorn and all sorts of hot and cold drinks.

6. FREE DIAPER SERVICE
FREE diaper service is provided in a special Ladies' Room "Diaper Den," through the courtesy of the Tidy-Didy Diaper Service and Loew's Sharpstown. Free bottle-warmers are provided in the air-conditioned refreshment building.

7. DUSTLESS PAVING
You'll not get sand or gravel in your shoes at Loew's Sharpstown. The entire theatre area has been topped with hard-top asphalt surface, eliminating the dust and grit nuisance.

8. TROPICAL LANDSCAPING
Imagination and artistry has gone into the landscape designs for Loew's Sharpstown. At night, unobtrusive ground-lighting transforms the theatre area into a veritable fairyland, bathed in the glow of artificial moonbeams.

9. CHILDREN'S ZOO!
Bring the kiddies to see "Honeysuckle," the bear; see the Monkey Jungle; visit Mr. and Mrs. Donald Duck; see the new Gnu, and Boffo, the Clown; nine trained animals.

10. EASY ACCESSIBILITY — AND QUICK ADMISSION
As the map below indicates, Loew's Sharpstown is easy to reach from all parts of Houston. From DOWNTOWN: Main St. to Holcombe, continuing on Bellaire Blvd. From NORTH: South on Hillcroft, Chimney Rock Rd., or Post Oak to Bellaire Blvd., then right. Shepherd Drive to Bissonnet, then right to Bellaire Blvd. Automatic, treadle type registers will speed up your admission.

CIRCUS PLAYGROUND · MINIATURE RAILROAD

Advertisement in the Houston Post for Loew's Sharpstown Open-Air Theatre.

TWELVE

★ ★ ★

THE
DRIVE-IN

★ ★ ★

A VIEW FROM THE CAR SEAT

*There will soon be so many drive-ins . . .
that you'll be able to get married, have a
honeymoon, and get a divorce without
getting out of your car.*

BOB HOPE

★ MUCH OF THIS BOOK deals with what
has been termed "vanishing Americana,"
a reference to integral aspects of a lifestyle that no longer exists. TV antennas,
typewriters, slide rules, milkmen, house
calls, rotary-dial telephones, eight-track
tapes, and vinyl records are but a few of
the vanquished—and so it is with drive-
in theatres.

Perhaps more so than any other aspect of the cinema, the outdoor theatre
reflected American values. Its beginnings,
rise in popularity, and eventual decline
paralleled the times and preferences of a
nation.

The drive-in originated in the early
thirties, rose to prominence in the postwar
years, and reached its zenith in the fifties
and sixties. The 1963 U.S. Census of Business recorded a nationwide total of over

3,500 drive-ins, with gross receipts of $253 million. By comparison, indoor theatres that year totaled over 9,000, with receipts in excess of $803 million.[1] The seventies saw a decline in the popularity of outdoor theatres, and their eventual demise followed thereafter. Only in the new century has there been a resurgence of interest in them.

Census statistics for Texas showed 88 drive-ins in 1948, jumping to 382 in 1958, and 263 in 1967. By 1977, when 192 theatres were operating, the figures had started to drop, sliding down to 137 in 1982. By 1987, only 56 theatres were in business. At its height, Houston was host to some 20 drive-ins.[2]

Author Kerry Segrave, in his exhaustive history of the drive-in, describes the outdoor theatre as a uniquely American institution; only Canada and Australia came close to matching the U.S. fervor for the huge screens. For drive-ins to be successful, a country must have a certain degree of wealth; an abundance of vacant, accessible, relatively cheap land; and a car-loving populace. America fit all these requirements.[3]

The drive-in was initially a family affair. Parents would pack up the kiddies in their pajamas; toss in picnic baskets, blankets, and pillows; then head for the nearest "ozoner." Crying infants caused little disturbance to the other patrons. Bottle warmers and playgrounds soon became common, which reinforced the idea of the drive-in as a source of entertainment for infants, children, and adults alike.

The drive-ins would come in all shapes and sizes, and might include extravagant concession stands, kiddie play areas, multiple screens, car service, speaker sound,

and, later on, radio sound. They went by many names, the most common one being the "ozoner" and the infamous "passion pit." Other names, according to Segrave, included "open-air operators," "auto havens," "outdoorers," "underskyers," "mudholes," "cow pastures," "rampitoriums," "fresh-air exhibitors," "under-the-stars emporiums," "autotoriums," and "autodeons."[4]

The outdoor theatre also offered a place for teens to hang out, its reputation as a "passion pit" not being groundless. While many drive-in supporters stated that such things never happened (they did), opponents denounced the outdoor theatres as places of sinnin' and fornication. While the reality was somewhere in-between the two extremes, more than one baby boomer's very existence is directly due to a steamy tryst under the stars there, and of those who ever attended a drive-in, few can state that they were never kissed at one. It was, in many ways, the perfect date site, offering privacy, intimacy, and little supervision. Unlike an isolated lover's lane, it offered the safety of others being nearby. Richard M. Hollingshead, Jr., who came up with the drive-in concept, caught heat from a number of angry parents, who felt that such places encouraged immoral conduct. Responded Hollingshead, "We always had a lot of criticism about kids necking, but I've always said that I'd rather see my daughter in a drive-in than parked in a dark alley somewhere."[5]

The first true drive-in theatre was built in 1933 in Camden, New Jersey. Hollingshead experimented with a 1928 Kodak projector set on the hood of his car and a screen nailed to a tree. Weather conditions were tested—the rain was simulated by a garden sprinkler—and a design of terraced rows, allowing cars to see over one another, was devised. The problem of sound was worked out by the RCA Victor Company, which neighbored the auto-parts plant owned by the Hollingshead family. The sound consisted of three centrally located speakers aimed at the rows of cars, a process that would annoy the neighborhood surrounding any drive-in.

THE DRIVE-IN SHORT REEL THEATRE

Texas wasted little time building its own outdoor movie theatre. The world's second drive-in was erected in Galveston, a cheaply built structure that lasted less than a month. Houston architect Louis P. Josserand designed and patented a drive-in in 1933 that was similar to the Hollingshead version. He, along with associate A. H. Emenhiser, attempted to lease land in Houston for a permanent structure that they estimated would cost $30,000. The skeptical landowner, T. D. Dunn, Jr., turned down the offer. To demonstrate the viability of an outdoor theatre, Josserand decided to build an inexpensive "experimental" model in Galveston at a cost of $1,500.[6]

The Drive-In Short Reel Theatre was located on the beach, just off 6th and Boulevard. Cars were faced out to sea, parked on sand that was terraced and ramped daily. Bench seats were located in front for walk-in customers (and the kids who would sneak in by way of the "unfenceable" ocean side of the theatre), and the parking area was lit for the convenience of the patrons.

The theatre was not without drawbacks. The sand was wetted down daily before the evening show, yet an occasional car would still get stuck. Wind would play havoc with the sand once it dried, making it necessary to regrade the lot almost every day.

The opening was on Thursday, July 5, 1934, and for the next twenty-one days it ran a steady stream of newsreels, cartoons, comedies, novelties, and other short subjects. Programs ran from eight to midnight, and on Saturdays until two. The short-lived theatre was leveled during a storm on July 26 and never rebuilt.

THE TEXAS/SOUTH MAIN
9900 *South Main*

By 1950, Houston was home to six outdoor theatres, and a number of new ones were set to open that year. By the end of the decade, there were more than a dozen, and additional theatres would be built during the sixties. In the beginning, however, it was quite simple, and the first Houston ozoner was named, appropriately enough, the Texas Drive-In.

"Drive out and be with us tonight," read the ads for its June 7, 1940, opening.[7] The Texas Drive-In was erected on an eighteen-acre tract of land on South Main "near the underpass." Built for an estimated $50,000, the 475-car theatre featured a seventy-three-by-eighty-foot screen onto which was projected a thirty-eight-by-fifty-two-foot image.[8] Houstonians flocked to the grand opening, which featured *The Under Pup*, starring child actress Gloria Jean, Robert Cummings, and Houston's Nan Grey. Musical shorts and a Universal newsreel were also pre-

Advertisement in the Houston Post *for Houston's full lineup of drive-ins, 1965.*

sented, all for an admission price that ranged from ten to twenty-five cents per person. The Texas Drive-In name was often shortened in advertisements to the Drive-In, but with little confusion, since there was no other in the vicinity. By 1946, its name would change to South Main Drive-In, and would later operate as part of the Interstate circuit.

THE EPSOM DOWNS (9700 *Jensen*), THE WINKLER (205 *Winkler*), AND THE SHEPHERD (6004 *North Shepherd*)

The northeast side of Houston was well known during the thirties as the location of the Epsom Downs horse track, pari-mutuel betting being legal at the time. This area became the home of Houston's second outdoor theatre, the Epsom Downs Drive-In. Located at 9700

Jensen Drive (formerly Humble Road), the Epsom would feature movies into the midseventies, operating for a time as the Bronco, "Houston's Drive-In Art Theatre." Features at this time, the midsixties, included *Nothing but Women* and *Cuties from Holland*.[9] It then changed its format, to Spanish-language films, and name, to the Películas Mexicano Auto-Cine, and later became a flea market. Unlike almost all of the other Houston drive-ins, the Epsom structure managed to survive into the current century.

The screen was still standing in 2005, albeit covered with graffiti. What was once the concession stand had been boarded up to keep out vagrants, and the six-by-six-foot ticket office showed signs of habitation—a worn-out mattress and a scattering of clothes. The only other addition to the property was a sign in front: FOR SALE by Big State Realty Northwest.

In 1947 came the Winkler and Shep-

The South Main Drive-In, c. 1953. Courtesy of the Center for American History, University of Texas at Austin, e_bb_1769.

The Epsom Downs Drive-In, later called the Películas Mexicano Auto-Cine, c. 1986. Courtesy of Ray M. Boriski.

The Epsom was used as a location for the feature The Locusts, *with Kate Capshaw, Ashley Judd, and Vince Vaughn, 1996. Courtesy of the Houston Film Commission.*

herd drive-ins. The Winkler, at 205 Winkler (off the Gulf Freeway near Woodridge), opened on March 21 with *Three Little Girls in Blue* plus a cartoon. It featured two shows nightly and a late show on Saturday. Unique to the Winkler were such child-friendly amenities as bottle warmers and a playground, which made use of the otherwise wasted space below the screen.[10] This became a com-

mon feature at drive-ins through the sixties, until made impractical by skyrocketing insurance rates and an increasingly lawsuit-happy America.

Two months later, the Shepherd, at 6004 North Shepherd, had its gala opening. The May 23 event featured the Ingrid Bergman–Robert Montgomery film *Rage in Heaven* (1941), plus a cartoon.[11] The Winkler closed down in the sixties. By 1977, the Shepherd had closed; the structure was razed, and the site is now occupied by Packaged Ice, Inc., maker of Reddy Ice.

Two key figures in these early drive-ins were Claude Ezell and W. G. Underwood, who operated a number of Texas ozoners under the U&E banner. By 1948, they had the Chief in Austin; the Buckner, Chalk Hill, and Northwest in Dallas; the Belknap and the Bowie in Forth Worth; the Cactus in Pharr; the Fredericksburg and the Trail in San Antonio; and the Circle in Waco.[12] Their U&E Houston drive-

ins were the Shepherd, South Main, and Winkler. Later still, a number of Houston drive-ins would operate under Ezell's Dallas-based Lone Star Theatre chain. Ezell founded the International Drive-In Theatre Owners Association, and is credited with being one of the first to install playground equipment for the kiddies (he did so in 1944, while a Detroit ozoner had included one the previous year).[13]

Some of Ezell's ozoners were recognizable by a standard image painted on the tower: a clown's head surrounded by a circus motif. The art is credited to artist Reed Hubnell.

Since sound was a problem at these early drive-ins, W. G. Underwood developed the "sound in the ground" system—speakers submerged in the ground and covered by a metal grate similar to a manhole cover. Because of a number of shortcomings, including an absence of a volume control, this technology never caught on, and the individual car speakers introduced by RCA became the standard.[14]

The Shepherd Drive-In, c. 1953. Courtesy of the Center for American History, University of Texas at Austin, e_bb_2106.

Advertisement in the Houston Post for the gala opening of the Shepherd Drive-In, May 1947.

THE MARKET STREET
8601 Market Street

A single outdoor theatre opened in Houston in 1948: the Market Street Drive-In. Two showings of the Robert Young film *Relentless* were presented for the August 26 premiere. The 670-car theatre featured such luxuries as individual speakers for each car, a children's playground, and a concession stand.[15]

The Market Street was operated by the Al Mortensen circuit of theatres. Alfred Mortensen had also been the founder and original owner of both the Southwestern Camera Company and the Southwestern Theatre Equipment Company. He passed away in May 2002 at the age of ninety-six. H. D. "Cotton" Griffith was a partner in the Mortenson group. He, along with his family, spent three decades in the drive-in business. Their last Houston operation was the I-45 Drive-In.

The Market Street Drive-In no longer stands. The site is now occupied by the Anheuser-Busch Brewery facilities.

THE TRAIL (3202 *Old Spanish Trail*), **THE AIRLINE** (4507 *Airline*), **THE HEMPSTEAD ROAD** (10600 *Hempstead*), **AND THE IRVINGTON** (8411 *Irvington*)

Four separate drive-ins sprang up in 1950:

the Trail, the Airline, the Hempstead Road, and the Irvington. First was the Trail, located at 3202 Old Spanish Trail and advertised as Texas's largest drive-in theatre, with a deluxe patio and concession stand and a capacity of 1,000 cars. A preview opening took place on Thursday, April 20, and the grand opening followed the next night, complete with a giant fireworks display and the feature film *Tulsa*.[16] The theatre was operated by Jack Farr, who also owned the Skyway Drive-In in Bryan. The Trail ceased operations in the late sixties.

The Airline Drive-In opened on June 10, 1950. Large newspaper ads heralded the twelve-acre theatre, located at 4507 Airline, as the most deluxe outdoor theatre in town. A fully equipped, adult-supervised playground and a snack bar, complete with car service and baby-bottle warmers, were heavily touted in the pro-

The Airline Drive-In, 1950. Courtesy of the Houston Metropolitan Research Center, Houston Public Library, MSS 200-112.

motions. Opening night featured the Randolph Scott western *Canadian Pacific* and three cartoons.[17]

With its bright flashing neon, the Airline was readily visible from the freeway. It operated as part of Claude Ezell's Lone Star Theatre circuit. Like many ozoners, the Airline would use numerous gimmicks to attract patrons. One such example was a display of marine equipment in May 1953, tied in with the featured film, *Battle Zone*. The equipment, set up by the 442nd Marine Infantry Battalion, included bazookas, machine guns, combat camera equipment, and bulletproof clothing.[18] During its later years, it would host events such as a live concert in September 1978 by Willie Nelson and family.[19]

During its early days, the Airline was recognized by the image of an airplane on the screen tower, accented by neon circles and the name overhead. Such representational paintings were standard for many early drive-ins. Later the Airline plane was gone, replaced with a set of three overlapping squares.

The Airline survived for three decades, eventually becoming the property of the Tercar Theatre Company before closing in 1981. The property was sold to Hines Industrial. Tercar executive Charles Paine claimed in a 1981 *Houston Post* interview that it was "one of the two or three top-grossing drive-ins in Texas," adding that location and taxes had "made it so expensive for us to operate that taking that offer [to sell] was the only sensible thing to do. We could run the Airline for the rest of our lives and not make that kind of money."[20]

September 15, 1950, marked the opening of Ezell's Hempstead Road Drive-In at 10600 Hempstead. Featured that evening was *My Friend Irma Goes West*, with

Firefighters work to extinguish the screen-tower fire at the Hempstead Drive-In, apparently caused by lightning, July 1964. Courtesy of the Houston Metropolitan Research Center, Houston Public Library, RGD6N-6855, #14.

Dean Martin and Jerry Lewis, along with a Donald Duck cartoon and a fireworks display.[21] It would stay in operation for a little over two decades. An office park now stands in its place.

The year was capped off with the opening of yet another Ezell drive-in, the Irvington, on November 3. Located at 8411 Irvington, the theatre premiered with *Singing Guns*, plus a live appearance by the "world famous thrill artist" Berosini.[22]

The Irvington staged another grand opening in May 1977. The dusk-to-dawn presentation on Friday the 13th featured *Beyond the Grave*, *Demon Seed*, *House of Insane Women*, *Burnt Offerings*, and *Killer Snake*. The grand-opening publicity ploy allowed free admittance to the following: the first thirteen cars, all those who could prove they were thirteen years old, all those who could prove they were born on the 13th, the first thirteen female drivers, any car with thirteen people in it (excluding vans and trucks), and the first thirteen redheaded drivers. Popcorn and soft drinks were sold that evening at the bargain price of . . . thirteen cents.[23] The theatre closed down around 1981.

Exploitation films always proved popular at the drive-in. If a movie featured car crashes, kung fu, monsters, or sex, it would pull in the crowds. Fright flicks were also guaranteed box-office draws. Jan Bettis, the manager of the I-45 during its final days put it best: "Horror films are always better at a drive-in."

THE POST OAK 1
(2900 *South Post Oak Road*)
AND 2 *(1255 North Post Oak Road)*

By 1951, Houston was building bigger and better theatres. On March 14 of that year, Jack Groves, Sr., opened the Post Oak Drive-In at 2900 South Post Oak Road. The double bill included the Zachary Scott flick *Pretty Baby* and *The Grass Is*

Always Greener, with Chill Wills.[24] Among the drive-in's unique features was the talking moose, a mounted moose head that the elder Groves had bagged years earlier and subsequently wired with a speaker. The moose was used for announcements, and occasionally would talk to the children.

In 1960, the Groves estate sold the land to developers, and the drive-in subsequently moved up the street. Jack Groves, Jr., partnered with Carroll A. Lewis, who owned a plot of land in the 1200 block of North Post Oak Road between the Katy and Hempstead highways. Much of the original drive-in was moved; the ninety-six-by-forty-eight-foot screen tower was cut into three sections and transported to the new site by house movers. Windows, doors, equipment–and the moose–from the old concession building were brought over for the new, larger building. Speakers and posts were removed, though the underground wiring was left. The move and new construction took about seven months.[25]

Everything about the new location was bigger, from the space between ramps and speaker posts to the concession stand and the playground space at the base of the tower. Construction was handled by the Oscar R. May Company of Fort Worth, which had already built forty-two drive-ins around the United States. More than likely, May had also handled the work on the original Post Oak, and, according to Lewis, is credited with the murals on the screen towers (Dinky Duck on the original, Bambi on the new).

The new Post Oak Drive-In, at 1255 North Post Oak Road, opened on June 16, 1960, with *Please Don't Eat the Daisies* and *Man on a String*.[26] Charlie Hillis, manager

Advertisement in the Houston Post *for the gala opening of the Irvington Drive-In, November 1950.*

of the older facility, and projectionist Horace Pitts resumed their duties at the new location. Groves eventually got out of the business, selling his share to Lewis.

Two years after the drive-in opened, Lewis added a new feature: Movieland Golf, a thirty-six-hole miniature golf course, each hole designed after a famous movie. Among the movies represented were *Giant* (with a large oil rig), *Tombstone Territory*, *The Vikings* (with a castle), *The Guns of Navarone*, *The Parent Trap*, *Fort Apache* (a large fort), *Tarzan's Secret Jungle*, *Dodge City*, *Mutiny of the Bounty* (a ship), *Treasure Island*, *Operation Petticoat*, and *The Bridge on the River Kwai* (a bridge, naturally). The standout was a 5,000-square-foot replica of the Alamo,

with all the ramparts, walls, and chapel fortifications—a logical choice, since Lewis was also quite knowledgeable about regional history.

Movieland Golf opened on March 22, 1962, while the theatre ran the 1953 Glen Ford movie *The Man from the Alamo*. Admission was fifty cents for each eighteen-hole course. Later, Lewis gave out "Oswalds," replicas of Academy Award trophies, to winning players on the course.[27]

Another feature was inspired by *King Solomon's Mines*. Lewis trucked in several truckloads of earth from the diamond mine in Murfreesboro, Arkansas, and kids could dig in the dirt and look for diamonds. This was no mere gimmick: diamonds were found in the soil. Later,

Aerial photo of Post Oak Boulevard, 1952. The area is now the site of Williams (Transco) Tower and Fountain. Beyond the drive-in is the "new" KPRC Channel 2 television station. Courtesy of KPRC Channel 2.

Lewis added a four-story giant slide to the attractions at the Post Oak complex.

Carroll Lewis sold the drive-in to the McLendon Corporation in 1970.[28] Its last listing was in the 1974 *Houston Directory*.

THE KING CENTER TWIN
6400 *Martin Luther King Boulevard*

The year 1952 marked the opening of the King Center Twin Drive-In, part of Beaumont's Jefferson Theatre circuit. The King was located at Holmes Road and South Park Boulevard, later listed as 6400 Martin Luther King Boulevard. Car capacity was 1,200, and the facilities included two playgrounds, a patio adjoining the snack bar, and two giant screens built back-to-back in the center of the lot.

The gala opening took place on June 25 amid spotlights and live appearances by Colleen Gray, Tim Holt, Preston Foster, and the Light Crust Doughboys. Screen one opened with *One Big Affair*, while the Tim Holt feature *Hot Lead* was shown on screen two.[29] Tercar took over the King Center in 1976.

Like other drive-ins, the King Center looked for ways to utilize the lot during the daylight hours. During the early seventies, the lot was used for the Swap-O-Rama Flea Market. Free helicopter rides were occasionally offered during these events.[30]

The King Center closed down at the end of 1981. Trammell Crow bought the property, intending to build a warehouse complex on the site.[31] In 2005, a portion of the property remained—nothing more than a fenced-in vacant lot and a few upright speaker poles.

THE HI-NABOR
7200 *Mykawa Road*

Ads that ran in the dailies on May 22, 1953, read "Hi Nabors! Tonight Is THE

Movieland Golf, 1962. Carroll Lewis sold ad space on some of the holes. The Dodge City hole, left, included advertising for Bob Webb, a barber located in Long Point; also visible are the holes themed around the Tombstone Territory, center, and the Gunfight at the OK Corral, far right. Courtesy of Carroll A. Lewis.

Night!" With this, Houstonians were invited to the grand opening of the deluxe Hi-Nabor Drive-In Theatre and Kiddie Play Park. Featured was a double bill of *She's Back on Broadway* and *The Red Snow*, plus cartoons. Free barbecue and ice cream were available for opening-night patrons, while kiddies were given free candy and free rides on the miniature electric train, one of the highlights of the playground.[32] The theatre stayed in operation until 1967.

INSECTS WERE ALWAYS a nuisance at the drive-ins. Concession stands usually would carry PIK, a coil-shaped incense that, when burned, produced a nauseating smell to humans and mosquitoes alike. Still, it kept the bugs away somewhat. While many patrons would come armed with their favorite brand of insect repellent, some drive-ins during the fifties and sixties would use insect foggers over the parking area. Operator Jack Farr, of the Trail Drive-In, turned insect fogging into a spectator sport, giving it top billing in his newspaper ads. People would turn out in droves to see the machine in action.

Moran McDaniel, of the La Marque Bayou Drive-In, also fogged his theatre. Both Farr and McDaniel were unaware of the dangers of DDT, the deadly poison that they used (which was subsequently banned by the federal government in 1972).[33] In a 1984 *Houston Post* interview, McDaniel said that before the county did any fogging, he was constantly asked to spray everything from football fields to outdoor party areas. In his early programs, he advertised, "We have large, powerful spraying machines, covering the entire area daily, building a concentration of DDT over the entire surface of the

drive-in. However, should any individual become annoyed with insects, we will be glad to spray their auto anytime."[34]

In 1978, *Houston Post* writer Eric Gerber reminisced about the insect-repellent ads at the Hi-Nabor (his family's favorite drive-in), which spawned his most vivid drive-in memory: "No, it has nothing to do with teen-age groping or dawn-to-dusk horror extravaganzas, but a silly intermission ad they ran for an insect repellant that sat smoldering on your dashboard: a mosquito took a big whiff and groggily testified, 'This stuff just kills me!'"[35]

THE RED BLUFF
Highway 225 at Red Bluff (Pasadena)

Before 1953 was out, one more outdoor theatre would open, and would, in years to follow, become the most scandalous of Houston's drive-ins. The Red Bluff Drive-In opened to the public on August 5 with the features *Shane* and *Navy Bound*.[36] The theatre presented a lineup of family-oriented films throughout the fifties and sixties, and was later operated by Phil Isley, who also controlled the Granada Theatre, as well as the nearby Capitan theatres.

As the motion-picture code was replaced by the new ratings system, filmmakers were given carte blanche to stretch the boundaries of what could be shown on film. The sexual revolution changed values on all fronts. It was inevitable that skin flicks eventually made their way to outdoor screens, leading to results that were also unavoidable.

On February 4, 1970, the Red Bluff officially changed formats, running what was described as "art films for adults." At the time, the theatre was part of Herb and

The Red Bluff Drive-In,
1980s. Courtesy of Parker
Riggs.

Harriet Hartstein's theatre circuit. The abundance of lust and naked skin did not sit well with the Pasadena neighborhood, especially since the screen was easily visible from outside the theatre walls. Action against the drive-in came quick.

On Tuesday, February 17, 1970, Pasadena police raided the Red Bluff, seizing three films and charging the manager and projectionist with possession of lewd and obscene films. Bond was set at $2,500 each. The films in question were *The Defilers*, *Suburban Pagans*, and *Orgy of the Dead*, which was written by legendary bad filmmaker Ed Wood (director of *Plan 9 From Outer Space*).[37]

Police again raided the Red Bluff the following night, arresting the assistant manager and the projectionist on the same charges as before. Shown that night was *Hot Skin and Cold Cash*. Bond was set at a more affordable $400 each.[38]

By April, the Hartsteins had filed a suit against the city for $150,000, naming the

mayor, councilmen, and the police as defendants. Court injunctions were filed. Mayor Clyde Doyal's office was besieged by letters to "keep smut out of Pasadena." The Pasadena city council also felt pressure from area residents.[39] Meanwhile, a self-appointed morality defender waged a personal fight against the theatre by shooting arrows into the theatre grounds; the notes attached were signed "The Night Rider."[40]

The Pasadena city council took action. In June 1970, an ordinance was passed to regulate both indoor and outdoor theatres. The ordinance required a twenty-five-dollar license for all theatres, and specific building regulations were aimed at preventing "bare buttocks and bare female breasts" from being seen from the street. Meanwhile, the nearby Capitan, an indoor theatre, was running X-rated films that were harder in content than anything shown at the *Red Bluff*.[41]

By August, the city had switched

tactics. The city building inspector condemned the concession stand, posting a
sign stating that it was not safe for human
occupancy. The concession-stand manager was arrested on three counts: operating a theatre without a license, and two
related to faulty electrical wiring.[42] The
battle between the Red Bluff and the city
would continue for years.

When the Golden Saddles Cinema,
at 3000 Spencer, began running X-
rated films in 1981, citizens were again
incensed, but most tactics had already
been tried with the Red Bluff. Said Police
Chief Doug Wilson, "We fought the battle with the Red Bluff Drive-In for years.
Our biggest accomplishment was a court
order telling us to leave them alone."[43]

The Red Bluff Drive-In would survive
into the nineties, well after most other outdoor theatres had given up the ghost, but it
wouldn't last out the century. It eventually
closed down and the site was razed.

THE TIDWELL
9603 Homestead

In 1955, the Tidwell Drive-In opened
its gates to the public. The grand opening on September 1 featured the James
Stewart western *The Man from Laramie*
as well as *5 Against the House*, with Kim
Novak. Advertisements claimed that the
Tidwell had the largest concession stand
on the Gulf Coast, offering candy, soft
drinks, sandwiches, hot dogs, hamburgers,
donuts, barbecue, chicken, shrimp, and
malts.[44] The theatre remained in operation through 1976, but is now gone, the
site occupied by the Swiss Village Apartment Homes.

IT WOULD BE TWO and a half years
before another drive-in would be built in
Houston—however, the result would be
well worth the wait, a venue larger and
more extravagant than anything yet built.

LOEW'S SHARPSTOWN
6366 Bellaire Boulevard

It cost over $1 million and took a year and
a half to build. It could hold 1,700 cars
on its thirty-six acres. This was the scope
of the Loew's Sharpstown Open-Air Theatre.[45] It was the largest drive-in theatre
built in Houston, rivaled only by the 1982
I-45 Drive-In, which housed six screens
on forty-eight acres.

Loew's hired New York architect John
McNamara, a veteran designer of motion-
picture and restaurant structures, to create
the outdoor theatre. His credentials were
impressive: he started in 1923 with Thomas W. Lamb, the architectural firm that
designed some of America's most spectacular movie palaces. The construction was
supervised by Harry Moskowitz of New
York, and David R. Hendrick of Waco
acted as general contractor. Nationally,
it was Loew's third drive-in, and its first
Houston theatre outside of the downtown
area. It was also Loew's most expensive
drive-in: construction was delayed four
months because of rain and cold weather,
and the cost eventually ran to $1,200,000.[46]

When it finally opened, patrons found
their way onto the massive site through
a set of entrance gates that counted each
car automatically, thereby eliminating
the need for printed tickets. Since it was
set in the middle of a residential area,
more than $40,000 worth of palm trees,
tropical plants, and other greenery was

February 26, 1958, the opening day of the spectacular Loew's Sharpstown Open-Air Theatre, was treated as a major media event. Courtesy of the Houston Metropolitan Research Center, Houston Public Library, RGD6N-2668, #17.

used to blend the theatre lot into the surroundings. An area was set aside for future expansion, allowing the car capacity to increase from 1,700 to 2,100 when completed. The 52-by-122-foot steel screen was mounted on a steel-and-concrete structure constructed to withstand hurricane-force winds. It was designed to accommodate various picture sizes, from those with flat ratios to ones shot in Cinemascope and VistaVision. Approximately seventy-five full- and part-time employees were hired to work the theatre.

More than ten acres were set aside for a fully supervised, deluxe kiddie playland set up in two separate areas, one directly behind the cafeteria building and the other, known as "Two Trigger Gulch," in the southwest corner. The latter was the originating spot for the *Sharpstown Flyer*, a spectacular four-car forty-eight-passenger miniature train that wound its way around a half-mile course. The train tracks passed through a secret diamond

mine of elves, eleven hand-painted scenes (including that of a fairy village), grandma's house, and a little red schoolhouse before circling the giant movie screen and returning to the gulch.

Other features of the southwest-corner playground included a thirty-horse carousel with two chariots, Boffo (the resident clown), a feature called "Judge Bean's Court–The Law West of the Pecos," and a petting zoo set up by the Houston Society for the Prevention of Cruelty to Animals. A 350-pound Coke-drinking black bear named Honeysuckle, belonging to Mrs. J. Moore of Sheldon Reservoir, was the featured attraction at the zoo. Other tenants included dogs that were available for adoption to qualified Houstonians.

Behind the concession stand was the 150-by-150-foot "circus playground," equipped with a ski slide, hobbyhorse, animal slide, sandboxes, and swings of the kindergarten, regular, belt, and glider varieties. Surrounding the area was a chain-link fence adorned with comic-strip characters.

The 3,720-square-foot cafeteria came equipped with air conditioning and automatic doors and served hot dogs, shrimp rolls, french fries, pizza, egg rolls, Smithfield hams, tortillas, enchiladas, and barbecue hamburgers. Bottle-warming services were available, as were free diaper services in the ladies' room "diaper den," courtesy of the Tidy Didy Diaper Service. A mobile "foodmobile" delivered food directly to patrons' cars during the performances. The cost of the concession stand was $400,000.

The grand opening took place on Wednesday, February 26, 1958, an unseasonable date for an outdoor event. The ceremonies began with a parade of antique cars, featuring Indianapolis racecar driver John Parsons, a Houston band, and four beauty queens from the University of Houston and Rice University. The parade stretched from Bellaire Circle along Bellaire Boulevard to the theatre, at the intersection of Hillcroft. At six, the ribbon cutting commenced, the scissors wielded by celebrities Barbara Lang and Chill Wills. Other notables included Mayor Pro Tem Lee McLemore, theatre manager Wayne Horton, and master of ceremonies Tim Nolan, of the popular Tim and Bob radio show on KPRC. On-the-spot radio broadcasts were fully covered by KXYZ, KNUZ, KILT, KTHT, KTRH, and KPRC. The featured attraction was the Jerry Lewis vehicle *The Sad Sack*, along with *Pawnee*, cartoons, and newsreels. Souvenirs were available for every patron that evening; however, the grand opening was planned to last fourteen days, during which daily cash door prizes of $100 and $50 spending sprees

at Sharpstown Center would be awarded.[47]

Claude Ezell's Lone Star Theatre circuit eventually took over the mammoth theatre, operating it during the sixties along with the Airline, Hempstead, Irvington, Pasadena, and Winkler drive-ins.[48] It was then taken over by Tercar in the seventies. Encroachment on the surrounding drive-in property by commercial and residential development raised both the land value and the property taxes. In 1974, taxes for the Sharpstown were $15,000; by 1975, they had jumped to $40,000.[49] The massive ozoner would eventually succumb to the inevitable. A retail center now stands in its place.

THE GULFWAY (9025 *Wald Road*) AND THE THUNDERBIRD (9510 *Clay Road*)

The Gulfway Drive-In, which opened in 1960 at an announced cost of $450,000, was puny in comparison with the extravagance of the Sharpstown. Its June 29 grand opening featured *Please Don't Eat the*

Loew's manager Homer McCallon sits behind the unidentified engineer of the Sharpstown Flyer train on opening day. Other officials behind McCallon are, right to left, Mayor Louis Cutrer, R. E. "Bob" Smith, and Frank Sharp. Courtesy of the Houston Metropolitan Research Center, Houston Public Library, RGD6N-2668, #5.

Daisies and *Never So Few*. It was located at 9025 Wald Road, off South Shaver near the Gulf Freeway.[50] Sold in 1970 to the McLendon circuit, it would be one of the last surviving drive-ins in the mideighties.

Five years later, the Thunderbird Twin, at 9510 Clay Road, opened. On the Thunderbird north screen was a triple bill of *Zebra in the Kitchen*, *Bus Riley's Back in Town* with Ann-Margret, and *Go Go Mania* ("with the international beat that's rockin' the world"). Presented on Thunderbird south was *Ski Party*, *Die! Die! My Darling!* and *That Man from Rio*. Opening night was July 1, 1965.[51]

Most notable about the Thunderbird was the spectacular neon Thunderbird logo stretching across the entire width of the screen's backside. The marquee listings for the north and south screens were located below the brightly colored bird. The theatre closed down in closed in 1979, and the site is now occupied by the Clay Campbell Business Park.

THE TELEPHONE ROAD TWIN, 11020 *Telephone Road (Pearland)*

Stanley Warner's Telephone Road Twin opened on June 29, 1967. Tickets for opening night were three dollars a car; the features were *The War Wagon* on screen one and *For a Few Dollars More* on screen two. The premiere night was held for the benefit of the Boy's Harbor of Houston, with guests Joe Ford of KNUZ and Miss Texas beauty Judi Lackey. Live performances by two local bands were lined up: Fever Tree and the Moving Sidewalks, the latter featuring Billy Gibbons, later of ZZ Top fame.[52] Tercar would take control of the twin theatre in

the seventies and operate it into the eighties, well after their other Houston ozoners had been closed (except their smaller screens in Baytown and Rosenberg). Stated Charles Paine in 1981, "Tercar's one Houston area drive-in that's holding steady is the Telephone Twin out near Hobby Airport, where commercial devel-

Advertisement in the Houston Post *for the grand opening of the Thunderbird Drive-In, July 1965.*

opment has not been quite so rapid. If the taxes don't get out of hand, we'll be okay."[53] The Telephone Road Twin would survive only a few more years before closing down.

THE MCLENDON 3
South Main at Hiram Clarke Road

In 1970 the McLendon Theatre Division of the Dallas-based McLendon Corporation announced plans for expanding into Houston. Barton R. McLendon and son Gordon were already well established in the media, operating one of the largest independent television and radio chains in the United States, which included Houston radio station KILT.[54]

Gordon gained recognition as a radio personality (nicknamed "the Old Scotsman") and a one-time candidate for the U.S. Senate. He also was responsible for several prime examples of drive-in fodder: *The Killer Shrews*, a 1958 movie he made for $125,000 with dogs dressed up as giant shrews; *The Giant Gila Monster* (1959); and the family-oriented *My Dog, Buddy* (1960).[55]

By 1969, the McLendons had purchased or expanded twenty-five Texas theatres, bringing their count up to forty-two. They acquired the Post Oak Twin from Carroll Lewis and made plans to expand it to a triple-screen theatre; and the Gulfway, bought from the Mortensen circuit. They also purchased the La Marque Bayou Twin Drive-In from M. C. McDaniel. Part of their announced master plan was the construction of a new theatre to be built on South Main at Hiram Clarke Road, along with a triple drive-in at West Road and Interstate 45. This latter project, origi-

nally called the Apollo Drive-In, would not take shape for another decade, when it would open as the I-45 Drive-In.[56]

Their plans for the three-screen McLendon Astro Drive-In ran into a snag during construction because of legal complications involving the registered "Astro" name, affiliated with the sports team and the neighboring Astrodomain complex. The McLendons withdrew the name; however, the injunction obtained by the Houston Sports Association caused the theatre to remain technically nameless as opening day arrived.[57] Premiere-day ads listed the outdoor theatre as the McLendon New Famous Drive-In. It would soon become known as, and remain, the McLendon 3.

A gala event was staged for the May 7, 1971, opening night. Featured were live appearances by stars George Peppard, Andrew V. McLaglen, Susan Stafford, and Big John Hamilton, along with Zay Winn, the clown, and Hudson and Harrigan from radio station KILT.

Presented for the gala on screen one

The McLendon 3, 1981. Courtesy of the Houston Metropolitan Research Center, Houston Public Library, RGD6N 4-27-81, #19.

was the southwestern premiere of *Big House Girls*, along with *Bloody Mama*. Screen two featured a dusk-till-dawn "Ghoul-arama" with *The Oblong Box*, *The Conqueror Worm*, *Horror House*, and *The Crimson Cult*. Featured on the third screen was the Texas premiere of George Peppard's *One More Train to Rob*, along with *The Hawaiians*.[58]

The McLendon 3 Drive-In closed down in August 1986. It then took on a new life for a while as the site of a flea market. By the turn of the century, the grounds remained closed, the asphalt lot overtaken by weeds. The screens were gone, but a graffiti-covered concession stand remained, as well as the foundation for the ticket booths. By 2005 even these last remnants had been swept away as the property underwent development into a new mecca for motor vehicles: the Lakeview RV Resort.

THE BAYOU (*La Marque*) AND OTHER OUTLYING THEATRES

During the fifties, outdoor theatres spread like wildfire, in large cities and small towns alike. While most of the drive-ins listed in the Houston newspapers were located either within or near the city limits, there were others scattered across the region, in some cases owned and operated by the same people who ran the major metropolitan drive-ins. These were the drive-ins' country cousins.

Of these, the Pasadena drive-ins were the best known, because of the city's proximity to Houston. The first, the Pasadena Drive-In, at 2221 South Shaver, opened on December 9, 1949, with the feature *Father Was a Fullback*.[59] Tercar would eventually take over the theatre, which would close down at the beginning of the eighties.

Later came the infamous Red Bluff Drive-In and the Town & Country Twin, the latter located at 4716 Pasadena.

The Pasadena Drive-In, c. early 1970s. Courtesy of Charles Paine.

Almost every town had an outdoor theatre within driving distance. Some had two. Bay City had the Showboat on Highway 35 East. The Hi-Y Drive-In in Conroe was located at Bowman and South Frazier Street and owned by C. M. Tinger. Alvin Guggenheim ran the Humble Drive-In in Humble. Tercar operated the Decker Drive-In in Baytown and the Twin City Drive-In in Rosenberg. The Tradewind Drive-In, at the Palmer Highway and 21st Street in Texas City, was operated by the Long theatre chain. Farther away to the east, Jefferson Amusements operated the Surf Drive-In in Port Arthur.

Of these, the best remembered was the Bayou Drive-In on Highway 1765 in La Marque—Galveston County's first drive-in. It was built in 1949 by locals Moran and

Lola McDaniel, who had previously built the Lamar, La Marque's only movie theatre, in 1940. The Bayou Drive-In could accommodate more than 600 cars and featured three screens, each measuring 60 by 100 feet, as well as a playground for the kids. The theatre was later relocated to the Gulf Freeway, fourteen miles north of Galveston, opening with the features *Flareup* and Roman Polanski's *The Fearless Vampire Killers (or Pardon Me, But Your Teeth Are in My Neck)*. Moran sold it to the McLendon theatre circuit in May 1970, and it remained operational until it was destroyed by Hurricane Alicia, which ripped through the area in August 1983 with 120 mph winds.[60]

In 1984, the McDaniels reminisced about their three decades in the movie business. From voodoo-potion gimmicks for a voodoo movie to problems with mosquitoes and hurricanes, they had experienced it all. Children were often dropped off at the drive-in but not picked up afterwards. "We couldn't take them home," explained Lola, "or we would be charged with kidnapping. Some of the children knew where they lived and some of them didn't, and sometimes we did take them home." Other times, the Morans would remain at the drive-in into the early hours of the morning, waiting for the parents to pick up their kids.

Another story related to their walk-in theatre in La Marque. They found a bundle underneath a theatre seat, which turned out to be a baby. As they explained, "The woman at the box-office said, 'Just a minute, I believe I know whose baby that is.' She then began calling around to all the beer joints for the mother. When the mother was found, she said, 'I knew that I left that baby someplace and somebody would be calling me about it.'"

EVEN WITHIN the Houston city limits, some drive-ins in operation garnered little advertising. According to various editions of the *Houston Directory*, the Chocolate Bayou Drive-In, at 10200 Cullen, was operational in the early sixties. By the early seventies, it had changed names to the Cullen Drive-In. The Three Way Drive-In, at 3101 Eastex Freeway, was operational in the seventies. The Pablos Drive-In was listed at 3920 Canal Street. The Parkway, at 7300 South Lake Houston Parkway in North Houston, operated through the late seventies.

The Mini Drive-In, an X-rated theatre at 15010 East Highway 90, bore the distinction of being Houston's only outdoor theatre-in-the-round. This "private

screen theatre" was the brainchild of Tom Smith and Bert Crowley of Buffalo, Missouri, who developed the idea in 1954. The Autoscope, as they called it, arranged 150 to 200 cars in a circle, like the rim of a wagon wheel, with a three-by-five-foot screen in front of each car. At the center of the circle was the projection booth, which utilized a "fly's-eye" projection lens to divide the image for each screen. Only three other such drive-ins were built, those being in Joplin, Missouri; Albuquerque, New Mexico; and Anchorage, Alaska.[61]

AS THE SEVENTIES drew to a close, so did the days of the drive-in, as insurmountable obstacles brought about a slow extermination. The luxury of spacious automobile interiors faded as cars were downsized. The movie industry had always given preference to indoor theatres, and drive-ins usually received second-run products. But by the late seventies this had changed. A steady flow of first-run features opened simultaneously at both indoor and outdoor theatres, but by this time the glut of indoor screens spread the audience base too thinly. As drive-in operator H. D. "Cotton" Griffith stated in 1981, "The studios are making stiffer deals these days. Film rental rates have gone up nearly 20 percent in the past few years. There's a lot less product around, too. Last year, there were only 175 films made. It's really tough for a drive-in to buy in on a first-run showing with that kind of competition for new movies."[62]

Additional nuisances inherent to the drive-in experience had never gone away. Bad weather, poor picture quality (especially on rainy nights), mosquitoes, and inferior sound were all there from day one. Even the improvement of having the sound broadcast on AM radio paled in comparison with the Dolby stereo and THX sound systems of the indoor screens.

The national implementation of daylight savings time in 1967 only increased the hardships. Operators found themselves pushing back showtimes to as late as nine during the summer, making double bills inconvenient for patrons, especially during the workweek. Said Moran McDaniel, "Twilight time came for the drive-ins when daylight saving time rolled in."[63]

Matters worsened with the coming of home video and cable in the eighties. However, the chief culprit in the downfall of the drive-ins was the value of the land itself. Many landowners had built drive-ins as a temporary source of income while patiently letting property values increase. Once the values rose to a certain point, profit margins could not justify keeping a drive-in operational, and the land was generally converted to retail purposes.

THE I-45
211 West Road

The last drive-in to be built was also the last to go. The Old Scotsman, Gordon McLendon, had laid out plans a decade earlier for the three-screen Apollo Drive-In. What was finally constructed in 1982 was a massive six-screen theatre on a forty-eight-acre site at West Road and I-45. Gordon was sixty-one years old at the time, and his father, Barton, was eighty-two. The elder McLendon died in October of that year.[64]

The construction of the $2.5 million I-45 Drive-In progressed even as the drive-in industry fell victim to home video. In a 1982 interview, Gordon said, "Drive-in the-

The Mini Drive-In. Courtesy of Jim Ohmart.

atres are less susceptible to the electronic form of competition because teenagers are simply far more restless than their elders." Yet his business sense predicted that while the property was valuable in the eighties, it would increase even more as the Houston building boom moved north. He further stated that should the drive-in gamble fail, "we'll simply move the timetable up to move the land into another phase of development."[65] The lease of the theatre was taken up by FLW Theatre Company of Detroit.

Opening day for "Texas' biggest drive-in theatre," with a 3,000-car capacity, took place on July 2, 1982. Of the six giant screens, only three were open for the gala. The features were *Star Trek II: The Wrath of Khan* and *Dragonslayer* on screen one, *The Thing* and *An American Werewolf in London* on screen two, and *Conan the Barbarian* and *Don't Go Near the Park* on screen three. At the time of the I-45's opening, the only remaining Houston drive-ins in operation were the Gulfway 3, the McLendon 3, the Red Bluff, and the Mini

The I-45 Drive-In, c. 1987. Courtesy of Parker Riggs.

Drive-In; the first two were McLendon theatres, and the others were independents running X-rated flicks.[66]

Absent from the I-45 were the familiar drive-in speakers; sound was simply transmitted to AM radio. Mondays became bargain nights, when admission was $1.50 a person. By 1988, regular pricing had changed to $4 a person for first-run films, while second-run tickets were $5 a carload. At the time of its closing, tickets would be $6 a person, not that different from indoor-theatre prices, although children eleven and under were still admitted free.

A notable highlight was the 1984 world premiere of *Yor: Spacehunter from the Future*, attended by film critic and champion of bad cinema Joe Bob Briggs (nom de guerre of writer John Bloom). Said Briggs in 1992 when the I-45 closed, "That's the drive-in way. It's also the Texas way. They can rip down those six drive-in screens, but they can't take away our memories. We'll always have *Yor*."[67]

In December 1987, Griffith Theatres leased the I-45. Owner H. D. "Cotton" Griffith had been in the business since 1950, and his daughter, Jan Bettis, had grown up with them, working the Tidwell candy counter as a teenager. Many area drive-ins, including the Thunderbird, Parkway, Tidwell, and Market Street, had all been either leased or owned by Griffith

No more movies at the I-45 Drive-In, 1992. When first constructed in 1982, speaker posts were installed, then went unused as a radio-transmitted system was adopted. Photograph by David Welling.

at one time or another. Improvements made by the Griffiths included additional security and the showing of first-run films. The latter change brought an end to car-load nights, since film-company contracts required a specific dollar amount be paid for each person; however, the I-45 was now showing first-run features at the same time as the indoor houses.[68]

The era of the Houston drive-in came to an end in February 1992. A long-term lease for the property was obtained by the Dallas-based Weber & Company development group, and construction plans, set for March, were made for a 355,000-square-foot retail center, including a K-Mart, a Builder's Square, and a Pace Membership Warehouse.[69] "Just what this town needs . . . another K-Mart," remarked more than one drive-in patron.

The Griffith management was given little time to wrap things up. Originally, they had hoped to stay open through Sunday, March 1, but were then told to vacate by first of March. The last day of operation was February 29–Leap Year Day.[70]

News of the I-45's closing attracted the media in droves, along with a huge boost in attendance by those wanting to experience the nostalgia of a drive-in one last time. On its final night, the I-45 played to a packed house (with this writer in attendance), and four of the six screens sold out. The last week of operation brought out young and old, regulars and some who had not been to an outdoor theatre in years, as indicated by a man who came up to the booth and (unaware of the radio-transmitted sound) reported that someone had stolen every single speaker and pole in the lot.[71]

During the final week, Bettis was asked by a reporter what she would miss most. Her reply was of the sky during the magic hour: "I've watched many beautiful sunsets over our west screens. The sunsets will still be there after the I-45 is gone, but they won't look the same over a shopping center."[72]

Perhaps *Houston Post* columnist Ken Hoffman noted it best in his weekly column: "I went to the last night of the I-45 drive-in theatre. The place was packed. Kids and their parents came dressed in

A new drive-in for the new century: the Showboat. Photograph by David Welling.

Map of drive-ins in Houston. Map by David Welling.

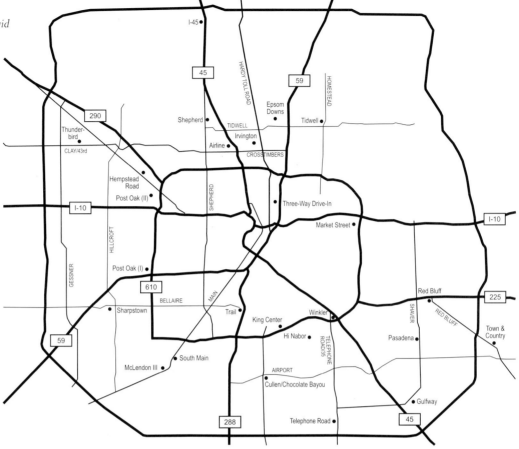

pajamas. People shared their insect repellent. It took me 45 minutes to get a Coke. It was so much fun that everybody wondered why they didn't go to the drive-in more often. Which explains why it's being torn down for another shopping mall. But the weirdest thing was, on closing night, they showed coming attractions."[73]

THOUGH THEY ARE NOW few and far between, outdoor theatres have never fully gone away. What is more, there has been a resurgence of interest in ozoners and, yes, new constructions to back up that interest. According to statistics assembled by the United Drive-In Theatre Owners Association in 2004, twenty-seven new drive-ins have been built since the 1990s, and fifty-

two older drive-ins have reopened.[74] In 2005, the owners of the Crossroads Drive-In in Shiner constructed a new drive-in theatre, the Starlite, on Highway 59 near Kingwood. The following year, the Showboat Drive-In opened in Tomball.

The drive-in will never reach the popularity that it once enjoyed; that time has forever passed, and the numbers are still going down. In the summer of 1999, there were 447 operational drive-ins in the United States. By July 2004, the number had dropped to 403.[75] The extension of daylight savings time would most likely take a further toll on the numbers. However, for the present, some outdoor theatres still operate, and the people who love them are willing to drive–and watch–by the carload.

The Windsor Theatre sold tickets well in advance for key features such as It's a Mad, Mad, Mad, Mad World, the first movie to take advantage of the new single-lens Super Cinerama projection process, 1963. Courtesy of Roy Bonario.

THIRTEEN

★ ★ ★

THE
SIXTIES

★ ★ ★

THE TIMES, THEY ARE A-CHANGIN'

We don't feel too dependent on Holly-wood product. We play almost all of it.

RICHARD SMITH, GENERAL CINEMA

★ THE SIXTIES were a decade of phenom-enal change and upheaval. Social and political reverberations stemming from the Vietnam War, the civil rights move-ment, feminism, and a complete rejection of the older generation's values by the youth of America were reflected in music, art, and the movies as the free-love gen-eration made its mark on the times. It was within this arena that theatre construc-tion would resume and, by the end of the decade, evolve radically.

The last two of Houston's grand-scale single-screen theatres were built dur-ing this decade—both by the Jefferson Amusement Company of Beaumont. By the time that Jefferson's Sharpstown/Gaylynn opened in 1965, a new trend had already been put into motion—that of housing multiple auditoriums in a

single building. The number of screens crammed under one roof continued to grow, and by the late nineties the city could boast of a thirty-screen megaplex— but in 1962 a single screen was enough for most.

THE WINDSOR
5078 Richmond Avenue

In the sixties, a new strategy in movie-house construction evolved: placing theatres either in or near shopping malls and large strip centers. Following this formula, the spacious Windsor Cinerama Theatre became the newest addition to the Windsor Plaza Shopping Center, which had opened in April 1959.

The theatre was built for Julius Gordon of Beaumont—president of the Jef-ferson Amusement Company. Gordon's father, Sol E. Gordon, had started up the company around 1924, and as a youth, Julius had worked for his father. He took over the company in 1940.[1]

Opening night was on December 20, 1962, with the Cinerama spectacle *The Wonderful World of the Brothers Grimm.* This marked the return to Houston of the ultrawide film process after the Rivoli's previous attempt to bring Cinerama to the city in 1960. The premiere-night crowd included astronaut Alan Shepard, Mayor Pro Tem Bill Swanson, Julius Gordon, and managing director Charles Paine. Up to showtime, Cinerama technicians from New York were making last-minute checks on the three enormous projectors and the separate, seven-channel sound track.[2]

Like Jefferson's Gaylynn Theatre, which would follow in 1965, the Wind-

The Windsor Theatre, 1988. Courtesy of the Houston Metropolitan Research Center, Houston Public Library, RGD6N 04-29-88.

sor was opulent in its large-scale simplicity. A long desk-like box office ran along the left wall of the enormous lobby. Past this were the stairs leading to the balcony and, farther back, a concession stand and restrooms. Food and drinks were not permitted inside the auditorium, a safeguard against spills on the deluxe seats and carpeting. This, of course, would eventually change. An ultrahigh ceiling, huge antique-style mirrors, dark wood lining the lobby walls, and rich carpeting completed the effect.

The decor of the auditorium was in deep reds and dark blues, with huge drapes covering the walls and rows of plush color-coordinated Heywood-Wakefield rocking-style armchair seats spaced a luxurious forty inches apart. The main floor seated 735 and the balcony held 270.[3] Based on the author's experience, those seats, along with the Gaylynn's, would remain the most comfortable accommodations in any movie house in Houston.

The movie screen was a massive curved structure, hidden from the audience by a pull-back curtain before showtime. It would then withdraw farther and farther until the full seventy-foot expanse was visible. Excellent viewing also available from the balcony, whose seats and decor matched those on the lower level.

Over the following years, the Windsor ran Cinerama exclusives, including *How the West Was Won* in 1963, along with regular features. On April 10, 1968, Stanley Kubrick's *2001: A Space Odyssey* premiered nationwide. The country was still reeling from the assassination of Martin Luther King, Jr., which had occurred six days earlier. A *2001* star, Keir Dullea, appeared at the Windsor premiere on Wednesday night, having arrived in town for an unofficial Keir Dullea film festival.[4]

The Windsor's ties to the Jefferson Amusement Company came to an end with the formation of the Tercar Theatre Company. Tercar was a business venture headed by Jack S. Josey, president of the Josey Oil Company, as chairman of the board; other Tercar officers included president Robert H. Park, also of Josey Oil Company, who had served as general counsel for Jefferson Amusement Company and East Texas Theatres; vice president and general manager Charles F. Paine, previously the director of theatre operations for Jefferson Amusement Company; and treasurer N. D. Lay, Jr.[5]

The Tercar name was derived from the name of the owners' daughters, Terry Park and Carolyn Josey. Other Houston theatres on their roster would include Jefferson's Sharpstown Theatre (renamed the Gaylynn), the Allen Center, the Bellaire, the East Park, the Memorial, the Park III, and the Southgate Red and Blue as well as the Airline, Pasadena, and Telephone Road drive-ins. Their out-of-town theatres included the Brunson and Decker Drive-in in Baytown; the Port and Colonial Drive-in in La Porte; the Cole and Twin City Drive-in in Rosenberg; the Cole in Halletsville; the Grand in Yoakum; the Palm in Sugar Land; and the Lamar in Richmond.[6]

When the Windsor ran a standard-format feature on its massive curved screen, even a modest film took on epic proportions. When a 70mm Cinemascope print

would show up, the results could be awe-some. In 1981, the Windsor landed one of the two 70mm prints of Steven Spiel-berg's *Raiders of the Lost Ark* shipped to Texas (the other went to Austin). As *Houston Post* writer Eric Gerber described at the time, "It's offering a 70 mm print that swells the screen from its already impressive 40-foot width to an eye-pop-ping, head-twisting 70-foot expanse which wraps around the curved outer edges. Audiences used to the compact dimen-sions of today's typical multicinema screen have been heard to actually gasp as the curtains open . . . and open . . . and open. Get a prime seat—center sec-tion, about a third of the way back—and the non-stop action of *Raiders* threatens to engulf you."[7]

Changing times caused the Wind-sor to eventually succumb to economics, and in 1979 the balcony was converted to a second theatre. Business continued to flounder under the onslaught of competi-tion from multicinemas, home video, and cable television.

In December 1982, the Tercar Theatre Corporation sold the Windsor II, Gaylynn III, and Memorial II to Jimmy Duncan, owner of the Cineplex Corporation.[8] Dur-ing this time, the theatre acted as one of the sites for the Houston International Film Festival, along with the Greenway and the Museum of Fine Arts.[9] Despite the new management, the Windsor never regained the stature of its former days, changing to a dollar cinema during its last year before shutting down entirely. On Sunday, January 15, 1989, the last features were shown, and then the projectors were silenced.

In 1989, Houston businessmen Sam Nogroski and Ron Marks spent more than a million dollars to renovate the

The Windsor lobby, mid-1970s, with a display for the movie Maneater, *a reissue of the 1969 Burt Reynolds film* Shark! *Courtesy of Charles Paine.*

theatre space into a 33,000-square-foot nightclub. The Avalon, as it was named, housed three clubs under one roof, the largest located in the main auditorium. Little remained of the cinema except for the metal stairway railing in the lobby and the jet black scaffolding that once supported the grand, seventy-foot-high screen, left as a tribute to a more glamorous era.[10]

The Avalon did not last long. By 1992, the club had reopened as Zazz, which also closed down after a time. The building underwent remodeling in late 1994, reopening the following February as the City Streets nightclub, actually a compound of six separate clubs, which would remain in operation through the end of the century. The main auditorium was renamed the Rose, a country-and-western nightclub that included a thirty-five-foot-high replica of the Alamo; the Cinerama screen scaffolding was left intact. The former lobby was renovated to house the Midway sports bar and Stray Cats, a sing-along bar with dueling pianos. An additional three bars were positioned upstairs: the Atlantis dance club, the Blue Monkey rhythm-and-blues club, and the Green Room, featuring mock gambling and billiards.[11] By 2006, this entertainment venue was gone as well. The space was eventually gutted and converted into retail space.

THE OAK VILLAGE/LONG POINT
10016 *Long Point*

Less than six months after the Windsor's opening, the Spring Branch area, in west Houston, gained its own theatre.

The Oak Village Theatre, set at the far end of a neighborhood shopping center on Long Point, opened on June 29, 1963. The massive auditorium housed 1,050 seats and a stunning sixty-foot-wide screen. Opening day began with a kiddie show featuring *The Three Stooges Meet Hercules* plus a serial and a cartoon carnival. Afterward came the opening presentation, Walt Disney's *Miracle of the White Stallions*.[12]

The Oak Village eventually changed its name to the Long Point Cinema, and by 1976 the theatre was operating as a dollar house with second-run features. It was during this time that Alvin Guggenheim took control of the theatre. By the eighties, most single theatres could no longer stay afloat, and the Long Point took to the most obvious solution: twinning. The massive auditorium and sixty-foot screen were lost when the space was divided in two. The Long Point limped into the nineties, at times operational, and other times not. Near the end of 1999 it was gutted and converted into retail space, a new drop ceiling obscuring the original deep blue one.

THE SHARPSTOWN/GAYLYNN
304 *Sharpstown Center*

Less than three years after the Windsor debuted, Jefferson Amusement Company opened its second major Houston theatre—one of the last of the large-scale Houston movie houses built before the multiplex era. The groundbreaking ceremonies for the 28,500-square-foot building took place on November 4, 1964. It was Gordon's intention for the Sharpstown

The Gaylynn and the Windsor were the last of the large-lobby theatres to be built before the multicinemas moved in. For ushers who swept up popcorn from the floor during every feature, the expansive lobby was a nightmare. Courtesy of Charles Paine.

Auditorium of the Gaylynn, its Cinerama screen undergoing final preparations, 1965. Courtesy of the Houston Metropolitan Research Center, Houston Public Library, RGD6N 10422.

Theatre to outdo the Windsor in opulence and appeal.[13]

A massive open lobby, measuring 50 by 175 feet and including an extrahigh ceiling, was ornamented by three fifty-six-inch-wide chandeliers. Three massive antique mirrors were located on the left sidewall, and a fourth ten-by-twelve-foot etched mirror was located behind the concession stand. Also adorning the walls was a vinyl wall covering imported from Holland. It was finished off with both white Alabama and Napoleon Gray marble set off by black slate trim. Gaylynn's architect, L. C. Kyburtz, also designed furniture specifically for the lobby.

The auditorium was one of ornate simplicity. The fabric-draped walls shifted attention to the 98-by-36-1/2-foot screen, which allowed for flat, Cinemascope, or Super Cinerama formats. Projection equipment was also set up to handle all major film formats: Cinerama, Cinemascope, and 70mm. Sound was carried through a transistorized six-track sound system.

As at its sister theatre, the Windsor, the auditorium seats were of the supersized Heywood-Wakefield rocking-chair variety that were the most comfortable seats in town. Seating capacity was 1,293.

The gala opening took place on May 27, 1965, with *Mirage* as the feature presentation. Master of ceremonies for the evening was radio personality Tim Nolan of KPRC's *Tim and Bob Show.* Also attending were Mayor Pro Tem Lee McLemore, Charles Paine, and manager Foy Myricks, who had previously run the King Center Drive-In and the Jefferson Theatre in Beaumont.

It operated briefly as the Sharpstown Theatre before taking on its permanent name, the Gaylynn, in June 1965. Construction on a second auditorium, the Gaylynn Terrace, began in 1968. Entry to the new theatre, which had its own lobby, was through two sets of double doors on the left side of the Gaylynn lobby.

Betty Cuthrell of Beaumont handled the Terrace's decor, which evoked a nature garden. The intimate lobby walls were latticed in shades of olive and white, with grass green and floral designs predominating. The design of the large, 827-seat auditorium was simple: olive curtains, plush seating, and a massive screen.[14]

The Terrace opened on December 22, 1968, with *The Lion in Winter.* Tickets for the reserved-seat performances were available at the box office and through the mail.[15]

The Gaylynn had its share of special events, such as a live appearance by Johnny Cash on November 16, 1973, when he was promoting his film *The Gospel Road.*[16] Another premiere was Russ Meyer's busty epic *Beneath the Valley of the Ultra-Vixens,* starring Francesca "Kitten" Natividad, whose bust line was one of exaggerated proportions. Both Meyer and Natividad were on hand for the April 1979 premiere. However, the pinnacle of the Gaylynn's success was the world premiere of *Urban Cowboy* on June 5, 1980. Tickets for the premiere and private party were $125, the proceeds benefiting the Houston Child Guidance Center; over $140,000 was raised from the event. In attendance were the cast and crew, including stars John Travolta and Debra Winger, Paramount executives, and Houston celebrities. Also pres-

The foyer of the Gaylynn Terrace was positioned directly off of the main Gaylynn lobby. Courtesy of Charles Paine.

ent were the Houston Derrick Dolls cheerleading team, several Dolly Parton look-alikes, and club owner Mickey Gilley. Following the world premiere, guests took a trip to Pasadena for the party held at Gilley's, the country and western nightclub featured in the film.[17]

The advanced projection setup at the Terrace made it a prime spot for wide-film-stock presentations such as *Ryan's Daughter*, *Sleeping Beauty*, *Logan's Run* (in Todd-AO 35), and the 1979 rerelease of *The Sound of Music*. Also in 1979, the Terrace's walls shook as the sci-fi

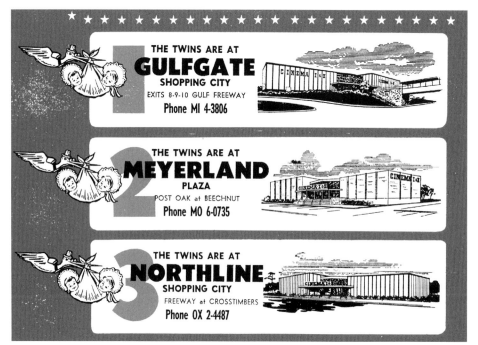

Advertisement in the Houston Post for the Gulfgate, Meyerland, and Northline twin theatres, April 1965.

feature *Battlestar Galactica* was shown in Sensurround.

Although business was substantial, competition from the multicinemas brought about the inevitable twinning of the main Gaylynn screen in November 1975. The grand Cinerama auditorium was split down the middle, evident afterwards by the seating arrangement still being angled inward for one large central screen. The eighties took their toll on the Tercar Company as more multicinemas were built in Houston, culminating in the sale of the Gaylynn, Windsor, and Memorial theatres to Cineplex. The Gaylynn closed for good during the week of September 4, 1988.

The building reopened in early August 1989 as Jungle Jim's Playland, a kiddie park operated by Children's Amusement, a San Antonio company. Auditoriums one and two were leveled, gutted, and opened to the main lobby area. Once finished, the playground of rides and games bore no resemblance to its former incarnation.[18] The Terrace was left alone, sans seats, and used as a storage area. Within three years, the park was closed. It then reopened as the Alpine Skate ice rink. By the end of the century, it too would vacate the building, and leaving the former movie house empty once more.

The Gaylynn served as a bookend in theatre architectural style. While it was not Houston's last single-screen theatre to be constructed, it was the last one to be built with grandiose flair. In the coming years, size and elegance would be downplayed in favor of functionality. A month before the Gaylynn's premiere, a trio of theatres that opened in Houston foreshadowed all that would come afterward.

This was the dawning of the age of the multicinema.

THE CINEMA II THEATRES: THE GULFGATE, MEYERLAND AND NORTHLINE

New theatre chains with names like AMC and General Cinema swept across the country during the sixties, taking their place alongside Loew's.

For Houston, it began in 1965, when the Boston-based General Cinema Corporation simultaneously opened three twin-screen theatres on the same date. The $3 million Cinema II Theatres at the Gulfgate, Meyerland, and Northline shopping malls opened on Thursday, April 13, 1965, with the world premiere of *Mister Moses*, with Robert Mitchum. A live appearance was made by Mitchum, first at Gulfgate, where he was met by a troop of the Harris County Sheriff's Office's Mounted Posse before being shuttled over to Meyerland and finally to Northline. The following day, Walt Disney's *Mary Poppins* began a rerelease showing on the second screens of the three theatres.[19] Each theatre featured widely spaced push-back seats, auditorium capacities of 1,000 and 500 patrons, and a lobby art gallery.[20]

"We're trying to get back people who haven't been to a movie in years," remarked Richard Smith, son of General Cinema's founder, at the time. "We'll never have the once-a-week audience the movies once had. But we'd like to get them back every two weeks."[21]

In June of the following year, the Meyerland hosted the world premiere of *A*

Big Hand for the Little Lady, with Henry Fonda, Joanne Woodward, and Jason Robards. Producer-director Fielder Cook appeared, along with stars Woodward, Paul Ford, Robert Middleton, and John Qualen.[22]

All three General Cinema theatres ceased operation in the nineties as competition from other multiplexes made them unprofitable. The Northline Cinema closed in 1996, a month before basketball star Earvin "Magic" Johnson announced plans to build a twelve-screen theatre at the mall.[23] The Meyerland Cinema stood until January 1995, and then was torn down and replaced with a new multicinema as part of the Meyerland Plaza renovation. According to its manager, the old theatre understructure was effectively built to last, resisting attempts at demolition. Big cranes were brought in to tear it down, but it still took days to level the building, and at one point the heavy machinery had succeeded in only bending the frame-

work at an angle.[24] It was replaced with a new, eight-screen theatre, which officially opened on March 17, 1995.

THE MEMORIAL

The 1,400-seat Memorial Theatre, constructed inside the Memorial City shopping mall in 1966, was one of the last single-screen theatres to be built in Houston. It was built for Stanley Warner Texas, Inc., which also operated the Winkler, Pasadena, and Airline drive-ins.[25] The Memorial opened on June 23, 1966, with the Steve McQueen feature *Nevada Smith*.[26] The auditorium also included what was now becoming obsolete in theatre design: a balcony. The Stanley Warner theatre was sold to Tercar in the seventies. Under Tercar, the auditorium was twinned, and operated until 1982, when it was sold to Cineplex. The Memorial would remain in operation for a few more years before it

The lobby stairs in the Memorial Theatre led up to the balcony and the projectionist's booth. Courtesy of Charles Paine.

James Coburn and an unidentified woman walk down the aisle of the Memorial Theatre during a special promotion in the early 1970s. Courtesy of Charles Paine.

closed down for good. The space was gutted and converted into a Miller's Outpost retail store.

The Memorial, the last of the single-screen theatres, marked the end of an era. The Cinema II houses at Gulfgate, Meyerland, and Northline malls were harbingers: theatres increased the number of auditoriums they contained while reducing the size of each space. Bigger in number, always bigger, was the attitude, but since the houses became akin to doll-houses, bigger did not necessarily mean better.

For a while, no one really cared.

The Golden Star Cinema, 912 Prairie, in the Packard's Troy Laundry Building (also known as the Shoe Market Building), 1981. The structure has since undergone a full restoration. Photograph by Jim Koehn.

FOURTEEN

★ ★ ★

THE
X-HOUSES

★ ★ ★

*A movie without sex would be like a
candy bar without nuts in it.*

EARL WILSON, GOSSIP COLUMNIST

*The freedom that enables me not to go to
porno films enables others to go.*

MOLLY HASKELL, CRITIC

★ DECENCY HAD BEEN an issue with the
movies from the earliest days of their existence. Some were outraged at the shame-
lessness of *The Kiss* when it first was
shown in 1896. Many felt that there
should be someone, preferably themselves, to dictate morality and keep the
populace in line.

In the forefront of this was the clergy,
whose job it was to save its citizens from
sin and eternal damnation. During Houston's early years, George C. Rankin, minister of Shearn Memorial Methodist
Church, led a constant attack on the city's
immorality. In 1894 he toured the tainted
areas of town incognito; his investigations
included spending several evenings at the
Variety Theatre, which he described as a
"disreputable and low flung manufactory
of vice, immorality and crime [where]
there are more young men in this city and

surrounding country traveling straight to hell than along any other one route now open to the public."[1] He blasted the "hellish" theatre during his Sunday sermon, having seen gamblers "swill beer and wine like swine in the gutter," while women danced with obscene gyrations and jests. Such behavior, he said, "would thoroughly impoverish the vocabulary of a pure-minded mortal."[2] Having heard ministers referred to as "God howlers" and "Bible yelpers," he yelped from the pulpit the names and places that he had seen in his travels.[3]

Houston acted by passing laws to curb such immorality, such as the 1905 "Goo-Goo Eyes" ordinance. "Any male person," the ordinance stated, "in the City of Houston who shall stare at, or make what is commonly called 'goo-goo eyes' at, or in any other manner look at or make remarks concerning, or cough or whistle at, or do any other act to attract the attention of any woman or female person" could be found guilty of the misdemeanor offence.[4] The city inflicted nationwide ridicule upon itself in 1968 when it revised the ordinance.

By the end of 1910, Houston had passed an ordinance creating a three-member board of censors to uphold standards of decency in places of public entertainment. The board had the power to levy fines ranging from $25 to $200 and to rescind an operator's license. The board's decisions were sometimes disputed, as when it condemned sixty feet of film in the movie *Don't Call It Love* (1923) for an "indecent" kiss. Theatre manager C. A. McFarland responded by stating it was merely a "plain, whole-souled smack."[5]

In 1923 alone the board banned twenty-eight movies. A *Houston Post* editor

The Village Theatre, 1984. Within ten years it would be torn down. Courtesy of Al Zarzana.

responded to such fanaticism by pointing out that a national board of censors was also in existence. "Considering this whole question of censorship," his column read, "the Post is wondering if the idea of a local censor board having unlimited power to pass upon all phases of a film is not impractical and unnecessary. As it is now, it is only a matter of the opinion of one person, or perhaps, a few against the opinion of others, perhaps just as capable of judging. Haven't we about reached the point in practice where we have set up an autocracy, or at least, an oligarchy, to rule in the realm of amusements?"[6]

In 1929 the board was expanded to eleven people. Mrs. Thomas H. Eggert, who had served as secretary to the three-person board for seven-plus years, felt that such censorship of the movies was vitally necessary and that Houston's standards were "second to none in the country."[7] When her position was eliminated, she responded by stating that of the 12,000 programs the board had reviewed, 2,600 ended up partially censored and an additional 225 were totally rejected for falling completely beneath its standards.[8] As previously mentioned, two films starring black Galveston boxer Jack Johnson, shown at the Lincoln Theatre, certainly offended its sensibilities, and were banned. After all, it was totally inappropriate to show a dignified black man interacting on-screen with white people.[9]

In 1922, to counteract a number of scandals, Hollywood created its own censorship board, complete with a production code. The murder of William Desmond Taylor and the rape trials of Roscoe "Fatty" Arbuckle had exposed the sordid excess of the movie business and brought a defensive Tinseltown to its knees. The studios appointed former postmaster Will Hayes censorship czar, empowering him to oversee future productions and make sure that, since Hollywood was doing its job, local censors would no longer be needed.[10] As Hays once stated, "Good taste is good business."[11] The association would keep a steel grip on studio output for the next four decades.

This all changed in the sixties. As the decade progressed, the Motion Picture Association of America (MPAA) production code, which had effectively controlled film content for so long, collapsed under the social and creative changes of the times. The new artistic expression found in films such as *Lolita* (1962), *Alfie* (1966), *Blow-Up* (1966), and *Who's Afraid of Virginia Woolf?* (1966) pushed the code to its limit. It soon became obvious that the current system had outlived its usefulness.

In May 1966, former Houstonian Jack J. Valenti took over as president of

The Academy Theatre, 4816 Main, once hosted legitimate stage productions before becoming an X-rated venue. Designed by Dixon and Greenwood, it was the first building in America constructed specifically for theatre-in-the-round. Photograph by Jim Koehn.

the MPAA. Valenti had worked as an usher at the Horwitz theatres during his youth, and later headed up an advertising and public relations firm. He was also a Saturday-morning columnist for the *Houston Post*.[12] When approached about taking the MPAA position, he was serving as special adviser to President Johnson. He was forty-five years old.

Under Valenti's guidance, the production code was dismantled in 1968 and replaced by a more contemporary rating system that allowed for artistic expression yet served as a barometer for delicate subject matter. The initial categories were four: the G rating was given to material suitable for general audiences; the M rating, to films for mature audiences; R was for restricted films, i.e., persons under sixteen would not be admitted to them unless accompanied by a parent or adult guardian; and an X rating, given to movies with graphic content or adult themes, meant that persons under sixteen would not be admitted. In an oversight that would cause numerous problems, the X rating was not copyrighted, while the other three were. The MPAA assumed that filmmakers could self-impose the X rating on their movies if they felt it pointless to submit them for classification; the MPAA did not expect the X rating to become synonymous with pornography.[13]

This did not occur right away. The first five years of the ratings system offered some notable X films, such as *The Killing of Sister George* and Brian De Palma's *Greetings*, both from 1968. *Midnight Cowboy* won the Oscar for Best Picture in 1969, and Stanley Kubrick's *Clockwork Orange* received the New York Film Critics Circle Awards for best film and best director in 1971. What was perhaps the last

great X film of the period, *Last Tango in Paris*, was released in 1972.[14]

As the seventies progressed, the X stamp came to be associated more and more with soft- and hard-core pornography. The previously discreet "nudie" films reached full bloom during this time.

The ratings system underwent modifications over the years. In 1971 the M rating was changed to GP, standing for "general audiences, parental guidance suggested," and was changed again the following year to PG. It was further expanded in 1984 to PG-13 in response to the intensity of Spielberg's *Indiana Jones and the Temple of Doom* and Joe Dante's *Gremlins*.

The X rating was another matter. Many theatres would not book an X film, whether it was pornographic or not. For Hollywood, the X rating was the kiss of death at the box office. Finally, after concentrated pressure from filmmakers, the X rating was scrapped in September 1990, replaced by a copyrighted NC-17 rating. Some in the industry argued that this was a cop-out, since changing the label would do nothing to change the "adults only" stigma. Regardless of whether a film was rated X or NC-17, some theatres, as well as some video-store chains, simply would not carry the product. What was needed was a new, respectable category in addition to X. None of this had been anticipated in 1968.

The new artistic license given to filmmakers during the sixties created its own problems. The X label seemed to invite protests by those who supported censorship. Such films were a major concern of civic-minded groups, and whenever such material was shown, the moralists came out in droves. When an X title was shown

The Franklin Street Cinema in 1983, well after it closed. The building was eventually razed. Photograph by Jim Koehn.

at an outdoor theatre, neighborhood groups felt that it was too visible and demanded it be shown indoors, if at all. When an indoor theatre ran X films, protesters wanted it shown elsewhere. If it was shown in another neighborhood, they would journey to the new theatre to protest anew, stating that such material should not be shown at all.

The previously mentioned battle between the Red Bluff Drive-In and the City of Pasadena was indicative of the general climate for all such establishments. The Heights Theatre is said to have gone up in flames in June 1969 because of its exhibition of the Swedish import *I Am Curious (Yellow)*, although a dispute at the time regarding union projectionists strongly suggests otherwise. Before the Heights showing, the film received its Houston premiere at the University Village Art Cinema in May. City officials quickly received letters of complaint from the locals. Harris County District Attorney Carol S. Vance, as quoted in a May 17 newspaper clipping, said, "We cannot prosecute a movie which has been

legally imported into this country." The Swedish film was cleared for import by a Second Circuit Court of Appeals opinion in 1968.[15]

While *I Am Curious* escaped the censor's wrath, others did not. Antismut campaigns gained strength in 1969, fueled by churches, the legislature, local leaders, and neighborhood groups. Several antiobscenity bills were passed through the Texas Senate that year, along with a resolution, passed by the Texas House, asking Congress to limit the power of the Supreme Court and leave obscenity judgments to the state. In separate cases, the Supreme Court had previously established a set of guidelines for determining obscenity: obscenity was to be established by community standards (*Roth v. United States*, 1957), and to be considered obscene, material must be "patently offensive" and "utterly without redeeming social value" (*Memoirs v. Massachusetts*, 1966).[16]

Newspaper advertising varied from the suggestive to the blatant. While the Paris, in 1969, advertised two big adult hits, *Dia-*

mond *Jim* and *Ramrodders*, the Art Cinema went for a more euphemistic approach:

> *Holiday special, especially filmed for this season. Limited engagement. Probably the most adult film shown ever. In good taste we have eliminated the title of this most adult color motion picture. So explicit and seen in such detail, you will be quite surprised and convinced you've made the right decision as to adult theatre. Rated XX, 100% everything.*[17]

What followed over the next decade became something of a routine. A theatre would run a film of a "questionable" nature, which would, in turn, bring about a number of complaints. Police would raid the offending theatre, usually arresting the manager, assistant manager, projectionist, ticket seller, and whomever else they could find, and confiscate the film. Bond would be set and paid, followed by court dates, injunctions, and appeals. Issues of morality, censorship, art, and pornography inevitably became an issue for the legal system.

One such instance was a "hardcore pornography sweep" and raid of adult houses in 1970. Twenty vice squad officers, reinforced by thirty uniformed policemen, raided fifteen Houston adult theatres and a lounge. During the October 8 raid, twenty-three employees were arrested, and bond was set at $400 each. In addition to the former Horwitz theatres–the Isis, Rivoli (Uptown), and Texan–those raided were the Academy, the Art Cinema, Cinema X, the Mini Park, the Zipper Lounge, the Movie

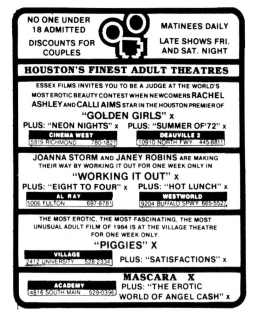

Advertisement from the Houston Post (1984) for six adult theatres: Cinema West, the Deauville 2, the Al*Ray, the Westworld, the Village, and the Academy.

House, Cinema Arts, Cinema Arts II, Tel-Art Cinema, Kitty Arts, Kazba Art Cinema, the Rex, and the Houston Mini-Art Theatre. The response was a lawsuit brought against District Attorney Vance and others. He filed for dismissal.[18]

On and on, back and forth, the process went, the courts serving as a battleground. Said a police sergeant at the time, "If they continue to run this type of lewd, obscene films banned by the state of Texas, we will continue to make raids and arrests."[19] Mel Friedman, the attorney for the theatres, responded by accusing the police of wrongfully "setting themselves up as censors for the entire adult community."[20]

Friedman, then a twenty-eight-year-old graduate of the University of Houston, successfully handled the defense. Said Friedman to the *Houston Post* in November 1970, "We made the first breakthrough here and the rest of the country followed. New York and Los Angeles might have more pornography now, but we won the first court case here and that opened it up."[21]

Theatres such as the Mini-Art appeared across town. The Mini-Art was nothing more than a forty-two-seat auditorium with a loudspeaker in front, blaring music to accompany the otherwise silent movie. Of the film, *Houston Post* reporter Ralph Williams described it as "one 20-minute sex orgy after another. Only the actors change."[22] He also noted that a mere year earlier a person could have been arrested for watching the same film in the privacy of his own home.

With 1972 came a film that radically changed the porn industry as well as how it was perceived. *Deep Throat* was initially released in June 1972 in New York. The $25,600 film made $1,300,000 over a thirty-nine-week run at the World Theatre in Manhattan and became a permanent part of the vocabulary of the times, supplying jokes for Johnny Carson and a

code name for a participant in the Watergate scandal. It also made a household name of Linda Lovelace, whose ability to overcome her gag reflex took X-rated films into new regions.[23] Police raids followed quickly wherever the film was shown. It was no different in Houston, but the ensuing trials redefined pornography from the legal stance.

Cinema West had been running adult features for three years when its owner acquired *Deep Throat*. Following several private screenings, it was opened to the public on April 10, 1973, and after three showings, the police raided the theatre and confiscated the film. Indictments, including a felony charge of conspiracy to exhibit obscene matter, were then issued for the owner and five other associates. Like federal law, the state's definition of pornography was threefold: the material in question had to have no redeeming social value, had to appeal to prurient interest, and had to affront contemporary community standards.[24]

A highly publicized trial ended with a hung jury. Another trial, on misdemeanor charges, ended in a mistrial. Meanwhile, the confiscated print was run numerous times, for the jury, prosecutors, defense lawyers—even for Rice University sociology students--and when the well-viewed film was returned, it was in virtually unusable condition.

Public opinion was divided, at least as expressed in the letters sections of the daily newspapers. While some condemned the material (and occasionally quoted scripture), others took a larger view of the trial and its ramifications. One reader questioned the police deployment's use of time and resources, asking if "the

The new Cinema West location, under construction at 5819 Richmond Avenue, c. 1978. Courtesy of Jim Ohmart.

department has caught up with all the murderers, thieves, swindlers, etc., who DON'T charge admission to their performances?" Said another, "I'm 35 years old, I have $5 and if I want to blow it on a skin flick, why should the fuzz care? I am also a woman and there's not a man alive who has the right to decide what I find disgusting and degrading. Only I can do that." Yet another commented, "I'm a 38-year-old married woman and I enjoyed *Deep Throat* so much last week in San Francisco that I had planned to see it again here in Houston."[25]

With the success of *Deep Throat*, porn films began to take on a new status, and a handful became the X equivalents of Hollywood blockbusters: *The Devil in Miss Jones* (1973), *The Joy of Letting Go* (1976), *The Opening of Misty Beethoven* (1976), and *Behind the Green Door* (1972), with Marilyn Chambers, who might be considered the industry's first real star. With Bernardo Bertolucci's *Last Tango in Paris*, the line between porn and mainstream art, already hazy to begin with, became forever blurred.

Film erotica could also show up in less likely surroundings, such as the University of Houston, when the Best of the Second Annual Erotic Film Festival was shown on campus in 1974. *Houston Post* writer Eric Gerber attended the presentation and commented that it drew "a very big crowd. The collection of erotic shorts was . . . uh, stimulating and amusing."[26] He also took note of the audience's reaction to several gay films. The first was a lesbian encounter, which was "greeted with silence and admiration." The second, a male homosexual liaison, "was met with nervous giggling and hooting—and not just from the males." Gerber found the sexual

Georgina Spelvin, star of the film Take Off, *with an unidentified friend on opening night of the new Cinema West, c. 1978. Courtesy of Jim Ohmart.*

prejudices in such matters interesting and somewhat embarrassing. "Remember," he added, "this wasn't your usual porno film crowd, but an honest to goodness, raised-consciousness college audience. It's no simple task to untangle the knot of threatened role concepts, social conditioning, and inherent psychic reactions that account for the contrasting attitudes to the two films, so I won't even try."

There were also confrontations with the Motion Picture Operators' Union, upset that certain theatres were using non-union projectionists. In December 1972, a restraining order was issued against the union for destroying property at four theatres: Cinema XX, the Academy, the Mini-Art, and Cinema One. The theatre owners claimed that union members had threatened them with bodily harm, threatened to burn the theatres out of business, damaged customers' cars, and destroyed movie equipment. The union vice president responded that union members were not guilty of such actions.[27]

Theatres such as Cinema West and the Village were still in operation in 1980, but the adult industry was undergoing a radical change at the time. The advent of home video would make most of these theatres obsolete, and a bare few survived into the nineties. At some of these, such as the Star, formerly the Santa Rosa Theatre, the lobby was converted into video-rental space. Now fans of X-rated fare could indulge their tastes in the safety of their own homes, which might be located in any neighborhood, next to a church or even a school. The irony was that video and cable meant such material, formerly isolated and visible, now invisibly pervaded every neighborhood.

The line separating porn and art continued to blur over the years, as demonstrated by films such as Pier Paolo Pasolini's *Salo* and Bob Guccione's *Caligula*. In the case of *Salo*, Houston vice officers raided the River Oaks Theatre in 1982 during the film's Houston engagement (see Chapter 8 for an account of the raid and subsequent trial). A year earlier, *Caligula* had been shown in an R-rated version despite a personal appeal from Mayor Jim McConn to the distribution supervisor for AMC. A special screening at the AMC Northwest was held for vice squad officers to determine if the film violated section 43.25 of the state penal code. Officers responded by saying it was "not worth the trouble." Said R. K. Hansen, an assistant district attorney and member of the officers obscenity committee, "In my opinion, it is a worthless movie. It was ridiculous--utterly ridiculous."[28]

Two decades later, sex on film could still arouse controversy. In 1996, John Cameron Mitchell wrote and directed *Shortbus*, which was shown at the Cannes Film Festival that year. It featured unsimulated sex in several scenes. Radio and TV personality Sook-Yin Lee was almost fired from her job at the Canadian Broadcasting Corporation because of her participation in the film.[29]

To date, porn has continued to flourish, becoming a multibillion-dollar industry. While some still watch it, and others still rally against it, the odds are that it won't be going away anytime soon. Meanwhile, the morality-minded groups have instead turned most of their energy toward other avenues, such as controlling sex, violence, and content on network television, cable, the Internet, and video games. The battle is still being fought; however, the playing field has changed radically since the ratings system was first installed.

Cinema XX, 306 Main, 1981. Photograph by Jim Koehn.

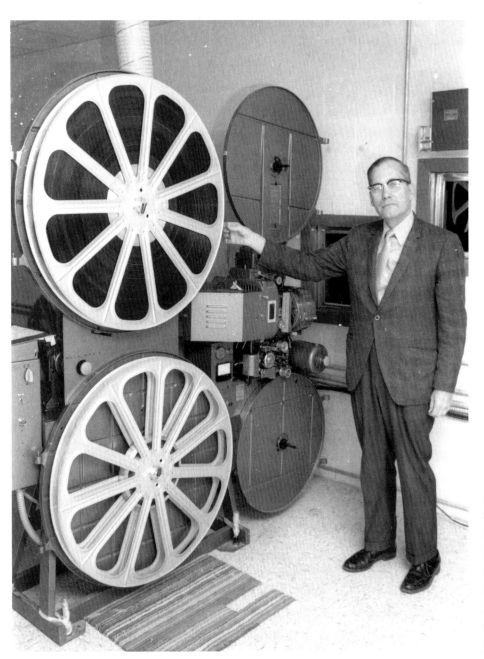

The state-of-the-art projector at the Southgate Theatre, 1972. Standing alongside is Elliott English, who would later manage Tercar's Gaylynn Theatre. Courtesy of the Houston Metropolitan Research Center, Houston Public Library, RGD6N 7076.

FIFTEEN

★ ★ ★

FROM MULTICINEMA
TO MULTIPLEX

★ ★ ★

SAFETY IN NUMBERS

Let's show the movies in the street — and drive the people back into the theatres.

NUNNALLY JOHNSON,
SCREENWRITER AND DIRECTOR

★ THE AMERICAN movie theatre, as a romanticized icon, effectively died with the evolution of the multiscreen cinema. Theatre functionality became tied to economics–more individual screens in a complex meant more people, hence more dollars. This new way of thinking also coincided with a steady decrease in the number of exclusive engagements and the concomitant spreading of any given movie across as many screens as possible. Auditoriums were reduced to matchbox-size rooms with little adornment.

For Houston, the change began in 1965 with General Cinema's Cinema II Theatres at the Gulfgate, Meyerland, and Northline malls. Patrons now had a choice of features in the same building and took to the concept with enthusiasm. A few single-screen theatres were built

The AMC Town & Country 6 Theatre undergoing demolition in 2002 after sitting dormant along with its neighbor, the Loew's Town & Country 3. Photograph by David Welling.

during this time, such as the Sharpstown and the Memorial, yet even they would eventually succumb to being twinned in order to compete. It took four more years before any more multiscreen theatres were built, and those were to be the first true multiple-screen venues in town.

THE ALMEDA 4, NORTHWEST 4, AND TOWN & COUNTRY 6

American Multi-Cinema (AMC) came to Houston on Christmas Day 1969 with three multicinemas that opened simultaneously. The Almeda 4, at Almeda Mall; the Northwest 4, at Northwest Mall; and the Town & Country 6, at Town & Country Village, were spread across the north, southeast, and west of the city. The theatres were constructed as separate buildings a short distance from the main shopping mall.

AMC did not get off to a good start in Houston, because of conflicts with the projectionists' union. Local 279 of the Motion Picture Operators' Union had been picketing all three theatres since their opening over lack of a contract with

the theatre chain. On January 15, 1970, stink bombs were set off in each of the Town & Country auditoriums, four of which had capacity audiences. Other incidents at the three theatres included tire slashings, acid poured on rugs, box office windows smashed, theatre seats cut, and stink bombs set off both inside and outside of the theatres.[1]

These tactics were not uncommon. Fourteen years later, when the projectionists' union was again on strike, the AMC Almeda was showing *Star Trek III* to a capacity crowd when someone opened the door at the rear of the auditorium and rolled a canister of tear gas down the middle aisle. Patrons ran from the theatre, suffering from stinging eyes, and twelve were taken to area hospitals for treatment. As a newspaper later reported, "Movie-goers got an extra dose of special effects on Friday night."[2]

The Almeda 4 changed its name to the Almeda 9 East in June 1976, when AMC built the new five-screen Almeda 9 West Theatre on the other side of the mall property. Both East and West theatres eventually closed down because of competition from neighboring multiplexes.

Advertisement in the Houston Post for the opening of the Galleria Cinema I and II, November 1970.

The Southgate Red and Blue Theatre, so-named because the separate auditoriums were identified by color, early 1970s. Courtesy of Charles Paine.

The AMC Northwest eventually closed, and was converted in 1992 into the Texas Longhorn Saloon, a country-and-western hangout with a giant longhorn cow skull positioned on the roof and a 2,300-square-foot dance floor inside. The Town & Country closed when AMC built the Town & Country 10 across the freeway in 1986. The older building would remain

vacant through the nineties, finally being razed in 2002 along with the neighboring Loew's theatre.

GALLERIA CINEMA II

The race for more screens per theatre was on. Next to be built was another General Cinema twin, the Galleria Cinema II, which opened on November 18, 1970, with *Scrooge* and *Five Easy Pieces*, two days after the official opening of the Galleria itself.[3] Unlike previous General Cinema theatres, the Galleria II was built in the mall interior, positioned at the far end of the bottom (ice rink) level.

The Galleria II is best remembered for its exclusive run of *Star Wars*, which opened on May 27, 1977, to packed houses and lines that would wrap around the Galleria ice rink for months. The George Lucas epic remained at the Galleria alone for well over a year before it was

released to other theatres in the city. Two additional screens were built also in 1977, in a separate section of the Galleria; the original two auditoriums closed down in 1994. The former space became a game arcade.

TWIN-, TRIPLE-, and quadruple-screen theatres became the new construction norm. Tercar's Southgate Red and Blue, located at 4333 West Fuqua, identified its two screens by color rather by number. It opened on March 17, 1971, with *Airport* in the red auditorium and *I Love My Wife* in the blue.[4] Tercar was, by this time, operating the Windsor, Gaylynn, Bellaire, and Memorial theatres along with the Pasadena, Airline, and Telephone Road drive-ins.

Two other theatres opened that year: the triplex Park III and the four-screen Shamrock. Tercar's Park III, at 1996 West Gray, opened on April 7, 1971, a block down from the River Oaks Theatre.

Opening night patrons were able to see *Little Murders* in auditoriums I and III–the second auditorium was still under construction.[5] Screen II would open on May 12 with *Investigation of a Citizen Above Suspicion*.[6]

The River Oaks–Park III rivalry lasted seven years, until the Park III closed on January 1, 1978.

AS THEATRE CONSTRUCTION evolved and changed, so did practices and policies. One such time-honored policy was that of the afternoon matinee. For decades, kids had always looked for ways of skipping school and slipping into the dark confines of a theatre. In the early seventies, midday presentations were being phased out, largely because of economics. ABC Interstate ceased daytime showings at the Tower, the River Oaks, and the Village. Tercar had done the same, and then reinstated them for the active Christmas season. General Cinema continued to

Tercar's Park III Theatre, on West Gray, early 1970s. Courtesy of Charles Paine.

offer matinees. As ABC Interstate's Art Katzen told the *Houston Chronicle* at the time, "Supermarkets will sell milk at cost just to get people in the stores, just to accommodate them. We feel the same way about matinees. If we were able to break even on matinees, we were glad to make them available. Now, we're losing money on them. We like to keep customers happy, and if some person on work shift can't get into a theatre during the day, he gets mad. And not having matinees hurts old ladies who just don't go out at night. But we lose money on them."[7]

The phasing out of matinees, in turn, affected the Motion Picture Operators' Union, whose members' employment went down by a third. Matinees could still be found downtown and in some of the larger shopping centers. In any case, this was only a sign of the times, and the afternoon matinee would eventually become the norm once more.

One policy that did stick was the no-smoking ordinance, although few smokers paid any attention when it was first implemented. Explained Katzen, "There's a city ordinance against smoking in theatres, and we try to enforce it. But there's just X amount of influence you can exert on a patron. People who want to smoke are going to smoke. You tell them to put it out, and they've lit up again before you're back up the aisle." Then he added, "This time of year, we're also short of ushers."[8]

A Houston Fire Department inspector told of the smoking complaints he had received the previous year during the Memorial Day closed-circuit telecast of the 1970 Indianapolis 500 at the Majestic, the Metropolitan, and the Alabama, an event at which beer sales were allowed.

The $6 telecast sold out at all three venues, and large volumes of beer were consumed. Said the inspector, "You just can't stop it then."[9]

Jeff Millar, in a 1971 article, suggested that nonsmoking patrons should unite and take action against such inconsiderate behavior by politely saying "excuse me," then placing a plastic laundry bag over the smoker's head and cigarette. His second suggestion was a water pistol.[10]

THE SHAMROCK
7017 South Main

The glamour of Glen McCarthy's Shamrock Hotel never quite carried over to the neighboring theatre of the same name. Robert Lippert's Shamrock 4, across South Main from the hotel, opened on July 14, 1971, with *Willard*, *The Andromeda Strain*, and *Love Story* (the last on two screens).[11] Lippert specialized in producing low-budget westerns and horror films in addition to managing his theatres. The Shamrock eventually came under the AMC banner, and was converted into a six-screen house. It closed, along with the Shamrock Hotel, in 1986. Mary Flood, then reporting for the *Houston Post*, wrote, "With all the ranting and raving about the closing of the Shamrock Hotel, I'm disappointed no one is even blinking an eye at the closing of a people's landmark right across the street. It was of so little consequence that no candidates even bothered to get their pictures taken in front of the Shamrock 6 Theatres when they were shut by the new owners, the Texas Medical Center."[12]

By this time, little care was being taken of the theatre, which mainly featured films such as *The Warriors* and *The Texas Chainsaw Massacre* as well as an occasional X title. The crowds were loud and unruly. In the same article, Flood wrote of watching John Carpenter's remake of *The Thing*, recalling that "every time gooey red stuff oozed from one crevice or another, some clown up in front started singing 'J-E-Double L-O Double Good.'" She also recounted stories of colorful goings-on at the Shamrock: her editor's car was stolen when he was inside; a jerk once sat down beside her and asked for a date; patrons occasionally would bring fried chicken into the theatre; and a crowd of Houston police scoured the auditorium while looking for someone on the lam. "But that's the stuff movies are made of, right?" she concluded. Both theatre and hotel were razed in 1986.

THE JERRY LEWIS CINEMA
2610 Fondren

In 1969, actor-comedian Jerry Lewis, in partnership with the Network Cinema Group, set out to establish a franchised chain of movie houses that would provide low-priced family-oriented entertainment. No X-rated films would be shown, and for a time, Lewis took issue with anything assigned other than a G rating.[13] The theatres were designed to be partially automated, so personnel was cut down to one or two employees.[14] The Jerry Lewis Cinema opened on February 25, 1972, with *Billy Jack* and *Summer of '42*. The theatre—two screens, 275 seats in each auditorium—was owned and operated by Mohawk Cinema Corporation.[15]

The Jerry Lewis banner was short-lived. The house reopened on November 2, 1973, as the Bijou Theatre, showing repertory classics such as Chaplin's *Limelight* and double features along the lines of Errol Flynn's *Captain Blood* and *The Sea Hawk*. Earl Blair, a Houston resident who was influential among local collectors of movie memorabilia, managed the theatre for Dan Lubbock.[16] The theatre eventually closed again, and then reopened several more times with new names and formats, once as the Southwest Cinema, which catered to Chinese-speaking audiences.

Loew's Town & Country Theatre, long after it had shut its doors in the late 1990s. Photograph by Tom Hannegan.

Parker Riggs, in the ape suit, poses in front of the Loew's Town & Country marquee, 1976. Courtesy of Parker Riggs.

In 1979, Farooq Khan moved from Pakistan to Houston and rented the theatre space as a venue for Hindi movies. At the time, there were no commercial Houston theatres regularly showing Hindi movies. He reopened the theatre as the Shalimar, beginning with the popular feature *Muqqadar ka Sikandar* (1978, directed by Prakash Mehra).[17] He closed the theatre in 1984, and in 2004 opened the Bollywood Cinema 6.[18]

LOEW'S TOWN & COUNTRY TWIN

More successful that year was Loew's Town & Country Twin, which opened on June 28, 1972, with *Last of the Red Hot Lovers* and *Conquest of the Planet of the Apes*. The building, which faced Beltway 8, was a short walk from its nearest competitor, the AMC Town & Country.[19]

It, like the early AMC houses, would best epitomize the matchbox design of the no-frills theatre. In his 1978 article on Houston's movie theatres, Peter Papademetriou said that the Loew's exterior

"might best be described as vintage shopping center, while the interior typically has the charm of a bowling alley (without the pins)."[20]

For the 1976 remake of *King Kong*, Loew's Town & Country dressed one of its teenage employees, Parker Riggs, in a rented gorilla suit and sent him into the neighborhood shopping malls. Riggs recalled wearing the costume with a cardboard sign advertising the movie—and being kicked out of Memorial City Mall by security after the Memorial Theatre manager complained about a competitor advertising outside his theatre. Eventually, Riggs would leave Loew's and work at Memorial. "It was probably six months later," said Riggs, "and I asked the manager, 'Do you remember when you kicked a guy out in a King Kong outfit?' And he said 'Sir, I remember that. That was not the proper thing for that person to do.' and I said, 'Well, that person was me.'"[21]

Loew's Town & Country closed down in the eighties. It, along with the AMC Town & Country, stood unused through the end of the century, and they were razed together in 2002.

DOWNTOWN HOUSTON had long since ceased to be a hot spot for movies (except for the Guggenheim houses), since the Majestic, Metropolitan, and Loew's State were no longer in operation. In an attempt to fill in the void, Tercar opened the Allen Center 3, at 500 Dallas in Allen Center. On opening day, screen one featured *40 Carats*, while the other two presented Roger Moore in *Live and Let Die*, his first appearance as James Bond.[22] The Allen Center 3 did last to the end of the decade. Another quarter century would pass before downtown saw another movie theatre, the Angelica, which opened in 1998.

THE GREENWAY

Unlike most theatres, the AMC Greenway 3 was not visible from the street; it was located underground in Greenway Plaza. The theatre opened on February 1, 1974, with *The Neptune Factor, Butterflies Are Free*, and *Play It Again, Sam*.[23] The theatre survived for a time with mainstream titles, but it would not really come into its own until 1978, when it began showing art and foreign films. As an art house, it ran a steady stream of specialty and foreign titles, and midnight movies were common fare. The Greenway also served as a home to the Houston International Film Festival/Worldfest Houston. "We were part of the vocabulary," noted manager Greg Reinhard during a 1994 interview. "When

The Greenway Theatre, 2006. Photograph by David Welling.

people said it was a Greenway film, you knew it was an art film."[24]

AMC decided to close the theatre when its lease expired. Competition and the limitations of only three screens cut down on traffic, so it was reduced to becoming a dollar house, showing second-run features for $1.25. The theatre closed down in January 1994, just three weeks shy of its twentieth birthday.

On March 11, 1994, Landmark Theatres reopened the Greenway with the Houston premiere of *Sirens* and *Highway Patrolman*.[25] Landmark had also recently taken over the former Loew's Saks space, but kept that space open only for a short time. Under Landmark's control, the Greenway flourished.

Reinhard once made a reference to the Greenway's orange walls, stating that for some people, orange walls and French films went together. Mindy Posey, Landmark's Houston manager, later confirmed this during a Greenway remodeling: "We're leaving some of the orange. After all, they have an image to maintain."[26]

LOEW'S SAKS TWIN
1800 *South Post Oak Road*

On July 24, 1974, close to six months after the Greenway opened, Loew's Twin (later called Loew's Saks) opened in the Galleria area. The features, *Death Wish* and *The White Dawn*, took a back seat to the unique design of the theatre. Past the ticket booth, a small corridor led to a set of escalators and the theatre proper downstairs. A sixty-foot mural of Hollywood's greatest stars, by Patrick Casey, was clearly visible as patrons rode down the escalator into the high-ceilinged lobby and conces-

sion area. On either side were entrances to the two 600-seat theatres.[27] When first planned, in 1965, the theatre was to have been called Loew's Magic Circle.[28]

Eventually, sagging business caused Loew's to close the theatre. Landmark took control in 1993, but the change never quite caught on, and the theatre shut down again in July 1995. Its location, right outside the 610 Loop, as well as the oversized auditoriums, worked against the inner-loop art-house crowd. Landmark's Mindy Posey explained at the time, "It was a constant battle to establish that theatre. For the most part, we were just getting by over there. But we were happy to continue that struggle. We didn't want to loose the extra screens."[29]

THEATRE CONSTRUCTION escalated during the midseventies. ABC Interstate's Woodlake Cinema 3 Theatre, at Westheimer and Gessner, opened on Christmas Day 1973 and would continue operations through the end of the eighties, eventually closing because of competition from newer multiplexes such as the neighboring Westchase Theatre. Other theatre openings included the Spring Branch Theatre, a twin-screen cinema at 10110 Hammerly, and Theatre Deauville, located on I-45 in Deauville Square. The latter kicked things off on July 11, 1975, with *The Great Waldo Pepper* and *Beyond the Door*.[30] Within three years, its format would change, and it began showing titles such as *Hot and Saucy Pizza Girls*, with John Holmes and Desiree Cousteau, and *The Opening of Misty Beethoven*. Other theatres built around this time included the General Cinema Greenspoint Cinema Center V, the Westwood Fashion Place Cinema III, and AMC's Southway 6 and Festival 6 theatres. Houses such as these eventually faded as bigger, better cinemas were built. The Festival 6 operated for over two decades, finally closing down in May 1999.

DESPITE THE GROWING number of new theatres and the additional screens at each house, moviegoing was being shortchanged as function came to dominate form. Theatres traded their glamour for utilitarian purpose.

"We are in the age of Movie-in-a-Box," noted Louis Parks of the *Houston Chronicle*. He described the modern movie experience as a no-frills flight; the first things to be stripped away were the once-standard newsreels, cartoons, and twin bills, and then the architectural flourishes–pulsing neon signs, ornate chandeliers, and exotic murals–were targeted for elimination. "Shopping mall theatres, with all the ambiance of K-Mart, are built for practicality and convenience."[31]

As the seventies progressed, this philosophy became the rule for theatre construction: smaller auditoriums (some seating as few as 150 people) and minimal interior decor. Multiple theatres allowed for film rotation, in which a new film was shown first on a larger screen, and then moved to a smaller auditorium as attendance dropped.

Constructed in 1977, the Briargrove 3 was part of a $1 million expansion and renovation program at the eighteen-year-old Briargrove Shopping Center. Operated by Transcontinental Theatres of San Francisco, venue had a brief life, opening on June 10, 1977, and closing in March 1978. The theatre then found new life as a dollar cinema, surviving well into the nineties–and with a final bit of notoriety.

In July 1994, while the initial hearings of the O. J. Simpson murder trial were underway, the Briargrove featured *Naked Gun 33 1/3*. According to News Radio AM 740, the Briargrove's telephone recording listed the film as featuring Leslie Nielsen and "the killer" O. J. Simpson. Once the news story broke, the recording was quickly changed. Briargrove management was not available for comment.[32] When the theatre closed down at the end of the nineties, it was gutted and converted into retail space.

ONE WEEK AFTER the Briargrove's opening, General Cinema unveiled its new extension to the two existing theatres in the Galleria. Cinema III & IV opened in the food-court area of the new second section of the Galleria, featuring a sunken lobby with stairs on either side of the box office. The absence of entry ramps led to criticism in May 1978. A new state law had already been enacted, requiring that all buildings constructed after January 1, 1978, be accessible to the handicapped. At the time, the Galleria III was showing *Coming Home*, which featured John Voight as a paraplegic veteran (the film garnered three Academy Awards and five nominations that year, including a statue for Voight). Those in wheelchairs who wanted to see the film found the theatre inaccessible. In response, a protest was held outside the theatre, organized by the Houston Coalition for Barrier-Free Living. The issue drew telegrams from John Voight and costar Jane Fonda, expressing their frustration over the situation. Explained one protester to Rick Barrs of the *Houston Post*, "This is embarrassing when you bring a date to the movies and someone has to carry you in."[33]

General Cinema had avoided possible protests two years earlier when it dropped *Cruising* from its listings. The film, which drew strong criticism from the gay community over its depiction of homosexuality, had been due to run at the Galleria, Westwood, and Greenspoint cinemas.[34]

The Galleria Cinema III & IV continued operations into the nineties, when they, along with Cinema I & II, closed for good.

Transcontinental Theatres opened up the Westchase 5, at 9749 Westheimer, on October 14, 1977. While following the matchbox guidelines for construction, it did include a one large auditorium with an oversized screen. This auditorium, complete with a Dolby four-track sound system and 70 mm capabilities, often showed blockbuster spectacles such as *Alien* in 1979 (along with the Alabama and Almeda East) and *The Empire Strikes Back* in 1980 (again with the Alabama).

Even this auditorium would be surpassed, however, as newer theatres were built. The Westchase closed down in 1999.

AS THE STRUCTURE of theatre entertainment changed, a new breed of cinema emerged. Cable and videotape emerged as the first serious threats to motion pictures since television. The surplus of second-run features, which still had the potential to make money, found a natural home at the dollar cinemas.

For Houston, the list of dollar cinemas was vast: the Briargrove, Longpoint, North Shore, Parkview, Bellaire, Westminster, and Windchimes, to name just a few. The dollar cinema evolved into a standard part of the motion-picture industry, becoming the last stop before a video release.

The most notable of these, the Cineplex Windchimes 8, at 13155 Westheimer, opened on December 11, 1981. The Windchimes, and the Westminster became

The Westchase 5 on opening day of The Empire Strikes Back, *1980. Courtesy of the Houston Metropolitan Research Center, Houston Public Library, RGD6N 5-21-80.*

dual dollar houses in the years to come. Nearly two decades later, the Windchimes earned a nod from the *Houston Press* in its "Best of Houston" issue. "Dollar movie theatres may be cheap," noted the *Press*, "but they also tend to be dumps. Windchimes Cinema 8 is not as dumpy as most. The trash here gets picked up more often; the floors are a little less sticky; the banal arcade games actually work; the popcorn is made often enough; and the restrooms are relatively clean, big, and easy to find. And of course there's the bargain (price)."[35]

THE BATTLE FOR SCREEN SUPREMACY

Houston was now on the verge of theatre oversaturation—not that this stopped new constructions. There had always been a kind of rivalry between theatre chains,

even during the simpler, single-screen days. Suddenly, chains began to announce the construction of more complexes, with more screens, than ever before. A war of sorts had begun.

In November 1986 there were fifty-seven theatres, with a total of 323 screens, in the Houston area, and three more theatres (with thirty more screens) were under construction. According to Wulfe & Company, a commercial and retail real estate brokerage firm, twelve new theatres (with eighty-five screens) had opened up within the last eighteen months alone. Said Wulfe president Ed Wulfe, "We've saturated the market. There are more theatres dividing up the pie, and they're not at the point level that they were."[36]

Casualties of the theatre glut included the locally owned Cineplex theatre chain, which filed for Chapter 11 bankruptcy. Of its seventy-five screens, a third of them had been converted to dollar houses, partly to conserve cash. The Cineplex theatres were eventually sold off to the Dallas-based Cinemark Corporation. AMC Theatres also took some hits, resorting to converting houses such as the Greens Crossings to $1.50 theatres.

Clearly, the public now wanted more than matchbox-sized auditoriums. Satisfying this need meant building sleeker new theatres, as well as performing major upgrades on the older houses. AMC spent $50,000 to renovate the Southway 6 Theatre. Despite this, the aging theatre still ended up as a dollar venue.

With theatres spread all across town, as well as cable and video at home, Houston audiences now had more choices than ever before. Over the last several decades, the magic of moviegoing had been lost, and the public wanted it back, complete

with surround sound, comfortable seating, and screens large enough to make it worth their while to leave cable at home. The theatre corporations were already attempting to respond. Plitt's multimillion dollar Presidio Square 6 incorporated an Italian marble floor in the lobby, imported wool carpet, cascading theatre drapes, and tiny white lights that adorned the floors, walls, and ceilings.

Many of the multiple-screen houses, built in haste under a "quantity, not quality" mentality, would be shuttered over the next decade. To survive, the theatre giants would have to reinvent themselves, effectively blending current theatre standards with the flair of the past.

Somehow, despite the odds, they managed to do just that.

Loew's Easton Commons Theatre under renovation, 2006. Photograph by David Welling.

Concession stand of the Loew's State, December 1953. Collection of Gary Warwick, courtesy of the Center for American History, University of Texas at Austin.

★ ★ ★

LET THEM
EAT CANDY

★ ★ ★

THE CONCESSION STAND

And there was popcorn in paradise.

BEN M. HALL, AUTHOR AND A
FOUNDER OF THE THEATRE HISTORI-
CAL SOCIETY OF AMERICA

The worse the pictures are the more stuff we sell.

UNIDENTIFIED DRIVE-IN OWNER

★ FOR MODERN AUDIENCES, the theatre experience would not be complete without a trip to the snack bar. It has long been standard for the theatre industry to provide a full array of candied confections, nachos, hot dogs, pickles, carbonated drinks, and the king of all munchies—popcorn—feeding, literally, a pleasurable addiction for the audience. In an age when theatres give 90 percent of their ticket sales right back to the studio and make the bulk of their profits from the candy counter, it is hard to imagine a time where there was no such thing—but in the beginning, the two were separate.

Patrons of the nickelodeons quickly discovered the hedonistic link between simultaneously eating and watching the "flickers." At that time, food was bought outside from neighboring confectionery shops, street vendors, or horse-drawn pea-nut wagons. Theatres initially resisted the idea of an in-house concession stand, since such a thing had been long associated with low-class entertainment such as carnivals and burlesque shows. Theatre owners were trying to fight the image of movies being entertainment for the lower classes. Most respectable people wouldn't be caught dead inside such a place. For the food vendors, locations near the the-atres proved to be profitable spots, since audiences turned over every twenty or thirty minutes.[1]

Eventually, movie theatres gained a more respectable status, yet snacks were still not part of their standard operation. By the twenties, some of the smaller the-atres sold prepackaged candy in the lobby, which, though it helped daily profits, the larger theatres had continued to resist. Others had a "candy butcher" who walked the auditorium aisles with an apron full of

candy, a method still used today at most sports arenas and ballparks. Some lobbies included candy machines, which were hidden away as a necessary though embar-rassing acknowledgment of popular demand.[2]

All this changed with the Great Depression, since concessions proved to be a ready way to increase profits without having to depend entirely on the popu-larity of a particular feature. Popcorn, purchased outside from wagons, had already been a favorite among moviego-ers for several decades. It also proved to be a food bought more than others dur-ing lean economic times, since it was easy to produce and less costly than other confections. The popcorn stand was moved into the theatre lobby, the treat's distinctive aroma permeating the entire building. The desirability of popcorn would eventually make it an important farm crop; harvests grew from five mil-

Lobby and concession stand of the Bluebonnet Theatre, July 1950. Collection of Roy Bonario, courtesy of the Center for American History, University of Texas at Austin.

lion pounds in 1934 to over a hundred million pounds only six years later. While Depression-era gimmicks such as bank nights helped bring patrons in, movie attendance was still down, and it has been claimed that popcorn sales kept many theatres afloat. The smell of coconut oil, the sound of popcorn popping, and the sight of the dancing yellow kernels emerging from the popper all served to entice patrons into buying a bag before entering. While there were early complaints of noisy popcorn bags, this was soon remedied by switching to less audible containers, leading up to the cardboard boxes and tubs used today.[3]

Salted popcorn made way for soda sales. The first beverages were fruity non-carbonated drinks and juices. The combination of candy, popcorn, and beverages redefined how theatres did business. Big profits were to be made from the concession stand, allowing operators to be less concerned about the movie itself. What was on the screen served to draw the customers in, but concession sales, which topped $10 million by 1936, kept theatres in the black.[4] Some theatres went for diversity, expanding well past the basics of popcorn and candy. According to resident Roy Bonario, the Wayside Theatre installed a fully operational, yet short-lived, soda fountain, which served shakes and malts to the patrons.[5]

World War II put a severe dent in the concession business, since sugar was rationed and wartime demands on agricultural acreage made popcorn scarce.[6] Interstate's Karl Hoblitzelle sponsored a popcorn research program at Texas A&M University, resulting in methods to improve yield. Ironically, Hoblitzelle had been initially reluctant to allow popcorn in his Majestics, envisioning the oily snack scattered across the elegant marble floors. Only after he was shown how pop-

Unique to the Wayside Theatre was a fully functional, although short-lived, soda fountain. Courtesy of Roy Bonario.

corn sales could increase the company's profits did he relent.[7]

After the war, vending machines, such as the Coke machine in the lobby of the Don Gordon Theatre, found their way into theatre interiors.[8] Other improvements—ice for drinks and multiple-sized cups—followed.

The intermission between features became standard break, allowing patrons time to go to the restroom and, naturally, stop off for some snacks. Concession-stand commercials, produced by food manufacturers to help increase sales, were supplied to theatres beginning in 1948. These became standard at drive-ins.[9]

The drive-in theatre took the concession stand concept and expanded it into a small cafeteria with a wide array of food, including shakes, ice cream, pizza, hamburgers, and steak sandwiches. Popcorn remained a top seller.

Jack Farr's Trail Drive-In housed a deluxe patio and concession stand. The Trail menu covered the basics—candy, soft drinks, and so forth—as well as chicken, tamales, shrimp, chili, and steak-burger dinners. Since a good 60 percent of the food sales occurred before the feature started, cooks would arrive at 5:45 p.m. to prep. When the theatre opened, a half hour later, the first batch of food was ready in the cafeteria.[10] The Trail concession area later found a rival in the Loew's Sharpstown Drive-In and its 3,720-square-foot cafeteria.[11]

The 1980s saw the arrival of alternative snacks, demanded by health-conscious consumers. Fruit juices, bottled water, air-popped popcorn, frozen yogurt, and imported candies all became part of the new trend. Coffees and herbal teas also entered the ranks at the concession stand, and a backlash occurred against the perennial favorite, popcorn.

Early on, theatres had learned how to manage popcorn supply and demand economically. While some theatres would pop

Concession stand of the Airline Drive-In, 1978. Courtesy of the Houston Metropolitan Research Center, Houston Public Library, RGD6N 9-12-78.

On a smaller scale: the concession stand of the Alvin Towne Plaza, c. 1970s. Photograph by Ray M. Boriski.

the corn on-site, others would buy pre-popped bags of stuff that usually tasted like stale cardboard; patrons were not usually fooled. Others would pop large quantities in advance, then bag them for reserve, again causing freshness to suffer. Some chains deemed popcorn-bagging taboo. As Dollar Cinema district manager Bob Lundry said in a 1988 *Houston Chronicle* interview, "If we catch any of our managers saving popcorn until the next day, they don't work for us anymore."[12] The policy differed from theatre to theatre and from chain to chain. In a 1978 *Houston Post* article, Loew's city manager Ed Orr explained that the popcorn "keeps for a long time while the bags are sealed. The popcorn we sell is, on the average, a couple of days to a week old, tops." Loew's could go through 50 to 400 pounds of popcorn a week.[13] Tercar also took to bagging popcorn in advance; its Gaylynn Theatre popped an excess of corn for weekend crowds and bagged extra for the slower times during the week, storing the bags in the room adjoining the snack bar.[14]

Other chains, such as AMC, Plitt, and General Cinema, went the fresh route, aware of the psychological aspect of an operational popper as a sales incentive. AMC's Jim Clark explained, "When you pop on the premises, people can watch the machine, they can hear it, the smell fills the lobby. It's really hard to ignore."[15]

Costing only pennies to make, popcorn received the biggest markup of any concession item. The more sold, the better for the theatre. While two kinds of popcorn were available—white and yellow—the latter became the standard, not only because it popped larger, but because it also looked more buttery. Prices, butter, bags, and bucket sizes varied from theatre to theatre. Tercar's Allen Center Theatre offered free refills for the hungry corn-a-holic, and General Cinema was noted for its monstrous 165-ounce popcorn bucket.[16]

The quest for epicurean popcorn involved more than freshness, as popping oil and butter toppings became part of the equation. The buttery topping, long used to finish off a tub of popcorn, had the downside of burning easily, filling the air with a lingering and unappealing burnt smell. In response, concession vendors created a new butter substitute that looked and tasted just like the real thing—or so they claimed. The product went by many names, such as "golden flavoring," and consisted of possibly as much as 10 percent butter, but the remainder was a mystery. The end product was cheaper, less likely to burn, and similar tasting. For purists, though, there was no comparison, and butter won hands down at the few theatres that carried it.[17]

Landmark's River Oaks Theatre was well aware of this fact and took the lead in

The Alamo Drafthouse West Oaks, 2006. Photograph by David Welling.

stocking one of the best concession stands for discriminating tastes. Fresh popcorn with real butter remained part of a stand that also offered imported chocolates, herbal teas, juices, Ben & Jerry's ice cream, and other items not found at standard theatres.[18]

With the megaplex came the in-theatre eatery, a deluxe cafeteria-style stand that provided goodies far beyond the normal popcorn and candy. Cinemark's Tinseltown theatres developed this idea fully with a small food court, independent of the concession stand, which featured pizza, cheesecake, salads, and specialty coffees as well as a moderately sized seating area.

While the River Oaks and Angelica theatres played up their epicurean snacks, the combination cinema and brewhouse took this trend to its next step: instead of

popcorn, give them pizza and burgers. Most importantly, give them beer.

This concept was hardly a new one. In 1997, the Alamo Drafthouse Cinema opened on Colorado Street in Austin. Patrons ordered food (pizza, hamburgers, salads) and drinks (beer and wine) from their seats, and the waitstaff brought it to them; food could also be ordered, and unobtrusively delivered, during the movie. The original did well enough to spawn additional locations, including three more in Austin. In June 2003, Houston's Alamo Drafthouse Cinema took up residence in the old Plitt West Oaks 7 at West Oaks Mall. For Alamo, it was an ideal setting, requiring only a refit. One of the seven auditoriums was converted into a kitchen, and a bar area was constructed in the main lobby. Alternate rows of auditorium seats were replaced with narrow bench tables to accommodate the food and drinks.[19]

The downtown Austin Alamo's popularity was due in part to its theme events, such as movie critic Harry Knowles's Butt-Numb-A-Thon (twenty-four straight hours of vintage movies and premieres), Weird Wednesdays (admission free, movies weird), and the ever-popular "Dark Side of the Rainbow," at which the 1939 *Wizard of Oz* is synced up to Pink Floyd's *Dark Side of the Moon*. The Houston chapter merely served as an extension of this concept.

The concept worked well enough for similar venues to follow, beginning in April 2005 with the Star Cinema Grill (in the former Loew's Bay Area 6, at 1020 Nasa Road 1). This was followed by a second Alamo location, at the old Mason Park Theatre in Katy. Others included an overhaul of the former Loew's Easton Commons on FM 1960 into the Studio Movie Grill; the Great Texas Movie Company's Movie Tavern–Richey Road (the former AMC 8 Theatre at The Commons at Commerce Park North Shopping Center, vacant since 1990); and the Deerbrook Movie Tavern (the former General Cinema 6 Deerbrook Commons in Humble, vacant since the late nineties).[20]

In the end, the concession stand is central to every theatre, primarily as a way to turn a buck. Since nearly all of its profits stem from snack sales, a theatre becomes, in essence, a confectionery store that just happens to show movies. As far back as the forties, a tagline at film-industry conventions ran "Location. Location. Location. Find the right spot for a popcorn stand, then build a movie theatre around it." In an age of vanishing Americana, some things haven't changed.[21]

The state-of-art concession stand of the new century, this one in the upper level of the Edwards Grand Palace, 2006. Photograph by David Welling.

Advertisement in the Houston Post for midnight movies on Friday the 13th, 1956. Midnight attractions have long been used to lure the public; whether as a time for showing horror movies on Halloween or the counter-culture films of the seventies any day, midnight has always been when, in the words of Eric Clapton, people would let it all hang out.

★ ★ ★

BEYOND
THE FRINGE

★ ★ ★

MIDNIGHT MOVIES AND THE ALTERNATIVE CINEMA

I see you shiver with antici . . . pation.

DR. FRANK-N-FURTER,
The Rocky Horror Picture Show

★ FOR EVERY ART FORM, there is a mainstream as well as a road less traveled. With motion pictures, the latter is the territory of art films, foreign and independent features, old movies and oddities. As this market developed, so came a need for a place to show them. Thus was born the alternative movie house. Universities and art centers served this need, as did more unconventional venues. The November 15, 1970, world premiere of Robert Altman's *Brewster McCloud*, which was partly filmed in the Astrodome, was held, appropriately enough, in the Astrodome, where a special 60-by-156-foot screen was set up for the occasion.[1]

In other instances, alternative cinema had nothing to do with locale, just time, since showings began on the stroke of midnight.

Welcome to cinema beyond the fringe.

THE MUSEUM OF FINE ARTS AND THE RICE MEDIA CENTER

The Houston Art League was formed in 1913, and soon after began laying plans for a public museum. The result, the Museum of Fine Arts of Houston, became Texas's first art museum. The museum sponsored a film series as early as 1939, and attendance was good: the five films shown that first year drew 3,371 people.[2] Before acquiring an auditorium, it had shown films at Sidney Lanier Junior High School and San Jacinto High School. Ludwig Mies van der Rohe's Brown Pavilion, added to the museum in 1974, included an auditorium specifically designed for film.

The new 325-seat theatre, located in the lower level of the Brown Wing, opened in July 1973, six months before the Brown Pavilion received its grand opening on January 15, 1974.[3] The film schedule kicked off with a children's film festival followed by a four-film retrospective of French director Jean Renoir.

As a repertory house and an American Film Institute affiliate, the museum excelled at presenting well-rounded retrospectives devoted to individual directors, actors, and genres. The first twelve months at the Brown, beginning in 1973, featured series on directors Sergei Eisenstein, Alfred Hitchcock, and François Truffaut; cinematographer Greg Toland; and themes such as horror and fantasy, femmes fatales, experimental films, pioneers of modern painting, and a festival of nations.[4]

In later years it would feature regional premieres, such as the Texas premiere of Wim Wenders's *Paris, Texas*, on January 20, 1985. Special guests for the event included actor Harry Dean Stanton.[5] The museum also took part in interrelated activities such as the Houston Interna-

Brown Auditorium, Museum of Fine Arts, Houston. Photograph by Laura Wells, courtesy of the Museum of Fine Arts, Houston, Archives.

Rice Media Center, 2006.
Photograph by David
Welling.

tional Film Festival. Despite fluctuating attendance, the museum film series, along with those at the Rice Media Center, have remained mainstays for the exhibition of repertory, foreign, and experimental films in the city.

The Rice University Media Center was established with funding from John and Dominique de Menil with the idea that the process of filmmaking belongs to all people. Because of the prohibitive cost of putting a movie together, the Menils established a film center to encourage experimentation and creativity in the medium. The corrugated-metal building, built by Houston architects Barnstone and Aubrey in 1969, was originally meant to be temporary. Instead, as the decades passed, the center served as a permanent part of Rice University's art and art history department.[6]

February 1970 marked the official opening; Italian director Roberto Rossel-

lini, invited by Dominique de Menil, was the featured guest. Rossellini, who shared Menil's vision, engaged in periodic meetings with students and teachers, and worked on a film, *Science*, based on the research of Rice scientists. The ten-hour film for television was never completed, and only fragments remain of the project.

The center's largest crowd on record took place soon after its opening, when Andy Warhol premiered *Lonesome Cowboys*. A young George Lucas presented his original film-school version of *THX-1138*. Other directors who showed their work included Michelangelo Antonioni, Martin Scorsese, Milos Forman, and Sam Peckinpah. Live appearances and lectures included those by George Stevens, Frank Capra, Spike Lee, special effects master Ray Harryhausen, Isabella Rossellini, King Vidor, and Richard Lester. Documentary filmmaker D. A. Pennebaker appeared for a retrospective in 1979 and

Film schedule for the Alley Theatre's Cinemafest, 1976. Courtesy of the Alley Theatre.

conducted a weekend workshop on cinema verité techniques. Also in the seventies, avant-garde artists Ed Emshwiller and Stan van der Beek presented an evening of psychedelia, projecting wild images onto the Media Center ceiling. Monty Python alumnus Eric Idle appeared for the preview of *Splitting Heirs* and led the audience in a sing-along of "The Philosopher's Song."

Yet the most unusual appearance of all was by Dennis Hopper, on hand in 1983 to screen his latest film, *Out of the Blue* (1980). Hopper refused to appear in front of the audience; instead, he spoke via video monitors from a nearby Media Center room. As described by Elena Rodriguez in *Dennis Hopper: A Madness to His Method* (1988), Hopper's life was out of control at this time because of alcohol and cocaine abuse.[7] According to Christopher Dow, who later recollected the experience for the *Rice News*, "He stayed in the projection booth and rambled on for 20 or 30 bizarre minutes. I couldn't tell you what he talked about, I'm not sure he really talked about anything. The one thing that did register, however, was that he wanted to blow himself up in the stadium parking lot."[8]

Hopper planned to perform what was called the Russian Suicide Death Chair Act, a stunt he had seen as a child. He would fold himself underneath a chair loaded with six sticks of dynamite and light the fuse. The stunt supposedly originated during the Russian Revolution, when the Bolsheviks faked the executions of those they wanted to save. In theory, the dynamite would obliterate the chair itself while creating a vacuum of safety for the person beneath. The reality could be deadly if the dynamite failed to explode

properly. Hopper had already performed the stunt once before, in Portland, Oregon.

The Houston fire marshals nixed the on-campus performance, so Hopper found an alternative site and bused the Rice audience to the Big H Speedway on Houston's north side. He took his position in what looked like a big foil-covered cardboard box and lit one match after another, only to have them extinguished by the wind. In frustration, he lit the entire box of matches at once and ignited the fuse. The expected big bang followed.

It was, Hopper later claimed, one of the craziest things he had ever done, leaving him unable to hear properly for weeks. The event was filmed and later run at the Media Center in a 1995 pairing with *River's Edge* (1986).[9]

The *Houston Press* listed the Media Center in its 1999 "Best of Houston" issue for the way its schedule reflected current events. After the April 20, 1999, Columbine High School massacre in Littleton, Colorado, Rice assembled the Kids Killing Kids series, which included Harmony Korine's *Gummo* (1997). Said the *Press*, "Janet Maslin of the *New York Times* called it the year's worst movie. She was wrong. Rice was right."[10]

THE ALLEY THEATRE

The repertory cinema reached its peak in the seventies, when a number of venues in town offered an eclectic mix of films, either regularly or periodically. Under the eye of director Bob Feingold, the Alley Theatre jumped into the fray with its Summer Film Festival, later to be called Cinemafest. Beginning in 1969, the Alley presented a ten-week series of movies each summer while the acting company was on vacation.

Titles covered the gamut of the film experience, from classic Hollywood fare to foreign cinema and silent films, the last usually with live musical accompaniment by Dr. William Glick. The epic Russian version of *War and Peace*, still on record as the most expensive movie ever made ($100 million at the time), was presented in 1971 to an audience mesmerized by its mammoth sweep and scope. Clocking in at 373 minutes, the film was shown over two nights, and would not be shown in Houston again until the River Oaks picked it up during the late seventies.

The Alley also offered a children's film series in 1974, and from 1975 to 1978 the Alley presented the Friday Night Sleaze Series alongside the regular schedule, with the weirdest of the weird cult features, all shown at the stroke of midnight. Among those shown: *Schlock*, Tod Browning's *Freaks*, *The Crazies*, *Beyond the Valley of the Dolls*, *The Corpse Grinders*, *Myra Breckenridge*, *Lisztomania*, *The Eyes of Hell (The Mask)* in 3-D, and *The Rocky Horror Picture Show*.[11]

Home video and cable effectively killed the repertory business. The Alley Theatre's final season was in 1980, and its last film was D. H. Lawrence's *The Fox*, shown on August 23 and 24.

Noted *Post* writer Eric Gerber in 1974, "If there is a moral to this story, it's probably something like 'It's always darkest before the first feature starts.' Waiting for the lights to dim, I looked almost wistfully at the crowd gathered for the last show of this summer's Alley Cinemafest. Too bad this festival has to end, I thought, but I

suppose the Alley really should get on with the business of live theatre."[12]

THE IMAX THEATRE

For lovers of big-screen high-definition cinema, little can compare to the clarity of an IMAX (Image Maximum) film. IMAX is a unique format: a special camera is required to shoot the film, since each frame measures 5.23 square inches, and the movie must be run on special projectors and shown a special screen, all housed in a special theatre. In 1989, an IMAX theatre opened in Houston as part of the Museum of Natural Science.

The theatre began its run in September with *The Dream Is Alive* (1985), a stunning depiction of the current space program. The screen alone, eighty feet wide and sixty-two feet tall, was enough to drop one's jaw. Even more moving for the opening-night crowd was seeing footage of Judith Resnik and Francis "Dick" Scobee, both featured in the film. They had perished in the space shuttle *Challenger* explosion three years earlier.[13]

Two more Houston-area IMAX theatres were later constructed: the Galveston 3-D IMAX Theatre in Moody Gardens and the Edwards Marq*E IMAX Theatre.

THE AURORA PICTURE SHOW

The avenues of expression for video-based art expanded in 1998 when the Aurora Picture Show Micro Cinema opened its doors. The cinema was founded as venue for artistic, experimental, and low-budget film and video works. Andrea Grover and

Patrick Walsh created the Aurora out of the most unlikely of places—an abandoned church. Built in 1924, the Church of Christ at 800 Aurora in the Heights was stripped of its faux wood paneling, the wallpaper beneath, and two sets of drop ceilings, each with a set of fluorescent lights. A nine-by-twelve-foot video projection screen was installed along with stereo sound. With its bare shiplap, church pews, and air conditioning, the alternative cinema space caught on quickly with the video-art crowd.[14]

"What we describe this as," explained Grover to the *Houston Press* in 1998, "is opening up our living room to a large group of friends." That year, the *Press* voted it "Best Secular Use of a Church Building" in the "Best of Houston" issue.[15] The theatre placed again in 2000 ("Best Movie Theatre That Will Never Show *Gladiator*") and 2002 ("Best Place to Genuflect Before Seeing a Movie"). The Aurora seated approximately a hundred people, and more inevitably filled the standing room at each show. From "The Nuts and Bolts Show" (about relations between the sexes) and "New 16mm Beatniks," to "Heebie Jeebies: Short Works in Horror" (a program organized in conjunction with the 1999 River Oaks opening of *The Blair Witch Project*), the presentations always served as an avenue for anyone with a camera.

As Charles Dove explained on the Internet site *Sidewalk*, "Movies are like churches--that neat little simile has been done to death and is more than a little inaccurate. Unless your local house of worship has a concession stand and teenagers necking in the back pew, movie theatres and chapels are miles apart. But they do share a certain longing for spirituality and community that sentient humans

The Aurora Picture Show, the best place to genuflect before seeing a movie, 2006. Courtesy of the Aurora Picture Show.

Midnight entertainment at the Heights Theatre, 1960s. Photograph by Ray M. Boriski.

fleetingly feel is gone during the commercial breaks and sitcom reruns of the long Houston summer."[16]

And, like a church, the Aurora charged no admission, just an appreciated donation, proportional to the amount of the spirit one would find during the evening.

THE MIDNIGHT MOVIE

Yes, Virginia, there were midnight movies before *Rocky Horror.*

Before the civil rights movement, Jim Crow laws prevented many blacks from seeing movies in a conventional manner. Instead, they were herded into balconies or sent to black theatres in other parts of town. Some of the early midnight shows were held specifically for black audiences. Midnight presentations also took the form of live ghost shows, with magicians, men in monster suits, and an occasional movie thrown in.

Midnight shows could also be found on special holidays, especially New Year's. For New Year's Eve 1940, a dozen Interstate theatres offered midnight shows, the majority of which were Boris Karloff thrillers, such as *The Human Monster* and *Before I Hang.* The downtowners went for the more upscale fare, with the Majestic showing *Chad Hanna,* with Henry Fonda, while the Kirby offered *A Night at Earl Carroll's,* billed as the most glamorous nightspot in the world.[17]

Meanwhile, the Horwitz theatres went for an entirely different audience that year, with combination live shows and movies. The Uptown offered the "Hollywood Review" stage show (and Gary Cooper in *The Westerner*). Daily ads for the show stated: "See! Living artist's models! See Chere oo-la-la! It's gaiety! It's naughty but nice!" The Texan likewise offered *Northwest Mounted Police* and the live "saucy French revue" "Midnight in Paris." No live acts were found at the Iris; instead was *Rebellious Daughters*, with "modern girls on the road to shame." A few streets over at the Ritz, *When the Daltons Rode* served as the film entertainment. Most patrons came instead to see the stage revue "New Year's Rambles," with "Naughty Nora, the peach blossom from Georgia."

The midnight hour served well for special promotions as well. For the opening of the 1963 Robert Wise film *The Haunting*, four patrons were selected for a midnight screening at the Metropolitan. Those that lasted through the entire film would divide a $100 prize.[18]

With the seventies came a new, hip attitude toward midnight showings. The counterculture of the period created a fresh audience that eagerly supported films outside of the norm. *Zabriskie Point* (1970), *Zachariah* (1971), *Alice's Restaurant* (1969), *Woodstock* (1970), and Alejandro Jodorowsky's *El Topo* (1970) were all shown during the early years, as was a popular favorite, *Harold and Maude* (1971). Rock concert films could always be found at midnight: Jimi Hendrix's *Rainbow Bridge* (1972), *The Last Waltz* (1978, about the final concert of The Band), Led Zeppelin's *The Song Remains the Same* (1976), Pink Floyd's *The Wall* (1982), and anything by the Beatles, particularly the psychedelia of *Yellow Submarine* (1968).

The midnight movie found a regular home at certain theatres around the city. ABC Interstate, along with rock radio station KLOL, established a continuous run of midnight classics. Interstate's success swayed other chains to try the midnight market as well, usually with mixed results. Tercar tried over the years with the Bellaire, Memorial, Allen Center, Windsor, and Gaylynn, as did Loew's, AMC, the

Houston International Film Festival, and the Alley Theatre (its Friday Night Sleaze Series, mentioned above).[19]

The crowds that attended the screenings varied; some liked the relaxed, bohemian atmosphere, while others stopped going for the same reasons. Said one "midnighter" patron to the *Houston Post* in 1973, "I used to go all the time, but it's getting out of hand. Too many young ones trying to be cool. Smoking cheap dope in your face."[20] While smoking ordinances prohibited such activity, the reality was different. KLOL's midnight-movie account executive, in the same article, explained, "I'm not going to tell you that there is none. But where in Houston isn't it? Fire regulations say no smoking and we try to enforce that. But I'd rather see that blue smoke than a crowd that'd be drinking."

The midnight-movie craze captured its biggest audiences during the seventies and eighties. During the mideighties, AMC and radio station 107.5 FM–97 Rock–presented the Midnight Movie Express. Movies at the Alabama East, Festival, Southway, and Northoaks theatres would sometimes be in as many as six auditoriums at a time.[21]

For the midnight crowd, weirdness ruled, and the stranger the film, the better. Monty Python was big, as were horror titles such as *The Texas Chainsaw Massacre*, *Night of the Living Dead* (1968), and *Basketcase* (1982). Yet perhaps the most bizarre feature to hit Houston's screens arrived in March 1979, when the Greenway III featured a black-and-white film by an unknown director named David Lynch. The film was *Eraserhead*.

Said Eric Gerber for the *Houston Post* in 1979, "No brag. Just fact. In my time,

I've been exposed to some pretty weird, mind-boggling, I-can't-believe-I'm-seeing-this films: *El Topo. Putney Swope. Rocky Horror Picture Show. Black Moon. Private Parts. Un Chien Andalou. Pink Flamingos.* But I've never–repeat–never been more a) befuddled b) offended and c) perversely fascinated by a film than *Eraserhead.*"[22]

However, none of these movies came close in popularity to the one film that redefined the midnight-movie phenomenon. From its first midnight showing in New York in 1976 to the present, *The*

Rocky Horror Picture Show has proved itself to be the big daddy of cult films.

The Rocky Horror Picture Show

In his book *Cult Movies,* author Danny Peary described *The Rocky Horror Picture Show* not as the undisputed king of the midnight-movie circuit, but as the queen; an apt title for what has stayed on an almost continuous midnight run for over a quarter century. Although the story was originally successful on the London stage,

*The queen of all midnight movies—*The Rocky Horror Picture Show—*celebrates its second anniversary as a midnight movie at the Alabama Theatre, June 1979. Eric Gerber noted at the time: "This should certainly quash any talk about Houston being a cultural wasteland." Courtesy of the Houston Metropolitan Research Center, Houston Public Library, RGD6N 8-9-79, #16a.*

the film version tanked when released in 1975; however, producer Lou Adler repackaged the film for the midnight crowd. The rest, as they say, is history.[23]

Rocky's first Houston appearances included a nonmidnight showing, on a double bill with *Phantom of the Paradise* at the River Oaks, which was then operating as a repertory house. It also appeared on July 22, 1977, as part of the Alley Theatre's Friday Night Sleaze Series. But it wasn't until it began its run at the Tower that it firmly established itself. Its Tower stay was brief, lasting until February 4, 1978, when it moved to the larger-capacity Alabama Theatre—*Rocky*'s home for the next six years.

ABC Interstate's run of the film was something of a fluke. When one of its Dallas theatres vied for the film, Twentieth Century–Fox insisted on bookings at a minimum of two theatres, so the second print was lined up for Houston. The theatre chain had no idea what would follow. Said Margaret Stratton of ABC Interstate in a 1978 *Houston Post* interview, "We planned to show it a few times and hope we didn't lose too much. Well, we started selling out the place! We were turning away from four to seven hundred people on Saturday night. So, around Christmas, we added a Friday midnight show as well. And that sold out!"[24]

It was during its Alabama years that *The Rocky Horror Picture Show* firmly established itself among Houston's alternative pop-culture crowd and quickly evolved into a form of weekly performance art, with audience participation. While the patrons sung, shouted dialogue, and threw rice during the wedding scene, a separate live stage show occurred at the front of the auditorium—hence the inside joke of the time: How can you tell if a theatre is running *Rocky Horror*? Answer: At cleanup time, there is more rice and glitter on the floor than popcorn and candy wrappers.

Despite a larger theatre and two showings a week, sell-out crowds were the rule rather than the exception. Lines would form well before midnight, extending past the theatre and the neighboring Cactus Records and on to the end of the building. Eric Gerber noted that patrons should "get there early. What you can see waiting in line is almost as good as what's in the movie."[25]

Despite an occasional box-office pull like *The Empire Strikes Back*, the Alabama was beginning to hit hard times. During this lean period, *Rocky Horror* served as a weekly boost to the cash register. *Rocky*'s stay at the Alabama came to an end in December 1983, when the theatre closed down for good. *Rocky* then went looking for another home.[26] The Gaylynn and Windsor theatres held showings for a time, as did the Bellaire in the early nineties. Eventually, *Rocky Horror* found its way back to the theatre where it had its debut—the River Oaks—and, perhaps fittingly, finished out the century there as well.

Even its eventual, long-awaited release on videotape and cable made hardly a dent in the weekly attendance. If anything, the film has continued to attract the youth crowd as well as the diehard fans. Others get their fill then move on. For some, the fun of *Rocky Horror* died when audience participation increased. As a DJ from radio station KPFT once quipped, "The *Rocky Horror Picture Show* was a good film until you geeks ruined it."[27]

The Edwards Grand Palace,
constructed in 1998, bears
its name well as it is the
modern equivalent of the
1920s picture palace. Photo
by David Welling.

EIGHTEEN

* * *

REDISCOVERY IN THE
AGE OF THE MEGAPLEX

* * *

Always remember, there's nothing too good for the audience.

IRVING THALBERG

★ BY THE EIGHTIES, theatre design had settled into a steady output of multiscreen cookie-cutter matchboxes. The opulence of the early days was out, not only because of simplicity of construction but for economic reasons as well. People no longer went to the theatre because of the theatre building itself, but because of the featured attraction . . . or so the exhibitors thought.

In actuality, audiences were becoming increasingly agitated by the shortcomings of the multiplexes. While sound and picture quality had reached new technological heights, sacrifices were being made in other areas, as when the state-of-the-art sound from one theatre distracted patrons in the adjoining auditorium. Ticket prices were higher and concessions cost more, yet the individual screens continued to shrink.

All this was about to change.

*The Cineplex Odeon
Spectrum Theatre, 1989.
Photograph by Jim Koehn.*

The first indicator appeared with the Cineplex Odeon Spectrum 9, at 2660 Augusta, which opened on June 24, 1988. Cineplex Odeon gained a foothold in the city with their takeover of the former Plitt theatres. With the Spectrum, matchbox design was discarded, replaced with high-tech wide-screened auditoriums, 70mm presentation capabilities, Dolby stereo sound, and advance same-day ticket purchases.[1]

Architecturally, the theatre tried to recapture the dazzle of older cinemas, not with opulent flourishes, but with grand scale and a multiple-level lobby. The mid-level entrance led to stairs and escalators for the secondary mezzanines above and below. The upper mezzanine's expanse was enhanced by the massive skylit window to one side.

The 3,500-seat Spectrum was the first Houston theatre to incorporate the newly designed Lucasfilm THX sound system in three of the nine auditoriums. Said *Houston Chronicle* writer Louis Parks of the THX impact on *Die Hard*, "When the windows explode out of a skyscraper, the 'KABOOM' goes right through you."[2]

On October 12, 1990, Cineplex Odeon followed up with the River Oaks Plaza Theatre, a twelve-screen version of the Spectrum, located on West Gray at Waugh Drive. Like the Spectrum, River Oaks Plaza was a multiple-level affair.

The old River Oaks Theatre management was less than excited about this new cinema, which was located only a few blocks away. Said Cineplex district manager Margaret Stratton to the *Houston Chronicle*, "We expect to be good neighbors."[3] Ironically, the similarity in names caused many of the early film shipments to be sent to Landmark's theatre.

Both the Spectrum and the River Oaks

Plaza would do brisk business for the next decade. Their demise came at the end of the century, brought about by the opening of two stadium-seat-designed Edwards theatres.

In 1995, General Cinema rebuilt its Meyerland theatre as part of a major overhaul of the entire mall. General Cinema razed the still-functional twin theatre, which had been operating since 1965, and built a new state-of-the-art cinema in its place, with a grand opening on March 17, 1995. Its operation under General Cinema was brief. In October 2000, General Cinema filed for bankruptcy reorganization. The Meyerland Theatre closed on October 19, just over a week after the filing.[4] It reopened under the Atlanta-based Entertainment Film Works Company, and later by the Nova theatre chain, but by the end of 2003 the theatre closed for good. The Meyerland 8 was razed and a new set of retail stores were constructed on the site.

Other new theatres constructed in

malls included those in Memorial City Mall (Loews, 1989) and Sharpstown Mall (Cineplex Odeon, 1992).

By the midnineties, movie attendance was on an upswing. As a result, the major chains set their sights on erecting theatres with an ever-growing number of auditoriums. Said a General Cinema executive, "Your chances are much better because you now have 12 rolls of the dice instead of one, two, or three."[5]

The new strategy was to create a destination theatre—one that included multiple large auditoriums, expansive lobbies, deluxe concession stands, and sleek decor. All of these would be overshadowed by one unique (yet simple) improvement— stadium seating. More than any other innovation, this single idea changed the motion-picture-exhibition industry in the later part of the twentieth century.

AMC led the charge in 1995 with a twenty-four-screen theatre in Dallas—the first true megaplex. This new breed of theatre swept across Houston the following year. AMC opened its Deerbrook 24 at Deerbrook Mall on May 24, 1996, its massive lobby advertised as being over a football field in length.

Deerbrook was not the first local theatre to embrace stadium seating. Cinemark beat it to the punch a month earlier with its new breed of theatre, the Tinseltown. The Woodlands Tinseltown, at 1600 Lake Robbins Drive, opened on April 5, 1996. It was an impressive site, although only two of its seventeen auditoriums were of stadium design.

Cinemark followed its construction in The Woodlands with two more theatres before the year was out. The sixteen-screen Tinseltown USA 290, at Highway

Stadium seating at the Angelica, 2006. Photograph by David Welling.

Cinemark's Tinseltown 290, 2006. Photograph by David Welling.

290 and Hollister, opened on November 15, 1996, and the twenty-four-screen Tinseltown USA Westchase, at Beltway 8 and Richmond, on December 13. Unlike the Woodlands, these theatres were fully stadium style in construction. The 290 location served as a prototype for a new exterior design. According to decorator Pamela Taylor, the color scheme originated with Tandy Mitchell, the owner's wife, who had walked in wearing a silk dress with a purple, green, orange, and pink design. Impressed with the colors, Taylor asked to borrow the dress and adapted it for the theatre design.[6]

AMC struck back less than a month later with the largest screen number to date, a whopping thirty auditoriums. The AMC Studio 30, at 2949 Dunvale, opened on May 16, 1997, and set a new world record for cinema size. Only two other theatres could boast of having thirty separate auditoriums under one roof—an

AMC theatre in Ontario, California, and the other across the globe in Belgium. With a space totaling 112,000 square feet, Studio 30 was larger than either.

THE ANGELICA FILM CENTER AND CAFE

Houston's downtown district experienced a major revitalization throughout the nineties, including a planned revamping of the old Albert Thomas Convention Center into a new entertainment center. Initial plans were announced in 1988 by Mayor Kathy Whitmire for its development, a joint venture between *Star Wars* filmmaker George Lucas and Century Development Corporation of Houston. The plans for Luminaire, as it was to have been called, died in 1990 when financing dried up. Developer David Cordish then stepped in with alternate plans for the building. The initial announcement of a Houston Angelica Theatre, in March 1997, was received with much enthusiasm, since the Angelica Film Center in New York's SoHo district had long established itself as a stylish art house. This would be the first new downtown movie theatre to open since the short-lived Allen Center Theatre in the seventies.

Featuring an adjoining restaurant and bar, the Angelica took its concession fare beyond even Landmark's standards. Beverages ranged from bottled water and "coffees with attitude" to imported beer, wines, and champagne, including Dom Perignon at the 1999 price of $175 a bottle. Full breakfasts, omelettes, soups, salads, pasta dishes, sandwiches, and pizza could all be found on the menu.[7] And for those who just had to have popcorn, a conventional snack bar was stationed in the lobby

The Angelica Film Center, part of the renovated Albert Thomas Convention Center, 2006. Photograph by David Welling.

as well.

The Angelica Film Center and Cafe opened on Christmas Day 1997, but held its official opening, an invitation-only benefit gala for the AIDS Foundation Houston, on January 8. Said manager Steve Buck to the *Houston Chronicle*, "One lady told me, 'Finally, a theatre for adults to enjoy. There are no video games and no kids running all through the lobby.'"[8] Buck's knowledge of the art-film scene was impressive: he had originally supervised the Greenway's transformation into a first-class art house during the seventies.

THE MAGIC JOHNSON THEATRE

Basketball legend Earvin "Magic" Johnson debuted his theatre chain in a minority area of Los Angeles in 1995, followed

by a similar theatre in Atlanta. His theatre concept was to nurture economic growth in the inner city, offer job opportunities for minority youth, and inspire them to succeed in the business world.[9]

Magic's Houston theatre took shape at Northline Mall (whose old General Cinema theatre had closed in 1996). The former Joske's building, which had been vacant for years, was to be torn down to make way for the theatre, a joint venture between Johnson and Sony theatres. The project was struck by tragedy on January 30, 1997, when a concrete wall and ceiling collapsed during construction, killing three women and injuring seven. Though the mall was closed at the time, people often used it as a place to walk for exercise before business hours.[10]

Despite the dark cloud, construction continued on the theatre, which opened on January 19, 1998, around Martin Luther King Day. The grand opening ceremonies included Johnson as well as Lee Brown, the first African American mayor of Houston.

Johnson's presence had been felt throughout the construction. Days before the opening, he arrived for a last-minute look-see. As described by Greg Hassell of the *Houston Chronicle*, "Around every corner, construction workers in hard hats suddenly dropped tough-guy postures and looked up at the 6-foot-9 Johnson with shining eyes. Rummaging through pockets, they held out pens, paper, even crumpled dollar bills for his signature."[11]

WITH ALL THIS NEW GROWTH came a few repercussions. "Economics aside, I think the neighborhood theatre identified neighborhood areas," said Susan McMillan to the *Houston Press* in 1999. McMillan, along with the Garden Oaks Civic Club, led an unsuccessful fight to save the Garden Oaks. "The neighborhood theatres were comfortable. They had some personality. They didn't look like every other theatre."[12]

Texas was at the forefront of the megaplex craze, primarily in Houston and Dallas, because of fairly inexpensive land prices and the sprawling nature of the cities.

The end of the twentieth century was showcased by four final complexes: AMC's Katy Mills 20, AMC's Willowbrook 24, and two theatres by the California-based Edwards Theatre Circuit. These last two complexes served as pinnacles of modern theatre construction and design in Houston.

Edwards entered the Houston market with the Grand Palace Stadium 24, near Highway 59 at Timmons. An advance gala was held on October 20, 1998, with proceeds from the $25-a-ticket event benefiting the Variety Club, a children's charity. The official grand opening took place on October 22.[13]

The theatre entrance featured an expansive, wide-open area with stairs and escalators leading to the second level (which later garnered it a *Houston Press* "Best of Houston" nod for 2005's "Best Cheap Thrill": sliding down the Edwards handrail).[14] The main inner lobby, where a small searchlight crossed the floor, featured one of six large hand-painted murals created by the Marv Brehm Studio of Newport Beach, California.[15]

The Edwards Theatre did not hold the spotlight for long. One week after the Grand Palace opening, AMC opened up

The return of grandeur to the theatre lobby: the Edwards Grand Palace, 2006. Photograph by David Welling.

its newest theatre, Katy Mills. Located inside the Katy Mills Mall, the theatre opened its doors to the patrons of the Houston suburb of Katy, on October 29, 1999. A media blitz promoted the opening of the new gargantuan mall: two hundred stores covering 1.3 million square feet, the equivalent of three Astrodomes, and enough parking for 8,000 cars.[16]

Less than a month after opening Katy Mills, AMC premiered another megaplex, this one out in the FM 1960 area on an eighty-acre tract of land that once belonged to entertainer Johnny Carson.[17] On November 19, the Willowbrook 24 effectively took the place of the older AMC Willowbrook 6 Theatre (which was immediately converted into a bargain house for second-run features).

As the final days of 1999 closed in, Edwards offered Houston one final theatre for the old year (and the first for the new one). The Edwards Marq*E 23 theatre complex was built on twenty-four acres at Interstate I-10 and Silber Road, once the location of the Cameron Iron Works. The Marq*E Houston Entertainment Center was planned to house a conventional megaplex and an IMAX theatre—both operated by Edwards—as well as food courts, apparel stores, specialty shops, and restaurants. Much of the design was patterned after that of the Irvine Spectrum Center in California, which also included an Edwards IMAX-megaplex combo.[18]

The twenty-two-screen theatre opened on Christmas Day, just slightly over two months after the Grand Palace, and was the first business to do so in the new complex. Unique to the Marq*E was setting the names of notable theatres of the past above the four largest auditorium entrances: the Coliseum, Lido, Egyptian, and Hollywood. Themed murals surrounding the entrances were painted by the Marv Brehm Studio, which was also responsible for the Grand Palace murals.

A week later—less than nine hours into the new year—Edwards opened the doors to the 410-seat Marq*E IMAX Theatre, showing Walt Disney's *Fantasia 2000.* Located in the same building as the other Marq*E auditoriums, the new IMAX was the third such house in the area, following those at the Museum of Natural Science and Moody Gardens in Galveston.

THE OVERSCREENING OF HOUSTON

The problem was hardly new; a multiplicity of multicinemas was all too evident in the eighties. In her 1986 *Houston Chronicle* article headlined "Houston's Other Glut: Too Many Screens," Judith Crown pointed out that the city's population growth had not kept up with the twelve new theatres (with a total of eighty-five new screens) that had opened up over an eighteen-month period. The repercussions of this included the bankruptcy of the local Cineplex theatre chain.[19]

The "more is better" attitude strengthened during the following decade, as both the goal of having more screens per complex and the allure of stadium seating intensified. Suddenly, all the major the-

atre chains were building stadium megaplexes, spelling certain death for the older multicinemas.

Theatre entrepreneur and publicist Alvin Guggenheim, the man who had built up the seventies Majestics, passed away in 1997, along with the era of the independent. In 1999 his son, Al Guggenheim, told the *Houston Press,* "There is no place for independent operators in this market. The megachains control just about everything. You might make a living as a mom-and-pop operator, but only if you were the only one in a small town."[20]

By the middle of 2000, Houston had over 430 individual theatre screens—more than double the number from five years earlier.[21] This coincided with a downturn in box-office revenues, which was attributable to higher ticket prices, higher concession prices, and a proliferation of entertainment choices offered to the public. The local effect was one of more theatre closings.

The larger result became clear as one theatre chain after another, overburdened by overbuilding, filed for bankruptcy. The cause was obvious to everyone except the theatre executives themselves. As journalist Richard Connelly stated in his March 2000 *Houston Press* cover story, "In the world of movie theatre chains, it's always the *other* guy that's overbuilding. *Your* brand new megaplex, on the other hand, is an example of strategically filling a little-noticed gap in the market."[22]

THE HOUSTON that entered the twenty-first century was a very different city from the one of a century earlier. So too were the movies, as well as the places that showed them. From the Vitascope and the nickelodeons came a high point during the silent days of the twenties, when the masses were entertained in grand, opulent palaces. Sound arrived, along with the Depression, and the downtown Gargantuas were replaced by smaller deco-style neighborhood theatres. Technicolor, Cinemascope, Cinerama, 3-D, VistaVision, and other innovations lured people from their homes (and television sets) and, for a while, kept them in their cars as drive-in theatres proliferated through out the fifties and sixties. Single screens were replaced by twins and triples, and then the multiplexes. These, in turn, fell into disuse with the rise of the megaplex.

Edison hadn't a clue. His Vitascope and its predecessor, the Kinetoscope, were little more than toys. He moved on to other things, and was concerned about his moving-picture machine primarily when

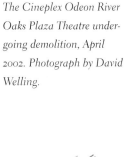

The Cineplex Odeon River Oaks Plaza Theatre undergoing demolition, April 2002. Photograph by David Welling.

his patent was infringed upon. So the art of film took its first baby steps despite Edison's lack of vision. Film was originally considered a novelty, far below the dignity of proper people. Sound was also considered a novelty. As Harry Warner prematurely blurted out, "Who the hell wants to hear actors talk?" He was quickly proved wrong, since a majority of moviegoers did want to hear them. Color and wide-screen also proved to be mainstays of the industry. Smell-O-Vision did not.

What has not changed is the communal experience: within the confines of the theatre, the viewer is held captive as part of a mass event. When a movie is seen at home on a television set, gone is the "sacred silence and purpose" of the collective audience. Distractions are introduced, such as ringing phones, conversations, and commercials. The viewing experience changes radically, even though the film itself, in content, may be exactly the same.

This is what defines the appeal of moviegoing.

Over the span of the last hundred years, a new art form invented itself, along with the buildings to experience it in. It then continued to reinvent itself, adapting to changes in the world as well as to its own technology. Who can doubt that this will not continue into the movies' second century? However, as long as there are movies, there will be a need for places to show them in.

And chances are, in the end, there will still be popcorn, preferably with real butter.

Since 1984, Houston artist Jim Koehn has created over 200 paintings and drawings of theatre exteriors. Using a variety of media—acrylic, watercolor, and pencil—Koehn has managed to capture the essence of an era now past while noting the juxtaposition of the old within contemporary settings. Many of the theatres he has photographed and painted no longer stand. The River Oaks Theatre, depicted here in a luminous night painting, is one of the fortunate ones. Painting by Jim Koehn ©1995, acrylic on canvas, 40 x 40 in.

PERSPECTIVES

AN AFTERWORD

We shape our buildings; thereafter they shape us.

WINSTON CHURCHILL

★ WHEN I WAS HALFWAY through writing the final chapter of this book, I happened across a 1983 issue of *Texas Highways* magazine. One of the feature stories, "The stars shine again at the Majestic," celebrated the restoration of John Eberson's Majestic Theatre in San Antonio. Built in 1929, the 3,743-seat theatre was among the largest movie theatres in the United States, along with the Fox Theatre in Atlanta, Georgia, and the Roxy Theatre in New York (holding an amazing 5,920 patrons). The Majestic had an opulent decor throughout the interior and the trademark atmospheric ceilings that had become Eberson's signature. After years of disrepair and neglect, the theatre was given a complete overhaul and reopened in December 1981 as the Majestic Performing Arts Center. The color pictures

printed in the magazine depicted a dazzling interior full of color and splendor.
The auditorium was so ornate, so textural,
and so very big, unlike the auditoriums of
today, that it is hard to believe that such a
thing was ever built. It was, in a word,
breathtaking.

Houston had had one very much like
it. Houston tore it down.

After the movies made their exodus to
the neighborhood theatres, downtown
theatres remained, making a slow, steady
descent into disuse. The story was the
same in other Texas cities: Dallas, San
Antonio, and Austin. Yet something
occurred in these other cities. Individuals
with vision foresaw reusing the old theatrical giants as a new form of performance
hall, in a way that linked the modern cultural art scene with the past. Austin's 1915
Paramount, originally an Eberson Majestic, made the transition, and reopened in
1980 as a home for many of Austin's arts
events, live performances, and films. The
1921 Dallas Majestic, another Eberson
construction, was restored in 1983. Restoration projects in San Antonio have
included the aforementioned Majestic as
well as the 1914 Empire Theatre and the
1926 Aztec.

So what happened in Houston? Quite
simply, the structures in other cities were
allowed to sit dormant for a while. Not so
with the Houston Majestic. It was razed in
February 1972, not even six months after it
closed. Of course, there were others: the
massive Loew's State, the Egyptian-
themed Metropolitan, and the Kirby, as
well as the Will Horwitz Homefolks theatres: the Texan, the Iris, and the Uptown.

Houston tore these down too. Only the
Ritz managed to survive.

When these houses closed, there was
no one to offer an economically sound
vision for preservation. Any restoration
effort had to be able to show a substantial
profitable return. At the time, there was
not a justifiable reason for keeping the
theatres intact. Left now are photographs
and newspaper clippings of those
structures.

With the revitalization of downtown
Houston in the late nineties, many

*That's all, folks. Courtesy
of Al Zarzana.*

neglected building have managed to find new life. The Rice Hotel, which seemed destined for destruction over the years, reinvented itself as lofts for those enamored with downtown living. Loft construction salvaged many other buildings as well. Even the old Isis building, at 1012 Prairie, was given an overhaul, although the theatre itself had long since vanished.

This single fact, perhaps more than any other, has played a large part in the formation of this book. The pictures of these buildings, the stories they told, their history, and the memories of those who attended are what remain–because for some unfathomable reason, respect for an architectural past seems possible only after a structure has been torn down, not before.

This is a book of and for memories. It is a book of amazement and wonder. As a ten-year-old, I remember standing in the Windsor during its first run of *2001: A Space Odyssey* and it *was* amazement, at a place so very big to someone so small.

I saw only one of the grand theatres–I believe it was the Majestic; I was five or six at the time, and I remember walking back up the aisle in awe of the decor. I never saw Loew's State. I never saw the Metropolitan or the Kirby. I wish I had.

My father did. He grew up in another age, without terrorists, postal bombings, drive-by shootings, and missing children's faces on milk cartons. He would rise early to deliver the newspaper on his bike, and then pedal downtown to see a movie. Sometimes it was at the Kirby, sometimes it was at the Majestic or the Delman further down on Main. It was all part of a Saturday-afternoon ritual, with an occasional treat at the drugstore. "Henke & Pillot's was over on Travis," he once told me, "and it was down a little south of the Delman Theatre. But they had a soda fountain. And whenever we had the money, we'd get a chocolate soda–it was a big one. Golly Moses, I used to love that thing. And then we would ride our bicycles all the way back home in West University Place."

That was a very different Houston from the one that closed out the century. Times have changed, as have people and social behavior. Put in the perspective of the present, that age seemed almost idyllic, despite the hardships brought by the Great Depression and the war. People did not have cable television, cell phones, or laptop computers. Many did not have air conditioning. But it was a time when people didn't need to lock their doors, and kids could walk or ride all over town without their parents wondering whether they would return safely. It was a simpler time, a time that is now long gone.

What is left of that time are pictures, and memories. I hope this book has managed to preserve a few of both.

Fade out. The end.

NOTES

ONE

1. Paul Hochuli, "Showcase: Former Mayor Says Houston's First Movie House Dates Back to 1898," *Houston Press*, June 10, 1948.

2. *Houston Directory*, 1900.

3. Joseph S. Gallegly, *Footlights on the Border* (The Hague: Mouton, 1962). The historical information in this section, "Houston's First Performances," comes largely from this source.

4. Dr. S. O. Young, *True Stories of Old Houston and Houstonians: Historical and Personal Sketches* (Galveston, Tex.: Springer, 1913; repr., Houston: Green Bottle Antique Shop, 1974), 22–24.

5. Sue Dauphin, *Houston by Stages* (Burnet, Tex.: Eakin Press, 1981), 18.

6. Ibid., 19–22.

7. Ann Holmes, "Archives Turn Up Interesting Incidents in City's Art Life," *Houston Chronicle*, September 2, 1956.

★ **TWO**

1. "Owner of First Movie House Here Recalls Rock-Tossing Days," *Houston Post*, April 14, 1940.

2. "Theatrical Houston 25 Years Ago Was Interesting Place," *Houston Post*, January 28, 1923.

3. Ibid.

4. Hochuli, "Houston's First Movie House."

5. Jeff Millar, "The Lincoln," *Houston Chronicle*, September 11, 1977, Zest section. The information in the next two paragraphs also comes from this story.

6. Linda Anderson Courtney, "The Evolution of Cinema Design in Houston from 1900–1920s," *Houston Review* 4, no. 1 (Winter 1982): 31.

7. King Vidor, *A Tree Is a Tree: An Autobiography*, (Hollywood, Calif.: Samuel French, 1953; rept., 1981), 16–20.

8. Ibid.

9. Advertisement, *Houston Post*, July 28, 1907.

10. "Has Leased the Lyric," *Houston Post*, December 5, 1907.

11. "A Theater Involved," *Houston Post* (clipping, date unknown).

12. "Auspicious Opening of the Prince Theater," *Houston Post*, September 25, 1908.

13. "Prince Theater to Dedicate $10,000 Organ This Week," *Houston Post*, March 2, 1919.

14. "The Bijou," *Houston Post*, October 11, 1908.

15. Advertisement, *Houston Post*, May 1, 1910.

16. "A New Theatre," *Houston Post*, December 19, 1909.

17. "Sentimental Visit Is Paid to Showhouse to Be Torn Down," *Houston Chronicle*, 1946.

18. "Houston Had 25 Theatres Two Decades Ago," *Houston Chronicle* (clipping, date unknown, in the files of the Houston Metropolitan Research Center).

19. Hochuli, "Houston's First Movie House."

20. "Houston Had 25 Theatres," *Houston Chronicle*.

21. "Movies Now Are Ranked over Stage," *Houston Chronicle*, February 22, 1938.

22. Madeleine McDermott Hamm, "Rebuilding Houston's Architectural History," *Houston Chronicle*, November 22, 1999.

23. "Old Cozy Theatre, Erected in Taft Administration, Razed," *Houston Chronicle*, September 4, 1941.

24. Ibid.

25. Thorne Dreyer and Al Reinert, "Montrose Lives," *Texas Monthly*, April 1973, http://www.texasmonthly.com/preview/1973_04-01/feature4 (subscription required).

26. "Ex-Actor Recalls Playing at Cozy, Now Being Razed," *Houston Chronicle*, 1941 (clipping, exact date unknown, in the files of the Houston Metropolitan Research Center).

27. "Old Cozy Theatre," *Houston Chronicle*. The information in the next several paragraphs comes from this article.

28. Mildred Stockard, "Movie-Going Has Been a Houston Habit," *Houston Chronicle* (clipping, date unknown, in the files of the Houston Metropolitan Research Center).

29. "The Plaza," *Houston Post*, May 12, 1912.

30. "The Isis," *Houston Post*, April 14, 1912. The information in the next several paragraphs comes from this article.

31. Advertisement, *Houston Chronicle*, April 16, 1912.

32. Thora Qaddumi, "Lounge Retains Architectural Elements of Old Theater," *Houston Business Journal*, September 24, 1999, http://houston.bizjournals.com/houston/stories/1999/09/27/focus9.html (accessed December 9, 2006).

33. Brenda Tavakoli, "What's Cooking in 002," *002*, September 2000, 46.

34. Bev Blackwood, "What Is Killing Houston's Brewpubs?" *Southwest Brewing News* 9, no. 1 (March 2001): 9.

35. Gerry Dawes, "The Best Bars in America," *Playboy*, May 2000, 94–158.

36. Brian D. Anderson, *The "Titanic" in Print and on Screen* (Jefferson, N.C.: McFarland, 2005), 132.

37. *Houston Post*, May 13, 1912.

38. Advertisement, *Houston Post*, January 21, 1915.

39. Advertisement, *Houston Post*, February 1915.

40. *Houston Directory*, 1910–1911.

41. "Theatrical Houston 25 Years Ago," *Houston Post*.

THREE

1. "New Queen Theatre Will Be Opened Wednesday," *Houston Post*, December 14, 1913. The information in the next several paragraphs comes from this article.

2. Advertisement, *Houston Post*, September 1920.

3. Advertisement, *Houston Chronicle*, May 31, 1932.

4. "Houston Had 25 Theatres," *Houston Chronicle*.

5. Advertisement, *Houston Post*, June 5, 1914.

6. Marguerite Johnston, *Houston: The Unknown City, 1836–1946* (College Station: Texas A&M Univ. Press, 1991), 145.

7. Advertisement, *Houston Post*, April 13, 1913.

8. "Houston Had 25 Theatres," *Houston Chronicle*.

9. "At the Theatre," *Houston Chronicle*, June 10, 1913.

10. Advertisement, *Houston Post*, February 6, 1916.

11. "'Are You Fit to Marry?' Film Due at Liberty," *Houston Post*, April 9, 1922.

12. "Movies Now Are Ranked over Stage," *Houston Chronicle*.

13. "Houston Had 25 Theatres," *Houston Chronicle*.

14. "Benefits at Pearce and Zoe for Bayland Orphans," *Houston Post*, January 4, 1915.

15. Courtney, "Cinema Design in Houston," 20–41.

16. Quoted in Courtney, "Cinema Design in Houston," 33.

17. Ibid.

18. Ibid., 33–36.

19. Advertisement, *Houston Post*, June 5, 1919.

20. "Theatre Is Ruined by Blaze," *Houston Post*, December 22, 1962.

21. Sarah H. Emmott, *Memorial Park: A Priceless Legacy* (Houston: Herring Press, 1992), 18.

22. Michael E. Wilson, *Alfred C. Finn: Builder of Houston* (Houston: Houston Public Library, 1983), 10.

23. "Houston Theater Owner Is Victim of Heart Attack," *Houston Post*, December 25, 1941.

24. "Rialto's Opening Program Draws Huge Attendance," *Houston Post*, April 14, 1922. The information in the next several paragraphs comes from this article.

25. Advertisement, *Houston Chronicle*, February 16, 1927.

26. Jane Preddy, "The Esperson Theatre," *Marquee* 20, no. 4 (1988): 18.

FOUR

1. Luthor Holcomb, message delivered at the funeral of Karl St. John Hoblitzelle.

2. Don Hinga, *Forty Years of Community Service: The Story of Karl Hoblitzelle and the Development of Interstate Theatres* (Dallas: Stellmacher and Son, 1946). The information about Hoblitzelle in this section of the chapter is taken from Hinga's book.

3. Ibid.

4. Ibid.

5. Ibid.

6. Ibid.

7. "Movies Now Are Ranked over Stage," *Houston Chronicle*.

8. "Empire Theatre Being Remodeled," *Houston Chronicle*, August 18, 1905.

9. Advertisement, *Houston Post*, November 6, 1905.

10. "Movies Now Are Ranked Over Stage," *Houston Chronicle*.

11. Ibid.

12. Hochuli, "Houston's First Movie House."

13. T. P. Luna, "Those Enterprising Exuberant Ebersons," *Marquee* 23, no. 1 (1991): 25–30.

14. "The New Majestic," *Houston Post*, February 20, 1910.

15. Johnston, *Unknown City*, 145.

16. "The New Majestic," *Houston Post*. The information in this paragraph and the next several is drawn from this article.

17. Ibid.

18. "Houston Had 25 Theatres," *Houston Chronicle*.

19. "Opening of New Majestic," *Houston Post*, February 22, 1910.

20. Ibid.

21. "Sentimental Visit Is Paid to Show House to Be Torn Down," *Houston Chronicle*, 1946 (clipping, exact date unknown, in the files of the Houston Metropolitan Research Center). The information in the next several paragraphs is drawn from this article.

22. "The New Majestic." *Houston Post*.

23. "Opening of New Majestic," *Houston Post*.

24. Ibid.

25. "Theatrical Houston 25 Years Ago," *Houston Post*.

26. Advertisement, *Houston Post*, October 16, 1914.

27. Advertisement, *Houston Post*, February 21, 1910.

28. Johnston, *Unknown City*, 184.

29. Hubert Roussel, *The Houston Symphony Orchestra: 1913–1971* (Austin: Univ. of Texas Press, 1972), 16–23.

30. Luna, "Exuberant Ebersons," 25.

31. Courtney, "Cinema Design in Houston," 40.

32. David Naylor, *American Picture Palaces: The Architecture of Fantasy* (New York: Van Nostrand and Reinhold, 1981), 68.

33. Courtney, "Cinema Design in Houston," 39–40.

34. Josie Weber, "It Was Houston's Vaudeville Palace and in a Word It Was . . . Majestic," *Houston Chronicle, Texas Magazine* section, March 8, 1970. The information in the next two paragraphs also comes from this article.

35. *Houston Post*, special section on the opening of the Houston Majestic, January 28, 1923.

36. Weber, "Houston's Vaudeville Palace."

37. Jane Preddy, *Palaces of Dreams: The Movie Theatres of John Eberson, Architect*, an exhibition catalogue (San Antonio, Tex.: McNay Art Museum, 1989).

38. Ibid.

39. Mildred Stockard, "The Rise and Fall of Houston's 'Flicker' Houses," *Houston Chronicle, Rotogravure Magazine* section, November 11, 1956.

40. "Great Changes Made in Play House Building," *Houston Post*, January 28, 1923, Majestic Opening section.

41. Preddy, *Palaces of Dreams*, n.p.

42. Luna, "Exuberant Ebersons," 26.

43. Lynn Ashby, "A Fitting Name . . . Majestic," *Houston Post*, September 22, 1968.

44. Weber, "Houston's Vaudeville Palace."

45. Ashby, "Fitting Name," 4.

46. Stockard, "Houston's 'Flicker' Houses," 11.

47. Advertisement, *Houston Post*, January 28, 1923.

48. "Movies Now Are Ranked over Stage," *Houston Chronicle*.

49. As quoted in Johnston, *Unknown City*, 245.

50. Mildred Stockard, "Houston Theaters Offer City Movie Goers Many Chances to See their Favorite Stars," *Houston Chronicle*, April 1962 (clipping, exact date unknown, in the files of the Houston Metropolitan Research Center).

51. Advertisement, *Houston Post*, October 31, 1938.

52. "Sentimental Visit Is Paid," *Houston Chronicle*.

53. Ibid.

54. Advertisement, *Houston Post*, January 28, 1923.

55. Ashby, "Fitting Name," 7.

56. Ibid.

57. "Big Accomplishments Highlight Theatrical History Made in City," *Houston Chronicle*, December 30, 1939.

58. Ashby, "Fitting Name," 7.

59. Bill Beck, *At Your Service: An Illustrated History of Houston Lighting and Power Company* (Houston: Gulf, 1990), 263–265.

60. "Majestic Will Be First Theater in South to Have Fox Movietone," *Houston Chronicle*, December 17, 1927.

61. Weber, "Houston's Vaudeville Palace."

62. "O'Rourke is Given Contract For Majestic Work," *Houston Chronicle*, August 9, 1950.

63. Advertisement, *Houston Post*, June 16, 1960.

64. "Premiere to Close Downtown Portions," *Houston Chronicle*, December 4, 1968.

65. "Meet the Lucky Couple Who'll 'Commit Marriage,'" *Houston Chronicle*, May 28, 1969.

66. Jeff Millar, "Majestic to Spin Its Last Dream," *Houston Chronicle*, September 15, 1971.

67. Jeff Millar, "Looping the Films," *Houston Chronicle*, September 26, 1971.

68. Ibid.

69. *Houston Post*, August 9, 1979.

FIVE

1. Michael E. Wilson, "Alfred C. Finn: Houston Architect," *Houston Review* 5, no. 2 (Summer 1983): 65–67.

2. Ibid., 70.

3. Ibid., 78.

4. Wilson, *Finn: Builder of Houston*, 30.

5. "Palace of Splendor to Stage Grand Show for Real Christmas Treat," *Houston Post*, December 25, 1926.

6. Ibid.

7. "Metropolitan Contains 2500 Splendid Seats," *Houston Chronicle*, December 24, 1926.

8. "Theatre Hailed as South's Greatest and Most Beautiful," *Houston Chronicle*, December 24, 1926.

9. "Disappearing Orchestra Pit Is a Feature," *Houston Chronicle*, December 24, 1926.

10. "New $2,000,000 Theatre Opens to Large Crowds," *Houston Post*, December 1926 (clipping, exact date unknown, in the files of the Houston Metropolitan Research Center).

11. "Stars Arriving for Opening of 'El Paso' at Met Today," *Houston Chronicle*, April 1, 1949.

12. "New Films," *Houston Post*, June 1, 1965.

13. Robert E. Carr and R. M. Hayes, *Wide Screen Movies: A History and Filmography of Wide Gauge Filmmaking* (Jefferson, N.C: McFarland, 1988), 52.

14. "Let's All Greet 'Vic,'" *Houston Chronicle*, April 5, 1929.

15. Advertisement, *Houston Post*, October 7, 1938.

16. "Mae West Turns Down Proposal but Obliges with Fine Show," *Houston Post*, April 15, 1939.

17. Advertisement, *Houston Post*, August 6, 1939.

18. "Charges Are Filed in Two Other Robberies," December 20, 1949 (clipping in the files of the Houston Metropolitan Research Center, newspaper unknown).

19. "Teen-Age Father, Friend Charged in Met Holdup," September 12, 1950 (clipping in the files of the Houston Metropolitan Research Center, newspaper unknown).

20. "Thieves Bind Watchman, Loot Theater," December 21, 1960 (clipping in the files of the Houston Metropolitan Research Center, newspaper unknown).

21. "Man Killed in Theater Restroom," *Houston Chronicle*, February 22, 1962.

22. "Yeggs Decline Instant Replay," July 23, 1972 (clipping in the files of the Houston Metropolitan Research Center, newspaper unknown).

23. "Simplicity Is Note in Decorations of New Movie Play House," *Houston Chronicle*, August 11, 1927.

24. "Experienced Movie Staff to Be in Charge of New Kirby Theatre," *Houston Chronicle*, August 11, 1927.

25. "Kirby Has Capacity Audience at Opening," *Houston Post*, August 13, 1927.

26. "Kirby Will Be Last Word in Picture Show," *Houston Post*, August 12, 1927.

27. "Kirby Has Capacity Audience," *Houston Post*.

28. Mildred Stockard, "Silents to Wide Screen," *Houston Chronicle*, April 6, 1956.

29. Johnston, *Unknown City*, 288.

30. Stockard, "Silents to Wide Screen."

31. Ibid.

32. "Ex-Convict Charged in Hijacking of Two Cashiers at Theatre," newspaper clippings dated January 20, 1949, Houston Metropolitan Research Center.

33. "Hundreds See Opening of Loew Theatre," *Houston Chronicle*, October 16, 1927.

34. *Houston Chronicle*, October 14, 1927.

35. "Hundreds See Opening," *Houston Chronicle*.

36. Ibid.

37. "New Theatre among Largest in the State Says Architect," *Houston Chronicle*, October 14, 1927.

38. Marge Crumbaker, "Palaces in Houston," *Houston Post*, August 29, 1965.

39. "New Theatre among Largest," *Houston Chronicle*.

40. Ibid.

41. Charlotte Phealan, "Nostalgia Is Interesting . . ." *Houston Post*, June 25, 1972.

42. Ibid.

43. Josie Weber, *Houston Chronicle*, date unknown.

44. Advertisement, *Houston Post*, February 7, 1940.

45. "'Gone With the Wind' Comes to Houston," *Houston Post*, February 8, 1940.

46. Phealan, "Nostalgia Is Interesting."

47. Jeff Millar, "It's a Heckuva Way to Have to End an Era," *Houston Chronicle*, October 15, 1972.

48. Phealan, "Nostalgia Is Interesting."

49. "Perpetual Crisp Spring Days in Loew's Theatre," *Houston Chronicle*, October 14, 1927.

50. "Technique of Keeping Theatres Comfortable during Summer Is Learned by House Managers," *Houston Chronicle*, 1932 (newspaper clipping, exact date unknown).

51. Ibid.

52. Don Looser, "A Musical Renaissance: The Growth of Cultural Institutions in Houston, 1929–1936," *Houston Review* 6, no. 3 (1984): 139.

53. Ibid., 143.

54. Ibid., 147.

55. Mildred Stockard, "'Goldfinger' Sets Record as Theatres Are Jammed," *Houston Chronicle*, December 29, 1964.

56. Millar, "It's a Heckuva Way."

57. Stockard, "Silents to Wide Screen."

58. Millar, "It's a Heckuva Way."

59. W. G. Roberts III, "Loew's State Theatre: Houston, Texas," *Marquee* 10, no. 1 (1978): 14.

60. Millar, "It's a Heckuva Way."

61. Ibid.

62. Phealan, "Nostalgia Is Interesting."

63. Millar, "It's a Heckuva Way."

64. "Veteran Manager to Retire Feb. 2," *Houston Post*, January 18, 1973.

65. Dick Willson, interview with the author, October 15, 2005.

66. Millar, "It's a Heckuva Way."

67. Louis Parks, "60 Years Ago, Loews Chain Opened Houston's Stately Movie Theater," *Houston Chronicle*, October 21, 1987.

68. "Restoration of the Ritz Theatre," *Houston Heights Tribune*, March 1988.

69. "Loew's State Theatre," Cinema Treasures.com, http://www.cinematreasures.com/theater/1703 (accessed August 2005).

70. Terry Mattingly, On Religion, "Big Hats and Black-Church Tradition," http://tmatt.gospelcom.net/column/1998/06/17 (accessed December 4, 2006).

71. Parks, "60 Years Ago."

72. Dan Grothaus, "Dynamite Reduces Skyscrapers to Rubble," *Houston Post*, April 15, 1985.

SIX

1. Larry Minor, "Scrapbook: Did You Know . . ." *Amusement Today*, February 1998, 30.

2. Juan Ramon Palomo, "Whatever Happened to . . . Houston's Luna Park" *Houston Post*, February 5, 1980.

3. Samuel Reaves, "Beauties Paraded at Luna Park," *Houston Chronicle*, August 13, 1950.

4. "Warwick Plans Restoration of Last Movie Palace," *Houston Downtown Maga-*

zine, January 25, 1988, 6.

5. Southwest Center for Urban Research and the School of Architects, *Houston Architectural Survey*, 6 vols. (Houston: Rice University, 1980–1981), 1:89.

6. Ibid., 88–90.

7. Advertisement, *Houston Post*, April 15, 1926.

8. Southwest Center for Urban Research and the School of Architects, *Houston Architectural Survey*, 90.

9. Gary Warwick, interview with the author, April 4, 2006.

10. "Ritz Theater Stage Show Keeps Vaudeville Alive in Houston," *Houston Post*, January 20, 1946.

11. Warwick interview, 2006. The information in the next two paragraphs is also from this interview.

12. Advertisement, *Houston Post*, October 4, 1946.

13. Warwick interview, 2006.

14. Fred Bunch, photo, *Houston Post*, December 26, 1976.

15. Advertisement, *Houston Post*, September 9, 1977.

16. Ann Holmes, "The Last Metro," *Houston Chronicle*, January 31, 1991.

17. Gary Warwick, interview with the author, January 1995.

18. "The Majestic Metro," *Houston Remodeling and Design Magazine* (clipping courtesy of Gary Warwick; author and date unknown).

19. Ibid.

20. Everett Evans, "Puttin' on the Ritz," *Houston Chronicle*, January 21, 1988.

21. Holmes, "Last Metro."

22. "Warwick Plans Restoration," *Houston Downtown Magazine*, 6.

23. Evans, "Puttin' on the Ritz."

24. Warwick interview, 1995.

25. *Houston Remodeling and Design Magazine*, "Majestic Metro."

26. Warwick interview, 1995.

27. "Houston Theatre Memories" (Bob Bailey Studios 1998 calendar, Houston, 1997).

28. Barbara Stones, *America Goes to the Movies* (North Hollywood, Calif.: National Association of Theatre Owners, 1993), 70–71.

29. Ibid., 71–73.

30. Randle G. Pace and Deborah Markey,

Houston Heights: 1891–1991 (Houston: Tribune, 1991), 47.

31. Ibid.

32. Jay Young, "Changing Times," *Houston Chronicle, This Week* section, December 13, 1989. The information in the next several paragraphs is also drawn from this article.

33. Ibid.

34. Pace and Markey, *Houston Heights*, 47.

35. Young, "Changing Times."

36. Advertisement, *Houston Heights Citizen*, November 10, 1939.

37. J. T. Chapin, "Movie Kings of Heights Theater," *Houston Chronicle, Texas Magazine* section, August 30, 1992.

38. Young, "Changing Times."

39. Don Moffitt, "Memo to the City Editor (internal memo)," *Houston Post*, October 16, 1959.

40. Cathy Harris and Ralph Williams, "'Radical Groups' Are Blamed for Fire at Sex-Film Theatre," *Houston Post*, June 7, 1969.

41. Ibid.

42. Young, "Changing Times."

43. Pace and Markey, *Houston Heights*, 59.

44. Eric Gerber, "In the Heights, Movies Could Be Special Again," *Houston Post*, August 30, 1981.

45. Young, "Changing Times."

46. Gerber, "In the Heights."

47. "'Rock Around the Clock' for Pacifica," *Houston Post*, April 16, 1982.

48. Raequel Roberts, "Anatomy of an Artist," *Houston Post*, August 30, 1989.

49. Angela Kerr Smith and Randy Cypret, *Heights Main Street Project: Final Report* (Houston: Greater Heights Area Chamber of Commerce), 7.

50. William Albright, "'Romp Thru Hell' is Sinfully Funny," *Houston Post*, November 1989 (clipping, exact date unknown).

51. "Heights Theater Restoration Will Receive Gold Brick Award," *Houston Leader*, January 21, 1993.

SEVEN

1. W. G. Jones, map of Houston, 1930.

2. Josie Weber, "The Santa Claus Houston Forgot," *Houston Chronicle, Texas Magazine*
section, December 24, 1967.

3. "Theater Owner Victim of Heart Attack," *Houston Post*.

4. Weber, "Santa Claus."

5. Ibid.

6. Advertisement, *Houston Post*, June 6, 1919.

7. Harold Scarlett, "Girls—Live—on Stage—," *Houston Post, Spotlight* section, April 11, 1965.

8. "Texan Theater Will Open Today," *Houston Post*, April 4, 1925.

9. Ibid.

10. "Texan Theatre, Opened in 1925, Will Be Razed," *Houston Chronicle*, 1953 (clipping, exact date unknown, in the files of the Houston Metropolitan Research Center).

11. Advertisement, *Houston Post*, January 4, 1929.

12. Weber, "Santa Claus."

13. Steven Long, "Depression-Era Santa Claus," *Houston Chronicle*, December 25, 1989.

14. Weber, "Santa Claus." The information in the next half dozen paragraphs is drawn from this article.

15. Ibid.

16. Scarlett, "Girls—Live."

17. Jeff Millar, "The Bulldozers Come for Last of the 'Homefolks' Theatres," *Houston Chronicle*, July 18, 1965.

18. Long, "Depression-Era Santa Claus."

19. Ibid.

20. Weber, "Santa Claus."

21. Long, "Depression-Era Santa Claus."

22. Weber, "Santa Claus."

23. "Theater Owner Victim of Heart Attack," *Houston Post*.

24. Weber, "Santa Claus."

25. "Theater Owner Victim of Heart Attack," *Houston Post*.

26. Ibid.

27. Weber, "Santa Claus."

28. "Last Zip on the Strip: Rivoli's Lights Go Out," *Houston Post*, July 19, 1969.

29. "Uptown Theater to Make Formal Opening Here," *Houston Post*, November 8, 1935.

30. "Foreign Film theater Will Have Premiere," *Houston Post*, December 1, 1935.

31. Advertisement, *Houston Post*, December 25, 1935.

32. "New Theatre Name to Be

Announced," *Houston Chronicle*, February 24, 1935.

33. "New Horwitz Theatre to Be Called 'The Tower,'" *Houston Chronicle*, February 28, 1935.

34. Warwick interview, 2006.

35. "New Horwitz Theatre Has Gala Opening," *Houston Chronicle*, November 10, 1935.

36. "History of New 'Uptown' Theater like Aladdin Tale," *Houston Post*, November 1935.

37. "Theater Owner Victim of Heart Attack," *Houston Post*.

38. Weber, "Santa Claus."

39. "Will Horwitz Funeral Rites to Be Held at 2:30 P.M. Today," *Houston Post*, December 26, 1941.

40. Jim Fisher and Nancy Simonds, *Houston: Remember When, Volume 1* (Houston: KHOU Channel 8, 1998).

41. Obituary of Frederick Royal Gibbons, *Houston Post*, July 21, 1981.

42. "Texan Theatre Will Be Razed," *Houston Chronicle*.

43. "Texan Theatre Says Farewell to Patrons," 1953 (clipping in the files of the Houston Metropolitan Research Center, newspaper and exact date unknown).

44. "Smashing Old Texan Theatre" (clipping in the files of the Houston Metropolitan Research Center, newspaper and date unknown).

45. "Mrs. Horwitz Rites Set in League City," *Houston Chronicle*, May 14, 1972.

46. "Iris Theater Closed For Remodeling," *Houston Chronicle*, May 5, 1958.

47. "Man Attacks Woman in Rest Room," *Houston Chronicle*, June 13, 1959.

48. Garvin Berry, "Oddities in Houston," *Inside Houston*, October 1996, 9.

49. "Uptown Will Change Name to Rivoli," *Houston Post*, December 15, 1959.

50. "Big Screens, Special Runs Top Film Scene," *Houston Chronicle*, January 29, 1961.

51. Scarlett, "Girls—Live."

52. Cecil Hodges, "JP Orders Hearing on Some Movies Here," *Houston Post*, May 27, 1962.

53. Scarlett, "Girls—Live."

54. Ralph Dodd, "Allright Buys Theatres' Land," *Houston Post*, March 1, 1964.

55. Ibid.

56. Nona Mewhinney, "His Theatres Die But Legacy of Love for Houston Lives On," *Houston Chronicle*, clipping date unknown.

57. Kay Gaston, "Farewell to a Landmark," *Houston Post*, July 26, 1965.

58. "Last Zip on the Strip," *Houston Post*.

59. Ibid.

60. "Theater Owner Victim of Heart Attack," *Houston Post*.

61. Obituary of Fred Valerio Cannata, *Houston Post*, February 16, 1990.

EIGHT

1. "Opening of New Delman Theater Draws Crowd," *Houston Post*, November 29, 1934.

2. "Decision to Stand in Delman Theatre Case," *Houston Post*, April 17, 1962.

3. "Big Screens Top Film Scene," *Houston Chronicle*.

4. H. Mewhinney, "Business Not Hurt," *Houston Post*, June 3, 1960.

5. Ernest Bailey, "Sneak Film Stops the Show," *Houston Post*, April 23, 1966.

6. Advertisement, *Houston Post*, December 21, 1969, *Spotlight* section.

7. Eric Gerber, "Death of a Theater," *Houston Post*, March 26, 1978.

8. "Delman Theater Undergoing Transformation into a Performing Arts Center," *Houston Chronicle*, January 25, 1986.

9. Nancy Sarnoff, "Theater Met with Demolition as Owners Picture New Use for Land," *Houston Business Journal*, June 28, 2002.

10. Earl Blair, letter to the author, February 21, 2006.

11. Stockard, "Houston Theaters Offer City Movie Goers Many Chances."

12. Advertisement, *Houston Post*, November 20, 1938.

13. Ione Kirkham, "Nan Gray Back Home Wearing Fame Easily," newspaper unknown, August 28, 1937.

14. "University Showhouse Joins Interstate," *Houston Post*, June 1, 1949.

15. "A Guide to West University Place," Roger Martin Properties, September 2005.

16. "Beautiful New Union Theater on Humble Road to Open Formally Today,"

Houston Post, October 8, 1938.

17. Advertisement, *Houston Post*, October 8, 1938.

18. "Big Accomplishments Highlight Theatrical History," *Houston Chronicle*.

19. Ibid.

20. Advertisement, *Houston Post*, November 16, 1939.

21. *Houston Directory*, 1956.

22. "Big Accomplishments Highlight Theatrical History," *Houston Chronicle*.

23. "New Theater Opens Tonight," newspaper unknown, November 22, 1939.

24. Advertisement, *Houston Post*, November 22, 1939.

25. "Big Accomplishments Highlight Theatrical History," *Houston Chronicle*.

26. Southwest Center for Urban Research and the School of Architects, *Houston Architectural Survey*, 3:699–700.

27. "New Suburban Showhouse to Open," *Houston Post*, November 26, 1939.

28. "Grand Opening of New River Oaks Theater Will Be Held at 7:30 p.m. Today," *Houston Post*, November 28, 1939.

29. Louis Parks, "Cinemystique," *Houston Chronicle*, January 12, 1984.

30. Dauphin, *Houston by Stages*, 116–123.

31. Jeff Millar, "Repertory Film Theater Plans New Approach," *Houston Chronicle*, March 23, 1977.

32. Ibid.

33. Ibid.

34. Louis Parks, "The Way They Were," *Houston Chronicle*, July 22, 1988, *Weekend Preview* section.

35. "Shouting Match Erupts at Rally," *Houston Post*, January 12, 1983.

36. Tupper Hull, "River Oaks Theatre Raided by Vice Police," *Houston Post*, September 13, 1982.

37. Vicki Macias, "'Salo' Not Obscene," *Houston Post*, April 12, 1983.

38. Michael Spies, "Rooms with a View," *Houston Chronicle*, May 16, 1986.

39. Cynthia Thomas, "Some Enchanted Evening," *Houston Chronicle*, December 7, 1996.

40. Louis Parks, "Film Notes: Silent Hamlet?" *Houston Chronicle*, December 20, 1996.

41. Bruce Westbrook, "'Blair Witch Project' Scaring Up Big Business Nationwide, in

Houston," *Houston Chronicle*, July 20, 1999.

42. "Best of Houston 2004," *Houston Press*, September 23–29, 2004.

43. Lisa Gray, "Historic Theatre Could Soon Fade into History," *Houston Chronicle*, July 22, 2006.

44. Lisa Gray, "Landmark's Supporters Take Plea to City Council," *Houston Chronicle*, August 2, 2006.

45. Lisa Gray, "Quiet, Color-Coordinated Efforts to Save Theatre," *Houston Chronicle*, August 31, 2006.

46. Richard Connelly, "Turkeys of the Year," *Houston Press*, November 23–29, 2006.

47. "Houston 1995" (Bob Bailey calendar).

48. "Big Screens Top Film Scene." *Houston Chronicle*.

49. "'Razzia' Opens Alray Tonight," *Houston Post*, April 20, 1960.

50. Advertisement, *Houston Post*, August 1, 1941.

51. Ed Henderson, interview with the author, January 1992.

52. *Houston Directory*, 1986.

53. Advertisement, *Houston Public News*, December 5, 1990.

54. Advertisement, *Houston Public News*, July 3, 1991.

55. Advertisement, *Houston Public News*, January 19, 1994.

56. "Best of Houston 1995," *Houston Press*, September 21–27, 1995.

57. Gerald Egger, "Farb Made Fortune on Local Realty," *Houston Post*, October 30, 1966.

58. Ibid.

59. "Sunset Theater, New Suburban Playhouse, Will Open Tonight," *Houston Post*, October 3, 1941.

60. Advertisement, *Houston Post*, October 3, 1941.

61. Egger, "Farb Made Fortune."

62. Ibid.

63. "Albert Farb, 80, Dies," *Houston Post*, August 17, 1979.

64. Advertisement, *Houston Post*, March 7, 1944.

65. *Houston Directory*, 1954–1986.

66. Advertisement, *Houston Post*, October 12, 1946.

67. Roy Bonario, interview with the author, December 28, 1991.

68. "Old Spanish Trail Theater Will Make Its Debut Today," *Houston Post*, February 15, 1947.

69. Advertisement, *Houston Post*, September 1, 1961.

70. Advertisement, *Houston Post*, November 22, 1961.

71. Advertisement, *Houston Post*, May 2, 1973.

72. "Project Grows in Popularity," *Houston Post*, November 17, 1973.

73. Rob Meckel, "Theater Will Be Renovated," *Houston Post*, April 27, 1985.

74. Dauphin, *Houston by Stages*, 256–258.

75. Ibid.

76. Ibid., 258.

77. Advertisement, *Houston Post*, September 1, 1961.

78. "New Theater in Bellaire Has Opening," *Houston Post*, April 17, 1949.

79. Advertisement, *Southwestern Times*, April 14, 1949.

80. "Bellaire Theatre," Cinema Treasures. com, http://www.cinematreasures.com/ theater/9910 (accessed August 2005).

81. Advertisement, *Houston Post*, May 1, 1969.

82. "Bellaire Theater Remodeling to Accommodate Live Entertainment," *Houston Chronicle*, June 13, 1982.

83. Parks, "Cinemystique."

84. "Bellaire Theater to Reopen This Fall," *Houston Post*, May 6, 1986.

85. Jeff Millar, "Bel Air: 1940s-Style Theater Reopens With 5 Screens," *Houston Chronicle*, November 26, 1986.

86. Ibid.

87. "The Red Eye: Mars," *Houston Post*, September 3, 1989.

88. Louis Parks, "Troubled Bel Air Theater to Close Its Doors in August," *Houston Chronicle*, July 25, 1992.

89. James Ward, "The Last Picture Show," *Houston Press*, August 6, 1992.

90. Greg Hassell, "Some Discovery Zone Locations Closed Here," *Houston Chronicle*, July 2, 1999.

91. Letter taped on business window, personal.

92. Greg Hassell, "Whole Foods Updating Format With 2 New Inner-Loop Stores," *Houston Chronicle*, January 13, 2000.

93. Whit Snyder, "Historic Theatre Awaits a New Fate," *Pasadena (TX) Citizen*, February 25, 1998.

94. Advertisement, *Pasadena (TX) Citizen*, November 13, 1949.

95. "Capitan's Decoration Will Set New Pattern in Local Theaters," *Pasadena (TX) Citizen*, November 13, 1949.

96. Advertisement, *Pasadena (TX) Citizen*, November 13, 1949.

97. Bob Newberry, "Pasadena Council Oks New Movie Law," *Houston Post*, June 10, 1917.

98. C. Leonard Holt, "Theater Becomes Christian Center," *Houston Post*, April 16, 1977.

99. Virginia Hahn, "Capitan Theater Once Had County's Largest Indoor Screen," *Pasadena (TX) Citizen*, January 9, 1997.

100. Kim Canon, "Historic Renovation," *Pasadena (TX) Citizen*, September 22, 1999.

101. Catherine Bray, "Capitan Re-lighting Prompts Memories of Yesteryear," *Pasadena (TX) Citizen*, June 22, 2000.

102. Greg Hassell, "Restoring Capitan a Sign of Change," *Houston Chronicle*, October 20, 1999.

103. Advertisement, *Houston Post*, December 7, 1949.

104. "Show Business," *Houston Post*, May 29, 1975.

NINE

1. Hinga, *Forty Years of Community Service*, 1.

2. Ibid., 12.

3. Conover Hunt Jones, *The Majestic Theatre, 1921–1983* (Dallas: *Dallas Morning News* and Neiman Marcus, 1983), 9–10.

4. "New Interstate Theaters Nearing Completion Here," *Houston Post*, November 10, 1935.

5. Advertisement, *Houston Post*, December 25, 1935.

6. Peter Papademetriou, "The Late, Great Picture Palaces," *Houston Home and Garden*, November 1978, 79.

7. Hinga, *Forty Years of Community Service*, 7.

8. "Tower Theater Ready to Open Doors

Tonight," *Houston Post*, February 14, 1936.

9. Papademetriou, "Late, Great Picture Palaces," 81.

10. Advertisement, *Houston Post*, April 3, 1960.

11. "Tower Theatre," Cinema Treasures. com, http://www.cinematreasures.com/ theater/6269 (accessed August 2005).

12. Eric Gerber, "The Last Picture Show," *Houston Post*, August 25, 1978.

13. William Albright, "Coming Attractions," *Houston Post*, August 25, 1978.

14. Barbara Canetti, "'Ipi-Tombi' Cast Rebels at Final Show," *Houston Post*, September 2, 1980.

15. Dan Hardy, photo, *Houston Post*, February 24, 1990.

16. "New Eastwood Theater to Be Opened Tonight," *Houston Post*, March 6, 1936.

17. Zarko Franks, "To Al Lever, It's Perpetual Spring and He's Stepping Down Smartly," *Houston Chronicle*, April 2, 1967.

18. Advertisement, *Houston Post*, May 20, 1938.

19. "Houstonian Leaves Theater Business After 46 Years," *Houston Post*, May 5, 1973.

20. Ibid.

21. Jeff Millar, "Another Houston Movie House—the Yale—Is Biting the Dust," *Houston Chronicle*, January 18, 1972.

22. "Bank Buys Theatre, Post Office Buildings," *Houston Post*, January 11, 1967.

23. Millar, "Another Houston Movie House."

24. Hinga, *Forty Years of Community Service*, 7–8.

25. Southwest Center for Urban Research and the School of Architects, *Houston Architectural Survey*, 4:746–747.

26. "Alabama Theater Opening Today to Be Gala Occasion," *Houston Post*, November 2, 1939.

27. Paul Hochuli, "Alabama Theater Opened at Gala First Night," *Houston Press*, November 3, 1939.

28. "Alabama Theatre," Cinema Treasures. com, http://www.cinematreasures.com/ theater/1462 (accessed August 2005).

29. "Todd-AO Outfit For Alabama," *Houston Post*, June 30, 1960.

30. Jeff Millar, "40 theatres Satisfy Variety of Appetites," *Houston Chronicle*, June 1966.

31. Papademetriou, "Late, Great Picture Palaces," 81.

32. Jeff Millar, "Era Ends as the Alabama Closes," *Houston Chronicle*, December 6, 1983.

33. "Old Alabama Theater Gets New Lease on Life," *Houston Post*, August 5, 1984.

34. Harriet Edleson, "Theater Shifts From Screen to Scribes," *Houston Chronicle*, October 5, 1984.

35. Ibid.

36. Barry Moore, "The Bookstop's Here," *Houston Press*, August 12, 1993.

37. William Albright, "Staging a Comeback," *Houston Post*, December 3, 1992.

38. "Best of Houston 1999," *Houston Press*, September 23–29, 1999.

39. "Ceremonies Will Mark Opening of Almeda Theater," *Houston Post*, August 3, 1040.

40. "Thousands Gather at Opening Celebration of Alabama Theatre," *Houston Post*, November 3, 1939.

41. *Houston Directory*, 1956–1969.

42. Hinga, *Forty Years of Community Service*, 10.

43. Ibid., 11.

44. Melissa Fletcher Stoeltje, "Restoring Magic at the Movies," *Houston Chronicle*, June 22, 1993.

45. Advertisement, *Houston Post*, August 15, 1941.

46. Elizabeth Bennett, "The Exorcist," *Houston Post*, January 14, 1974.

47. Mike Avalos, "Vice Arrest Sours Porno Star's Visit," *Houston Post*, August 10, 1978.

48. "Court Hearings Held on Theater Orgy Charges," *Houston Post*, November 2, 1983.

49. Elizabeth Bennett, "Ratings War," *Houston Post*, November 20, 1983.

50. Jeff Simmon, "Village Theater Closes Its Doors," *Houston Post*, February 19, 1987.

51. Barry Moore, "The Last Picture Show," *Houston Press*, June 25, 1992.

52. Fletcher Stoeltje, "Restoring Magic at the Movies."

53. D. J. Wilson, "Lights, Camera, Demolition," *Houston Press*, September 2, 1993.

54. Lisa Singhania, "Lights Out Forever at Village Theater," *Houston Post*, January 7, 1994, A21–24.

55. Claudia Feldman, "It's the End of the World," *Houston Chronicle*, January 12, 1993.

56. "Wayside Theater to Open with Ceremonies Tonight," *Houston Post*, April 24, 1942.

57. Hinga, *Forty Years of Community Service*, 14.

58. Ibid.

59. Ibid., 13–15.

60. Ibid., 14.

61. Ibid., 15.

62. Ibid., 14–16.

63. Advertisement, *Houston Post*, December 20, 1946.

64. Southwest Center for Urban Research and the School of Architects, *Houston Architectural Survey*, 3:700.

65. "Show Business," *Houston Post*, May 29, 1975.

66. "Broadway Theater to Open Friday," *Houston Post*, May 23, 1947.

67. Millar, "Another Houston Movie House."

68. Advertisement, *Houston Post*, July 10, 1947.

69. Parks, "Cinemystique."

70. "Show Business," *Houston Post*, May 29, 1975.

71. Advertisement, *Houston Post*, May 30, 1975.

72. Advertisement, *Houston Post*, November 6, 1987.

73. David Plesa, "City Hopes to Reverse Historical Trend," *Houston Post*, February 5, 1993.

74. Rob Vanya, "A Grand 'Old Lady' Gets a Second Chance," *The Leader*, July 23, 1992.

75. Plesa, "City Hopes to Reverse Historical Trend."

76. Advertisement, *Houston Post*, September 26, 1947.

77. *Houston Directory*, 1958–1969.

78. Stones, *America Goes to the Movies*, 140–161.

79. Franks, "To Al Lever, It's Perpetual Spring."

TEN

1. Douglas Gomery, *Shared Pleasures: A History of Movie Presentation in the United States* (London: British Film Institute, 1992), 155–156.

2. Renée Kientz, "Days of Promise," *Houston Chronicle*, February 6, 2000.

3. Gomery, *Shared Pleasures*, 157–158.

4. Advertisement, *Houston Post*, April 21, 1912.

5. F. H. Richardson, *Motion Picture Handbook: A Guide for Managers and Operators of Motion Picture Theatres* (New York: World Photographic, 1910), 160.

6. Cab Calloway and Bryant Rollins, *Of Minnie the Moocher and Me* (New York: Crowell, 1976), 138–140.

7. Millar, "The Lincoln."

8. Fisher and Simonds, *Houston Remember When*, Volume 1.

9. Ibid.

10. David G. McComb, *Houston: The Bayou City* (Austin: Univ. of Texas Press, 1969), 160–161.

11. Kientz, "Days of Promise."

12. Millar, "The Lincoln."

13. Alvin Guggenheim, interview with the author, January 1995.

14. Barbara Cleland, "'Conquest' Brings Ape Movie Chain Full Circle," *Houston Chronicle*, June 29, 1972.

15. Louis Parks, "Movie Publicist Guggenheim Succumbs to Heart attack at 73," *Houston Chronicle*, June 25, 1997.

16. Advertisement, *Houston Chronicle*, September 11, 1977.

17. Parks, "Movie Publicist Guggenheim."

18. Millar, "The Lincoln."

19. *The Red Book of Houston* (Houston: Sotex Publishing, 1915), 170.

20. *Motion Picture Trade Directory* (New York: Seibert, 1928), 834–835.

21. "Citywide Street Smarts," *West U Magazine*, December 1993, 21.

22. Sigman Byrd, *Sig Byrd's Houston* (New York: Viking, 1955), 148–149.

23. Advertisement, *Metropolitan Civic News*, May 1, 1947.

24. Interstate Theatres interoffice communication from John Q. Adams to all city managers, June 10, 1954.

25. Gomery, *Shared Pleasures*, 166–168.

26. Ann Hodges, "Houston's Silent Battle," *Houston Chronicle*, February 4, 1998.

27. David Berman, director, *The Strange Demise of Jim Crow* (Galveston, Tex.: Institute for the Medical Humanities, Univ. of Texas Medical Branch 1997).

28. Hodges, "Houston's Silent Battle."

29. Berman, *Strange Demise of Jim Crow.*

30. Rob Meckel, "100 Years of The Post: 'White Only' Signs Gone, But Bad Memories Linger," *Houston Post*, Centennial Edition, 1985.

31. Thomas H. Kreneck, *Del Pueblo: A Pictorial History of Houston's Hispanic Community* (Houston: Houston International Univ., 1989), 47–48, 64, 68. The information in the next paragraph also comes from this source.

32. Parks, "Cinemystique."

33. Tara Dooley, "Bollywood in Our Backyard," *Houston Chronicle*, August 12, 2005.

34. Joey Guerra, "Cinema en Español," *Houston Chronicle*, June 8, 2005.

ELEVEN

1. Maggie Valentine, *The Show Starts on the Sidewalk: An Architectural History of the Movie Theatre, Starring S. Charles Lee* (New Haven, Conn.: Yale Univ. Press, 1994), 164–165.

2. Mildred Stockard, "Summer Boom Gives Theaters a Boost," *Houston Chronicle*, June 16, 1961. The information in the next paragraph also comes from this article.

3. Valentine, *Show Starts on the Sidewalk*, 164.

4. *Houston Directory*, 1951–1960.

5. Carr and Hayes, *Wide Screen Movies*, 11–56.

6. "Big Screens Top Film Scene," *Houston Chronicle.*

7. Advertisement, *Houston Post*, December 20, 1962.

8. "Big Screens Top Film Scene," *Houston Chronicle.*

9. "Uptown Will Change Name to Rivoli," *Houston Post.*

10. "Big Screens Top Film Scene," *Houston Chronicle.*

11. Ibid.

12. "Parade, Revue Set For 'Thrillarama' Premiere," *Houston Post*, August 1956.

13. Carr and Hayes, *Wide Screen Movies*, 52.

14. Gomery, *Shared Pleasures*, 230–231.

15. Carr and Hayes, *Wide Screen Movies*, 207–232.

16. Gomery, *Shared Pleasures*, 239–241.

17. Richard Schroeder, *Lone Star Picture Shows* (College Station: Texas A&M Univ. Press, 2001), 141.

18. Interstate Theatres interoffice communication from Raymond Willie to theatre managers, September 28, 1953.

19. Mark Walker, *Ghostmasters: A Look Back at America's Midnight Spook Shows* (Boca Raton, Fla.: Cool Hand Communications, 1991), 85.

20. Ibid., 22.

21. Stockard, "Summer Boom."

TWELVE

1. Kerry Segrave, *Drive-In Theaters: A History from Their Inception in 1933* (Jefferson, N.C.: McFarland, 1992), 235–236.

2. Ibid., 234.

3. Ibid., vii–x.

4. Ibid., 18–20.

5. Ibid., 148.

6. Ibid., 17–18. The account of the Drive-In Short Reel Theatre in the next several paragraphs is taken from these pages.

7. Advertisement, *Houston Post*, June 7, 1940.

8. "Houston's Drive-In Theatre on South Main," *Houston Chronicle*, April 21, 1940.

9. Advertisement, *Houston Post*, 1965 (clipping, exact date unknown).

10. Advertisement, *Houston Post*, March 21, 1947.

11. Advertisement, *Houston Post*, May 23, 1947.

12. *Theatre Catalog*, 1948–1949 (Philadelphia: Emanuel, 1948); available online at http://www.drive-ins.com/libtc48.htm (accessed December 9, 2006).

13. Segrave, *Drive-In Theaters*, 43, 70.

14. Schroeder, *Lone Star Picture Shows*, 134.

15. Advertisement, *Houston Chronicle*, August 26, 1948.

16. Advertisement, *Houston Post*, April 20, 1950.

17. Advertisement, *Houston Post*, June 10, 1950.

18. "Marine War Gear Shown at Drive-In," *Houston Chronicle*, May 22, 1953.

19. Advertisement, *Houston Post*, September 24, 1978.

20. Eric Gerber, "What's Driving Drive-Ins Out?" *Houston Post*, June 21, 1981, Parade section, 11.

21. Advertisement, *Houston Post*, September 15, 1950.

22. Advertisement, *Houston Post*, November 3, 1950.

23. Advertisement, *Houston Post*, May 11, 1977.

24. Advertisement, *Houston Post*, March 14, 1951.

25. "Moving the Drive-in," *Boxoffice*, 1960 (clipping courtesy of Carroll A. Lewis, exact date unknown).

26. "New Post Oak Drive-In Opens," *Houston Post*, June 16, 1960.

27. "World's Only Movieland Golf to Open Here Friday," 1962 (newspaper clipping courtesy of Carroll A. Lewis, newspaper and exact date unknown).

28. Carl Hooper, "McLendon Sets Theatre Investment in Houston," *Houston Post*, June 5, 1970.

29. "Film Stars Here Tonight for New Drive-In 'Preem,'" *Houston Post*, June 25, 1952.

30. Advertisement, *Houston Post*, March 5, 1971.

31. Gerber, "What's Driving Drive-Ins Out?"

32. Advertisement, *Houston Chronicle*, May 22, 1953.

33. Segrave, *Drive-In Theaters*, 124.

34. Sandy Warren, "Life at the Movies," *Houston Post*, November 4, 1984, Magazine section, 16.

35. Eric Gerber, "Back Row at the Drive-In," *Houston Post*, September 15, 1978.

36. Advertisement, *Houston Post*, August 5, 1953.

37. "3 Movies Seized; 2 Charged," *Houston Post*, February 18, 1970.

38. "Drive-In Movie Raided Again," *Houston Post*, February 19, 1970.

39. Bob Newberry, *Houston Post*, March 27, 1970 (clipping; headline unknown).

40. Ibid.

41. Bob Newberry, "Fight Between City, Drive-In Flares," *Houston Post*, October 1, 1970.

42. Ibid.

43. "New X-Rated Theater Cuts Council Off at Pass," *Houston Post*, March 20, 1981.

44. Advertisement, *Houston Post*, September 1, 1955.

45. "Latest Wrinkles in New Drive-In," *Houston Post*, August 29, 1957.

46. *Houston Post*, February 26, 1958, special section. The information in the next half dozen paragraphs is drawn from this source.

47. Ibid.

48. Stockard, "Houston Theaters Offer City Movie Goers Many Chances."

49. Gerber, "What's Driving Drive-Ins Out?"

50. Advertisement, *Houston Post*, June 29, 1960.

51. Advertisement, *Houston Post*, July 1, 1965.

52. Advertisement, *Houston Post*, June 29, 1967.

53. Gerber, "What's Driving Drive-Ins Out?"

54. Hooper, "McLendon Sets Theatre Investment in Houston."

55. "Radio Innovator Off the Air," March 25, 1984 (clipping in the files of the Houston Metropolitan Research Center, newspaper unknown).

56. Hooper, "McLendon Sets Theatre Investment in Houston."

57. "Drive-In Theatre Banned From Using 'Astro' In Name," *Houston Post*, May 19, 1971.

58. Advertisement, *Houston Post*, May 7, 1971.

59. Advertisement, *Houston Post*, December 4, 1949.

60. Warren, "Life at the Movies." The information in the next paragraph also comes from this article.

61. Don and Susan Sanders, *The American Drive-In Movie Theatre* (Osceola, Wisc.: Motorbooks International, 1997), 62.

62. Gerber, "What's Driving Drive-Ins Out?"

63. Segrave, *Drive-In Theaters*, 127.

64. "Radio Magnate B. R. McLendon Dies in Dallas," *Houston Post*, October 13, 1982.

65. Sharon Donovan, "Entertainment Czar McLendon," *Houston Chronicle*, June 17, 1982.

66. Advertisement, *Houston Post*, July 2, 1982.

67. Joe Leydon, "Your Last Chance to Enjoy the Great Outdoors," *Houston Post*, February 29, 1992.

68. Ibid.

69. Ralph Bivins, "Final Frame Nears as Last Drive-In in Area Gives Way to Retail Center," *Houston Chronicle*, February 8, 1992.

70. Leydon, "Your Last Chance."

71. Bob White, "Curtain Drops on Last Picture Show," *The Leader*, February 27, 1992.

72. Ibid.

73. Ken Hoffman, "Those New Voices behind the Talk," *Houston Post*, March 3, 1992.

74. "Statistics," www.driveintheatre-owners association.org/media.html (August 2005).

75. Ibid.

THIRTEEN

1. "Sharpstown Theatre Opens," *Houston Post*, May 27, 1965.

2. George Christian, "Cinerama Returns," *Houston Post*, December 21, 1962.

3. Parks, "Cinemystique."

4. "Show Business," *Houston Post*, April 11, 1968.

5. Tercar corporate publicity: corporate biographies.

6. Tercar corporate publicity: theatre listings.

7. Eric Gerber, "'Raiders' Thrills Range Far, Wide," *Houston Post*, August 14, 1981.

8. "3 Theaters Acquired," *Houston Post*, December 12, 1982.

9. Jeff Millar, "Film Fest Toasts Huston, Berlin," *Houston Chronicle*, April 12, 1987.

10. Beverly Narum, "Former Windsor Theater Soon to House Nightclub," *Houston Post*, December 7, 1989.

11. Advertisement, *The 104 Zone: KRBE's Lifestyle Magazine*, n.d.

12. Advertisement, *Houston Post*, June 29, 1963.

13. "Sharpstown Theatre Opens," *Houston Post*. The information in the next several paragraphs is drawn from this article.

14. "Gaylynn Terrace Already Popular," *Houston Post*, March 9, 1969.

15. Advertisement, *Houston Post*, December 22, 1968, Spotlight section, 18.

16. Advertisement, *Houston Post*, November 16, 1973.

17. Marilyn Marshall, "For Everybody Else, It's Been Travolta Watching Time," *Houston Post*, June 7, 1980.

18. Claudia Feldman, "A Jungle of Giggles," *Houston Chronicle*, August 30, 1989.

19. George Christian, "A World Premiere and Three New Twins, With Robert Mitchum," *Houston Post*, April 15, 1965.

20. "Twin Theaters in 3 Shopping Centers," *Houston Post*, April 14, 1965.

21. Christian, "World Premiere and Three Twins."

22. Advertisement, *Houston Post*, June 1, 1966.

23. Ralph Bivins, "Northline Gets Assist from Magic," *Houston Chronicle*, June 4, 1996.

24. Author's personal recollection and discussions with the Meyerland's manager.

25. Ralph Dodd, "Total Boosted to $4 Million: New Theatres Planned," *Houston Post*, March 14, 1965.

26. Advertisement, *Houston Post*, June 23, 1966.

FOURTEEN

1. McComb, *Houston: The Bayou City*, 153–154.

2. Ibid.

3. Ibid., 154.

4. Ibid., 155–156.

5. Ibid., 152–155.

6. Ibid., 153.

7. Ibid., 152–153.

8. Ibid., 153.

9. Ibid., 161.

10. Frank Miller, *Censored Hollywood: Sex, Sin, and Violence on Screen* (Atlanta: Turner, 1994), 20–36.

11. Quoted in the biographical note for Will W. Hays by Bob Sorrentino on the Inter-

net Movie Database, http://www.imdb.com/ name/nm0371655/bio (accessed December 6, 2006).

12. Jack J. Valenti, *Ten Heroes and Two Heroines* (Houston: Premier Printing, 1957).

13. "Reasons for Film Ratings," www.film ratings.com/about (August 2005).

14. Jack Boulware, *Sex American Style* (Venice, Calif.: Feral House, 1997), 179.

15. "Vance Says He Can't Close Movie," *Houston Post*, May 17, 1969.

16. Charles Layton, "Anti-Smut Drive Gains in Texas," *Houston Post*, May 18, 1969.

17. Advertisement, *Houston Post*, December 1969 (clipping, exact date unknown).

18. "DA Asks Movie Suit Dismissal," *Houston Post*, November 6, 1970.

19. George Rosenblatt, "Police Arrest 23 in Raids on 16 'Lewd Films' Spots," *Houston Chronicle*, October 9, 1970.

20. Ibid.

21. Ralph Williams, "It's the Real Stuff . . ." *Houston Post*, November 15, 1970.

22. Ibid.

23. Boulware, *Sex American Style*, 31–34.

24. John Durham, "DA Drops Prosecution on Films like 'Deep Throat,'" *Houston Chronicle*, February 18, 1974.

25. *Houston Post* and *Houston Chronicle* (undated clippings, courtesy of Jim Ohmart).

26. Eric Gerber, "The Shows Must Go On—and They Will at Museum," *Houston Post*, September 22, 1974.

27. "Theatrical Union Members Given Restraining Order," *Houston Chronicle*, December 14, 1972.

28. "Vice Officers Say Controversial Film Violates No Laws," *Houston Post*, October 17, 1981.

29. Wikipedia, s.v. *Shortbus*, http:// en.wikipedia.org/wiki/Shortbus (accessed December 6, 2006).

FIFTEEN

1. "Stink Bombs Force Movie House Audiences to Flee," *Houston Post*, January 16, 1970.

2. "Theater Gas-Bombed," 1984 (newspaper clipping in the files of the Houston Metropolitan Research Center, exact date and newspaper unknown).

3. Advertisement, *Houston Post*, November 18, 1970.

4. Advertisement, *Houston Post*, March 17, 1971.

5. Advertisement, *Houston Post*, April 7, 1971.

6. Advertisement, *Houston Post*, May 12, 1971.

7. Jeff Millar, "Rising Costs Blamed for Matinee Failure," *Houston Chronicle*, January 9, 1971.

8. Jeff Millar, "Non-Smokers' Last Escape Is Going," *Houston Chronicle*, April 28, 1971.

9. Ibid.

10. Ibid.

11. Advertisement, *Houston Post*, July 14, 1971.

12. Mary Flood, "Tribute to a B-Movie Palace," *Houston Post*, July 8, 1986.

13. "Lewis Won't Permit Showing of X Films," *Houston Post*, February 19, 1972.

14. Vernon Scott, "Minis in the Malls," *Houston Post*, November 28, 1969.

15. "First Jerry Lewis Cinema Here in Piney Point Center," *Houston Chronicle*, October 31, 1971.

16. "New Bijou Movie House to Feature Classics," *Houston Chronicle*, September 28, 1973.

17. Lavina Melwani, "Showtime," *Little India*, September 15, 2005, http://www.little india.com/news/123/ARTICLE/1320/2005-09-15.html (accessed December 6, 2006).

18. Tara Dooley, "Bollywood in Our Backyard," *Houston Chronicle*, August 12, 2005.

19. Advertisement, *Houston Post*, June 28, 1972.

20. Papademetriou, "The Late, Great Picture Palaces," 83.

21. Parker Riggs, interview with the author, September 1999.

22. Advertisement, *Houston Post*, June 27, 1973.

23. Advertisement, *Houston Post*, February 1, 1974.

24. Louis Parks, "After Nearly 2 Decades, AMC Greenway to Close," *Houston Chronicle*, January 11, 1994.

25. Greenway Theatre advertising flyer, March 1994.

26. Theis, "Film Forums," *Houston Press*, March 10–16, 1994.

27. "A New Addition," July 21, 1974 (newspaper clipping in the Houston Post library).

28. Ralph Dodd, "Total Boosted to $4 Million," *Houston Post*, March 14, 1965.

29. Louis Parks, "Sunday to Mark Last Screenings at Saks Cinema," *Houston Chronicle*, July 7, 1995.

30. Advertisement, *Houston Post*, July 10, 1975.

31. Parks, "Cinemystique."

32. Heard by the author on KTRH, July 1, 1994.

33. Rick Barrs, "Protesters in Wheelchairs Criticize Access to Theaters," *Houston Post*, May 14, 1978.

34. "Film Attacked by Gays Dropped by Nation's Top Theater Chain," *Houston Post*, February 1, 1980.

35. "Best of Houston 2004," *Houston Press*, September 23–29, 2000.

36. Judith Crown, "Houston's Other Glut: Too Many Screens," *Houston Chronicle*, November 23, 1986. The information in the next two paragraphs is also drawn from this article.

SIXTEEN

1. Gomery, *Shared Pleasures*, 79.

2. Stones, *America Goes to the Movies*, 101–102.

3. Gomery, *Shared Pleasures*, 80–81.

4. Ibid., 80.

5. Bonario interview.

6. Gomery, *Shared Pleasures*, 81.

7. Tom Peeler, "Silver-Screen Empire," *Texas Highways*, January 1999, 43.

8. Bonario interview.

9. Stones, *America Goes to the Movies*, 111.

10. Segrave, *Drive-In Theaters*, 97.

11. "Cafeteria Is Built to Speed Food Service," *Houston Post*, February 26, 1958, special section.

12. Louis Parks, "Food for Thought on Popcorn," *Houston Chronicle*, July 22, 1988.

13. Eric Gerber, "Popcorn," *Houston Post*, October 27, 1978.

14. Personal recollection. The author worked at several of the Tercar Theatres during the time and popped (and bagged) many a kernel of corn.

15. Gerber, "Popcorn."

16. Ibid.

17. Christi Foster, "A Junk Food Lover's Guide," *Houston Post*, December 28, 1984.

18. Ibid.

19. See www.drafthouse.com for complete information on the Drafthouse Cinema concept.

20. Louis B. Parks, "Dinner at the Movies," *Houston Chronicle*, July 20, 2006.

21. Gomery, *Shared Pleasures*, 81.

SEVENTEEN

1. Advertisement, *Houston Post*, November 15, 1970, Spotlight section.

2. "Annual Report Summary," *Bulletin of the Museum of Fine Arts of Houston, Texas*, July 1939, vol. 3, no. 1.

3. "Museum of Fine Arts Opening Brown Pavilion," *Houston West Side Reporter*, January 2, 1974.

4. Annual Report 1973–1974, Museum of Fine Arts, Houston.

5. Advertising flyer, Museum of Fine Arts, Houston, January 1985.

6. Lia Unrau, "Celebrating 25 Years: Rice Media Center," *Rice News*, September 14, 1995. The information in the next two paragraphs also comes from this article.

7. Elena Rodriguez, *Dennis Hopper: A Madness to His Method* (New York: St. Martin's, 1988), 140–143.

8. Christopher Dow, "Dennis Hopper Blew Away Houston with 1983 Dynamite Death Chair Act," *Rice News*, September 14, 1995. The information in the next two paragraphs is also from this article.

9. Ibid.

10. "Best of Houston 1999," *Houston Press*, September 23–29, 1999.

11. Alley Theatre Film Festival schedules, 1969–1978.

12. Gerber, "The Shows Must Go On."

13. Claudia Perry, "The Big Picture," *Houston Post*, September 8, 1989.

14. Holly Glentzer, "In the Niche of Time," *Houston Chronicle*, October 23, 2001.

15. "Best of Houston 1998," *Houston Press*, September 24–30, 1998.

16. Charles Dove, "The Next Picture

Show," *Sidewalk*, September 3, 1998.

17. Advertisement, *Houston Post*, December 31, 1940. The information in the next paragraph is also drawn from this source.

18. "Brave Four Defy Eerie Ghost Film," *Houston Chronicle*, October 1963.

19. Eric Gerber, "Midnight Movies Sunny Success," *Houston Post*, November 10, 1973.

20. Ibid.

21. Advertisement, *Houston Post*, May 24, 1985.

22. Eric Gerber, "Eraserhead," *Houston Post*, March 9, 1979.

23. Danny Peary, *Cult Movies* (New York: Dell, 1981), 302.

24. Eric Gerber, "It's a Real Horror . . . But Fans of the Other 'Rocky' Are Super-Devoted," *Houston Post*, March 10, 1978.

25. Ibid.

26. Millar, "Era Ends as the Alabama Closes."

27. Author's recollection.

EIGHTEEN

1. Advertisement, *Houston Post*, June 24, 1988.

2. Louis Parks, "The Sound of Movies," *Houston Chronicle*, July 22, 1988, Weekend Preview section.

3. Louis Parks, "Showtime: 12-Screen Theater Opens near Downtown," *Houston Chronicle*, October 12, 1990.

4. Louis Parks, "General Cinema to Close Its Last Houston Theater," *Houston Chronicle*, October 17, 2000.

5. Greg Hassell, "Renewed Popularity for Movies," *Houston Chronicle*, February 28, 1995.

6. "Theater Boasts New 'Star' Attractions,"

The Leader, November 14, 1996, vol. 13, no. 1, 1.

7. Angelica Cafe and Bar menu.

8. Louis B. Parks, "Downtown's Angelica Officially Opens Tonight," *Houston Chronicle*, January 8, 1998.

9. Bivins, "Northline Gets Assist."

10. S. K. Bardwell, "Death Toll in Mall Collapse Likely to Rise," *Houston Chronicle*, January 31, 1997.

11. Greg Hassell, "Will Movies Again Do the Trick?" *Houston Chronicle*, January 24, 1998.

12. Ibid.

13. Advertisement, *Houston Press*, October 11–17.

14. "Best of Houston 2005," *Houston Press*, September 29–October 5, 2005.

15. Author's notes from opening day, October 22, 1998.

16. Greg Hassell, "Mall Opens with Mega-hoopla," *Houston Chronicle*, October 29, 1999.

17. Laura A. Stromberg, "Entertainment Complex Planned on Tract Once Owned By Johnny Carson," *Houston Business Journal*, March 20, 1998; available online at http://houston.bizjournals.com/houston/stories/1998/03/23/newscolumn1/html (accessed December 9, 2006).

18. Ralph Bivins, "I-10 Center's Main Draw to Be Theater," *Houston Chronicle*, February 9, 1999.

19. Crown, "Houston's Other Glut."

20. Kimberly Reeves, "Megascreen Cinemas March In," *Houston Press*, March 4–10, 1999.

21. Richard Connelly, "Battle of the Megaplex Monsters," *Houston Press*, March 2–8, 2000.

22. Ibid.

BIBLIOGRAPHY

BOOKS

Anderson, Brian D. *The "Titanic" in Print and on Screen*. Jefferson, N.C.: McFarland, 2005.

Beck, Bill. *At Your Service: An Illustrated History of Houston Lighting and Power Company*. Houston: Gulf, 1990.

Berger, John. *Ways of Seeing*. New York: Penguin, 1977.

Blum, Daniel. *The Pictorial History of Silent Film*. New York: Putnam, 1953.

Boulware, Jack. *Sex American Style*. Venice, Calif.: Feral House, 1997.

Bowers, David Q. *Nickelodeon Theatres and Their Music*. New York: Vestal Press, 1986.

Byrd, Sigman. *Sig Byrd's Houston*. New York: Viking, 1955.

Calloway, Cab, and Bryant Rollins. *Of Minnie the Moocher and Me*. New York: Crowell, 1976.

Carr, Robert E. and Hayes, R. M. *Wide Screen Movies: A History and Filmography of Wide Gauge Filmmaking*. Jefferson, N.C.: McFarland, 1988.

Chase, Linda. *Hollywood on Main Street: The Movie House Paintings of Davis Cone*. Woodstock, N.Y.: Overlook, 1988.

Dauphin, Sue. *Houston by Stages*. Burnet, Tex.: Eakin Press, 1981.

Emmott, Sarah H. *Memorial Park: A Priceless Legacy*. Houston: Herring Press, 1992.

Everson, William K. *The Hollywood Western*. Secaucus, N.J.: Citadel Press, 1969/1992.

Fuhrman, Candice Jacobson. *Publicity Stunt*. San Francisco: Chronicle, 1989.

Gallegly, Joseph S. *Footlights on the Border: The Galveston and Houston Stage before 1900*. The Hague: Mouton, 1962.

Giesberg, Robert I. *Houston Grand Opera: A History*. Houston: Houston Grand Opera Guild, 1981.

Gomery, Douglas. *Shared Pleasures: A History of Movie Presentation in the United States*. London: British Film Institute, 1992.

Haines, Richard W. *Technicolor Movies: The History of Dye Transfer Printing*. Jefferson, N.C.: McFarland, 1993.

Hall, Ben M. *The Best Remaining Seats: The Golden Age of the Movie Palace*. New York: Bramhall House, 1961.

Halliwell, Leslie. *Halliwell's Filmgoer's and Video Viewer's Companion.* 9th edition. New York: Harper & Row, 1988.

Henry, Jay C. *Architecture in Texas, 1895–1945.* Austin: Univ. of Texas Press, 1993.

Hinga, Don. *Forty Years of Community Service: The Story of Karl Hoblitzelle and the Development of Interstate Theatres.* Dallas: Stellmacher and Son, 1946.

Hutton, Jim, and Jim Henderson. *Houston: A History of a Giant.* Tulsa, Okla.: Continental Heritage, 1976.

Johnston, Marguerite. *Houston: The Unknown City.* College Station: Texas A&M Univ. Press, 1991.

Jonas, Susan, and Marilyn Nissenson. *Going, Going, Gone: Vanishing Americana.* San Francisco: Chronicle, 1994.

Katz, Ephraim. *The Film Encyclopedia.* New York: Perigee, 1979.

Kreneck, Thomas H. *Del Pueblo: A Pictorial History of Houston's Hispanic Community.* Houston: Houston International Univ., 1989.

Lent, Joy. *Houston's Heritage: Using Antique Postcards.* Houston: D. H. White, 1983.

Margolies, John, and Emily Gwathmey. *Ticket to Paradise.* Boston: Little, Brown, 1991.

Mazar, Nergal Ory, and the editorial staff of Unibook. *Houston: City of Destiny.* New York: Macmillan, 1980.

McAshan, Marie Phelps. *A Houston Legacy: On the Corner of Main and Texas.* Houston: Hutchins House, 1985.

McComb, David G. *Houston: The Bayou City.* Austin: Univ. of Texas Press, 1969.

Miller, Frank. *Censored Hollywood: Sex, Sin, and Violence on Screen.* Atlanta: Turner, 1994.

Miller, Ray. *Ray Miller's Houston.* Houston: Cordovan Press, 1984.

Motion Picture Trade Directory. New York: Seibert, 1928.

Naylor, David. *American Picture Palaces: The Architecture of Fantasy.* New York: Van Nostrand and Reinhold, 1981.

———. *Great American Movie Theaters.* Washington, D.C.: Preservation Press, 1987.

Pace, Randle G., and Markey, Deborah. *Houston Heights, 1891–1991,* Houston: Tribune, 1991.

Peary, Danny. *Cult Movies.* New York: Dell, 1981.

Pildas, Ave. *Movie Palaces: Survivors of an Elegant Era.* New York: Potter, 1980.

Pratt, George. *Spellbound in Darkness: A History of the Silent Film.* Greenwich, Conn.: New York Graphic Society, 1966, 1973.

Ramsaye, Terry. *A Million and One Nights: A History of the Motion Picture through 1925.* New York: Simon and Schuster, 1926.

The Red Book of Houston. Houston: Sotex Publishing, 1915.

Richardson, F. H. *Motion Picture Handbook: A Guide for Managers and Operators of Motion Picture Theatres.* New York: World Photographic, 1910.

Robinson, Willard B. *Gone from Texas: Our Lost Architectural Heritage.* College Station: Texas A&M Univ. Press, 1981.

Rodriguez, Elena. *Dennis Hopper: A Madness to His Method.* New York: St. Martin's, 1988.

Roussel, Hubert. *The Houston Symphony Orchestra, 1913–1971.* Austin: Univ. of Texas Press, 1972.

Sanders, Don, and Susan Sanders. *The American Drive-In Movie Theatre.* Osceola, Wisc.: Motorbooks International, 1997.

Schroeder, Richard. *Lone Star Picture Shows.* College Station: Texas A&M Univ. Press, 2001.

Segrave, Kerry. *Drive-In Theaters: A History from Their Inception in 1933.* Jefferson, N.C.: McFarland, 1992.

Slide, Anthony. *Nitrate Won't Wait: Film Preservation in the United States.* Jefferson, N.C.: McFarland, 1992.

———. *Silent Portraits.* New York: Vestal Press, 1989.

Southwest Center for Urban Research and the School of Architects. *Houston Architectural Survey.* 6 vols. Houston: Rice University, 1980–1981.

Stones, Barbara. *America Goes to the Movies.* North Hollywood, Calif.: National Association of Theatre Owners, 1993.

Tarkington, Booth. *The Magnificent Ambersons.* New York: Doubleday, 1918.

Theatre Catalog, 1948–1949. Philadelphia: Emanuel, 1948.

Thompson, Frank. *Lost Films: Important Movies That Disappeared*. New York: Citadel, 1996.

Tornabene, Lyn. *Clark Gable: Long Live the King*. New York: Putnam, 1976.

Valenti, Jack J. *Ten Heroes and Two Heroines*. Houston: Premier Printing, 1957.

Valentine, Maggie. *The Show Starts on the Sidewalk: An Architectural History of the Movie Theatre, Starring S. Charles Lee*. New Haven, Conn.: Yale Univ. Press, 1994.

Vidor, King, *A Tree Is a Tree: An Autobiography*. Hollywood, Calif.: Samuel French, 1953; reprinted 1981.

Von der Mehden, Fred R. *The Ethnic Groups of Houston*. Houston: Rice Univ. Studies, 1984.

Walker, Mark. *Ghostmasters: A Look Back at America's Midnight Spook Shows*. Boca Raton, Fla.: Cool Hand Communications, 1991.

Wilson, Michael E. *Alfred C. Finn: Builder of Houston*. Houston: Houston Public Library, 1983.

Young, Dr. S. O. *True Stories of Old Houston and Houstonians: Historical and Personal Sketches Covering Houston's First Seventy-five Years*. Galveston, Tex.: Springer, 1913. Reprint, Houston: Green Bottle Antique Shop/Press of Premier, 1974.

VIDEO AND DOCUMENTARIES

Berman, David. *The Strange Demise of Jim Crow*. Galveston, Tex.: Institute for the Medical Humanities, Univ. of Texas Medical Branch, 1997.

Fisher, Jim, and Nancy Simonds. *Houston: Remember When, Volume 1*. Houston: KHOU Channel 8, 1998.

The Amazing Years of Cinema: The Immortals. A Polymedia/RM Productions coproduction.

Historic Building: Tower Theatre For Sale. News report by Charles Hadlock for KHOU-TV Channel 11, March 3, 1995.

PERIODICALS

Berry, Garvin. "Oddities in Houston." *Inside Houston*, October 1996, 9.

Blackwood, Bev. "What Is Killing Houston's Brewpubs?" *Southwest Brewing News* 9, no. 1 (March 2001).

Courtney, Linda Anderson. "The Evolution of Cinema Design in Houston from 1900–1920s." *Houston Review* 4, no. 1 (Winter 1982): 28–43.

Dawes, Gerry. "The Best Bars in America." *Playboy*, May 2000, 94–158.

Dove, Charles. "The Next Picture Show," *Sidewalk*, September 3, 1998.

Dreyer, Thorne, and Al Reinert. "Montrose Lives." *Texas Monthly*, April 1973.

Houston Downtown Magazine. "Warwick Plans Restoration of Last Movie Palace." January 25, 1988.

Looser, Don. "A Musical Renaissance: The Growth of Cultural Institutions in Houston, 1929–1936." *Houston Review* 6, no. 3 (1984): 135–154.

Luna, T. P. "Those Enterprising Exuberant Ebersons." *Marquee* 23, no. 1 (1991): 25–30.

Melwani, Lavina. "Showtime." *Little India*, September 15, 2005. http://www.littleindia.com/news/123/ARTICLE/1320/2005-09-15.html (accessed December 6, 2006).

Minor, Larry. "Scrapbook: Did You Know . . ." *Amusement Today*, February 1998, 30.

Papademetriou, Peter. "The Late, Great Picture Palaces." *Houston Home and Garden*, November 1978, 76–83.

Peeler, Tom. "Silver-Screen Empire." *Texas Highways*, January 1999, 40–43.

Pinkard, Tommie. "The Stars Shine Again at the Majestic." *Texas Highways*, January 1983, 18–23.

Preddy, Jane. "The Esperson Theatre." *Marquee* 20, no. 4 (1988): 18.

Qaddumi, Thora. "Lounge Retains Architectural Elements of Old Theater." *Houston Business Journal*, September 24, 1999. Available online at http://houston.bizjournals.com/houston/stories/1999/09/27/focus9.html.

Roberts III, W. G. "Loew's State Theatre: Houston, Texas." *Marquee* 10, no. 1 (1978): 14.

Scardino, Barrie. "A Legacy of City Halls for Houston." *Houston Review* 5, no. 3 (Fall 1982): 155–163.

Stromberg, Laura A. "Entertainment Complex Planned on Tract Once Owned By Johnny Carson." *Houston Business Journal*,

March 20, 1998. Available online at http://
houstonbizjournalscom/houston/stories/
1998/03/23/newscolumn1/html.
Tavakoli, Brenda. "What's Cooking in 002."
002, September 2000, 46.
Variety. "Spotlight: Cineplex Odeon 15th
Anniversary." January 25–31, 1994, 31–56.
Wilson, Michael E. "Alfred C. Finn: Hous-
ton Architect." *Houston Review* 5, no. 2
(Summer 1983): 64–79.

PROGRAMS AND PAPERS

Conover Hunt Jones. *The Majestic Theatre
1921–1983: Publication Developed Courtesy
of the "Dallas Morning News" and Neiman
Marcus.* Dallas, Texas, 1983.
Preddy, Jane. *Palaces of Dreams: The Movie
Theatres of John Eberson, Architect.* Exhibi-
tion catalogue. San Antonio, Tex.: McNay
Art Museum, 1989.
Holcomb, Luthor. Message delivered at the
funeral of Karl St. John Hoblitzelle.
Wilson, Michael E. *Alfred C. Finn: Builder
of Houston—A Catalogue of Drawings of
the Firm in the Houston Public Library/
Houston Metropolitan Research Center.*
Houston: Houston Public Library, 1983.

NEWSPAPERS AND PERIODICALS

002
The 104 Zone
Alvin Sun
Boxoffice
Dallas Morning News
Dallas Observer
Dallas Times Herald
Heights Citizen (Houston)
Houston Chronicle
Houston Post
Houston Press
Inside Houston
Leader (Houston)
Metropolitan Civic News (Houston)
Pasadena Citizen (TX)
Public News (Houston)
Southwest Brewing News
Southwestern Times (Houston)
Texas Highways
West Side Reporter (Houston)
West U Magazine (Houston)

INTERVIEWS

Jan Bettis, February 1992.
Roy Bonario, December 28, 1991.
Keith Curtis, August 1994.
Alvin Guggenheim, January 1995.
Ed Henderson, March 25, 1992.
Gus and Sharon Kopriva, November 1994.
Parker Riggs, September 1999.
Gary Warwick, January 1995 and April 4,
2006.
Al Welling, September 26, 1999.
Dick Willson, October 15, 2005.
Al Zarzana, 1993.

WEB SITES

The Handbook of Texas Online: www.tsha
.utexas.edu/handbook/online/index.html
Magic Lanterns: www.geocities.com/Colos
seum/Field/1844/past_magic.htm
University of North Carolina at Chapel Hill:
www.unc.edu/~lbrooks2/magic.html
Cinema Treasures: www.cinematreasures.org
Cinerama Top Cities: www.cinerama.topci
ties.com
Drive-Ins.com: www.drive-ins.com
A Guide to West University Place: rogermar
tin.com/pdf_files/wuguide_downtown.pdf
Guidry News Service Online: www.guidry
news.com/03lang/19303lang.htm
Saenger Amusements: www.saengeramuse
ments.com
Brad Light's Drive-In Workshop: www.drive
inworkshop.com
Film Ratings: www.filmratings.com
American President.org, "Thomas Woodrow
Wilson (1913–1921)," http://www.american
president.org/history/woodrowwilson (Sep-
tember 8, 2005)
United Drive-In Theatre Owners Association:
http://www.driveintheatre-ownersassocia
tion.org

EPHEMERA

Bob Bailey Studios. 1995 calendar. Houston:
Champagne Printing, 1994.
———. 1998 calendar. Houston: Champagne
Printing, 1997.

INDEX